THE FIRST WORLD WAR
AN ILLUSTRATED HISTORY

THE FIRST WORLD WAR

AN ILLUSTRATED HISTORY

JOHN KEEGAN

HUTCHINSON

LONDON

© John Keegan 2001

The right of John Keegan to be identified as the Author of this work has been asserted by John Keegan in accordance with the Copyright, Designs and Patents Act 1988.

All rights reserved

1 3 5 7 9 10 8 6 4 2

This edition first published in 2001 by Hutchinson.

Random House (UK) Limited
20 Vauxhall Bridge Road,
London SW1V 2SA

Random House Australia (Pty) Limited
20 Alfred Street, Milsons Point, Sydney,
New South Wales 2061, Australia

Random House New Zealand Limited
18 Poland Road, Glenfield,
Auckland 10, New Zealand

Random House South Africa (Pty) Ltd
Endulini, 5A Jubilee Road,
Parktown 2193, South Africa

A CiP record for this book is available from the British Library

Papers used by Random House UK Limited are natural, recyclable products made from wood grown in sustainable forests. The manufacturing processes conform to the environmental regulations of the country of origin.

ISBN 0 09 179392 0

Page i: Original design for poster, *Kitchener Needs You,* by Alfred Leete.
Pages ii–iii: Battle of Champagne, September 1915.
Pages iv–v: German troops advancing to assault Picardy, March 1918.
Page vii: *Battle of Hermada,* northern Italy, August 1917, by A. Mallier.
Page viii: *Battle of the Skagerrak,* 1916, by Claus Bergen.
Pages x–xi: American troops advancing along with French tanks, the Somme.
Pages xii–xiii: Russians besieged at the Battle of Przemysl, September–October 1914.
Page xiv: French soldiers in trench in forest of Apremont near St. Mihiel, 30 metres from the enemy, on January 23, 1915, by J. F. Bouchor.
Pages xvi–1: Australians passing along a duckboard track, October 29, 1917.

CONTENTS

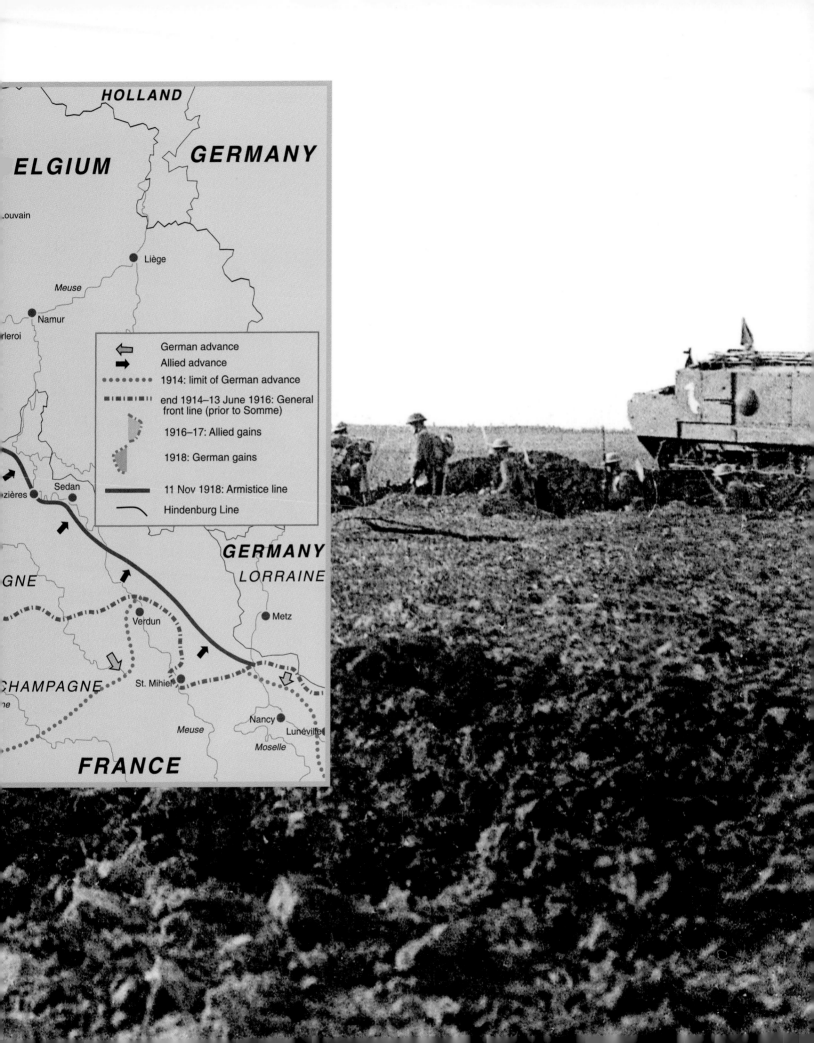

HOLLAND

BELGIUM

GERMANY

Louvain

Liège

Meuse

Namur

arleroi

German advance

Allied advance

1914: limit of German advance

end 1914–13 June 1916: General front line (prior to Somme)

1916–17: Allied gains

1918: German gains

zières

Sedan

11 Nov 1918: Armistice line

Hindenburg Line

GERMANY

LORRAINE

GNE

Metz

Verdun

CHAMPAGNE

St. Mihiel

Nancy

Lunéville

Meuse

Moselle

FRANCE

SWEDEN

FINLAND

GERMANY

RUSSIA

RUSSIA

AUSTRIA-HUNGARY

SERBIA

BULGARIA

ROMANIA

EAST PRUSSIA

GALICIA

TRANSYLVANIA

WALLACHIA

MOLDAVIA

BESSA-RABIA

MONTE-NEGRO

ST. PETERSBURG (Petrograd)

Revel · Narva

Pskov

Riga

Libau

Dvinsk

Königsberg · Kovno

Danzig

Tannenberg · Vilna

Grodno

Prasnysz · Minsk

Vistula · Warsaw · Brest-Litovsk · Pinsk

Lodz

Pripet Marshes

Radom · Lublin

Lutsk · Rovno · Kiev

Cracow · Jaroslav · Lemberg · Brody

Przemysl · Tarnopol

Gorlice

Stanislau

Budapest

Kishinev · Odessa

Danube

Tisza

Drava

Sava

Belgrade

Bucharest

Danube

Dvina

Desna

Vorskha

Dnieper

Bug

Dniester

Pruth

Nikolaiev

Legend:

⇦ German advance

➡ Allied advance

▪—▪ 1914–15: limit of Russian advances

···· 1915–16: limit of German advance

June–Aug 1915: Brusilov offensive

Sept 1917: German gains

— 3 March 1918: German gains into Russia (Treaty of Brest-Litovsk)

200 miles

ACKNOWLEDGEMENTS

My principal thanks go to Anne-Marie Ehrlich and Jock Craven, who undertook the picture research for this book. Working in archives all over Europe and in North America, they assembled many pictures not previously published. They were, as always, the kindest and most helpful of collaborators. My thanks also go to my editors in England and the United States respectively, Anthony Whittome and Ashbel Green, and to Jonathan Fasman. I am grateful, as ever, to my literary agent, Anthony Sheil, and to my invaluable assistant, Lindsey Wood. Nothing, of course, could have been achieved without the help of my darling wife, Susanne, and the support of our family.

A EUROPEAN TRAGEDY

French Zouave soldiers enjoying a moment of relaxation.

Europe in the summer of 1914 enjoyed a peaceful productivity so dependent on international co-operation that a belief in the impossibility of general war seemed the most conventional of wisdoms. In 1910 an analysis of prevailing economic interdependence, *The Great Illusion,* had become a best-seller; its author, Norman Angell, had demonstrated that the disruption of international credit inevitably to be caused by war would either deter its outbreak or bring it speedily to an end. It was a message to which the industrial and commercial society of that age was keenly sympathetic. After two decades of depression, industrial output had begun to expand again in the last years of the nineteenth century. New categories of manufactures had appeared to tempt buyers; new sources of cheaply extractable raw materials had been found; so, too, had new deposits of precious metals to fertilise credit; rising population—a 35 per cent increase in Austria-Hungary between 1880 and 1910, 43 per cent in Germany, 26 per cent in Britain, over 50 per cent in Russia—enlarged the size of internal markets; emigration—twenty-six million people left Europe for the Americas and Australasia from 1880 to 1910—increased demand for goods there also, while the enormous expansion of overseas empires drew millions of their inhabitants into the international market, both as suppliers of staples and consumers of finished goods. A revolution in transport greatly accelerated and expanded the movement of commerce overseas, while the extension of the railway network in eastern Europe and in Russia added that enormously rich region to the integrated international economy. It is scarcely surprising that, by the beginning of the century, bankers had recovered their confidence, gold-based capital was circulating freely and return on overseas investment had come to form a significant element of private and corporate incomes in Britain, France, Germany, Holland and Belgium.

Russian railways, South African gold and diamond mines, Indian textile factories, African and Malayan rubber plantations, South American cattle ranches, Australian sheep stations, Canadian wheat fields and almost every sector of the enormous economy of the United States devoured European capital as fast as it could be lent. The greater proportion passed through the City of London. Its worldwide connections made it the principal medium of buying, selling and borrowing for all advanced countries. Its predominance fed the belief so persuasively advanced by Norman Angell that any interruption of the smooth, daily equalisation of debit and credit it masterminded must destroy the very monetary mechanism by which the world lived. Speaking to the Institute of Bankers in London on January 17, 1912, Angell argued that "commercial interdependence is surely doing a great deal to demonstrate that morality after all is not founded upon self-sacrifice, but upon enlightened self-interest, to create a consciousness which must make for more efficient human co-operation, a better human society." W. R. Lawson, a former editor of the *Financial Times*, observed at the end of the speech that "it is very evident that Mr. Norman Angell had carried this meeting almost entirely with him."

It was not only bankers who accepted the interdependence of nations as a condition of the world's life in the first years of the twentieth century. The revolution in communications required international co-operation to service the new technologies and bureaucracies of travel and messaging. An International Telegraph Union was established in 1865 and the International Postage Union in 1875. An International Conference for Promoting Technical Uniformity in Railways was set up in 1882. The International Meteorological Organisation appeared in 1873 and the International Radiotelegraph Union, which allotted separate wavelengths for the new invention of wireless, in 1906. All these were governmental organisations. The world of commerce was meanwhile establishing its own international associations: for the Publication of Customs Tariffs in 1890, of Patents and Trademarks in 1883, for Industrial, Literary and Artistic Property in 1895, of Commercial Statistics in 1913; an Institute of Agriculture was established in 1905. Particular industries and professions meanwhile set up their own international bodies: the International Congress of Chambers of Commerce in 1880, the Congress of Actuaries in 1895, the Association of Accountancy in 1911, the International Electrotechnical Commission in 1906, the Committee for the Unification of Maritime Law in 1897. An International Bureau of Weights and Measures had been organised in 1875 and the first International Copyright Conventions were signed in the 1880s.

Internationalism, however, was not merely commercial. It was also intellectual, philanthropic and religious.

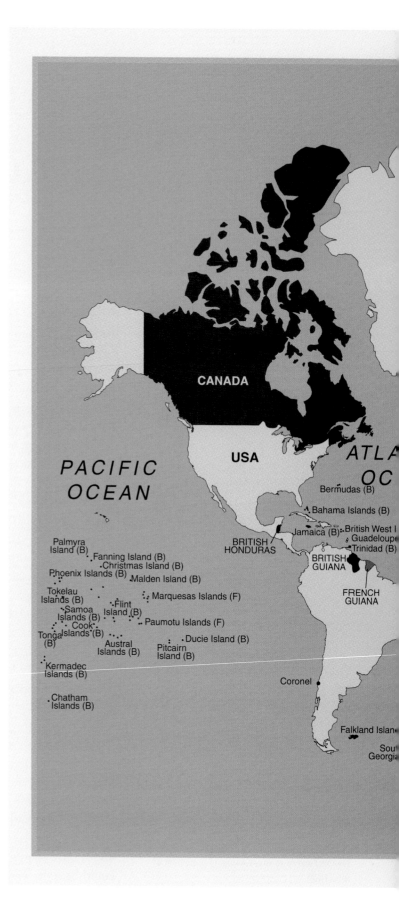

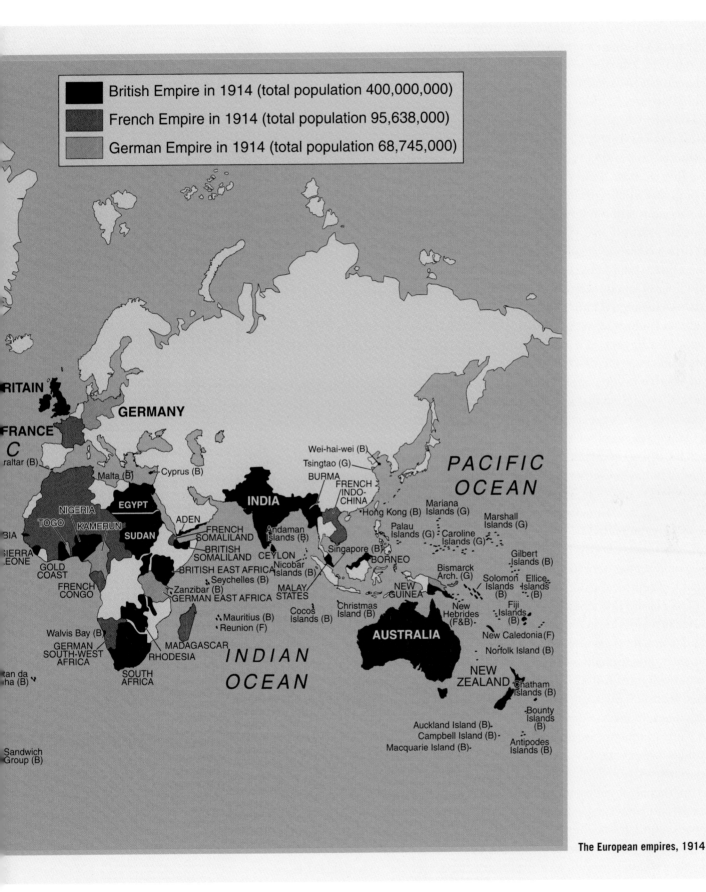

British Empire in 1914 (total population 400,000,000)

French Empire in 1914 (total population 95,638,000)

German Empire in 1914 (total population 68,745,000)

RITAIN

GERMANY

FRANCE

C

raltar (B)

Malta (B)

Cyprus (B)

Wei-hai-wei (B)

Tsingtao (G)

BURMA

PACIFIC
OCEAN

NIGERIA

TOGO

KAMERUN

EGYPT

SUDAN

ADEN

FRENCH
SOMALILAND

BRITISH
SOMALILAND

CEYLON

BRITISH EAST AFRICA

Seychelles (B)

Zanzibar (B)
GERMAN EAST AFRICA

INDIA

FRENCH
INDO-
CHINA

Hong Kong (B)

Andaman
Islands (B)

Singapore (B)

Nicobar
Islands (B)

MALAY
STATES

BORNEO

Mariana
Islands (G)

Palau
Islands (G)

Caroline
Islands (G)

Marshall
Islands (G)

Gilbert
Islands (B)

Bismarck
Arch. (G)

NEW
GUINEA

Solomon
Islands
(B)

Ellice
Islands
(B)

New
Hebrides
(F&B)

Fiji
Islands
(B)

BIA

SIERRA
LEONE

GOLD
COAST

FRENCH
CONGO

Walvis Bay (B)

GERMAN
SOUTH-WEST
AFRICA

RHODESIA

MADAGASCAR

SOUTH
AFRICA

Mauritius (B)

Reunion (F)

Cocos
Islands (B)

Christmas
Island (B)

INDIAN

OCEAN

AUSTRALIA

New Caledonia (F)

Norfolk Island (B)

NEW
ZEALAND

Chatham
Islands (B)

tan da
ha (B)

Auckland Island (B)

Campbell Island (B)

Macquarie Island (B)

Bounty
Islands
(B)

Antipodes
Islands (B)

Sandwich
Group (B)

The European empires, 1914

The only truly transnational religious movement remained the Catholic Church, with bishoprics throughout the world centred on that of Rome. Some denominations nevertheless succeeded in co-operating in the missionary field at least. The China Inland Mission, uniting several Protestant churches, dated from 1865. A World Missionary Conference held at Edinburgh in 1910 broadened that impetus and in 1907 Christians in universities had founded the International Christian Movement at Tokyo. Common Christianity found an easier expression in philanthropy. Opposition to slavery had been an early issue. In 1841 Britain, France, Russia, Austria and Prussia had signed a treaty that made slave-trading an act of piracy, a policy Britain was already energetically enforcing through the anti-slavery patrols of the Royal Navy off West Africa. The traffic in women and children for prostitution, "White Slavery," also stimulated international action and in 1910 a convention, subsequently signed by nine states, decreed the traffic to be a crime punishable by their domestic law wherever committed.

Conditions of labour were also a philanthropic concern. By 1914 many European states had entered into bilateral treaties protecting workers' rights to social insurance and industrial compensation, while restricting female and child labour. They may best be seen as a state response to the activities of the international working man's movements, particularly the First International, founded by Karl Marx in London in 1864, and the Second, in Paris in 1889. It was their preaching of social revolution that had driven governments, particularly Bismarck's in Germany after 1871, to enact labour welfare laws as a measure of self-protection. Other, older measures of self-protection were present in international agreements to check the spread of disease, usually by the quarantining of ships in the distant trade and of immigrants from the Near East, identified as the main source of epidemic outbreaks in Europe. The sale of liquor and drugs was also subject to international control; an Opium Conference between twelve governments met at the Hague in 1912, an undertaking which was evidence of a growing willingness by governments to act collectively. They had done so with success to suppress piracy. Europe could act together when it chose to.

It could, of course, also think and feel together. Europe's educated classes held much of its culture in common, particularly through an appreciation for the art of the Italian and Flemish renaissance, for the music of Mozart and Beethoven, for grand opera, for the architecture of the Middle Ages and the classical revival, and for each other's modern literature. Tolstoy was a European figure; so, too, were other writers of Europe's present or recent past. Victor Hugo, Balzac, Zola, Dickens, Manzoni, Shakespeare, Goethe, Molière and Dante were familiar, at least as names, to every European high school child, and French, German and Italian were commonly taught then in their foreign-language classes. Homer, Thucydides, Caesar and Livy were set-books in all of them and the study of the classics remained universal. Through the teaching of Aristotle and Plato there was a congruence of philosophy. Europe's university graduates shared a corpus of thought and knowledge which preserved something recognisable as a single European culture. It was enjoyed by an ever-increasing number of European cultural tourists. By the beginning of the twentieth century travel had become a middle-class pleasure as well. Karl Baedeker's guides were in 1900 in their thir-

Kaiser Wilhelm II, Emperor of Germany, and Winston Churchill at the Imperial Manoeuvres at Würzburg, September 14, 1909. Churchill, who had met the Kaiser once before in 1907, was now a Cabinet minister as President of the Board of Trade. He is wearing the uniform of a major in the Queen's Own Oxfordshire Hussars, a Territorial (volunteer) cavalry regiment which he had joined after giving up his regular commission. He was an enthusiastic Territorial soldier. The Kaiser is in the uniform of a Prussian field marshal. His cloak disguises his withered arm, a birth defect of which he was acutely conscious.

Churchill could not speak German but the Kaiser both spoke and wrote English fluently. His mother, the Empress Frederick, was the eldest daughter of Queen Victoria. Her husband died in 1888 after he had been on the throne for only a hundred days. The Empress Frederick was emphatically a liberal and a democrat but her efforts to transmit English political values to her son failed. His instincts were autocratic. Churchill on his visit noted German rigidity. "Anything they have not considered officially and for months upsets them dreadfully. With us there are so many shades. Here it is all black and white."

teenth edition for Rome, their ninth for the Eastern Alps and their seventh for Scandinavia. The most visited locations were Venice and Florence, the Holy City, the castles of the Rhine, and Paris, "City of Light"; but there were also large annual migrations to the spa towns of Central Europe, to the French and Italian rivieras and to the Alps. Some travellers were venturing further afield. Baedeker's guide to Austria included Bosnia, with an entry on Sarajevo: "The numerous minarets and the little houses standing in gardens give the town a very picturesque appearance . . . the so-called Konak is the residence of the Austrian commandant."

The most important visitor to Sarajevo in 1914 would be Franz Ferdinand, heir to the Austrian throne. He, of course, was travelling within his own territory

Queen Victoria Diamond Jubilee Review at Spithead, June 26, 1897, painted by Charles Dixon (1872–1934).

but the members of the royal houses of Europe were great international travellers and their marriages one of the most important of bonds between states. The offspring of Queen Victoria were married into most of the Protestant royal families of the continent. It was broadly true that all European royalty were cousins; even the Habsburgs of Austria, most imperious of sovereigns, occasionally mingled their blood with outsiders; and since every state in Europe, except France and Switzerland, were monarchies, that made for a very dense network of inter-state connections indeed. Marital relationships were, however, not hard currency in foreign affairs. Nineteenth-century Europe had produced no solid instruments of inter-state co-operation or of diplomatic mediation. The "Concert of Europe" had withered; so, too, had the anti-revolutionary League of the Three Emperors. It is commonplace to say that Europe in 1914 was a continent of naked nationalism: it was true all the same. Some effort had been made to supply the deficiency through the establishment of a code of international law. It remained a weak concept, for its most important principle was that of the sovereignty of states, which left each, in effect, unfettered by anything but judgement of self-interest. The only area over which states had agreed to limit the operation of self-interest lay at sea, which the leading powers had agreed at Paris in 1856 should be one where neutrality was respected. The decision of Tsar Nicholas II in 1899 to convene an international conference dedicated to the limitation of armaments and the founding of an international court for the settlement of disputes was therefore a creative innovation. Historians have perceived in his summons of the powers to the Hague an admission of Russia's military weakness. At the time, people of goodwill thought differently. It was to some degree in deference to that public opinion that the 1899 Hague Conference did consent both to a limitation of armaments and to the creation of the International Court.

A EUROPE OF SOLDIERS

The flaw in the provision for an International Court was that its convening was to be voluntary. "The greatest thing," wrote the American delegate, is that it "relieves the dread of a sudden outburst of war at any moment." A German delegate more realistically noted that the court's "voluntary character" deprived it of "the very last trace of any compulsion, moral or otherwise, upon any nation." The truth of Europe's situation at the turn of the century lay rather with the German than the American. There was, admittedly, a fear of war in the abstract. Stronger by far was the fear of failure to face the challenge of war itself. Each state—Britain, France, Germany, Russia, Austria-Hungary—felt its position threatened in some way or other. The three great European empires, German, Austrian and Russian, felt threatened by the national dissatisfactions of their minorities. It was the burden of a different sort of empire that weighed upon Britain and France, the administration of vast overseas dominions which were a source of enormous national pride but also a spur to aggressive jealousy among their European neighbours. The British believed that Russia had ambitions on India, which its Central Asian possessions closely abutted. The Germans were ever ready to quarrel with France over the few remaining areas not yet subject to European rule.

In a continent in which a handful of powers exercised control over a large cluster of subordinate peoples, and from which two, Britain and France, ruled much of the rest of the world, it was inevitable that relations between all should be infused by suspicion and rivalry. The worst of the rivalries had been provoked by Germany, through its decision in 1900 to build a fleet capable of engaging the Royal Navy in battle. The British rightly decided to regard the enactment of the Second Naval Law as an unjustified threat to its century-old command of the seas and reacted accordingly; by 1906 the race to outbuild Germany in modern battleships was the most important popular element of British public policy. There was a strong and complementary military rivalry between the continental powers, exemplified at its starkest by the decision of France, a nation of forty million

French mountain troops on manoeuvres in the Alps in 1912. They are wearing their distinctive large, floppy beret, *"la marmite."* Known as *"Chasseurs alpins,"* the thirteen regiments were recruited and based in the mountain *départements* on the frontier with Italy. The Italian army had been the first to recruit specialist mountain troops. By 1882 it had six regiments of *Alpini*, supported by batteries of mountain artillery equipped with guns that could be dismantled into portable loads. The *Alpini* wore an eagle's feather in their caps.

Austria had recruited in the mountainous Tirol since 1801 and the regiments gradually evolved into the famous *Tiroler Kaiserjäger*, the Habsburg army's élite infantry. They were not, however, trained specifically as mountain troops, a role assigned in 1906 to the Tirolean militia, the *Landesschützen*. Their distinctive dress included a ski cap, decorated with capercaillie feathers, and the edelweiss badge. After the outbreak of war in 1914, the German army raised several units of mountain troops, including the Württemberg Mountain Battalion, in which the young Rommel won the *Pour la Mérite*, Germany's highest award for bravery, at Caporetto in October 1917. It then formed part of the Bavarian *Alpenkorps*, one of several mountain divisions which had been brought into being to fight in the Alps, the Carpathians and the Vosges. Mountain troops were regarded as an élite in all armies.

9   A European Tragedy

people, to match the strength of Germany, with sixty million, in number of soldiers. There were other rivalries, not least between Britain and France, by 1900 mutual allies in the face of Germany's rising aggressiveness, who nevertheless managed to quarrel over colonial interests in Africa. What uniformly characterised all these disputes was that none were submitted to the process of international arbitration foreshadowed by the discussions at the Hague in 1899. When issues of potential conflict arose, as they did over the first (1905) and second (1911) Moroccan crises in Franco-German relations and over the First (1912) and Second (1913) Balkan Wars, the great powers made no effort to invoke the Hague provisions but settled affairs by international treaty. Peace, temporarily at least, was the outcome; the ideal of supra-national peacemaking, towards which the Hague Conference had pointed the way, was in no case invoked.

European policy was indeed, in the opening years of the twentieth century, guided not by the search for a secure means of averting conflict but by the age-old quest for security in military superiority. That meant, as the Tsar had so eloquently warned at the Hague in 1899, the creation of ever larger armies and navies, the acquisition of more and heavier guns and the building of stronger and wider belts of frontier fortification. Fortification, however, was intellectually out of fashion with Europe's advanced military thinkers. Power had transferred, it was believed, from static defence to the mobile offensive. It was on numbers of infantrymen taught to accept that casualties would be heavy until a decision was gained that the generals counted upon to achieve victory. The significance of entrenchments thrown up at speed had been noted, but discounted. Given enough well-motivated infantry, the European military theorists believed, no line of trenches could be held against them.

Among the other great industrial enterprises of Europe in the first years of the twentieth century, therefore, the industry of creating soldiers counted among the first. Since the triumph of Prussia's army of conscripts over the Austrians in 1866 and the French in 1870, all continental European states had accepted the necessity of submitting their young men to military training. The result of this requirement was to produce enormous armies of serving and reserve soldiers. In the German army, model for all others, a conscript spent the first two years of full adulthood in uniform. During the first five years after his discharge he was obliged to return to the reserve unit of his regiment for annual train-

Soldiers of a French infantry regiment at the South-Western Manoeuvres, September 1913. The horses of a dragoon regiment are tethered in front of the infantrymen. Their officer stands to the right. A senior officer's car is parked beyond him, displaying the dragoons' regimental standard.

All are wearing uniforms scarcely changed since the 1830s, the infantry dark blue overcoats and red trousers, the dragoons a plumed Grecian helmet. The infantrymen are burdened with the enormous *chargement de campagne*, crowned with a cooking pot. They are armed with the modern Lebel magazine rifle and also carry, beside a long brass-handled bayonet, an entrenching tool. They are not, however, dug in but have merely taken cover in a convenient ditch. Everything in the picture—conspicuous clothing, overweight equipment, lack of concern for entrenchment—testifies to the French army's unreadiness for modern war.

Soldiers and non-commissioned officers of the 78th Regiment of Infantry at their barrack room at Guéret, in the Creuse, 1910. It is the hour of "*la soupe*," the most important of the peacetime day. French army food was rough but tasty and copious. There was also a generous wine ration and ample bread. The soldier sitting on the left has one of the large military loaves under his arm. Conscripts were often better fed during their two years of military service (three after 1913) than they were at home. This was probably particularly true in the Creuse, one of the poorest rural departments in France.

The 78th Regiment belonged to the 23rd Division in the XII Military District. In August 1914 the 23rd Division formed part of the Fourth Army, which took part in the Great Retreat and fought in the Battle of the Marne. The headquarters of the XII Military District was at Limoges, to which Joffre posted unsuccessful generals, because it was far from the battlefront. Hence the expression "*limogé*," meaning, effectively, disgraced.

Generals and staff officers on manoeuvres, 1913. Their appearance—overweight, overage—implies much of what was wrong with the pre-war French army. Its senior officers were on average eight years older than their German equivalents. During the crisis of August 1914, Joffre sacked one of the five army commanders, three of the twenty-one corps commanders and thirty-one of the 103 divisional commanders. In September he sacked another thirty-eight divisional commanders, in October eleven and in November twelve.

French infantry on the march during the South-Western Manoeuvres of 1913. Pre-war training did little to prepare soldiers for the realities of the coming war. The infantry deployed in dense columns, as in this photograph, and charged with fixed bayonets. The cavalry charged in dense masses with drawn swords. French doctrine stated that casualties would be heavy but that the side which accepted losses and pressed home the offensive nonetheless would triumph. It made no allowance for the crippling effect of artillery, machine-gun and concentrated rifle fire on massed ranks. At the end of the campaign of 1914, over 300,000 French soldiers had been killed.

Belgian soldiers on manoeuvres before 1914. Belgium's neutrality had been guaranteed by the Great Powers in 1839 and its army was subsequently maintained as a home defense force. Not until 1912 did the country introduce general conscription. It was slow to take effect. In 1914 the Belgian army was one of the most old-fashioned in Europe, poorly equipped, under-trained and dressed in antiquated uniforms. The soldiers in the foreground are carabineers, manning Maxim machine guns drawn by dogs, as were the Belgian milk carts so popular with tourist photographers. Those standing are lancers, wearing Napoleonic uniforms. The Belgian army fought with great bravery in 1914 but was eventually driven into the western corner of its homeland, where it took refuge behind inundations.

ing. Then, until the age of thirty-nine, he was enrolled in a unit of the secondary reserve; thereafter, until the age of forty-five, in the third-line reserve. There were French, Austrian and Russian equivalents. The effect was to maintain inside European civil society a second, submerged military society, millions strong, of men who had shouldered a rifle and learnt to obey orders.

Submerged, also, below the surface of Europe's civil geography was a secondary, military geography of corps and divisional districts. France, a country of ninety administrative departments, was also divided into twenty military districts,

Left: The battlecruisers of the Grand Fleet at anchor in the Firth of Forth, swinging to the tide, with the Forth railway bridge in the background. The photograph is taken from the airship R.9, one of whose gondolas is visible at the upper left. By 1914 the Admiralty had concentrated its battleships and battlecruisers, with their attendant cruisers and destroyers, in Scottish waters, withdrawing them from the Channel and East Coast ports, so as to guard the exit from the North Sea against a sortie by the German High Seas Fleet into the Atlantic, as far north as possible. For most of the war the Grand Fleet was stationed at Scapa Flow, in the Orkney islands, with the Battle Cruiser Fleet at Rosyth, in Scottish mainland waters. This strategy successfully ensured that the High Seas Fleet was contained in the North Sea and brought to battle—at the Dogger Bank in 1915 and Jutland in 1916—whenever it emerged from its harbours.

Opposite bottom: The German dreadnought *König* in dock. The *König* class—also including *Kronprinz*, *Grosser Kürfurst* and *Markgraf*—were the penultimate class of battleships laid down by Germany in the Great War period. *König*, launched in October 1914, mounted ten 12-inch guns, all on the centerline, unlike those in the *Westfalen* class, and achieved a speed of 21.5 knots. *König* took part in a successful encounter with the Russian Baltic fleet in 1915. In 1916 she sailed in the Third Squadron of the High Seas Fleet against the Grand Fleet in the Battle of Jutland, sustained eight heavy-calibre hits and was so badly damaged that she returned only with difficulty back into harbour.

each the peacetime location of a corps of the "active" army, the source in war of an equivalent group of divisions of the reserve. The forty-two active divisions would, on mobilisation, take with them into the field another twenty-five reserve divisions, raising the war strength of the army to over three million. From the I Corps District to the XVIII the military replicated the civil geography of France at every layer. So, too, did it in Germany, also divided into twenty-one Corps Districts. The I Corps District in East Prussia was the peacetime station of the 1st

Above: The First and Second Squadrons of the German High Seas Fleet at anchor in Kiel in 1911. The battleship in the foreground belongs to the first group of German dreadnoughts—*Westfalen, Nassau, Posen* and *Rheinland*—laid down in 1906–07, following the launch of the revolutionary British *Dreadnought*, the original turbine-driven, "all-big-gun" battleship, in 1906. The ship beyond also belongs to the same class. They were armed with ten 12-inch guns and achieved a speed of 21 knots.

Germany decided to challenge Britain's naval supremacy in 1898. Thitherto the Royal Navy out-numbered the fleets of the other naval powers several times over, for much of the nineteenth century being larger than the next half-dozen combined. Admiral Tirpitz, the father of the new German navy, set out to build a fleet which, if not equal to the British in size, would subject it to the "risk" of defeat in advantageous circumstances. Its ships were designed from the outset to be superior to their British equivalents in armoured protection and striking power. Britain rightly regarded the Tirpitz policy as a direct challenge to its world position and Anglo-German hostility dates from its initiation.

Despite the adoption of the high-velocity magazine rifle, accurate to 500 yards or more, European armies proved reluctant to abandon their traditional and conspicuous uniforms in the last decades of the nineteenth century. By 1900, however, the British army's experience of colonial campaigns, usually fought in barren, treeless terrain where its historic scarlet showed up with lethal results, had opted for Indian khaki (drab brown) service dress. The Germans soon followed suit, choosing a grey-green *feldgrau* colour, then the Austrians and Russians also, the former deciding for "pike-grey," the latter for an olive-green colour, cut as a loose *"ghymnasterka"* (gymnastic) blouse. Among leading armies, only the French clung to their old garb, a dark blue overcoat and madder-red trousers. Even it, however, had been experimenting with an inconspicuous *"mignonette"* (light green) outfit.

The appalling casualties suffered by the French in 1914 (600,000 dead) prompted a rapid change to a grey-blue (*bleu d'horizon*) uniform, worn as tunic and breeches, tucked into puttees, on the British pattern. Conditions of trench warfare led to the introduction of a steel helmet, worn by all major armies (except the Russian) from late 1915 onwards. The most distinctive was the German "coal scuttle"; the elegant French *casque André* was adopted by the Italians and Belgians, the British "tin hat" by the Americans.

Yet, despite the universal change to camouflage dress, tradition retained its hold. The German field-grey uniforms retained the historic cut of the different arms of service, the plastron front for uhlans, braid frogging for hussars. The French Zouaves kept their baggy trousers, Russian Cossacks their astrakhan hats. British highlanders wore the kilt, under a khaki apron. The most successful item of equipment adopted during the war was the British officer's Sam Browne belt, eventually worn by the French, Americans and Belgians as well and, after 1918, by the Germans and the Red Army. It had been designed by the one-armed Sam Browne as a convenient means of carrying a sword. Swords were worn by the cavalry throughout the war, sometimes by infantry officers in the trenches.

Die graue Felduniform der Offiziere.

Husar.   Ulan.   Jäger zu Pferde.   Offizier der Feldartillerie.   Offizier eines Linien-
Offizier v. 16. Hus.-Reg.   Offizier v. 2. Garde-Ul.-Reg.   Offizier v. Reg. Jäg. z. Pf. Nr. 2.   Pionier-Bataillons.

The German army, like the British, had adopted camouflage uniforms well before the outbreak of the First World War. The colour chosen was *feldgrau* (field-grey), in actuality a sort of green-brown.

When the British, however, abandoned all connection with its old full-dress uniform, opting for what a German officer of the 1914 campaign would describe as "a golfing suit," the Germans clung to many of the features of their traditional ceremonial dress, as these illustrations of the new uniforms for Bavarian soldiers and officers reveals. Thus the Bavarian *chevauxleger* (light cavalry) soldier continues to wear his cross-belt and the guardsman of the *Leibregiment* (Body Guard) his spiked helmet, under a canvas cover. The officers, respectively a hussar, a lancer (uhlan) and a mounted rifleman (last three), all wear field-grey versions of their traditional costume.

Die graue Felduniform der Mannschaften-Bayerische Truppenteile.

Infanterie · Leib-R.   Jäger   Infanterie   1. Ul.-R.   Fussartillerie.   Pionier.   1. schw. Reiter-R.
   II. A.-K.   III. A.-K.   3. Chevauleger-R.   Train.   Feldart. III. A.-K.

and 2nd Infantry Divisions, but also of the wartime I Reserve Corps and a host of additional *Landwehr* and *Landsturm* units, dedicated to the defence of the Prussian heartland against the danger of Russian attack. Russia's military geography resembled Germany's; so, too, did that of Austria-Hungary.

Whatever the diversity of the European armies' component units there was a central uniformity to their organisation. That was provided by the core fighting organisation, the division. The division, a creation of the Napoleonic revolution in military affairs, normally comprised twelve battalions of infantry and twelve batteries of artillery, 12,000 rifles and seventy-two guns. Its firepower in attack was formidable. In a minute of activity, the division could discharge 120,000 rounds of small-arms ammunition and a thousand explosive shells. There were in Europe, in 1914, over two hundred divisions, in full existence or ready to be called into being, theoretically deploying sufficient firepower to destroy each other totally in a few minutes of mutual life-taking.

What had not been perceived is that firepower takes effect only if it can be directed in timely and accurate fashion. That requires communication. Undirected fire is wasted effort unless observers can co-ordinate the action of infantry with its artillery support. The communication necessary to such co-ordination demands the shortest possible interval in time between observation and response. Nothing in the elaborate equipment of the European armies of the early nineteenth century provided such facility. Their means of communication were at worst word of mouth, at best telephone and telegraph. As telephone and telegraph depended upon preserving the integrity of fragile wires, word of mouth offered the only standby in a failure of communication, consigning commanders to the delays and uncertainties of the earliest days of warfare. Radio communication, wireless telegraphy as it was then known, offered a solution to the difficulty in theory, but not in practise. Contemporary wireless sets were not practicable tools of command in the field. Though wireless was to play a minor strategic role early in the coming war, it was to prove of no tactical significance at any time. That was to prove true at sea also, because of the failure of navies to solve the problem of assuring radio security in the transmission of signals in action and in close proximity to the enemy. In retrospect, it may be seen that a system existing in embryo lagged technically too far behind its potentiality to prove effective.

If the potentiality of modern communications failed those dedicated to waging war, how much more did it fail those professionally dedicated to preserving the peace. The tragedy of the diplomatic crisis that preceded the outbreak of the fighting in August 1914 is that events successively and progressively overwhelmed the capacity of statesmen and diplomats to control and contain them. Honourable and able men though they were, the servants of the chancelleries and foreign officers of the great powers in the July crisis were bound to the wheel of the written note, the encipherment routine, the telegraph schedule. The potentialities of the telephone, which might have cut across the barriers to communication, seem to have eluded their imaginative powers. The potentialities of radio, available but unused, evaded them altogether. In the event, the states of Europe proceeded, as if in a dead march and a dialogue of the deaf, to the destruction of their continent and its civilisation.

WAR PLANS

2

The French 28th Regiment in camouflage uniform in 1912. Britain had adopted khaki as the color of its service dress after the Boer War (1899–1902). Germany adopted field-grey in 1910. The traditionalist French army clung to its dark blue overcoat and red trousers, the costume in which it had fought all its wars since 1830. By 1912, however, anxiety about the uniform's conspicuousness was creeping in and, after much debate, a new outfit, known as the Réséda after its designer, was issued experimentally. The colour was light green (*mignonette*) but the cut followed that of the traditional uniform, while the leather helmet was modelled on an eighteenth-century pattern. It did not find favour, so the army went to war in 1914 still in blue and red. The helmet, however, influenced the design of the steel helmet, the *casque Adrian*, adopted in 1915 and copied by the Belgians, Italians and many minor combatants on the Allied side.

All European armies in 1914 had long-laid military plans, notable in most cases for their inflexibility. None was integrated with what today would be called a "national security policy," made in conclave between politicians, diplomats, intelligence directors and service chiefs, and designed to serve a country's vital interests, for such a concept of national leadership did not then exist. Military plans were held to be military secrets in the strictest sense, secret to the planners alone, scarcely communicable in peacetime to civilian heads of government, often not from one service to another. The commander of the Italian navy in 1915, for example, was not told by the army of the decision to make war on Austria until the day itself; conversely, the Austrian chief of staff so intimidated the foreign minister that in July 1914 he was left uninformed of military judgements about the likelihood of Russia declaring war. Only in Britain, where a Committee of Imperial Defence formed of politicians, civil servants and diplomats as well as commanders and intelligence officers had been instituted in 1902, were military plans discussed in open forum; even the C.I.D., however, was dominated by the army, for the Royal Navy, Britain's senior service and heir of Nelson, had its own plan to win any war by fighting a second Trafalgar, and so held magnificently aloof from the committee's deliberations. In Germany, where the army and the Kaiser had succeeded by 1889 in excluding both the War Ministry and parliament from military policy-making, war planning belonged exclusively to the Great General Staff; the navy's admirals were fed crumbs and even the prime minister, Bethmann-Hollweg, was not told of the central war plan until December 1912, though it had been in preparation since 1905.

Yet that plan, the "Schlieffen Plan," so-called after its architect, was the most important government document written in any country in the first decade of the twentieth century; it might be argued that it was to prove the most important official document of the last hundred years, for it was to have consequences that persist to this day. Its importance must never be exaggerated. Plans do not determine outcomes. In no sense did it precipitate the First World War; the war was the result of decisions taken, or not taken, by many men in June and July 1914, not by a group of officers of the German Great General Staff years beforehand. Nevertheless, Schlieffen's plan, by his selection of place for a war's opening and proposal of action in that theatre by the German army, dictated, once it was adopted in the heat of crisis, where the war's focus would lie and, through its innate flaws, the possibility of the war's political widening and therefore the probability of its protraction. It was a plan pregnant with dangerous uncertainty: the uncertainty of the quick victory it was designed to achieve, the greater uncertainty of what would follow if it did not attain its intended object.

Schlieffen's was a war plan in the abstract par excellence. He was appointed Chief of the German Great General Staff in 1891 and began at once to consider how best to secure his country's security in the political circumstances prevailing. The plans inherited from his predecessors, the great Moltke the Elder and Waldersee, took the predicament of Germany's interposition between France, implacably hostile since the defeat of 1870 and the loss of Alsace-Lorraine, and Russia, long France's friend, as their starting point. That presaged, in worst case, a two-front war. Both discounted the likelihood of a success against France, which was protected by a chain of fortresses, and therefore concluded that the German army should fight defensively in the west, using the Rhine as a barrier against a French offensive, and deploy its main strength in the east. So, it must be said, did Schlieffen; but he, though a pupil of Moltke, understood only his military, not his political thinking. Moltke had always taken trouble to adjust his strategic ideas to the spirit of his country's diplomacy. Schlieffen was uninterested in foreign affairs. He believed in the primacy of force. Because of the young German Kaiser's ill-judged repudiation of Bismarck's "reinsurance" treaty with Russia in 1890, a treaty holding Russia to neutrality with Germany unless Germany attacked France, and Germany to neutrality with Russia unless it attacked Austria-Hungary, Germany's ally, he was allowed, on succeeding as Chief of Staff, to give his preoccupation with force full rein. Chessboard thinking came to possess him. The pieces he identified were few: a France weaker than Germany but protected by forts; a Russia weaker than Germany but protected by great space; a weak Austrian ally, but hostile to Russia and therefore useful as a distraction and perhaps even as a counterweight; a very weak Italy, allied to Germany and Austria, which therefore did not count; a Britain which could be ignored, for Schlieffen was so uninterested in seapower that he even despised the German navy.

Given the relativities of force, and they alone influenced his thinking, he arrived in progressive stages at a plan to commit seven-eighths of Germany's strength, in the contingency of war, to an overwhelming offensive against France. Already by August 1892 he had decided that the west must be the centre of effort. By 1894 he was proposing a scheme for destroying the French fortresses along the Franco-German frontier. In 1897, having accepted that Germany's heavy artillery could not do sufficient damage to the forts, he began to argue to himself that the "offensive must not shrink from violating the neutrality of Belgium and Luxembourg," in other words, neutralising the French fortresses by outflanking them. Plans written between 1899 and 1904 envisaged an advance through Luxembourg and the southern tip of Belgium with more than two-thirds of the army. Finally, in the so-called Great Memorandum of December 1905, completed just before his

The Kaiser Manoeuvres, the annual summer exercises of the German army at which the German Emperor observed his troops practising for war. The officers are dressed in the regimental uniforms worn before the adoption of field-grey. Third from the left, on horseback, is General von Schlieffen, Chief of the Great General Staff, 1891–1906, the author of the

retirement after fourteen years in the highest military post, he cast moderation aside. Belgian neutrality—guaranteed jointly by Britain, France and Prussia, since 1839—was not tepidly to be infringed but violated on the largest scale. Almost the whole of the German army was to march forward in a huge wheeling movement, first through Belgium, then across the plains of Flanders to reach, on the twenty-second day after mobilisation, the French frontier. On the thirty-first day,

German war plan of 1914. He is dressed as an officer of the Guard Uhlans. The Kaiser is in the center, mounted, behind the cuirassier in white. The officers in the foreground, with white armbands and helmet covers, are umpires, who adjudicated the outcome of encounters between "friendly" and "enemy" forces.

the German line was to run along the Rivers Somme and Meuse and from that position the right wing was to turn southward, envelop Paris from the west and begin to drive the French army towards the left wing advancing from Alsace-Lorraine. A great semi-circular pincer, four hundred miles in circumference, the jaws separated by two hundred miles, would close on the French army caught in between. Under inexorable pressure the French would be pinned to the ground of a decisive battlefield, fought to a standstill and crushed. By the forty-second day from mobilisation, the war in the west would have been won and the victorious German army freed to take the railway back across Germany to the east and there inflict another crushing defeat on the Russians.

French army manoeuvres in the south-west, September 1913.

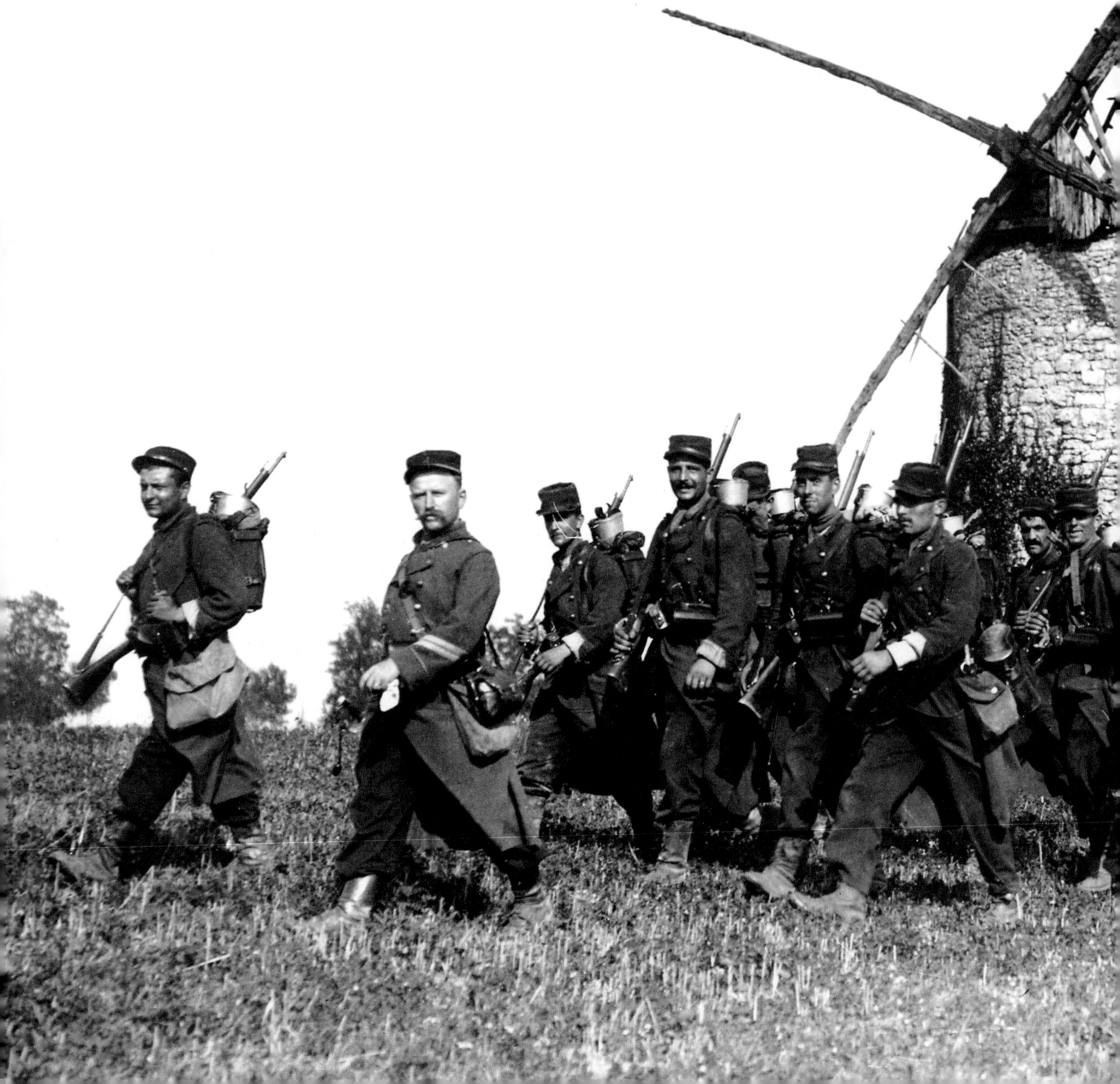

The progress of the German armies of the right wing during the advance from Belgium into France, August–September 1914. The dotted line shows that reached by August 23. The Schlieffen Plan then required the First and Second Armies to wheel inwards, encircle the left wing of the retreating French and bring them to a concluding battle in the vicinity of Paris. The plan failed in practise because von Kluck, commanding First Army, could not decide as he approached the heavily fortified city of Paris whether to pass to its north or south. Either route was dangerous. He decided eventually to pass to the north and was attacked by the Paris garrison in the opening stages of the Battle of the Marne, a great French victory. Schlieffen had foreseen such an outcome, conceding that his plan, on which he laboured for a dozen years, was an enterprise for which "we are too weak."

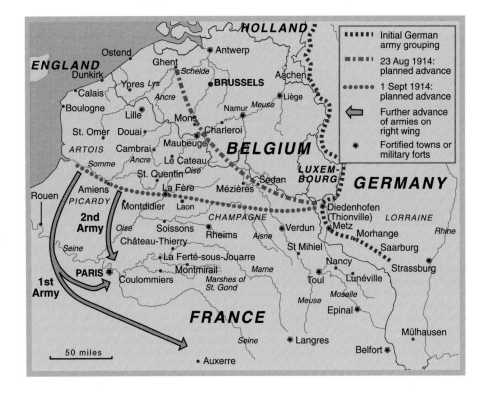

Schlieffen continued to tinker with his plan until his death in 1912. He had no other occupation. He was a man without hobbies. It was the dispositions of armies on a map that interested him. He had an obsession with Cannae, the battle in which Hannibal had encircled the Roman legions in 216 B.C. Hannibal's crushing victory was a major inspiration of his Great Memorandum of 1905. In Cannae he perceived the pure essence of generalship, untainted by politics, logistics, technology or the psychology of combat. Aloof, sarcastic, intellectually arrogant, he had by the end of his career succeeded in reducing war to a pure abstraction, so many corps here, so many there. An extract from the Great Memorandum gives the flavour: "If possible, the German Army will win its battle by an envelopment with the right wing. This will therefore be made as strong as possible. For this purpose eight army corps and five cavalry divisions will cross the Meuse by five routes below Liège and advance in the direction of Brussels-Namur; a ninth army corps will join them after crossing the Meuse above Liège." Odder still, given his obsession with troop movements, Schlieffen had objections to enlarging the size of the German army so as to ensure its capacity to overwhelm the enemy. The intellectual problem he had set himself was how to win a short war with the resources available. His ambition was to repeat the triumphs of the great von Moltke in 1866, against Austria, and 1870, against France, wars of six and seven weeks respectively. Above all he wanted to avoid a "wearing-out" war. "A strategy of attrition," he wrote, "will not do if the maintenance of millions costs billions."

The dream was of a whirlwind; the calculations warned of a dying thunderstorm. Even in the Great Memorandum of 1905 Schlieffen took counsel of his fears. "It is therefore essential," he wrote, "to accelerate the advance of the German right wing as much as possible" and "the army commanders must be constantly on the alert and distribute the marching routes appropriately." This is not the only note of desperation in the Great Memorandum. There are others. Schlieffen yearns for more troops at the decisive point, the right wing of the great wheel through Belgium and northern France: "Still greater forces must be raised . . . Eight army corps must be raised." Schlieffen urges the creation of these eight corps, an addition of a full quarter to the strength of the army, from the reserves and the *Landwehr* (over-age reservists), even though he apparently shared his brother generals' fear of enlarging the army through the enlistment of unreliable elements. The note of desperation grows stronger: "How many [of the eight corps] can be transported [to the right wing] depends on the capacity of the railways . . . [they] are needed for the envelopment of Paris . . . How they advance and the attack on the position are shown on Map 3."

It is at this point that a careful reader of the Great Memorandum recognises a plan falling apart: Map 3 in no way shows how the new corps are to advance or to invest Paris, the central strong point of the "great fortress" that was Schlieffen's France. The corps simply appear, with no indication of how they have reached Paris and its outskirts. The "capacity of the railways" is irrelevant; railways, in Schlieffen's plan, were to carry the attackers no further than the German frontier with Belgium and France. Thereafter it was the road network that led forward, and the plodding boots of the infantry that would measure out the speed

Opposite top: Von Moltke the Younger (1848–1916) was Chief of the German Great General Staff in 1914. His father had also been Chief of Staff and had masterminded the great Prussian victories over Austria in 1866 and France in 1870. The Kaiser believed that the son would repeat the father's successes in a new war with France and so appointed him to succeed Schlieffen in 1906. The younger Moltke, however, lacked his father's iron will and certainty of thought. Dreamy, cello-playing and interested in Oriental religion, he suffered a nervous breakdown after the failure of the invasion of France in 1914 and was replaced by the more decisive von Falkenhayn.

Opposite bottom: Field Marshal Alfred Graf von Schlieffen (1833–1913) became Chief of the German Great General Staff in 1891, four years after von Moltke the Elder had given up the post. Like the elder Moltke, whose intellectual influence upon him was strong, he spoke little and had few interests outside military affairs. Unlike Moltke, who benefited from Bismarck's policy of keeping on good terms with Russia, he had to face the problem of fighting a "two-front" war, with France as well. His solution was the famous "Schlieffen Plan," designed to defeat France in six weeks, making enough time to transfer the army to the east, for victory over Russia. In 1914, it failed, with disastrous consequences.

of advance. Schlieffen himself reckoned that to be only twelve miles a day. For the "eight new corps," needed by Schlieffen as his plan's clinching device, to arrive at the decisive place of action, they would have actually needed to march not only further and faster, which defied probabilities, but to do so along the same roads as those occupied by the corps already existing, a simple impossibility. It is not surprising, therefore, to find buried in the text of the Great Memorandum its author's admission that "we are too weak" to bring the plan to a conclusion. He had run into a logical impasse. Railways would position the troops for his great wheel; the Belgian and French roads would allow them to reach the outskirts of Paris in the sixth week from mobilisation day; but they would not arrive in the strength necessary to win a decisive battle unless they were accompanied by eight corps—200,000 men—for which there was no room. His plan for a lightning victory was flawed at its heart.

It was pigeonholed for use nonetheless. Moltke the younger, nephew of the victor of 1866 and 1870, tinkered with it when he succeeded as Chief of the Great General Staff in 1906. Schlieffen did so himself, literally up to the eve of his death on January 4, 1913. Neither solved the inherent difficulties. Moltke is conventionally accused of compounding them, by strengthening the left of the planned German deployment at the expense proportionately of Schlieffen's massive right; that is scarcely the point. Moltke's staff certainly abbreviated the time needed to entrain and offload the troops at the frontier deployment points. That was scarcely the point either; beyond the railways lay the roads. There the inflexible average of the twenty marched miles a day cramped the calculations of the finest minds. The Schlieffen Plan was left to lie in its pigeonhole, to be extracted and instituted in August 1914 with calamitous results.

Yet the French war plan that lay in its pigeonhole in 1914, Plan XVII, proposed exactly that "favour" to Germany Schlieffen had discounted France making. It was a plan for a headlong attack across the common Franco-German frontier, into Lorraine and towards the Rhine, judged by Schlieffen the least well suited to serve French interests. France had spent vast quantities of money since the 1880s in improving the fortifications that protected its territory. The provinces of Alsace and Lorraine, annexed to the new German Empire in 1871, had, under German imperial government, the fortifications of Metz and Thionville expensively modernised. Those cities were the gateways from France to Germany. Schlieffen presumed that the French high command would shrink from planning to attack them.

In the period while the Great Memorandum was in preparation, Schlieffen's presumption was correct. The French Plan XIV, completed in 1898, predicated defence of the common frontier in the event of war with Germany. A French attack was thought impossible by reason of disparity of numbers. A static French population of forty million could not challenge an expanding German population already fifty million strong, and rising fast. Moreover, the French high command was intimidated by Germany's proven ability to enlarge its army rapidly in time of crisis by incorporation of reservists. The French reserve system had failed in 1870. The French generals of 1898 did not trust that the system would work any better in the future.

The rise of the popular forces at the beginning of the twentieth century had made advertising an enormous and influential industry. Its members—artists, graphic designers, and copywriters—applied their talents to war propaganda from the outset. They addressed a variety of themes, but particularly appeals to enlist, to subscribe to war loans and to take up war work.

In Britain, where mass-circulation newspapers were better established than in any European country, advertising was a highly developed art. Its practitioners applied themselves particularly to the need for manpower, for until 1916 the British army was recruited entirely by volunteering. Three of the most famous posters of the war are recruiting appeals. Two play on male pride: "Daddy, what did YOU do in the Great War?"—which became a catchphrase, still current—and "Women

of Britain say 'GO!' " A third is perhaps the most famous of all Great War images, the face of Kitchener, Britain's War Minister, his pointing finger and the words "needs YOU."

In France and Germany, which conscripted their soldiers, advertising was largely directed at civilian leaders, since loans, rather than taxation as in Britain, was a principal means of financing the war. One, by Jules Faivre, popularized the phrase *"On les aura!"*—"We'll get them," which became a long-lasting French catchphrase. In Germany, a popular means of raising money was to sell iron nails, which were then hammered into wooden statues of Hindenburg.

As the war intensified, and enthusiasm flagged, propaganda increasingly took the form of vilifying the enemy. Curiously, the most effective demonizer was a neutral, the Dutchman Louis Raemaekers, whose depictions of the Germans as baby-killers, rapists and mass-murderers remain among the most graphic of Great War propaganda.

By 1911 fears of a large German offensive through Belgium, reinforced by massive reserves, were becoming acute and a new French Chief of Staff, Victor Michel, proposed a radical departure from the strategies of Plans XIV–XVI: all available French reserves were to be amalgamated with the active units, and the army was to be deployed on mobilisation along the whole French frontier from Switzerland to the North Sea. Michel's plan mirrored, though he could not know it, Schlieffen's; it even proposed an offensive into northern Belgium which would have met Schlieffen's "strong right wing" head on; with what results cannot be guessed, though surely not worse than those produced by the totally different French war plan of 1914. Michel, unfortunately, was a military odd-man-out, a "Republican" general whose politics were disliked by his fellows. He was soon ousted from office by a new right-wing government. Plan XVII, which came into force in April 1913, reversed his scheme. The amalgamation of reserve with active units was set aside. The deployment northwards to the sea was curtailed, leaving only the left-hand Fifth Army to deal with the danger of a German advance through northern Belgium from a position opposite southern Belgium. Most important, the operations on the common frontier were designed to be offensive. "Whatever the circumstances," Plan XVII laid down, "the intention of the commander-in-chief is to advance with all forces united to the attack on the German armies."

There were several reasons for the adoption of Plan XVII, the brainchild of Michel's successor, Joseph Joffre. One was an absence of any firm assurance by the intelligence services that the Germans would indeed risk a drive through northern Belgium. Another was the anxiety induced by Germany's known ability to deploy reserve formations at mobilisation, which put a premium on using the strength of the French peacetime army as forcefully as possible, before the reserves of either side could come into play. That meant attacking, and attacking at a point that the Germans must defend and where they could be found quickly, which was across the common frontier. A final reason for the adoption of Plan XVII was supplied by the developing relationship between France and her associates. Since 1905 the British and French general staffs had been in active conclave. By 1911 there was between them a firm understanding that in the event of Germany's violation of the Anglo-French-Prussian treaty of 1839 guaranteeing Belgium's neutrality, a British Expeditionary Force would take its place on the French left.

Moreover, the French generals believed the Plan XVII offensive to be a necessity if their Russian allies were to lend the help France would need at the outset of a German war. Russia's strategic difficulties both resembled and differed from those of France. Like France, it would be slower than Germany to utilise its reserves in a crisis. Unlike France, its difficulties of reinforcement were more geographical than organisational. It was the vast distance between population centres within Russia which would delay deployment to the front. Yet those distances were also an advantage to Russia, since it would not be pressed, in the crisis of mobilisation. It could accept an initial loss of territory while it rallied its army, something France could not afford. Plan XVII was therefore justified in one sense because the great battle it was designed to provoke was motivated by

The arrival of Grand Duke Nicholas Nicholaevich (in motorcar, escorted by French cuirassiers) at Montcontour, Vienne, for a banquet given in his honour during the manoeuvres of 1912. The Grand Duke was Tsar Nicholas II's uncle and became Commander-in-Chief of the Russian armies in 1914. Russia and France had been allies since 1894, when a treaty was signed guaranteeing that either would come to the other's assistance if attacked by a third party. The treaty was directed against Germany which, under the young Kaiser Wilhelm II, had abandoned Chancellor Bismarck's former policy of maintaining friendly relations with Russia. It led to detailed Franco-Russian planning for war from 1911 onwards, which laid the basis for Russia's offensive into East Prussia in August 1914.

the need the French felt to convince the Russians at the outset that the struggle was one of life and death. The bigger and quicker the crisis, the greater the danger to France, the sooner the subsequent threat to Russia and therefore the more imperative the need for it to march rapidly to the help of France also.

Yet Russia had a reputation for dilatoriness. It rightly exasperated the French generals. It took new staff talks, convoked by a thoroughly alarmed Joffre in August 1910, to win from General Sukhomlinov, the Russian War Minister, an assurance that the Russian army would "undertake some offensive action on the sixteenth day in the hope of tying down at least five or six German corps otherwise employable on the western front." The Russians were not wholly to be

blamed. The first decade of the century was for them a time of troubles, revolution at home, defeat in war with the Japanese in the Far East. The years 1906–9 were those in which the Schlieffen Plan would have worked. By 1909 the Russians had recovered enough to write a Mobilisation Schedule, Number 18, which at least included provision for an offensive. In June 1910 the Russian staff had become more positive. Mobilisation Schedule 19 accepted that Germany would be the chief enemy. Further debate within the general staff ensued, over the relative weights of what was operationally possible, what was owed to Russia's traditional commitments in south-eastern Europe and what was due to the French alliance. The outcome was a compromise, known as Variants A and G to Schedule 19, A for a main effort against Austria, G against Germany.

Variant A, had the French known of it, would have confirmed their worst fears. Fortunately for them, in the same month, August 1912, that the Russian general

General Kuropatkin, Commander of Russia's army in Manchuria, greets officers during a tour of inspection during the Russo-Japanese War of 1904–5. The officer on the right is General Meyendorf, one of the numerous Tsarist officers of German origin. Japan's invasion of Manchuria in 1904 and its attack on Russian naval forces in the Far East was an effort to establish itself as the dominant military power in the north-western Pacific. It resulted in a decisive Japanese victory, much to the surprise of Europe and the United States. The character of the war, fought from entrenchments with heavy losses of infantry on both sides, anticipated that of 1914–18.

Right: A Russian gunboat sinking off Port Arthur in the Russo-Japanese War, May 1904, from a popular print.

Below: The survivors of the Russian 1st Rifle Regiment after the Battle of Mukden in Manchuria, Russo-Japanese War, 1905. A third of the Russian defending force, 300,000 strong, were killed or wounded in this last battle of the war. Though Russia conceded defeat to Japan in the war, its army had not been beaten. Its soldiers fought with great bravery and its officers learnt lessons which stood it in good stead against the Germans in 1914. Russia was obliged eventually to sue for peace because of civil discontent, not military failure, a pattern to be repeated in 1917.

MILITARY MEDICINE

The First World War was the first in which deaths by enemy action exceeded those caused by disease. That was the outcome of improved field hygiene, particularly the provision of clean drinking water, disinfestations of clothing, pest control and obligatory bathing. Such conditions prevailed, however, only in Europe. In the East African campaign, disease casualties exceeded those caused by the enemy a hundredfold. The great influenza epidemic of 1918, moreover, killed more people than the war itself had done and the victims included many soldiers.

Battle deaths in all armies totalled over ten million, of which two-thirds were caused by shell fire. Bullets killed most of the rest; gas deaths were only 3 per cent of the total. Many of those who died did so because, in the conditions of trench warfare, they could not be brought quickly enough to first aid before shock, usually caused by loss of blood, supervened. The journey on stretcher from point of wounding to dressing station might, in the most waterlogged battlefields, take several hours and require relays of carriers. Sometimes, as on the Somme on July 1, 1916, the number of wounded overwhelmed the carrying parties and wounded, left untreated for several days, died where they had been hit.

Military surgery, under anaesthesia, by 1914 universally available, was skilful and effective, but too often radical. Amputation was a common treatment of wounds to the extremities. The deficiencies, by modern standards, were lack of blood transfusion and of antibiotics. Shock was therefore a great killer and so too was infection, particularly by soil organisms carried into open wounds on the heavily manured fields of northern France and Belgium. A new phenomenon was that of "shell shock," today called "combat stress." At first unrecognised, and treated as a symptom of cowardice, it became during the war one of the most common causes of disablement, leaving hundreds of thousands of post-war victims in all countries.

The toll of severe wounds among those who survived may be measured by figures from Germany. In that country after 1918 there were 44,657 who had lost a leg, 1,264 who had lost both legs, 20,877 who had lost an arm and 2,547 war blind. Figures were similar in France, where post-war sanatoria were set up for those so facially disfigured as to embarrass the public.

Opposite: A Russian field hospital.

Right: French health outpost on the Marne front, near Reims.

Below: *The Workroom of the Gerrard's Cross War Hospital Supply Depot,* 1918. Watercolour by J. Barnard Davis (1861–c.1942), British.

British casualties of the gas attack on Hill 60, May 1, 1915, receiving open-air treatment at Number 8 Casualty Clearing Station, Bailleul, Second Battle of Ypres.

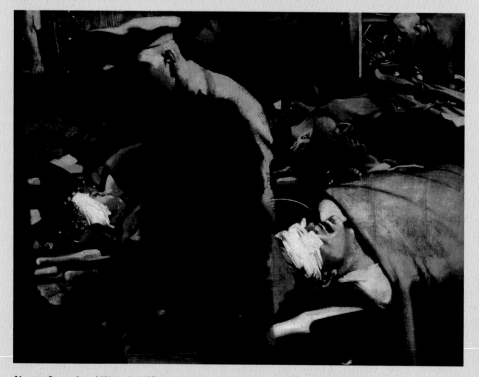

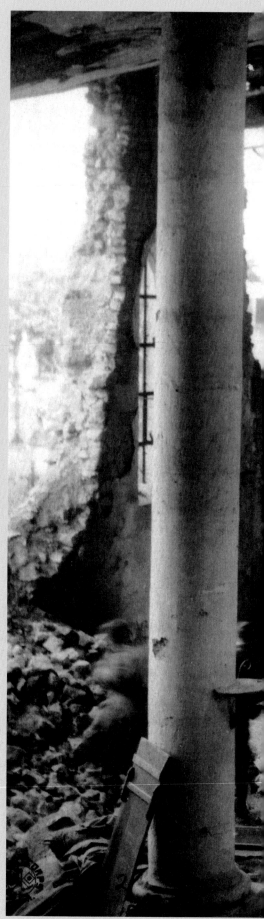

Above: *Gassed and Wounded.* Oil by Eric Henri Kennington (1888–1960), English.

Right: Wounded American soldiers resting in the ruined church of Neuvilly during the advance at Argonne, 1918.

staff completed the drafting of the two variants, they were able to extract from General Zhilinsky, the Russian Chief of Staff, a promise that his army would attack Germany with at least 800,000 men fifteen days from mobilisation. This sudden show by the Russians of wholehearted commitment to their ally has been explained in a variety of ways. One is that by 1913 the Russian army had largely recovered from the chaos into which it had been thrown by defeat at the hands of the Japanese. A second reason was misleading intelligence. In 1913 Russia had an "agent in place," the Austrian Colonel Alfred Redl, who had sold them the plans for his army's mobilisation, plans which appeared to minimise the dangers foreseen in Variant A. "A third explanation for Russian conduct was the weight of the [French] alliance . . . Russia and France either rose or fell together and . . . Russia should strain to the utmost in meeting its obligations." Finally, there is the suggestion that the Russian generals abruptly closed their minds to the dangers into which an offensive war would lead them. In that, however, they differed from the French and the Germans only in the lateness of their decision to gamble.

If Russia alarmed France by procrastination in the years 1906–14, so did Austria her German ally. The two countries, enemies in the war of 1866 which had given Germany the leadership of Central Europe, had made up their differences by 1882. The alliance then signed, however, contained no military provisions. There things rested. The Austrian staff found Schlieffen, when he came into office, "taciturn" and "hardly forthcoming." It was not until after his retirement that productive negotiations commenced, in Jan-

Foreign officers, at the French manoeuvres of September 1913, held in south-western France. The officer on the left is Bulgarian, the other two Austrian. The Second Balkan War, in which Bulgaria had attacked the Greeks and the Serbs, had just ended in a Bulgarian defeat, by which it lost all the territory it had gained in the First

Balkan War of 1912, when it, Greece and Serbia had combined to fight Turkey. In 1915 Bulgaria entered the First World War on the side of Germany, hoping to recover the ground lost in 1913, a bad decision which put it among the losers at the Peace Conference of 1919.

A French officer briefs foreign observers at the eastern manoeuvres of 1911. Two are Chinese. The officer on the right is Mexican, the officer second left from the French colonial troops.

The armies of the smaller powers greatly valued the opportunity to observe the latest military practise at the great annual training exercises in the major states.

Franz Graf Conrad von Hötzendorf (1852–1925), Chief of Staff of the Austro-Hungarian army from 1906 to 1917. Conrad was a highly intelligent military technician, with a keen understanding of the latest developments in military technology and practise. He was also, however, an aggressive nationalist, who believed that military action against Austria's enemies offered the best hope of preserving the loyalty of the Habsburg empire's many different component nationalities. He had a violent hatred for the independent kingdom of Serbia, believing correctly that many of the Emperor Franz Josef's subjects of Serb ethnicity were disloyal and hoped that a break-up of the empire would lead to the creation of a Greater Serbia of which they would become citizens. He had long advocated a pre-emptive war against Serbia and was a moving force behind the policy of confronting Serbia with an ultimatum in the crisis of July 1914, following the assassination by Serb terrorists of the Emperor's heir, the Archduke Franz Ferdinand, at Sarajevo.

uary 1909. Moltke the Younger knew what he wanted. The Schlieffen Plan lay in its pigeonhole. It required of the Austrians the largest and speediest deployment possible against Russian Poland. The initiative for the talks, however, had come from his Austrian opposite number, Franz Graf Conrad von Hötzendorf. The solution he suggested was the division of his army into three at mobilisation: a *Minimalgruppe Balkan* of ten divisions, to deploy against Serbia, a *Staffel-A* of thirty divisions for the Polish theatre and a *Staffel-B* of twelve divisions, to act as a "swing" force reinforcing either, as need be.

The scheme offered little to Moltke. He assured Conrad that the war in the west would be over before Russia could fully mobilise and that Germany would by then have sent strong forces to the east; but he gave no timetable, an omission to cause Conrad anxiety, since he had a two-front war of his own to plan. He warned Moltke that Germany could not count on the transfer of *Minimalgruppe Balkan* to Poland before fifty days from mobilisation. Could Germany guarantee to send support within forty days? If not, he had better stand on the defensive in Poland and destroy Serbia in an all-out offensive. The destruction of Serbia was Conrad's real desire; like many German-Austrians, he detested the small Slav kingdom, not merely because it failed to show due deference to Austria's unofficial imperium over the Balkans but also because it was a magnet of attraction to dissident Serbs within the Habsburg empire.

Moltke replied with a mixture of assurances and dismissals. He was concerned, above all, to arrange that Russia should also have to fight on two fronts—a Polish western front where the Germans would be temporarily weak, a Polish southern front where he hoped the Austrians would be strong—and he stifled any irritation Conrad's prevarication provoked and promised to join with Austria in an offensive: "I will not hesitate to make the attack to support the simultaneous Austrian offensive." That was a promise he should not have given and could not certainly make good. The Schlieffen Plan, indeed, stipulated that the fraction of the German army left in East Prussia while the great western battle was fought should stand on the defensive. When he and Conrad had their final pre-war meeting in May 1914, the German Chief of Staff responded to the Austrian's request for the commitment of additional troops in the east, with the vague assurance, "I will do what I can."

What he had not counted upon was the intervention of the British. Since military conversations between France and Britain did not begin until December 1905, the month in which the Great Memorandum was finished, Schlieffen had no indication that they might. Moreover, the British themselves remained in two minds over what they should do with their army if it were committed to the continent. In April 1906 the Committee of Imperial Defence drew up plans to send troops directly to the Low Countries. There was then a lapse of five years, brought about by Belgian unwillingness to admit a British army and by French inability to design a convincing war plan. All changed in 1911, with the appointment of Joffre as French Chief of Staff and Henry Wilson as British Director of Military Operations. Joffre was formidable, Wilson dynamic. When they met for the first time in Paris in November, Joffre unveiled the outlines of Plan XVII. Wilson, in August, had already outlined to the Committee of Imperial Defence how best a

British Expeditionary Force might be employed, small though it would be, for spending on the navy and the country's continued resistance to conscription allowed it to keep an army of only six divisions at home. Those six divisions, by operating against the German right wing, might tip the balance by forcing the Germans to divert strength to deal with it. The British were nevertheless cautious. Ardently Francophile though he was, Wilson succeeded in denying to the French any specific indication as to where the expeditionary force would take the field, right up to August 1914, while it was only in November 1912 that the French extracted from the Foreign Secretary, Sir Edward Grey, something like a commitment to common action. The principle of splendid isolation, for all the dangers offered by diminishing economic power and growing German naval strength, could still cause Britain to hesitate at binding herself to an ally.

Britain, of course, enjoyed a luxury of choice the continental powers did not, the choice between "taking as much or as little of a war" as it wanted; Bacon's summary of the advantages of sea power remained as true in the twentieth as it had been in the sixteenth century. France and Germany, Russia and Austria, did not benefit from the protection of saltwater frontiers. Separated from each other at best by river or mountain, at worst by nothing more substantial than a line on the map, their security resided in their armies. That threw them into a harsh and mutual predicament. The danger most acutely threatened Germany: if it failed to move to the offensive as soon as the troop trains disgorged their passengers at the unloading points, the unequal division of force between west and east would be pointlessly revealed and so, worse, would be the concentration against Belgium. The Schlieffen Plan would have been betrayed, France given the time to recoil from the peril of Plan XVII, Russia the incentive to invade East Prussia in overwhelming force and Austria the unsought and probably undischargeable burden of guaranteeing the security of Central Europe. The existence of a permanent medium of negotiation between the European powers might have robbed the war plans that lay in their pigeonholes of their menacing instantaneity. Before 1914 technology, however, could not offer the opportunity of frequent and immediate communication, but more important than that lack was the absence of a mood to seek an expedient. The mood was absent not only from diplomacy, which clung to the stately rhythms of past times, but also within governments. Britain's Committee of Imperial Defence, bringing together service chiefs, diplomats and statesmen, was unique but also imperfect; the Royal Navy, insistent on its seniority, kept its own counsel. The French army behaved likewise in the much more makeshift Superior War Council. In Germany, Russia and Austria, countries of court government, where the sovereign was commander-in-chief both in name and fact, and each organ of the military system answered directly to him, communication between them was beset by secretiveness and jealousy. The system, disastrously, took its most extreme form in Germany, where "there was no governmental process that corrected . . . the concentration of the assessment [of plans and policy] in a single person, the Kaiser." In the crisis of 1914, when he alone might have put brakes to the inexorable progression of the Schlieffen Plan, he found he did not understand the machinery he was supposed to control, panicked and let a piece of paper, the Schlieffen Plan, determine events.

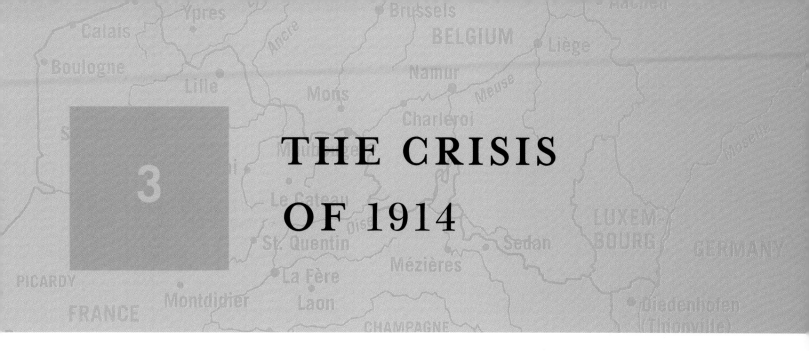

THE CRISIS OF 1914

3

The Kiss: Young women bid farewell to a troop train; a picture postcard after a coloured drawing by Brynold Wennerberg (born 1866).

Secret plans determined that any crisis not settled by sensible diplomacy would, in the circumstances prevailing in Europe in 1914, lead to general war. Sensible diplomacy had settled crises before, notably during the powers' quarrels over position in Africa and in the disquiet raised by the Balkan Wars of 1912–13. Such crises, however, had touched matters of national interest only, not matters of national honour or prestige. In June 1914 the honour of Austria-Hungary was touched to the quick by the murder of the heir to the throne at the hands of an assassin who identified himself with the monarchy's most subversive foreign neighbour. The chief source of subversion was Serbia, an aggressive, backward and domestically violent Christian kingdom which had won its independence from the rule of the Muslim Ottoman Empire after centuries of rebellion. Independent Serbia did not include all Serbs. Large minorities remained, by historical accident, Austrian subjects. The most extreme among them were prepared to kill. It was the killing by one of them of the Habsburg heir that fomented the fatal crisis of the summer of 1914.

The Habsburg army's summer manoeuvres of 1914 were held in Bosnia, the former Ottoman Turkish province occupied by Austria in 1878. Franz Ferdinand, nephew to the Emperor Franz Joseph, arrived in Bosnia on June 25 to supervise. After the manoeuvres concluded, on June 27, he drove next morning with his wife to the provincial capital, Sarajevo, to carry out official engagements. It was an ill-chosen day. June 28 is the anniversary of the defeat of Serbia by the Turks in 1389, the event from which they date their long history of suffering at the hands of foreign oppressors. The provincial administration had been warned that his visit was unwelcome and might be dangerous. The warnings he ignored. In this case a murder team was in place. On the Archduke's way to the residence of the provincial governor, one of the terrorists threw a bomb at his car, but it bounced off. The imperial party proceeded on its way. Three-quarters of an hour later, however, the archducal couple's chauffeur took a wrong turning and came to a momentary halt. The stop brought the car opposite one of the undetected conspirators, Gavrilo Princip, who was armed with a revolver. He stepped forward

41

and fired. The Archduke's wife died instantly, he ten minutes later. Princip was arrested on the spot.

Investigation swiftly revealed that the terrorists had been armed in Serbia and smuggled back across the Austrian border by a Serbian nationalist organisation. In fact the responsible organisation was the clandestine "Union or Death," commonly known as the Black Hand, which lay under the control of the colonel commanding the intelligence section of the Serbian army's general staff.

The evidence of Serb complicity, official or not, in the assassination was enough to persuade the imperial government that a war against Serbia was now a necessity. An Austrian emissary was ordered to Berlin. Count Berchtold, the Austrian foreign minister, gave the emissary, Count Hoyos, verbal authority to warn the Germans that Vienna would ask Belgrade for guarantees as to its future conduct, to be followed by military action if refused. Within six days of the assassination, therefore, Austria had staked out her position. It remained to be seen whether

The Archduke Franz Ferdinand, heir to the Emperor of Austria-Hungary, with his wife, leaving the residence of the governor of Bosnia-Herzegovina in Sarajevo, June 28, 1914. One of the group of Serbian terrorists had already made an attempt on their lives earlier that morning. It failed but an officer in the car following had been wounded. The archducal couple are on their way to visit the casualty in hospital.

the German Emperor and his government, without whose backing the Austrians dared not act, would support them. With the arrival of Berchtold's emissary in Berlin, on July 5, calculations of the import of war planning switched to the German side. Over lunch Wilhelm II authorised him to tell Emperor Franz Josef that Austria could "rely on Germany's full support." The possibility of Russian intervention was discussed but discounted. So it was also in the discussions with the Kaiser's ministers and military advisers whom the Austrian ambassador then saw. General von Falkenhayn, the Minister of War, asked if preparatory measures should be taken and was told not. Bethmann Hollweg, the Chancellor, had been independently advised by his foreign office that Britain would not involve herself in a Balkan crisis nor would Russia if it came to the point. The following day, Monday, July 6, after repeating his own judgement to a number of military officers that Russia, and France also, would not involve themselves and that precautionary measures were consequently necessary, the Kaiser departed on the imperial yacht, *Hohenzollern*, for his annual cruise in the Norwegian fjords. He was to be absent for three weeks. The Chief of the Great General Staff and the Secretary of the Navy were already on leave and he left no orders for their recall.

En route their chauffeur took a wrong turn and, while reversing, brought the car to a halt opposite another of the terrorists, Gavrilo Princip. Armed with a revolver, he stepped forward and shot both. The Archduke's wife died immediately, he ten minutes later. Princip was arrested on the spot. The murders provoked the Austrians into issuing an ultimatum to Serbia which, when rejected, precipitated the attacks leading to the general outbreak of the First World War. Princip died of tuberculosis in the fortress of Theresienstadt, later to be Hitler's "model ghetto" for Jews, in April 1918.

The Kaiser had, however, insisted both to the Austrian ambassador and to his officials on one point: that it was for Austria to come to a firm resolution about what it wanted to do. Austrian prevarication was a constant irritant to the emphatic Germans. The first week of July 1914 therefore brought a strange reversal of attitudes. Austria was for once in a hurry; Germany went on holiday. The Austrians, though under pressure to make up their minds, dithered. The Imperial Council of Ministers did not meet until Tuesday, July 7, already ten days after the assassination. Berchtold, who sensed justification and time slipping away equally rapidly, proposed military action. Count Tisza, the Hungarian Prime Minister, held out. He insisted that the taking of military measures be preceded by the issue of a note of demands. Only if they were rejected would he agree to an ultimatum leading to war. That was not what Berchtold desired to hear. His position was steadily hardening, towards that of Field Marshal Conrad, who had wanted war from the outset. He sustained his pressure. By Tuesday, July 14, when Tisza and Berchtold met again, the Hungarian Prime Minister won his case against an ultimatum but was forced to concede the shortest possible time limit attaching to a note. The terms of the note were drafted and so was the date of the ministerial meeting at which it would be finally approved.

That date, however, was Sunday, July 19, the twenty-first day since the assassination. Worse, Berchtold told Tisza that the note would not formally be presented for another week after that. He had a justification. The French President, Raymond Poincaré, who would leave to make a state visit to Russia on July 16, would not, it was believed, begin his return until Saturday, July 25. The delivery of an Austrian note to Serbia in the days when the Russian and French heads of state—respectively the Serbs' protector and his chief ally—would be in intimate contact was likely to throw them into diplomatic and strategic conclave. Hopes of localising the dispute and of isolating Serbia would be dangerously reduced thereby. That was the explanation given to Berlin for the further postponement. The Austrian note, conclusively agreed on Sunday, July 19, listed ten numbered demands. Points 5, 6, 7 and 8 stipulated the arrest, interrogation and punishment of Serbian officials implicated in the assassination and also demanded that Austro-Hungarian officials should take part in the necessary processes on Serbian soil. Serbia, in short, was not to be trusted to police the crime itself; Austria should supervise. The time limit for an answer attached to the note was forty-eight hours from delivery. That would take place on the day Berchtold had now learnt the French President would leave Russia, Thursday, July 23. The document would reach Belgrade at six o'clock (local time) in the afternoon of that day and expire on Saturday, July 25.

It was then the twenty-fifth day since the assassination and the Serbian government had been warned that the note was on its way. Nicholas Pasic, the Serbian Prime Minister, had nevertheless decided to leave the capital for the country and, even after word reached him that the Austrian ambassador had brought the document to the foreign ministry, proceeded with his journey. Only during the night did he decide to return and it was not until ten o'clock in the morning of Friday, July 24, that he met his ministers to consider what answer should be made. By the following morning, Saturday, July 25, however, both the British and French delegations in Belgrade reported home that Serbia would agree to the Austrian demands, excepting the condition that imperial officials be admitted onto Serbian territory to supervise the investigations.

Even on that sticking point, however, the Serbians had as yet not made up their minds. As late as the twenty-seventh day after the assassination, it therefore seemed possible that Austria would arrive at the result it might very well have achieved had it exercised its right as a sovereign power to move against Serbia from the outset. The vital interest of no other power was threatened. Even at noon on Saturday, July 25, therefore, six hours before the time limit attached to the Austrian note would expire, the crime of Sarajevo remained a matter between Austria-Hungary and Serbia, diplomatically no more than that.

The night and most of Saturday remained for it to be seen what the Serbians would do. On the morning of July 25 they were still reconciled to capitulation, though reluctantly and with occasional bursts of belligerence. Then, during the afternoon, word was received from their ambassador at the Tsar's country palace that the mood there was fiercely pro-Serbian. The Tsar, though not yet ready to proclaim mobilisation, had announced the preliminary "Period Preparatory to

An artist's impression of the Emperor Franz Josef of Austria and the Archduke Franz Ferdinand discussing pre-war strategy.

Kaiser Wilhelm II (center) with Prince Heinrich of Prussia (left), one of his six sons, and Archduke Karl Stephan of Austria, in naval uniform, aboard the German imperial yacht *Hohenzollern* in 1910. The Kaiser was a committed navalist, believing that Germany must build a fleet large enough to challenge the supremacy of Britain's Royal Navy if it were to achieve its ambition of becoming a true world power. In the period 1896–1914 the Imperial German Navy was transformed from a coast defence force to an oceanic fleet of the most advanced types. In 1914 the High Seas Fleet consisted of sixteen modern battleships and four battlecruisers, giving it a strength of two-thirds of the British Grand Fleet.

War" at eleven o'clock. The news reversed everything the Serbian ministers had decided. In the morning they had agreed to accept all ten Austrian demands, with the slightest reservations. Now they were emboldened to attach conditions. In the hurried hours that followed, the reply to the note was drafted and re-drafted, lines crossed out, phrases corrected in ink. The finished document was an undiplomatic palimpsest of revisions and afterthoughts. Within an hour of its delivery, however, the personnel of the Austrian legation had boarded the train and left Belgrade.

There followed a curious two-day intermission, Sunday and Monday, July 26–27. Serbia mobilised its little army, Russia recalled the youngest reservists to the units in its western military districts, there were scenes of popular enthusiasm in Vienna over the government's rejection of the Serbian reply and similar scenes in German cities. On Sunday, however, the Kaiser was still at sea, while Poincaré and Viviani, the French Foreign Minister, aboard *La France*, did not receive a signal urging their immediate return until that night. Meanwhile there was much talk. Bethmann Hollweg instructed the German ambassadors in London and Paris to warn that the military measures Russia was taking could be judged threatening. The German ambassador in St. Petersburg was told to say that the measures, unless discontinued, would force Germany to mobilise, which "would mean war." The British Foreign Office perceived a hope that the Russians were ready to acquiesce in a mediation by the United Kingdom, France, Germany and Italy. There was, briefly, the circulation of a feeling that the crisis, like those of 1909 and 1913, might be talked out.

The weakness of that hope was the ignorance and misunderstanding among politicians and diplomats of how the mechanism of abstract war plans, once instigated, would operate. Only Sir George Buchanan, the British ambassador in St. Petersburg, and Jules Cambon, the French ambassador in Berlin, fully comprehended the trigger effect exerted by one mobilisation proclamation on another. Buchanan had already warned the Russians that their mobilisation would push the Germans to a declaration of war. Cambon had come to the same conclusion. Mere ambassadors as they were, however, their voices failed to convey urgency. It was those at the point of decision—in the entourages of the Tsar and Kaiser, in Paris, in Vienna, in London—who were heard. They, moreover, did not equally share the information available, nor understand what they did share in the same way. Information arrived fitfully but was always incomplete. There was no way of correlating and displaying it. In 1914, lack of information consumed time as men puzzled to fill in the gaps between the facts they had. Time, in all crises, is usually the ingredient missing to make a solution. It is best supplied by an agreement on a pause. In 1914 there were none. Any pause would have to be arranged by men of goodwill. Grey, the British Foreign Secretary, was such a man. He had raised the proposal for a four-power conference on Sunday, July 26, and spent Monday trying to convene one. Had it been the only proposal in circulation he might have succeeded but others were set in motion and that deflected attention. Finally, when Berchtold, in Vienna, learnt of Grey's conference proposal he informed the German ambassador that he intended "to send official declaration of war tomorrow, at the latest the day after, in order to cut away the ground from any attempt at mediation."

In the event, Austria-Hungary declared war on Serbia on Tuesday, July 28. It was Berchtold rather than Conrad who was now in a hurry. His urge to act was heightened by the discovery that his own country's war plans impeded what prospect remained of a speedy resolution. Conrad's tripartite division of forces precluded, the Field Marshal warned him, an immediate offensive against Serbia unless it could be guaranteed that Russia would not mobilise. Small though Serbia's army was, only sixteen weak divisions, it outnumbered Austria's "minimal" group; operational prudence therefore required the commitment of the "swing" grouping if a quick Serbian war were to be brought off. If the "swing" grouping went south, however, the northern frontier with Poland would be left dangerously exposed. All therefore depended on what Russia would do next.

Russia had already done much. On the previous Saturday, when news of her emphatic support for Serbia had encouraged the Belgrade government to reject the Austrian note, she had instigated the military measures known as the Period

A Serbian machine-gun team, taking up a fire position. The team commander is beyond the gun, the number two is prone in the foreground, the three ammunition handlers kneel to the rear. The Serbian army in 1914 was enlisted on the basis of universal obligation to serve and contained stripling youths and grandfathers. It was an experienced force, having fought in both the Balkan Wars of 1912–13, and was notable for the physical hardihood of its soldiers and tactical resilience, learnt in decades of irregular mountain warfare against the Turkish oppressors. The Austrians greatly underestimated its military worth, which led to the failure of their two offensives into Serbia in 1914. Not until 1915, when the Germans and Bulgarians joined in, were the Serbs forced from their positions and driven into retreat through the mountains to refuge on the Greek island of Corfu.

Preparatory to War. The procedure was only precautionary. In practice, much more had been done. Under cover of the Period Preparatory to War half the Russian army was coming to a war footing. France had been informed and approved; indeed, Messimy, the minister of war, and Joffre were pressing the Russians to achieve the highest possible state of readiness. The Russian generals at least needed little urging. Their responsibility as they saw it was to prepare for the worst if the worst came. The worst for them would be that their preparations provoked Germany into full-scale mobilisation. That would come about if their partial mobilisation prompted a full Austrian mobilisation, which required a full German mobilisation also. On Tuesday, July 28, therefore, the Russian Chief

of Staff, Janushkevich, agreed that the Period Preparatory to War must now be superseded by formal mobilisation announcements. Privately they accepted the sequence Russian partial mobilisation against Austria = Austrian general mobilisation = German general mobilisation = war, which stood stark before them. They decided, however, that publicly they would announce only partial mobilisation, while preparing with the order for it another for general mobilisation.

Sazonov, who had received word of Austria's declaration of war on Serbia that Tuesday morning, attempted to palliate the fears the proclamation would certainly arouse by telegraphing Vienna, Paris, London and Rome (though not Berlin), with "stress on the absence of any intention on the part of Russia to attack Germany." Nevertheless, that evening Janushkevich informed all military districts

COMMUNICATIONS

Communication was the weak link in the machinery of war-making throughout the First World War, both at sea and, above all, on land. Wireless telegraphy, radio, recently demonstrated as practicable by Marconi, rapidly assured strategic communication over long distances, with great benefit to the control of fleets, as was proved in the British campaign against the German commerce raiders in 1914. Wireless as a means of tactical communication at sea failed, however; overcrowded long-wave networks proved inferior to traditional flag-signalling, defective as that was, in the handling of battleships in fleet actions, particularly at Jutland in 1916. The use of wireless in communication between armies in fluid operations, as during the Tannenberg campaign of 1914, was compromised by overhearing, usually the result of poor cipher security.

Radio failed as a means of tactical communication on land, because of the inability to develop a compact, portable wireless set. The British "Trench Set" of 1918 required twelve men to carry its components, largely heavy, wet-cell batteries. In consequence commanders were forced to rely on telephone lines, inevitably broken when heavy fighting began. Cables were buried, the British developing a network of "six-foot bury" under their trench system. While it assured secure communication even under heavy bombardment, it failed to provide useful communication during offensives, when the leading infantry moved forward of the cable head. Then units were thrown back on such traditional means as runners, dogs, flares, heliograph, carrier pigeons or even flags. The inadequacy of signalling had lamentable effects, particularly on communication between advancing infantry and their supporting artillery. Gunners, unable to identify what position the infantry had reached, fired blind, usually onto the wrong targets, sometimes on their own men. The result was that senior commanders were obliged to devise increasingly rigid attack plans, requiring both infantry and artillery to conform to pre-determined timings, which events frequently falsified. The problem of communication was never solved during the war, and its difficulties largely determined its brutal, mechanistic character.

Left top: A messenger dog bringing food to troops in forward trenches.

Left: Telephone post, Vaux Verdun.

Opposite top: Hoisting signals on the British ship H.M.S. *Titania*.

Opposite bottom: A German army field telephone station at Suvalki, Poland.

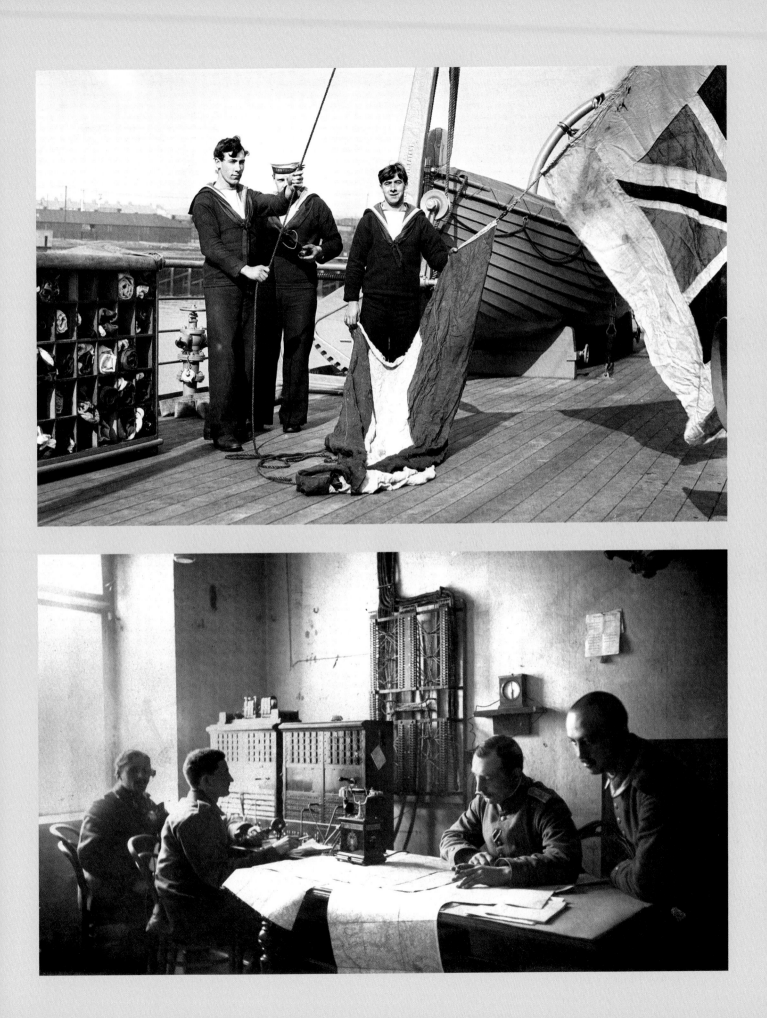

Above: Canadians releasing a homing pigeon from a trench on the Western Front, May 17, 1917.

Left: *Valve Testing: The Signal School RN Barracks at Portsmouth,* by Arthur David McCormick (1860–1943), British.

that "30 July will be proclaimed the first day of our general mobilisation" and on the following morning, having seen Sazonov, called on the Tsar and secured his signature to the orders for full mobilisation. This decision to order general mobilisation "was perhaps the most important . . . taken in the history of Imperial Russia and it effectively shattered any prospect of averting a great European war." It was also unnecessary. Sazonov's support for the soldiers seems to have been supplied by his learning of a bombardment of Belgrade by Austrian gunboats on the Danube on the night of July 29. The attack was a pinprick. On the wider front, Russia's security was not threatened by the Austrian mobilisation. Indeed, Austria's war with Serbia precluded its fighting a larger war elsewhere. Small as Serbia's army was, its size required, even by Vienna's calculation, the commitment against it of over half the Austrian force available. The "minimal" and "swing" groupings totalled twenty-eight of Austria's divisions and the twenty remaining were too few to launch an offensive into Russian Poland.

Below: A Russian Cossack regiment parades before departing for the front on Russia's western border in 1914. The Cossacks were originally fugitives from Tsarist authority who set up independent settlements on the Russian steppes border with Central Asia in the sixteenth century. Eventually they become loyal military servants of the Tsar, providing numerous regiments of light cavalry for the wars against Napoleon in 1812–15 and the Caucasian and Central Asian principalities in the nineteenth century.

Russia might, therefore, without risk to its security, have confined itself to partial mobilisation on July 29. General mobilisation, including that of the military districts bordering Germany, would mean general war. That awful prospect was now taking shape in all the European capitals. Those who most feared the military preparations of others—Janushkevich, Moltke, Conrad, Joffre—were looking to their own lest they be taken at a disadvantage. Those who more feared war itself were scrabbling for stopgaps. Bethmann-Hollweg, the German Chancellor, was one of them. The Kaiser was another. On the afternoon of July 29, he telegraphed his cousin the Tsar, in English, urging him "to smooth over difficulties that may still arise." In reply the Tsar pathetically suggested, "It would be right to give over the Austro-Servian problem to the Hague conference," that weakling brainchild of his not scheduled to meet again until 1915. Later that evening a second telegram from the Kaiser reached the Tsar. "It would be quite possible," he suggested, "for Russia to remain a spectator of the Austro-Servian conflict without involving Europe in the most horrible war she has ever witnessed." Immediately on receipt of this telegram, the Tsar ordered the cancellation of general mobilisation. He intervened only just in time, for at 9:30 in the evening of July 29 the Russian quartermaster-general was actually standing over the typists at the Central Telegraph Office in St. Petersburg as they tapped out the orders onto telegraph forms.

The cancellation should have brought the pause which the search for peace required. At the opening of the day following, Thursday, July 30, the British were

Opposite bottom: Russian conscripts reporting to the recruiting officer at Bogorodsk, near the Volga, east of Moscow, at the outbreak of the First World War. The Russian empire had both the largest peacetime army in Europe and the largest reserves of manpower. Most Russian conscripts, however, were landless, illiterate peasants. Though loyal to Mother Russia and to their father, the Tsar, they had little understanding of why they were fighting and were easily disheartened. Brave fighters, they were taken prisoners in tens of thousands by the Germans and Austrians when involved in strategic setbacks.

still seeking to arrange a mediation, France had not taken any substantial precautionary measures, the Austrian troops mobilised were marching against Serbia only and Germany had mobilised no troops at all. The leaders of the German army were nevertheless in a state of acute anxiety. General von Falkenhayn wanted to mobilise at once, Bethmann Hollweg did not. He was still hoping that Berchtold would deal directly with the Russians and succeed in persuading them to accept the offensive against Serbia as a local war. Moltke, the Chief of the Great General Staff, was less bellicose but wanted at least the proclamation of the *Kriegsgefahrzustand,* which would match Russian preparations. The Austrian liaison officer to the German Great General Staff outlined to him his army's current dispositions which, Moltke instantly grasped, would leave Germany's eastern fron-

tier desperately exposed if war came. ("He needed forty Austro-Hungarian divisions in [Austrian Poland] ready to attack; what he was getting were twenty-five divisions standing on the defensive.") He at once expressed his extreme alarm to the Austrian military attaché; later that evening he telegraphed Conrad in Vienna, as one Chief of Staff to another, "Stand firm against Russian mobilisation. Austria-Hungary must be preserved, mobilise at once against Russia. Germany will mobilise."

That announcement in itself would have ensured a reconsideration of the Tsar's decision to cancel general mobilisation in the evening of July 29. In fact, it had already been reconsidered. Throughout Thursday, July 30, Sazonov, Sukhomlinov and Janushkevich—Foreign Minister, War Minister, Chief of Staff—had badgered the Tsar with their fears. Between three and four o'clock on the afternoon of Thursday, July 30, Sazonov rehearsed his anxieties to the Tsar, who listened, pale and tense, occasionally showing an uncharacteristic irritation. General Tatistchev, his personal representative to the Kaiser, who was present, at one point observed, "Yes, it is hard to decide." The Tsar replied in a rough, displeased tone, "I will decide." Shortly he did. Sazonov left the audience chamber and telephoned Janushkevich with the order to proclaim general mobilisation. "Now you can smash your telephone," he concluded.

The hour had come. That evening the posters announcing mobilisation went up in the streets of all cities in Russia. It was not what Bethmann Hollweg wanted to hear. He had retained the hopes up to the moment the news arrived that Austria could be brought directly to negotiate with Russia and that Russia could be brought to accept the war against Serbia as local and limited. Now he had to accept what seemed inevitable. News of Austria's general mobilisation arrived half an hour after noon. Germany proclaimed the "State of Danger of War" half an hour after that. With Austria and Russia mobilising, the Germans concluded that they must mobilise also unless Russian general mobilisation was reversed. An ultimatum to that effect was sent soon after three o'clock on the afternoon of July 31 to St. Petersburg and another to Paris. The relevant sentence in each read: "[German] mobilisation will follow unless Russia suspends all war measures against ourselves and Austria-Hungary." That to Russia demanded, within twelve hours, "a definite assurance to that effect," that to France included the warning that "mobilisation inevitably means war" and required a declaration of neutrality "in a Russo-German war . . . within eighteen (18) hours."

The afternoon of July 31 thus brought to a crux the crisis which had begun thirty-four days earlier with the murders at Sarajevo. Its real duration had been much shorter than that. From the murders on June 28 to the conclusion of the Austrian judicial investigation and the confessions of the conspirators on July 2 was five days. It was in the period immediately following that the Austrians might have decided for unilateral action, and taken it without strong likelihood of provoking an intervention by the Serbs' protectors, the Russians. Instead, Austria had sought a German assurance of support, given on July 5; elapsed time from the murders, eight days. There had then followed an intermission of nineteen days, while the Austrians waited for the French President to conclude his state visit on July 23. The real inception of the crisis may thus be dated to the delivery of the Austrian "note with a time limit" (of forty-eight hours) on July 24. It was on its expiry on Saturday, July 25, twenty-eight days from the murders, that the diplomatic confrontation was abruptly transformed into a war

Kaiser Wilhelm addresses the crowd from the balcony of his Berlin palace on August 1, 1914, the first day of mobilisation. Next day many of the men waving their straw hats would be at the barracks of their regiments, drawing field-grey uniforms and spiked helmets from the quartermaster's stores. The prospect of war generated intense popular enthusiasm in all the capitals of the combatant states but deep foreboding in their rulers. At the last moment, both the Kaiser and the Tsar, who were cousins, tried to draw back from the brink.

A rail wagon of a German troop train moving to the front, August 1914. The occupants have decorated it with flowers, a common motif of departure for the war. Soldiers stuck flowers in the muzzles of their rifles. These men have made a dummy of a French soldier and some of the slogans scrawled in chalk read "Only for the boys," "Holiday outing to Paris," "Password Paris," and "Moulin Rouge." The caricature depicts a German soldier bayoneting a French officer, who is brandishing a cat-o'-nine-tails. German troop trains did not enter French or Belgian territory but unloaded at the frontiers, beyond which the passengers marched.

crisis. It was not a crisis which the participants had expected. Austria had simply wanted to punish Serbia. Germany had wanted a diplomatic success that would leave its Austrian ally stronger in European eyes; it had not wanted war. The Russians had certainly not wanted war but had equally not calculated that support for Serbia would edge the danger of war forward. By July 30, thirty-three days from the murders, the Austrians were at war with Serbia, but were not concentrating against Russia. Russia had declared partial mobilisation but was concentrating against nobody. The German Kaiser and Chancellor still believed that Austria and Russia could be brought to negotiate their mobilisations away, even if the Chief of the Great General Staff by then wanted a mobilisation of his own. France had not mobilised but was in growing fear that Germany would mobilise against her. Britain, which had awoken to the real danger of the crisis only on Saturday, July 25, still hoped on Thursday, July 30, that the Russian would toler-

ate an Austrian punishment of Serbia but were determined not to leave France in the lurch.

It was the events of July 31, therefore, the dissemination of the news of Russian general mobilisation, and the German ultimata to Russia and France, which made the issue one of peace or war. The day following, August 1, the thirty-fifth since the murders, would bring Germany's mobilisation against Russia—thus making "war inevitable"—unless Germany withdrew its ultimatum to Russia. German mobilisation would, under the terms of the Franco-Russian Convention of 1892, require both to mobilise and, if either was attacked by Germany, to go jointly to war against her. As the hours drew out on July 31 only a hair's breadth kept the potential combatants apart. There was still a hope. The Russo-French Convention of 1892 required that Germany actually attack one country or the other before the two went to war against her. German mobilisation entailed only their mobilisation. Even a German declaration of war would not bring the treaty into force. Nevertheless, the Germans had warned France that their mobilisa-

Left: French civilians exchanging paper currency for gold at the Banque de France, Paris, in the last days of July 1914. The placards specify that only denominations between 20 and 5 francs ($10–$2.50) will be accepted, an attempt by the bank to prevent the depletion of its gold reserves. The French had a traditional suspicion of paper money, originating in the debasing of the value of *assignats*—paper bonds—in the early days of the French Revolution. Much private French wealth was always kept in gold. In practise governments were remarkably successful in preserving the value of money during the First World War. Only in 1917–18 did serious inflation take hold, and then only in Germany, Austria and Russia.

Opposite top: A coloured photograph of General Joseph Joffre (1852–1931), French Chief of Staff, in 1914. Joffre, an engineer officer whose career had been made in the colonies, became enormously popular as "Papa" Joffre, the imperturbable commander whose refusal to be panicked by defeat and retreat after the Battle of the Frontiers led to the victory of the Marne in September. Eventually removed from office in 1917, he was made a Marshal of France, the first to be created since the Second Empire (1851–70).

Opposite bottom: Leading citizens demonstrate their enthusiasm for the war in a Paris boulevard, August 2, 1914. Mobilisation swept up only the younger classes of reservists, those under thirty. As the war protracted, and losses grew, the draft reached out to take older men, including perhaps some of those in the photograph.

tion meant war with Russia. The twelve hours given by Germany to Russia for acceptance of the ultimatum was the last twelve hours of available peace.

That, by July 31, was certainly the view of the French army. News, true or exaggerated, of German military preparations had thrown even Joffre, "a byword for imperturbability," into a state of anxiety. The loss of advantage was a fear that now afflicted him as acutely as it had Janushkevich on July 29 and Moltke on July 30. He foresaw the secret approach of German troops to their deployment positions while his own soldiers were still in barracks. On the afternoon of Friday, July 31, he handed to Messimy, the Minister of War, a short note which epitomises the state of mind which possessed the military professionals of the age. "It is absolutely necessary," he warned, "for the government to understand that, starting with this evening, any delay of twenty-four hours in calling up our reservists and issuing orders prescribing covering operations, will have as its result the withdrawal of our concentration points by from fifteen to twenty-five kilometres for each day of delay; in other words, the abandonment of just that much of our ter-

Left: Tsar Nicholas II of Russia appears on a balcony of the Winter Palace in St. Petersburg on August 1, 1914, to address the crowd. He has just prayed before the famous Vladimir icon of the Virgin Mary, believed by pious Russians to have turned back the hordes of the Tartar leader Tamerlane in the fourteenth century. It was also venerated by General Kutuzov before his successful resistance to Napoleon during the French invasion of Russia in 1812.

Below: A Protestant pastor calls for a blessing on German reservists of the *Landwehr* in a small southern German town, August 2, 1914. The *Landwehr* were third-line troops but would play a significant part in East Prussia in the defeat of the Russian invasion of August–September.

Above: Mobilisation in Belgium. The group includes representatives of many branches of the kingdom's tiny army, regular infantrymen in peaked shakos, cavalry in tasselled caps, a carabineer of the Civic Guard militia in his leather top hat. Though untrained and ill-equipped, the Belgians resisted the German invasion with great bravery.

Right: A sergeant marches backwards before his advancing soldiers as they make their way to the railway station down a Paris boulevard during the days of mobilisation in August 1914. This, one of the most atmospheric photographs of the outbreak, catches many moods—pride but apprehension in the faces of the men in uniform, burdened under the enormous weight of their equipment, patriotic jollity among the older male onlookers, sharp anxiety in the expressions of the women, whose sons or husbands may be among the marching ranks. A third of those who marched away would become casualties.

Above: A patriotic postcard of Marianne, feminine symbol of France, carrying the Tricolor. *"Enfin"*—at last— invokes the idea of revenge for defeat by the Germans in the war of 1870–71.

Right: The day of general mobilisation at Porte St. Denis, Paris, on the outbreak of the First World War, August 8, 1914, painting by André Leveille (b.1880), French.

Overleaf: Volunteers for military service parade behind a civilian band in a London street, August 1914. The all-regular British army, 200,000 strong, had few reserves, and the part-time Territorial Force could not be used to make good losses in its ranks. Field Marshal Kitchener, the victor of the Boer War of 1899–1902 who became Secretary of State for War at the outbreak, immediately called for 100,000 more to volunteer "for three years or the duration." The response was overwhelming. Five contingents, 100,000 strong, joined up in 1914–15 and the eventual total of volunteers reached two million before the government introduced conscription in 1916.

Kitchener's volunteers formed the bulk of the divisions which attacked on July 1, 1916, the first day of the Battle of the Somme.

A. Léveillé. 1914

ritory. The Commander-in-Chief must decline to accept this responsibility." That evening he formally requested the President to order general mobilisation at once. The first day of mobilisation, to be August 2, was proclaimed at four o'clock that afternoon.

Yet the irrevocable did not yet seem done. The Tsar still hoped, on the strength of a telegram from the Kaiser begging him not to violate the German frontier, that war could be averted. The Kaiser, meanwhile, had fixed on the belief that

the British would remain neutral if France was not attacked and was ordering Moltke to cancel the Schlieffen Plan and direct the army eastward. Moltke was aghast, explained that the paperwork would take a year, but was ordered to cancel the invasion of Luxembourg, which was the Schlieffen Plan's necessary preliminary. In London this Sunday, August 2, the French ambassador, Paul Cambon, was thrown into despair by the British refusal to declare their position. Britain had, throughout the crisis, pursued the idea that direct talks between the involved parties would dissolve the difficulties. As a power apart it had concealed its intentions from all, including the French. Now the French demanded that the understanding between them and the British be given force. Would Britain declare outright its support for France and, if so, on what issue and when? The British themselves did not know. Throughout Saturday and Sunday, August 1 and 2, the cabinet debated its course of action. The treaty of 1839, guaranteeing Belgian neutrality, would force it to act, but that neutrality was still intact. It could give no firm answer to France, any more than it could to Germany, which had requested a clarification on July 29. Precautionary measures had been taken; the fleet had been sent to war stations, France was even secretly assured that the Royal Navy would protect its Channel coast; but further than that the cabinet would not go.

Far left: An Australian newspaper of August 5, 1914, signals the outbreak of the war with the artist's impression of French soldiers in action against the Germans. Australia, with Canada and New Zealand, responded with enormous enthusiasm to Britain's entry. Though self-governing, those independent states' parliaments all voted to declare war on Germany immediately and began to ship their troops to Europe at once. The youth of the Dominions volunteered as readily as the young men of Britain. A Canadian division reached France in February 1915, while the Australian and New Zealand Army Corps (ANZAC) formed a major component of the Allied force that attacked the Turks at Gallipoli in April 1915, winning an immortal reputation.

Left: In 1914 the horse was still the main means of mobility in all combatant armies. The value of the motorcar, however, for liaison work and, when armoured, as a fighting reconnaissance vehicle, was well established. Private motorcars, often driven by their owners, were soon conveying commanders and staff officers around the fronts.

Opposite: Battleships of the *King Edward* class moored at Sheerness, at the entrance to the Thames, in August 1914. A passenger ferry passes in the foreground. The *King Edward*s, designed in 1902, were the last British battleships to be launched before the *Dreadnought* (1906), the revolutionary, turbine-powered, all-big-gun warship which rendered all existing capital ships, in all navies, obsolete when it appeared. Armed with four 12-inch guns, and many of smaller calibre, the *King Edward*s were regarded as best of their type when launched but the introduction of the *Dreadnought* banished them from the battle line. None ever formed part of the Grand Fleet. In supporting and escorting roles they continued in service, nevertheless, until 1918. *King Edward* was mined in 1914 and *Britannia* torpedoed in 1918.

Then, on August 2, Germany delivered the last of its ultimata, this time to Belgium, demanding the use of its territory in operations against France and threatening to treat the country as an enemy if she resisted. The ultimatum was to expire in twenty-four hours, on Monday, August 3. It was the day Germany also decided, claiming violation of its own territory by French aircraft, to present France with a declaration of war. The expiry of the ultimatum to Belgium proved the irrevocable event. On Tuesday, August 4, Britain sent an ultimatum of its own, demanding the termination of German military operations against Belgium, which had already begun, to expire at midnight. No offer of termination in reply was received. At midnight, therefore, Britain, together with France and Russia, were at war with Germany. The First World War had begun.

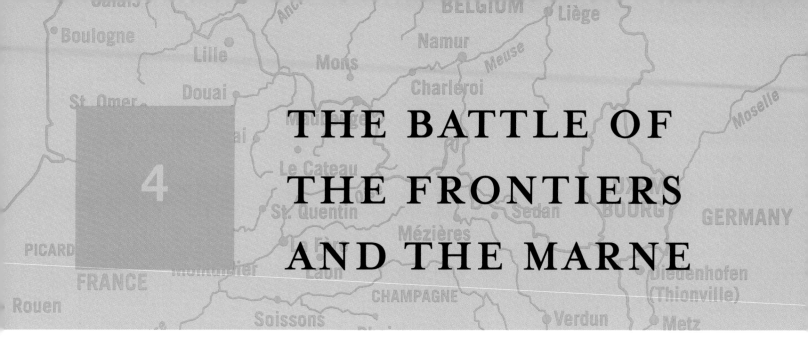

4

THE BATTLE OF THE FRONTIERS AND THE MARNE

A British infantry battalion entrains for the front at a railway station in England, 1914. The soldier in the foreground carries his large pack, water bottle, ammunition pouches and haversack, and his Lee-Enfield rifle with loose sling, while he looks for a place to board. The officer wears his sword and leather Stohwasser gaiters of Boer War vintage. The British Expeditionary Force, initially of four infantry divisions and one cavalry division, left English ports in the second week of August and by August 23 was in action on the Belgian frontier in the Battle of Mons. After helping to blunt the advance of the German First Army, it took part in the Great Retreat, which culminated in the successful counter-offensive on the Marne in early September.

The coming of war was greeted with enormous popular enthusiasm in the capitals of all combatant countries. In St. Petersburg an enormous crowd congregated with flags, banners, icons and portraits of the Tsar. The Emperor appeared on the balcony. The entire crowd at once knelt and sang the Russian national anthem. In Berlin the Kaiser appeared on his palace balcony, dressed in field-grey uniform, to address a tumultuous crowd: "A fateful hour has fallen upon Germany. Envious people on all sides are compelling us to resort to a just defence. The sword is being forced into our hands."

There were to be similar scenes in London on August 5. In Paris it was the departure of the city's regiments to the railroad stations which brought forth the crowds. "Cries of *'Vive la France! Vive l'armée'* could be heard everywhere, while people waved handkerchiefs and hats. The young men were shouting: *'Au revoir! A bientôt!'* "

Reservists not yet called were already putting their affairs in order; in most armies the day before the stipulated date for reporting was a "free day" for farewells to family and employer. "Complete strangers," recorded Richard Cobb, the great historian of France, "could be heard addressing one another in bizarre fashion, in a new sort of calendar. 'What day are you?' And, before the other could get in an answer, 'I am on the first' (as if to suggest: 'beat that'). 'I am the ninth' ('Bad luck, you'll miss all the fun, it'll be over by then')." A German officer-candidate reservist gives a more prosaic account of how the procedure swept up the individual. He was on business in Antwerp. His military document told him he had to report "to the nearest regiment of field artillery on the second day. On August 4, I presented myself to the army as a reservist and was told I now belonged to Reserve Field Artillery Regiment No. 18, which was forming in Behrenfeld near Hamburg. All soldiers and most of the officers were reservists. The horses were reservists, too. Owners of horses had to register them regularly and the army knew at all times where the horses were."

Horses, like men, were mustering in hundreds of thousands all over Europe in the first week of August. Even Britain's little army called up 165,000, mounts

67

for the cavalry, draught animals for the artillery and regimental transport waggons. The Austrian army mobilised 600,000, the German 715,000, the Russian—with its twenty-four cavalry divisions—over a million. The armies of 1914 remained Napoleonic in their dependence on the horse; staff officers calculated the proportion between horses and men at 1:3.

Trains were to fill the memories of all who went to war in 1914. The railway section of the German Great General Staff timetabled the movement of 11,000 trains in the mobilisation period and no less than 2,150 fifty-four-waggon trains crossed the Hohenzollern Bridge over the Rhine alone between August 2 and 18. The chief French railway companies had since May 1912 a plan to concentrate 7,000 trains for mobilisation. Many had moved near the entraining centres before war began. "Travellers coming in [to Paris] from Melun brought extraordinary accounts of empty, stationary trains, engineless, and often of mixed provenance, the carriages from different companies strung up together, passenger ones mixed up with guard trucks, many with chalk marks on their sides . . . waiting on side-lines the whole way to the approaches of the Gare de Lyon."

Feet were as important as trains in August 1914, horses' feet as well as men's feet for, after detrainment in the concentration area, cavalry and infantry deployed onto the line of march. That, for the Germans, presaged days of marching west and southwards. The telltale clink of a loose nail warned a cavalryman that he must find the shoeing-smith. There were five thousand horses in an infantry division in 1914, more than five thousand in a cavalry division. All had to be kept shod and healthy if the twenty miles of the day were to be covered to timetable. Fourteen miles of road was filled by an infantry division on the march and the endurance of horses counted with that of the infantry in the race to drive the advance forward.

The race was tripartite. For the French it was north-eastward from their detraining points at Sedan, Montmédy, Toul, Nancy and Belfort behind the 1870 frontier. For the British Expeditionary Force, which began to disembark at Boulogne on August 14, it was south-eastward towards Le Cateau, just before the Belgian border. General von Kluck's First Army on the right faced a march of two hundred miles from its detraining points at Aachen to the French capital.

Before Paris, however, there was Liège and Namur and the other fortresses of the Belgian rivers which impeded any easy crossing for a German army into France. The strength of the Belgian forts had alarmed Schlieffen and his general staff successors. They were, indeed, immensely strong, subterranean and self-

The crowd in the Odeonplatz in Munich, August 1, 1914, celebrating the declaration of war. Circled is the face of Adolf Hitler, by his own identification. Hitler, an Austro-Hungarian subject, was then living in the city and at once petitioned the King of Bavaria to be allowed to join up as a volunteer. He was accepted and posted to the 16th Bavarian Reserve Infantry Regiment in the 6th Bavarian Reserve Division. After a few weeks of training the regiment was sent to the Western Front to take part in the final autumn offensive, an attempt to break the line in front of Ypres and resume the outflanking manoeuvre checked by the French victory on the Marne. The German attacks at Ypres were opposed by the British Expeditionary Force and defeated, with very heavy losses on both sides.

The Guard Pioneer Battalion entrains for the front, Berlin, August 1914. It belonged to the Guard Corps, which in August formed part of von Kluck's First Army, the right-hand formation of the German line which wheeled through Belgium to the Marne. During the advance it had much work to do in repairing blown bridges and general combat engineering. Unlike their French and British equivalents, however, the German Pioneer troops were trained and equipped to fight as infantry. Many of the well-wishers are former members of the battalion, dressed in their best to see it off to war.

contained, surrounded by a ditch thirty feet deep. Their thick skins would have to be broken by aimed artillery fire, and quickly, for a delay at the Meuse crossings would throw into jeopardy the smooth evolution of the Schlieffen Plan. No gun heavy enough for the work existed at the time of Schlieffen's retirement in 1906. By 1909, however, Krupp had produced a prototype of a 420-mm (16.8-inch) howitzer. The Austrian Skoda company was meanwhile working on a 305-mm (12.2-inch) model. It had the advantage of being road-transportable. The Krupp howitzer, in its original form, had to be transported by rail and embedded for action at the end of a specially built spur track. Austria lent Germany several of its 305s; only five of the Krupp rail and two of the new road-transportable guns had been finished by August 1914.

Yet Liège had to be taken. Such was the urgency that the German war plan provided for the detachment of a special task force from Second Army to complete the mission. Commanded by General Otto von Emmich, its start line was drawn between Aachen and Eupen, at the north of the narrow corridor of French territory lying between Holland and Luxembourg. The time allotted for the mission was forty-eight hours. It was expected by the Germans that Belgium would either not resist an invasion of its neutral territory or, should it do so, that its resistance would be swiftly overcome.

Both expectations were to be proved wrong. One of the clauses of the oath sworn by the Belgian sovereign on accession to the throne charged him with defence of the national territory. Albert I, King of the Belgians, was a man to take

his responsibilities to heart. The German ultimatum, fictively alleging a French intention to violate Belgian territory, was delivered on the evening of Sunday, August 2. King Albert, acting as president of a council of state, considered it two hours later. There were divided counsels. The Chief of Staff, General Antonin de Selliers, confessed the weakness of the army and advocated retreat to the River Velpe, outside Brussels. The Sub-Chief demanded a spoiling attack into Germany: "Send them back where they belong." This fantasy was rejected. So, too, was Selliers' defeatism. Eventually a middle way was decided. Belgium would not appeal for French or British assistance until her territory was physically violated, but the German ultimatum would meanwhile be rejected. The reply was delivered to the German Legation at seven o'clock on the morning of August 3. Later that evening the Kaiser sent a personal appeal to Albert restating his "friendliest

A German transport column traverses a shuttered and almost deserted main street in Brussels, August 1914. The small carts are carrying soldiers' large packs, often done to lighten their burden on long marches. The nearer four-wheeled cart has picked up footsore stragglers. German regiments on the right wing often marched over twenty miles a day during the advance from the Belgian frontier to the Marne and, though they held together well, there were inevitably some men whose feet were ruined by the hard, nailed military boot. The horses, too, suffered. Germany requisitioned over 700,000, many of which broke down under the strain of unrelenting advance.

intentions" and claiming "the compulsion of the hour" as justification for the invasion that was about to begin. On its receipt, the Belgian King gave way to his first outburst: "What does he take me for?" He immediately gave orders for the destruction of the bridges over the Meuse at Liège and the railway bridges and tunnels at the Luxembourg border. He also charged the commander of the Liège fortress, General Gérard Leman, "to hold to the end."

Leman was a man of honour and, despite his advanced age, of courage. The Meuse, which he was entrusted to hold, is a mighty river. At Liège the river runs in a narrow gorge 450 feet deep. It cannot be crossed in the face of a determined defence. So Emmich was to discover. His command entered Belgium early on the morning of August 4. Soon they came under fire from Belgian cavalrymen and cyclist troops. Pressing on to Liège, the Germans found the bridges above and below the city already blown, despite the warning given that demolitions would be regarded as "hostile acts." They responded as threatened. Germany interpreted international law to mean that an effective occupying force had the right to treat civilian resistance as rebellion.

The "rape of Belgium" served no military purpose whatsoever and did Germany untold harm, particularly in the United States. The reputation of the German army was dishonoured also. On August 4, six hostages were shot at Warsage and the village of Battice burnt to the ground. "Our advance

A Krupp 420-mm (16.8-inch) howitzer, one of the guns which destroyed the defences of the Belgian fortifications at Liège and Namur between August 12 and 24, 1914. The Krupp howitzer, however, developed in 1909, came in two versions, the earlier having to be transported by rail and embedded on a concrete platform before firing. The later model, of which this is an example, was road transportable when broken down into three loads carried on separate motor vehicles. Only two were available for the attack on the Belgian forts. They fired armour-piercing shells, in a steep trajectory, which were in flight for sixty seconds. The noise and shock of the detonation shattered not only thick concrete but the nerves of the defenders.

in Belgium is certainly brutal," Moltke wrote on August 5, "but we are fighting for our lives and all who get in the way must take the consequences." Within the first three weeks, there would be large-scale massacres of civilians in small Belgian towns. At Andenne there were 211 dead, at Tamines 384, at Dinant 612. Worst of all the outrages began on August 25 at Louvain. This little university town was a treasure store of Flemish Gothic and Renaissance architecture. At the end of three days of incendiarism and looting, the library of 230,000 books had been burnt out and 1,100 other buildings destroyed. The worldwide condemnation of Germany's war against "culture" bit deep in the homeland. Germany's scholars and writers responded with a "Call to the World of Culture," claiming that if it had not been for German soldiers, German culture would long have been swept away. The call fell on deaf ears. The damage had been done.

Emmich's task force crossed the Belgian frontier on August 4. It headed straight for Liège, twenty miles to the east. With it the task force brought two batteries of 210-mm (8.4-inch) howitzers, the heaviest available until the Skoda and

Krupp monsters could be got forward. On the morning of August 5 Captain Brinckman, recently the German military attaché in Brussels, appeared in Liège to demand Leman's surrender. He was sent packing. The German bombardment on the eastern forts opened shortly afterwards. When the infantry and cavalry attempted to advance, however, they found the way barred. The garrisons of the forts returned fire steadily, while the "interval troops" manning the hastily dug entrenchments fought manfully whenever the German advance guards tried to

penetrate the line. Throughout the night of August 5–6 German casualties mounted steadily.

Early in the morning of August 6, General Erich Ludendorff, the liaison officer between Second Army and Emmich's command, rode forward into the confusion to find that the commander of the 14th Brigade had been killed. Instantly assuming the vacancy, Ludendorff fought his new command to a high point from which he could look down into Liège itself. From his vantage point, Ludendorff ordered forward a party under a flag of truce to demand Leman's surrender, which was again refused. Ludendorff's bold sally nevertheless prompted Leman to leave the city and take refuge in Fort Loncin. A moment of equilibrium ensued. The situation map showed a French army aligned towards Lorraine, a German army whose weight had not yet crossed either the Belgian or French frontier, a British army still mobilising, a Belgian army concentrated in the centre of its homeland

Regular infantry of the Belgian army, distinguishable by their peaked caps, man a roadblock in a Belgian village in the face of the German advance. Barricades of this sort, hastily thrown up in dozens across the route of the German invasion, were no impediment at all to the German onset. The invaders pressed inexorably forward, pushing the Belgians before them in flight, only to be checked by the deliberate flooding of the Yser estuary, in western Belgium, in October.

and, at Liège, a small German striking force immobilised by a handful of Belgian fortress troops guarding the crossings on the possession of which the future of military events in the west turned.

The equilibrium was upset by Ludendorff. Large in physique and personality, he resolved on the morning of August 7 to launch the 14th Brigade into the centre of Liège. Driving up to the gates of the old citadel, he hammered on the door with the pommel of his sword. The surrender of the garrison gave him possession of the city. His bold sortie had put the bridges into his hands. He decided to return posthaste to Aachen and urge forward Second Army to complete his success.

While he was away Emmich's task force broke the resistance of Forts Barchon and Evegnée. The first road-transportable Krupp 420 eventually arrived within range of Fort Pontisse on August 12. The crew lay prone three hundred yards away while the gun was fired electrically. "Sixty seconds ticked by—the time needed for the shell to traverse its 4,000-metre trajectory—and everyone listened in to the telephone report of our battery commander." The first of the shells, delay-fused to explode only after penetration of the fort's protective skin, fell short. The eighth struck home. Then the gun fell silent for the night but next morning, joined by the other which had completed the journey from Essen, the bombardment reopened. By 12:30 Fort Pontisse was a wreck and it surrendered. Fire then shifted to Fort Embourg, which surrendered at 5:30; Fort Chaud-

Two of the armoured cupolas of Fort Loncin, Liège, dislodged from their concrete mountings by shells fired by a Krupp 420-mm howitzer. The Krupp guns had already destroyed Forts Barchon, Evegnée, Embourg, Chaudfontaine, Liers, Fléron, Boncelle and Lautin. The fortifications at Liège and Namur were the most modern in Europe and were believed to be invulnerable to artillery fire. They had been completed, however, before the development of the mammoth Krupp guns. Loncin was the head-quarters of General Leman, Chief of Staff of the Belgian army. After 140 minutes of bombardment on August 15, 1914, its crust was penetrated and the magazine detonated. The attacks on Liège and Namur were the most successful operations of the war by siege artillery but succeeded largely because Belgium lacked sufficient infantry to keep the enemy's guns at a distance.

Belgian women and German soldiers amid the ruins of the center of Louvain, September 1914. Louvain was the kingdom's leading university town, "the Oxford of Belgium," architecturally a gem of high medieval architecture, scholastically a treasury of ancient manuscripts and early printed books. Its destruction, on August 25–27, was both systematic and senseless. A false alarm stampeded the German occupiers into a search for non-existent snipers. In the ensuing disorder, the university library was burnt out, together with its stock of 230,000 priceless books, over a thousand other buildings destroyed and irreversible damage done to the structures of the university. Over 200 civilians were killed and, inexplicably, the population of 42,000 was forcibly expelled from the city.

Assailed by the outraged denunciations of professors in every neutral country, including most weightily the United States, the German university community attempted to justify the atrocity, without avail. The devastation of Louvain was correctly recognised to be an attack against civilisation.

"This will make room for our colonists," reads the caption to this anti-German cartoon by Louis Raemaekers, 1914. The German army committed widespread atrocities during the first days of its advance into Belgium in 1914, murdering women and children, as well as unarmed civilian men, in hundreds, at Andenne, Tamines, Seilles and Dinant. Neurotic folk memory of guerrilla activity by civilians during the invasion of France in 1870 seems to have motivated this psychopathic behaviour. It outraged civilised opinion around the world and besmirched the reputation of the Kaiser's Germany, a setback from which it did not recover throughout the war. Raemaekers, a neutral Dutchman, became the most effective cartoonist of the conflict, his images imputing, with eerie foresight, a German inclination to policies of mass murder and racial extermination.

Belgian regular infantrymen man the parapet of a railway bridge, Louvain, August 20, 1914.

German reservists of a Guard regiment take their rest from a training march, with packs, piled rifles and spiked helmets in rear. The majority are in pre-war blue uniform, only a few in wartime field-grey. Germany, unlike France, had a surplus of young men in 1914 who had not yet done their military training. During August–September they were hastily inducted, fitted out with whatever uniforms and equipment were on hand, and thrown into the line during the manpower crisis of the autumn as they became available.

fontaine had been destroyed by the explosion of its magazine at nine o'clock. On August 14 it was the turn of Fort Liers, at 9:40 a.m., and Fléron, 9:45. Finally, on August 15, the howitzers reduced Forts Boncelle, at 7:30 a.m., and Lautin, 12:30 p.m., before turning their fire onto Fort Loncin, to which General Leman had shifted his headquarters nine days earlier. After a hundred and forty minutes of bombardment the magazine was penetrated and the fortress destroyed. Amid the ruins General Leman was found lying insensible. To Emmich, he said from the stretcher on which his captors placed him, "I ask you to bear witness that you found me unconscious."

Left: General Joffre in 1915, with French soldiers in the new "horizon blue" uniforms.

Below: An artist's impression of Joffre in his headquarters on the eve of the French counter-offensive on the Marne, September 4, 1914. A dragoon reports with a message. Joffre's headquarters was known as *Grand quartier général* (G.Q.G.) and was located then at Bar-sur-Aube, finally (September 5) at Châtillon-sur-Seine. Unlike the British and Germans, who chose luxury hotels or châteaux as their general staff headquarters, the French located themselves in simpler buildings, typically village schools. When Joffre eventually decided to dismiss Lanrezac, Commander of Fifth Army, the spot he chose to convey the message, on September 3, was the playground of the school in Sezanne, a small provincial town in the department of the Marne.

The last two forts, Hollogne and Flémelle, surrendered without further fight on August 16 and the Krupp and Skoda guns were then broken out of their emplacements and diverted towards the forts or Namur, where they would repeat the victory of Liège after three days of bombardment on August 24. These two "naval battles on land" spelt the end of a three-hundred-year-old military trust in the power of fortresses. That trust had never been more than conditional in any case. The Prince de Ligne, one of the leading generals of the eighteenth-century

fortress age, had written, "The more I see and the more I read, the more I am convinced that the best fortress is an army, and the best rampart a rampart of men." Ramparts of men, not steel or concrete, would indeed form the fronts of the First World War.

Just such a rampart was in the making far to the south of the Meuse crossings. If the Emmich element in the German plan was bold, the French plan for the opening of the war was bolder in a different dimension. "Whatever the circumstances," Plan XVII stated, "it is the Commander-in-Chief's intention to advance with all forces united to attack the German armies." Those the French expected to find deployed along the common frontier between Luxembourg and Switzerland. Joffre's scheme of operations was to throw forward his five armies in two groups, Fifth and Third on the left, Second and First on the right, with Fourth echeloned slightly in the rear to cover the gap between the two masses, into which topography and fortification, the French calculated, would funnel any successful German advance. The two thrusts, by the Fifth and Third and the Second and First Armies respectively, were the essence of Plan XVII.

Before either could be set in motion, however, Joffre had unleashed a preliminary assault to open the way for the larger offensive to follow. On August 7 General Bonneau's VII Corps moved forward to seize Mulhouse in Alsace. Bonneau expressed reluctance and allowed himself to be driven out within twenty-four hours when the Germans counter-attacked. The humiliation incensed Joffre. He dismissed Bonneau on the spot. Joffre was a sacker. By the end of August he would have dismissed an army commander, three out of twenty-one corps commanders and thirty-one out of 103 divisional commanders. In September he was to dismiss another thirty-eight divisional commanders, in October eleven and in November twelve. "My mind was made up on this subject," Joffre would write later. "I would get rid of incapable generals and replace them with those who were younger and more energetic." Right was on his side. French generals were too old—in 1903 their average age had been sixty-one against fifty-four in Germany—or, if younger, often unfit. Joffre, admittedly, set no example. Heavily overweight, he was devoted to the table and allowed nothing, even at the height of the crisis in 1914, to interrupt lunch. He was, for all that, shrewd, imperturbable and a keen judge of character, the qualities that would see the French army through the coming campaign as the crisis deepened.

THE BATTLE OF THE FRONTIERS

The Lorraine offensive opened on August 14, when Dubail's First Army, with Castelnau's Second echeloned to its left, crossed the frontier and advanced towards Sarrebourg. The French advanced as liberators and conquerors. The thought that the Germans might have plans of their own appears to have crossed no mind in the French high command. Its intelligence underestimated the Germans' strength. In fact the German Sixth and Seventh Armies comprised eight, not six, corps and were preparing to strike the French a weighty counter-blow as soon as they overreached themselves.

They were shortly to do so. For four days the Germans fell back, contesting

50 miles

HOLLAND

GERMANY

Ostend
Antwerp
Belgian Army
1st Army
Ghent
Rhine
Cologne

Maastricht
Aachen
Eupen

Ypres
Lys
Schelde
BRUSSELS
BELGIUM
Liège
Coblenz

Lille
Ancre
Mons
2nd Army
Meuse
Namur
Moselle

Douai
Maubeuge
Charleroi
3rd Army

Cambrai
LUXEM-BOURG

Ancre
Le Cateau
Oise
GERMANY

Somme
St. Quentin
Mézières
Sedan
4th Army
LUXEMBOURG

La Fère
Aisne
LORRAINE

Montdidier
1st Army
Laon
5th Army
Diedenhofen (Thionville)

Oise
Soissons
2nd Army
3rd Army
Rheims
Metz
Morhange

6th Army
4th Army
Verdun
3rd Army
St. Mihiel
6th Army
Saarburg

Coulommiers
Marshes of St. Gond
Châlons-sur-Marne
2nd Army
Toul
Lunéville
7th Army

PARIS
British Expeditionary Force
9th Army
4th Army
Marne
Moselle

5th Army
Provins
Epinal
1st Army

FRANCE
Meuse
Mülhausen

Seine
Langres
Saône
Belfort

Dijon
Montbéliard

Besançon

Legend:
- German advance
- 17 Aug 1914 — German positions
- 5 Sept 1914 — German positions
- French — Allied positions, 5 Sept 1914
- British
- Belgian
- Fortified town/ military fortress

Map: The strategic situation on the Western Front on the eve of the Battle of the Marne, September 5, 1914, showing the line of advance of the seven German armies since August 17. The route taken by the German First Army shows the length of the great wheeling movement, intended to outflank the French line, and of the retreat of the French Fifth and Fourth Armies and the British Expeditionary Force in its path. The French Ninth and Sixth Armies were formed during the campaign, the latter from the garrison of Paris. Its appearance helped to drive the German First Army away from Paris and, by threatening its exposed flank, to win the Battle of the Marne. The Belgian army, defending Antwerp, later made its escape along the coast to new defensive positions on the River Yser between Ypres and the sea.

Background: A German patrol in the ruins of the Belgian village of Visé, on the Meuse north of Liège, one of the first places to be entered during the invasion, on August 4. The soldiers belong to the task force of General Emmich, whose role was to seize the crossings of the Meuse at Liège and Namur in advance of the arrival of von Kluck's First Army.

but not firmly opposing the French advance. Then the front lost its sponginess. The French infantry found German resistance stiffening. First Army was not firmly in contact with Second; west of the Saar Valley, Dubail and Castelnau were not in operational touch at all. Dubail was conscious of the weakness and intended on August 20 to mend it by launching an attack that would both restore contact and open a way through Conneau's Cavalry Corps to debouch into the enemy's rear; but even as he set the attack in motion on the night of August 19–20, the Germans were preparing to unleash their planned counter-offensive.

Rupprecht's and Heeringen's armies had been temporarily subordinated to a single staff. Thus, while the French Second and First Armies co-ordinated their actions only as well as sporadic telephoning could arrange, the German Sixth and Seventh fought as a single entity. Dubail's night attack was checked as soon as begun. The setback was followed by a simultaneous offensive along the whole line of battle by the eight German corps against the French six. Heavy artillery did even worse damage to Second Army on August 20. The XV and XVI Corps abandoned their positions. Only the XX, on the extreme left, held firm. It was fighting on home ground and was commanded by General Ferdinand Foch, of exceptional talent and determination. While his soldiers clung on, the rest of the army was ordered by Castelnau to break contact and retreat behind the River Meurthe, from which it had begun its advance six days earlier. It had completely lost touch with the First Army, which Dubail was therefore obliged to disengage from battle also. By August 23 it, too, had returned to the Meurthe and was preparing to defend strong positions which Foch had established on the high ground of the Grand Couronné de Nancy. There the two armies entrenched to await further German assaults which, between August 25 and September 7, broke on the stout French defences.

The significance of the French recovery on the Meurthe would take time to emerge. Elsewhere disaster persisted. Next above the First and Second Armies stood the Third and Fourth, given by Joffre the mission of penetrating the forest zone of the Ardennes and striking towards southern Belgium. General Headquarters (G.Q.G.) had assured both Fourth and Third Armies, on August 22, that "no serious opposition need be anticipated."

The Germans were better informed than the French. Their aviators had reported significant enemy movements on the front of Fourth Army and alerted the Germans to Joffre's real intentions. On August 20 Sixth Army had remained in its positions but on the morning of August 22 both it and Fifth Army were on the march. Fourth Army was particularly concerned with the danger of being outflanked and its headquarters issued orders for the corps on its left to take particular care to maintain contact with its neighbour.

In fact, it was the French, not the Germans, who risked being unhinged. Their formations were disposed *en echelon*, like a flight of steps descending in a shallow easterly direction from north to south. Were the Germans to push hard against the top of the French front, there was a danger that the steps of the French line would separate in sequence, leading to the wholesale collapse of Fourth and Third Armies. That, on August 22, was exactly what happened. It was Third Army which collapsed first. Advancing at daybreak, its vanguard ran into unexpected German

General Edouard de Castelnau (1851–1944) (right) at the 1913 manoeuvres. A devout Catholic, known as *le Capucin botté*, "monk in boots," because of his membership in the Third Order of Franciscans, his career suffered because of his religious beliefs in the anticlerical atmosphere of the pre-war Third Republic. He was favoured by Joffre, nevertheless, and became Deputy Chief of Staff in 1911, helping to draw up the French war plan, Plan XVII. In 1914 he commanded Second Army and in 1915 was promoted to command Army Group Centre. Later that year he became Joffre's chief of staff and was instrumental in 1916 in forming the decision to hold Verdun. When Joffre was relieved in December 1916, Castelnau was considered as his replacement but his Catholic associations told against him. He ended the war, in which he had lost his three sons, as commander of the Eastern Army Group.

The campaign of August–September 1914 drove civilians to flee from their homes at the approach of the fighting in hundreds of thousands. These are Germans, dislodged by the French advance of August into Alsace. The greatest number of refugees were Belgian who, rightly terrified by the initial German atrocities against civilians in the eastern regions of their country, fled westward in dense columns, cluttering the roads and impeding the movement of the retreating Belgian and French armies. Tens of thousands of Belgians were evacuated to Britain where, with the greater part of their country occupied by Germany, they spent the rest of the war. The French government itself left Paris on September 2 for Bordeaux, whither it had transferred during the Franco-Prussian War of 1870–71, and did not return to the capital until after the victory on the Marne.

resistance and the infantry were panicked into flight. The rest of the army was stopped in its tracks and had to fight hard to hold its position. Fourth Army also failed to advance, except in the centre, a position held by the Colonial Corps. This was composed of white regiments which in peacetime garrisoned the empire. Its soldiers were hardened and experienced veterans. That was to be their undoing. Pressing forward with a determination the unblooded conscripts of the metropolitan army could not match, it rapidly became embedded in a far larger mass of Germans. The harder the Colonials pressed, the higher their casualties mounted. By the evening of August 22, the 3rd Colonial Division had lost 11,000 men killed or wounded, the worst casualties to be suffered by any French formation in the Battle of the Frontiers. Its effective destruction spelt an end to Fourth Army's efforts to take ground forward.

Plan XVII had thus been brought to a standstill along a crucial section of front. Joffre at first refused to credit the outcome. On the morning of August 23 he signalled de Langle de Cary to say that there were "only . . . three [enemy] corps

before [you]. Consequently you must resume your offensive as soon as possible."
De Langle obediently attempted to do as ordered, but his army was only driven
further back that day. Unsuccessful, too, were the Third and the recently assembled Army of Lorraine. On August 24, the Fourth Army retired behind the protection of the River Meuse and Third Army shortly followed. Much of Maunoury's
Army of Lorraine was meanwhile withdrawn to Amiens, where a new army, the
Sixth, was to be created.

THE BATTLE OF THE SAMBRE

On two sectors of the French frontier, Alsace-Lorraine and the Ardennes, the
Germans had, by the end of the war's third week, achieved significant victories.
The scene of action was now to shift to the frontier with Belgium. It was there
that Germany's offensive plan must succeed if Schlieffen's dream of a six-week
war were to be realised. The seizure of Liège had laid the ground. The conse-
quent retreat of the Belgian field army had opened the way. The fall of Namur
would complete the clearing of the theatre of major obstacles. Most important
of all, the French high command remained apparently and obstinately blind to
the danger that threatened. Lanrezac had begun to warn G.Q.G., even before
war was declared, that he feared an envelopment of his left—northern—flank by
a German march into Belgium. Joffre dismissed these anxieties. As late as August
14, within earshot of the guns, the Commander-in-Chief continued to insist that
the Germans would not deploy any major force inside Belgium north of the
Meuse.

Over the next six days, Joffre began to reconsider, issuing orders that first
directed Lanrezac's Fifth Army into the angle between the Meuse and the Sambre, then to join with the British Expeditionary Force in operations against the
left wing of the German battle line, whose appearance in great strength in Belgium could no longer be denied. Events at a lower level then took charge. Rivers,
unless wide, are always difficult to defend. Meanders create pockets that soak up
troops and cause misunderstandings between neighbouring units as to where
responsibilities start and end. Bridges are a particular problem: does a bridge
which marks a boundary between units lie in one sector or another? Lanrezac,
with perfect orthodoxy, had ordered the bridges to be held only by outposts, while
the bulk of the Fifth Army waited on higher ground, whence it could advance to
repel a German crossing or mount its own offensive across the bridges into Belgium. The outposts at the bridges, however, found themselves in a dilemma. They
discovered more bridges than their orders indicated had to be defended. While
they were making their dispositions, German patrols from the Second Army
appeared opposite, sensed an opportunity and requested permission to chance
a crossing from corps headquarters. It was that of the Imperial Guard, which,
fortuitously, Ludendorff happened to be visiting when the message arrived. He
took personal responsibility for approving the venture. The 2nd Guard Division
attacked, found an undefended bridge and established a foothold. To the west of
Auvelais a patrol of the German 19th Division found another unguarded bridge

Above: A patrol of French dragoons falls on a German cavalry scouting party, August 1914. An artist's impression; in practice, there was very little contact between the cavalry of either side during the opening days. The French cavalry corps commanded by General Sordet combed southern Belgium for many days in August seeking contact with the Germans but, though several thousand strong, failed to find them.

Right: Belgian carabineers, with their dog-drawn machine guns, retreating to Antwerp, August 20, 1914. The carabineers, who wore distinctive leather top hats, formed part of the country's *Garde Civique*, a part-time militia. In the opening days, the Germans refused to recognise the militia as a legitimate force and threatened reprisals against its members unless they lodged their weapons at town halls. Some local militias obeyed the invaders' instructions.

and crossed without asking for orders. By the afternoon of August 21, therefore, a gap four miles wide had been opened across the river front.

Yet Lanrezac might still have retrieved the situation had he stuck to his original plan of holding the high ground south of the Sambre as his main position. Inexplicably, however, he now acquiesced in the decision of his two subordinates commanding III and X Corps to counter-attack. They tried and on the morning of August 22 their troops were repelled with heavy loss. Strategically the result was even worse. Nine French divisions had been defeated by three German, and forced to retreat seven miles, contact with the Fourth Army, on the Meuse, had been broken, contact with the British Expeditionary Force at Mons had not been established and Sordet's Cavalry Corps was drawing back through Fifth Army's positions, its men exhausted and its horses worn out. The situation did not improve during August 23. An hour before midnight Lanrezac concluded he was beaten and telegraphed Joffre that as the "enemy is threatening my right on the Meuse . . . Givet is threatened, Namur taken . . . I have decided to withdraw the Army tomorrow."

THE BATTLE OF MONS

Lanrezac made no mention of the situation on his left, though there his British allies had also been locked in combat with the Germans throughout August 23. The British Expeditionary Force had arrived on the Mons-Condé Canal on August 22. By the morning of August 23 it was deployed on a front of twenty miles, II Corps to the west, I Corps to the east, with the whole of von Kluck's First Army bearing down on it from the north. General Sir John French, the B.E.F. Commander, had expected to march level with Lanrezac in an advance into Belgium. News of Lanrezac's defeat on the Sambre ruled that out but, when a message arrived from French Fifth Army headquarters just before midnight on August 22, asking for assistance, he agreed to defend the canal for twenty-four hours.

The B.E.F. was equal to the task. Alone among those of Europe, the British army was an all-regular force, composed of professional soldiers whom the small wars of empire had hardened to the realities of combat. Many of them had fought in the Boer War fifteen years earlier, against skilled marksmen, and they had learnt from them the power of the magazine-rifle and the necessity of digging deep to escape its effects.

The Germans, who outnumbered them by six divisions to four, were unprepared for the storm of fire that would sweep their ranks. "The dominating German impression was of facing an invisible enemy," hidden behind freshly turned earth in trenches much deeper than the inexperienced French or amateur Belgians thought to dig. The British Lee-Enfield rifle, with its ten-round magazine, was a weapon superior to the German Mauser, and the British soldier a superior shot. "Fifteen rounds a minute" has become a catchphrase, but it was the standard most British infantrymen met. A German officer of the 12th Brandenburg Grenadiers was among the first to experience the effect of long-range, well-aimed rifle fire. "No sooner had we left the edge of the wood than a volley of bullets whistled past our noses and cracked into the trees behind. Five or six cries near

Above: Field Marshal Sir John French, Commander-in-Chief of the British Expeditionary Force. French, "the little Field Marshal," was a cavalryman who had won his reputation during the Boer War. Of peppery temperament and personally brave, he was disheartened by the heavy losses his units suffered in the Battles of Mons and Le Cateau and thereafter sought to disengage, in the hope of reorganising the B.E.F. at a distance from the enemy. At one point he even warned the British government that he intended to retire behind the Seine, breaking contact with the French Fifth Army, in whose commander, Lanzerac, he had lost confidence. It took a personal visit by Kitchener, the British Secretary of State for War, to stiffen his resolve. Eventually, the strains of command overwhelmed him and he was replaced by the tougher Douglas Haig in December 1915.

Opposite bottom: Soldiers of the 4th Battalion the Royal Fusiliers resting before the Battle of Mons, August 22, 1914. The Royal Fusiliers were recruited in London and were one of the oldest and most distinguished regiments of infantry in the British army, with battle honours going back to the seventeenth century. Lieutenant Dease, a Royal Fusilier officer, won the Victoria Cross, Britain's highest award for bravery, at Mons, the first award of the V.C. during the First World War. He was killed in the action.

Right: Soldiers of the Royal Artillery disembarking at Rouen, a main point of entry for the British Expeditionary Force in France, in mid-August 1914. By a remarkable feat of organisation, four British infantry divisions and a cavalry division were mobilised and transported to the continent in two weeks. By August 22, the advanced guards of the B.E.F. were in position on the Belgian frontier at Mons, where they fought a successful delaying action throughout August 23. The batteries of the Royal Artillery, equipped with quick-firing 18-pounder guns, were particularly successful at breaking up German attacks.

me, five or six of my grey lads collapsed in the grass . . . The firing seemed at long range and half-left . . . Here we were as if advancing on a parade ground . . . away in front a sharp, hammering sound, then a pause, then a more rapid hammering—machine guns!"

The soldiers opposite the Brandenburg Grenadiers belonged to the 1st Battalion Queen's Own Royal West Kent Regiment and it was their rifles, not the battalion's two machine guns, that were causing the casualties. By the end of the day, Bloem's regiment was "all to pieces." Five hundred had been killed or wounded, including three out of four of his battalion's company commanders. Bloem was lucky to be untouched. The results were the same in many other units, for every British battalion held its ground and the supporting artillery had kept up a steady supporting fire throughout the action. Total British casualties were 1,600 killed, wounded and missing. German casualties, never fully disclosed, must have reached nearly 5,000.

That evening the Germans of von Kluck's army slept where they tumbled down, exhausted, on the north bank of the canal, with the day's work of carrying crossings over it to do all over again on the morrow. The British, exhausted too, prepared to fall back on positions a little to the canal's south. They were flushed with the emotion of a fight well fought. They expected to sustain their defence of the Allies' left flank the following day. Even as they began to retire to their night positions, however, new orders came in. They were for retreat.

On the morning of August 24, the B.E.F. began a general retirement. At 9:35 Joffre explained in a message to the Minister of War why the whole front must be withdrawn. "In the north, our Army operating between the Sambre, the Meuse and the British Army, appears to have suffered checks of which I still do not know the full extent, but which have forced it to retire . . . One must face facts . . . Our army corps . . . have not shown on the battlefield those offensive qualities for which we had hoped . . . We are therefore compelled to resort to the defensive, using our fortresses and great topographical obstacles to enable us to yield as little ground as possible. Our object must be to last out, trying to wear the enemy down, and to resume the offensive when the time comes."

THE GREAT RETREAT

The great retreat had begun, a retreat which would carry the French armies, and the B.E.F. on their left, back to the outskirts of Paris during the next fourteen days. Yet Joffre's despatch, doleful as it must have read to Messimy, Minister of War, remains one of the great documents of the war. In its few sentences it sketched out a plan of recovery, even of eventual victory. The great fortresses, Verdun foremost, were indeed still in French hands. The topography which defends France from the east, the mountains of the Vosges, the waterways of the Seine River system, were unviolated. The spirit of the French army survived unbroken. Could it but retain its cohesion as it fell back on the capital, the opportunity for a counterstroke remained. "Future operations," Joffre wrote in his General Instruction

Opposite: A corporal and private soldiers of the London Scottish sightseeing in a Paris street in the autumn of 1914. The London Scottish were a regiment of the Territorial Force (T.F.), Britain's part-time volunteer reserve army, and the first T.F. unit to move to France. They wore a distinctive "hodden grey" kilt with their standard khaki jackets. The kilted Scottish regiments fascinated the French, as the expression of the onlookers reveals. On November 30 the London Scottish fought a night battle outside Ypres in Belgium, which helped to turn the tide of the First Battle of Ypres and terminate the final German offensive of the year.

Right: The commanding officer, adjutant and second-in-command of the 1st Cameronians (Scottish Rifles) conferring before the Battle of Le Cateau, August 25, 1914. Photography was forbidden on active service in the British army, lest photographs fall into the hands of the enemy and reveal sensitive information. An officer of the Cameronians disobeyed the rule. His photographs, which survived, form one of the few visual images of the campaign. The Cameronians were a Lowland regiment which did not wear the Highlanders' kilt, but disclosed their Scottishness by their ribbed Glengarry caps. Engaged at Mons in August, the Cameronians also fought later at the Battle of the Marne, the Aisne and First Ypres.

No. 2 of August 25, "will have as their object to reform on our left a mass capable of resuming the offensive. This will consist of the Fourth, Fifth and British Armies, together with new forces drawn from the eastern front, while the other armies contain the enemy for as long as possible."

The location indicated by Joffre for the positioning of the "new offensive mass" was the line of the River Somme near Amiens, seventy-five miles south-west of Mons. Thus Joffre already envisaged a long retreat before his redeployment of forces could permit a resumption of the attack. The reality of the coming retreat was to be grimmer by far than anything Joffre anticipated. The German infantry of the right wing, despite twelve days of fighting and marching through Belgium, remained fresh. Buoyed up by victories already gained, hardened by days on the road, they were ready to step out with a will if the defeat of distance would defeat the French army. "This frantic, everlasting rush," Bloem's battalion commander told him on the seventh day after Mons, "is absolutely essential . . . use all your powers to keep up spirits at any price." Bloem's Brandenburgers needed little encouragement. Despite "inflamed heels, soles and toes . . . whole patches of skin rubbed off to the raw flesh," they kept up the pace under the grilling sun of one of the century's most brilliant summers for day after day. Falling back before them, the 1st Battalion the Gloucestershire Regiment, for example, recorded a distance covered of 244 miles in thirteen days, with only one of rest (August 29) and two successive marches of over twenty miles on August 27 and 28. What the British and French endured, the Germans did likewise.

Both sides fought as well as marched. The British I Corps had to fight at Landrecies and Maroilles on August 26 but disengaged easily and resumed its retreat; II Corps, battered by Mons, was forced to fight at Le Cateau on the same day an even bigger battle in order to get away. General Smith-Dorrien, commanding II Corps, had three infantry divisions under command, supported by the Cavalry Division. His tired men were assaulted on the morning of August 26 by three German infantry and three cavalry divisions, reinforced during the day by two more infantry divisions, a total of eight against four. Such an inequality of force offered the Germans an opportunity. As dusk fell, II Corps, which had lost 8,000 killed, wounded and missing during the battle—more than Wellington's army at Waterloo—summoned its reserves of strength to slip away and resume the retreat. Thirty-eight guns, half a divisional artillery, were lost nonetheless, despite desperate attempts to save them.

On the day of Le Cateau, Joffre met Sir John French at St. Quentin, together with Lanrezac. It was not a happy meeting. Lanrezac and French had got on badly since their first encounter ten days earlier. The atmosphere of the conference, held in a darkened room in a private house, was uneasy. French denied having received Joffre's General Instruction No. 2, for a future counter-offensive. All he could talk of was his own difficulties. Lanrezac's manner implied that the B.E.F. was an embarrassment rather a support. Moreover, the Frenchmen did not speak English, French scarcely any French; General Henry Wilson, Deputy Chief of Staff, translated. There were also personal differences. Joffre and Lanrezac, big, heavy men in dark blue, gold-buttoned uniforms, looked like station masters, the vulpine Wilson and the peppery French, in their whipcord breeches and glittering riding boots, like masters of foxhounds.

The conference came to no clear decision and, when it ended, Lanrezac declined to lunch with French. Joffre, however, accepted and, when he left, returned to G.Q.G. with the intention of stiffening Lanrezac's backbone. He perceived that the British needed a breathing space, for he was aware of the risk that a beaten B.E.F. might head for safety in the Channel ports, and so sent orders to Lanrezac to counter-attack the German Second Army, treading close on his heels in its path towards Paris. Lanrezac complained but obeyed. His instructions were to align

Fifth Army along the upper course of the River Oise with two corps facing north in defence and another to attack to the west where the river turned south to join the Seine at Pontoise, above Paris. A fourth corps, commanded by the very determined Franchet d'Esperey, was to stand in reserve. The battle—known to the French as Guise, to the Germans as St. Quentin—opened on the morning of August 29 in thick mist. The Imperial Guard Corps and Plattenburg's X Corps stepped out with a will, their commanders believing that no serious French resistance was to be met before the River Aisne, thirty-five miles distant. They were surprised by the strength of the opposition, against which they began to suffer heavy casualties.

During the course of the day, however, the Guard and the Hannoverians of

Unsere gefürchtete Kavallerie
Harczok Páris körül. Német gyözelmek.

"Our terrifying cavalry," a German propaganda postcard of 1914. The artist portrays an imaginary scene. No massed cavalry charges took place in any of the Western Front battles of 1914, since dense formations of horsemen attracted instant and devastating counter-fire by rifles, machine guns and quick-firing artillery. Such images remained popular for a time with artists and their publics but reality quickly broke in.

X Corps advanced some three miles and, as evening approached, were preparing to consolidate the ground won. At that moment the character of the battle was transformed. Franchet d'Esperey had been ordered shortly after noon to intervene in support and at six o'clock he did so in person. Riding a chestnut charger at the head of regiments advancing behind their unfurled colours and the braying brass of their bands, with the corps artillery thundering overhead, he led his soldiers forward in counter-attack. Franchet d'Esperey made his reputation at Guise. "Desperate Frankie," as his British admirers christened the fire-eater, would soon succeed Lanrezac at the head of the Fifth Army. It would be a just reward, for his spectacular intervention had halted the Germans in their tracks and won an extra day and a half for the army to reposition itself for the counter-stroke which Joffre remained determined to deliver.

Whether he could or not now depended more on the movements of the German armies than his own. Were they to persist in their march to the southwestward, aiming to pass Paris to the right, Joffre's scheme of forming an offensive mass to drive into their flank might be defeated by distance and logistic difficulty. Were they, on the other hand, to press to the south-east, leaving Paris on the left, they would be doing the French what Schlieffen, in another context, had called a "willing favour." Schlieffen had, as his Great Memorandum reveals, come to fear that whichever decision was taken, it would favour the French. To aim to pass Paris to the right would expose the German outer wing to a thrust launched from the Paris fortified zone by its strong garrison; to pass Paris to the left would open a gap between the outer German force and those with which they should keep station, for Paris, like a breakwater, would then divide the tide of the German onset. This "problem of Paris" had driven Schlieffen to "the conclusion that

HOME FRONT

With the precipitate departure to the battlefronts of millions of conscripts and reservists in August 1914, life on what soon came to be called the "home front" changed. Acute labour shortages suddenly appeared, not made good until women began to substitute in both factories and fields. There was also very rapidly a severe shortage of supply in certain categories of military stores, particularly shells. States had planned and provided for a short war. When it protracted, they were caught out. In Britain, France and Germany the solution adopted was to place production under ministerial control; the co-operation of employers and workers was secured by the provision of high profits and wages respectively. As needs were identified, skilled workers were released from the army to resume their essential occupations.

War profits and wages created inflation. It was controlled successfully in Britain and France by fiscal and monetary measures but less so in Germany and Austria, where poverty became common as the war drew out, heightened by the effects of the Allied blockade and the domestic black market. In Russia, failures of supply and price control did much to prepare the way for the two revolutions of 1917.

Politically, the outbreak of the war brought a suspension of conflict in most countries. The parties in France declared a *Union sacrée,* in Germany a *Burgfrieden,* both implying parliamentary truce. In Britain, the Conservative opposition cooperated with the Liberal government until party positions were overtaken by the creation of a coalition in 1915. As the war intensified, however, power passed to the strong-minded: in Germany to the military duumvirate of Hindenburg and Ludendorff, in Russia eventually to the Bolsheviks.

The home front proved a better place in the victor nations than the vanquished, where by 1918 malnutrition, infant and adult mortality and deprivation of every kind had increased far above peacetime levels. The most potent non-military weapon employed by the Allies was the blockade, perpetuation of which after the war obliged Germany to sign the Peace of Versailles.

Opposite: Peasants receiving their bread rations, Champagne.

Above: Berlin residents receiving food from a mobile soup kitchen.

Right: Territorials examine a bombed-out building in London after a Zeppelin raid.

93

we are too weak to continue operations in this direction." The fault of conception Schlieffen had recognised in his study the German general staff was now discovering in the field, as its troops marched southward, while their chiefs dithered about their eventual destination.

The difficulty of choice had revealed itself soon after the Supreme Army Command, *Oberste Heersleitung,* or O.H.L., as it became in war, had displaced from Berlin to Coblenz, on the Rhine, on August 17 (its next location would be in Lux-

embourg and its final station the little resort town of Spa, in Belgium). Moltke's decision to allow von Bülow, of Second Army, to oversee the operations of First and Third Armies, began to have unfortunate consequences soon after the move to Coblenz had been completed. Bülow's anxiety to assure mutual support between the armies of the right wing deprived Hausen, Third Army, of the chance to strike into Lanrezac's rear as he disengaged from the Sambre on August 24. Then Moltke allowed anxieties of his own about the predicament of the Eighth Army, defending East Prussia against the Russians, to distort his control of the larger and more critical operations in the west. Seeing in the fall of Namur a chance to economise force, he decided to redirect the troops thus released across Germany to the eastern frontier.

Meanwhile the marching armies had been further weakened by the detachment of III Reserve Corps to contain the Belgian army in Antwerp, of IV Reserve

The original caption of this picture, a watercolour by Hans Schmidt, 1915, reads *Destruction of the British 18th Hussars and 4th Dragoon Guards on Thulin, 24 August 1914, by the fire of German Landwehr troops.* It is a wildly exaggerated depiction of a minor incident during the retreat for Mons. Neither regiment was destroyed nor were the *Landwehr*—Germany's third-line reserve—deployed with the first-line troops. The picture, nevertheless, is typical of many painted early in the war by artists who were trying to represent its scenes in terms of traditional military painting. It would take time for the reality of industrial warfare to be accepted and longer still for a new generation of artists to find the means to depict it.

Corps to garrison Brussels and of VII Reserve Corps to besiege Maubeuge. The loss of five corps from the fighting line—one-seventh of the western army—actually eased Moltke's logistical difficulties. Nevertheless, preponderance of force at the decisive point is a key to victory. On August 27, moreover, Moltke further diminished his chance to secure a concentration of superior force by ordering the outer armies to fan out. First Army was to pass west of Paris, Second to aim directly for the fortified city, while Third was to pass to the east and Fourth and Fifth, still battling with the French armies defending the lower Meuse, to press westward to join them. Sixth and Seventh, operating where the French had launched their opening offensive of the war, were to attempt to reach and cross the River Moselle.

The march west of Paris was the manoeuvre which Schlieffen had deemed the German army "too weak" to realise. If attempted, it might have proved so but the practicability of Moltke's directive was not put to the test. The day after its issue, August 28, von Kluck independently decided to change his line of march and move south-eastward, inside Paris, giving as his reasons the disappearance of any threat from the B.E.F. and the desirability of finally disabling Fifth Army by a drive into its flank. Moltke, despite his quite precise order of August 27 that Kluck should go west of Paris, acquiesced and on September 2 went further. In a message to First and Second Armies he announced that it was "the intention of the High Command to drive the French back in a south-easterly direction, *cutting them off from Paris* [italics supplied]. The First Army will follow the Second in echelon and will also cover the right flank of the armies." This was an acceptance of events rather than an effort to determine them. Second Army had halted to recuperate from the effects of fighting and the long march, so that for First to echelon itself with it would entail a pause also. The French Fifth Army meanwhile was slipping away to the east, so eroding the danger of an attack into its flank and distancing itself from Paris in so doing. The B.E.F. was not disabled but had merely disappeared into the countryside while the growing assemblage of Joffre's new striking force in and around Paris remained undiscovered by the enemy altogether.

Meanwhile the marching armies tramped on, fifteen and twenty miles a day in the heat of a brilliant late summer. Joffre, out on inspection of the French armies on August 30, passed "retreating columns . . . Red trousers had faded to the colour of pale brick, coats were ragged and torn, shoes caked with mud, eyes cavernous in faces dulled by exhaustion and dark with many days growth of beard. Twenty days of campaigning seemed to have aged the soldiers as many years." The French and British were at least falling back on their lines of supply. The Germans marched ahead of theirs. A French witness noticed on September 3, when a unit of the invaders reached their billets for the night, "they fell down exhausted, muttering in a dazed way, 'forty kilometres! forty kilometres!' That was all they could say."

On September 3 von Kluck's headquarters were installed at Compiègne. It was there that he received Moltke's wireless message of September 2 directing his First Army to follow Bülow's Second "in echelon" to the south-east, in order to cut the French off from Paris. Kluck decided to interpret the order literally,

General Alexander von Kluck (1846–1934), commander of the German First Army in the invasion of Belgium and France and the Battle of the Marne. Von Kluck was unusual among German commanders of his generation and seniority in that he had no general staff experience. He had a reputation for competence, however, and was given heavy responsibilities in the opening stages of the war. First Army had a successful passage though Belgium and northern France but, as it approached Paris in early September, Kluck proved unable to resolve the fatal ambiguity in the Schlieffen Plan: whether to pass to west or the east of Paris. He chose to pass to the east but, in so doing, he allowed a gap to open between his army and Second, commanded by von Bülow, to his left. It was into that gap that the new formations assembled by Joffre, notably Foch's Ninth Army, attacked with such effect during the Battle of the Marne. In 1915 Kluck was badly wounded and did not serve again.

to cross the River Marne and to initiate the decisive battle that Moltke actually intended to be delivered by the armies of the center. The German strategic effort was beginning to fall apart. "Moltke," a French historian comments, "had never much believed in the possibility of manoeuvring masses . . . like his uncle [the elder Moltke], he thought it necessary to leave each army commander a wide freedom of movement." Laxity of control had not mattered in 1870, when the front of battle was narrow. Moltke the Younger's easy reign over the far wider battlefront of 1914 had resulted in his right-hand army, on which all depended, first slipping to the south, then turning south-eastward, at right angles to the direction which the plan of campaign laid down it must maintain for victory to be achieved.

Apologists argue that Kluck was doing the right thing by keeping on Lanrezac's heels. The truth is that he was being led by the nose. Every mile he marched in pursuit of the Fifth Army served Joffre's purpose. For the further Kluck widened the gap between his army and Paris, the more space he created for Joffre to position the "mass of manoeuvre" against the German flank.

The creation of this "mass of manoeuvre" had been fore-shadowed in Joffre's General Instruction No. 2 of August 25. By September 1 it consisted of VII and IV Corps, taken from First and Third Armies, and the 55th, 56th, 61st and 62nd Reserve Divisions, the whole forming Sixth Army under General Maunoury; with it was associated the garrison of Paris. Together they constituted the Armies of Paris, under the overall command of General Gallieni. Gallieni was sixty-five in 1914, Maunoury sixty-seven; even in a war of old generals—Moltke was sixty-six, Joffre sixty-two—they might have appeared too elderly to find energy sufficient to mastermind a counter-stroke against the largest army ever deployed in the field. They, however, were men of vitality, Gallieni exceptionally so. Recalled from retirement on August 25, he had at once warned Messimy, Minister of War, that the enemy would be at the gates in twelve days. He demanded reinforcements, which could only be got from Joffre, who was unwilling to release any and, as supreme commander with war powers, could not be overruled even by the President. Gallieni's demands provoked a government crisis. Messimy, finding himself blamed for the dangers of which Gallieni was now warning, insisted on being dismissed and by so doing brought about the resignation of the whole ministry.

Meanwhile the French railway system was hurrying to the front the forces with which Joffre planned to deliver his counter-stroke. Its network brought troops rapidly from the increasingly stabilised eastern sector to the critical points. By September 5, the IV Corps was on route from Fourth Army. The Ninth Army, commanded by the newly promoted Ferdinand Foch, comprised the IX and XI Corps transferred from Fourth Army, together with the 52nd and 60th Reserve

General Joseph Gallieni (1849–1916) shared with Joffre a background in colonial operations but was regarded by him as a rival. He had retired before the war but was recalled as Joffre's deputy at the outbreak. In late August, as the Germans approached the capital, Gallieni was appointed Military Governor of Paris and began to put the city into a state of defence. He was responsible for assembling "the taxis of the Marne," which carried reinforcements to the battle but, more importantly, for creating the Sixth Army, which crucially attacked the German First Army in flank, from the city's garrison. In October 1915 Gallieni replaced Briand as Minister of War but he and Joffre remained on bad terms and he resigned in March 1916. He died two months later of chronic bad health. In this portrait he is standing in front of a "75," the famous French quick-firing field gun.

Divisions and 9th Cavalry Division, the 42nd and 18th Divisions from Third Army. Between the Paris Entrenched Camp and the Marne, Joffre therefore disposed of, at the opening of the great battle named after the river, thirty-six divisions, including the B.E.F., while the German First, Second, Third, Fourth and Fifth Armies opposing totalled just under thirty. Schlieffen's "strong right wing" was now outnumbered, the result of Moltke's failure to control his subordinates and of Joffre's refusal to be panicked by early defeat.

THE BATTLE OF THE MARNE

"It is the thirty-fifth day," the Kaiser exulted to a delegation of ministers to his Luxembourg headquarters on September 4. The thirty-fifth day had an acute significance to the German general staff of 1914. It lay halfway between the thirty-first day since mobilisation, when a map drawn by Schlieffen himself showed the German armies poised to begin their descent on Paris, and the fortieth, when his calculations determined that there would have been a decisive battle. That battle's outcome was critical. Schlieffen had calculated that the deficiencies of the Russian railways would ensure that not until the fortieth day would the Tsar's armies be assembled in sufficient strength to launch an offensive. Between the

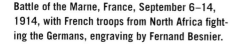

Battle of the Marne, France, September 6–14, 1914, with French troops from North Africa fighting the Germans, engraving by Fernand Besnier.

thirty-fifth and the fortieth day, therefore, the outcome of the war was to be decided.

On September 4 and 5, the commanders issued the orders which would set the engagement in motion. "The enemy," von Moltke admitted, on September 5, "has eluded the enveloping attack of First and Second Armies and has succeeded, with part of his forces, in gaining contact with Paris." First and Second Armies were therefore to stand on the defensive, while Third Army was to advance towards the upper Seine and Fourth and Fifth Armies were to attack to the south-east, with the object of opening a way for the Sixth and Seventh and complete the encirclement of the enemy. This was the opposite of what Schlieffen had intended. On September 4, Joffre had issued General Instruction No. 6 which

An impression by Paul Thiriat of an action between French and German troops at Mailly-le-Camp during the Battle of the Marne. Mailly-le-Camp, which lies south of the River Marne in the department of the Aube, marks almost the furthest point of penetration by the German Fourth Army during its advance. Fighting in the marshes of the St. Gond, to the west, brought any further advance to a halt, soon to be followed by retreat to the Aisne.

exactly anticipated Moltke's recognition of his predicament and proposed means to exploit it. Accordingly, the Sixth Army, at the outermost extremity, was to cross the Ourcq, a tributary of the Marne, and advance round the Germans' flank, while the B.E.F., the Fifth Army and Foch's Ninth Army were to make a fighting advance northward; effective date of the order, September 6. The biter was to be bit. The German, not the French, army was to be the target of an encirclement.

What stood between conception of the order and realisation were water barriers, not the Marne itself, but its tributaries. None of the waterways were serious obstacles. They defined, nevertheless, the lines on which action was to be joined and required preparation for deliberate attack. That necessity, as it proved, was to favour the Germans rather than the French, thanks to tactical quick-

Right: The transport of a British infantry battalion comes under shell fire during the Battle of the Marne, September 8, 1914.

thinking by a commander on the spot at a critical point. The man was General von Gronau, an artillery officer commanding IV Reserve Corps. On the morning of September 5, as Maunoury's Sixth Army probed forward to take up attacking positions for the following day, he was seized by disquiet at the reports sent back by his attached cavalry division. Its patrols found advancing French troops all across its front. As the IV Reserve Corps was aligned at right angles to, and to the rear of, von Kluck's First Army, that meant that the enemy was manoeuvring to take First Army in flank and roll it up. His response was instantaneous and courageous. He decided to attack.

As Maunoury's advance guard breasted forward towards the Ourcq in the mid-morning of September 5, they were suddenly brought under fire by the Germans who were occupying terrain supposed empty. The French went to ground. As darkness fell, von Gronau wisely judged he had won the time necessary to save First Army from surprise attack and disengaged his troops. In bright moonlight the French followed, launching attacks against positions the Germans had already abandoned.

The Battle of the Marne had therefore opened a day earlier than Joffre had intended. Thanks to von Gronau's independent action, the beckoning open flank which offered the opportunity for an encirclement had been covered and von Kluck given the warning necessary to hurry reinforcements from his centre to his right before the danger heightened. Kluck reacted with an energy he had not shown during the days when he had let his army drift eastward in the footsteps of Lanrezac's retreat. By the morning of September 6, he had transferred his II Corps from south of the Marne and he would successively transfer northward the IV Corps on September 7, the III Corps on September 8 and the IX Corps on September 9. What strategists call "interior lines" were now working in von Kluck's favour.

There was this difference. It was critical. Joffre's transfers had not altered the strategic situation on the eastern front, which had stabilised as soon as the French found strong defensive positions behind the Meuse and Moselle. Kluck's withdrawals, by contrast, weakened his principal front when the French were gathering to deliver their counter-offensive over the same ground. Indeed, by September 9, the fortieth day itself, the German First Army was not on the Marne at all. Between the German First Army and Second an enormous gap had opened, thirty-five miles wide, which the Germans could disregard only because they believed that the enemy troops opposite, the British Expeditionary Force, lacked the strength to penetrate.

The high command of the B.E.F. had given the Germans reason for so believing. Sir John French, "the little Field Marshal," stout, florid, had proved a dashing cavalry leader in the British army's small wars. At the head of his country's only field army in the largest war ever to involve it, he displayed an increasing tendency to nerves. The losses at Mons had unsettled him, the far heavier losses at Le Cateau had shaken his resolve altogether. He feared that the B.E.F. would fall to pieces unless given a respite. What heightened his anxieties was his conviction that Lanrezac had let him down. Before August was out, he had come to hate Lanrezac and to distrust the French generally. For Joffre he retained a personal regard but, as he told Kitchener on August 30, "my confidence in the ability of the leaders of the French Army to carry this campaign to a successful conclusion is fast waning." It took Kitchener's visit to Paris on September 2 to check this defeatism but French remained unwilling to rejoin battle. As late as September 5 he continued to prevaricate. Only when Joffre found the time to visit his headquarters and make a personal appeal did he stiffen. French was an emotional man. Joffre's clutching of his hands set tears running down his cheeks. He tried his ally's language, fell tongue-tied, then blurted at a staff officer who spoke French better, "Damn it, I can't explain. Tell him that all man can do our fellows will do."

The Esplanade of Les Invalides, Paris, filling with taxis waiting to take reinforcements to the Battle of the Marne. Only five thousand soldiers were transported but the news of the "taxis of the Marne" had a powerful effect on French morale at the time and has become a legend in French popular memories of the Great War.

Difficulties remained. The B.E.F. had fallen too far to the rear to join at once in the general offensive. "Desperate Frankie," the new commander of Fifth Army, fell into a rage at his ally's apparent unco-operativeness. Sixth Army faltered under one counter-attack after another. It would have been surprising if it had not. It lacked both the quality and numbers to stand up to Kluck's First Army, which contained eight active divisions. It deployed intact and in vigour. One critical situation had been saved for the French only by a dashing intervention of the 45th Division's artillery, led by Colonel Nivelle, a future commander of the French army, another by the arrival from Paris of a portion of the city's garrison mounted in commandeered taxicabs, an episode of future legend. The Battle of the Ourcq, between September 5 and 8, nevertheless tended Kluck's way. On the evening of September 8, he felt confident enough to signal his subordinates that "the decision will be obtained tomorrow by an enveloping attack." The Schlieffen Plan, in short, might be about to work after all.

Geography spoke otherwise. The aggressiveness Kluck's army had shown against Maunoury's had actually worked to enlarge the gap that now loomed between it and Second Army. They were, moreover, too weak to oppose the force marching

up to exploit the weakness. True to his reluctant word, Field Marshal French started the whole of the B.E.F. forward on September 6 and it soon covered the distance. The intervention of the British alarmed von Kluck. Even more alarmed was von Bülow, whose Second Army was heavily engaged throughout the day against the French Fifth Army, galvanised by the leadership of Franchet d'Esperey. On September 7 Bülow radioed the high command to warn that he was withdrawing the troops on the east of the gap, into which the B.E.F. was marching, behind the Petit Mourin River. Worse, he was obliged to swing his right wing northward, thereby further widening the gap between his army and von Kluck's and leaving the way open for a full-scale allied advance to the Marne.

The German right wing was now divided into three sections, with Kluck's First Army north of the Marne, the right of Bülow's Second south of the Marne but falling back towards it across the Grand and Petit Morin, and his left, which connected only weakly with von Hausen's Third, positioned on the Petit Morin itself, in the Marshes of the St. Gond. The whole region "is a country of great open spaces; highly cultivated, dotted with woods and villages. It is cut from east to west by deep valleys." The Marshes of the St. Gond are a topographical exception, "a broad belt of swamp land . . . five lesser roads and three foot-paths cross [the marshes] from north to south, but they are otherwise impassable." Von Bülow's right, and the left of von Hausen's Third Army were, on September 6, firmly embedded on the northern edge, with Foch's new Ninth Army positioned on the other side. The mission given him by Joffre was to protect the flank of Fifth Army, battling to drive von Bülow beyond the Marne. It was in character that he chose to interpret it offensively. While his centre and right stood fast, he ordered his left to advance. During September 6 and 7 it battled valiantly to

German dead on the battlefield of the Marne, September 1914. A regimental side drum lies beside the body in the foreground. Attacking to the sound of drums and bugles remained a common practise in 1914 and continued even into 1915, after the trenches had been dug. Some regiments unfolded their regimental colours, just as they had in the wars of the eighteenth century. Many of those who fell in battle might have been saved had the medical services been prepared for the scale of the casualties. They were not. For lack of bearers to carry them, the wounded lay out where they had been hit, to die of shock, loss of blood or thirst.

work its way round the western end of the marshes, while the rest of Ninth Army and the Germans opposite conducted artillery duels over the sodden ground of the marshes themselves. The battle of the marshes threatened to descend to a stalemate. Then it was transformed by the uncharacteristic boldness of von Hausen. This Saxon general has been described as too deferential to the wishes of the Prussian Kluck and Bülow on his right, too overawed by the German Crown Prince who commanded on his left, to take forthright decisions in the handling of his own army. On September 7 he displayed an independence that contradicted both judgements. He decided to launch a surprise night attack. In the moonlit early morning of September 8, the Saxon 32nd and 23rd Reserve Divisions and the 1st and 2nd Guard Divisions advanced through the marshes, fell on the French with the bayonet and drove them back three miles. This was a local victory that shook the confidence of Foch's Ninth Army, which lost further ground on its right during the day.

The events of September 8 prompted Foch to draft the later legendary signal,

"My centre is giving way, my right is in retreat, situation excellent. I attack." It was probably never sent. Nevertheless, the general's actions bore out the spirit of those words. During September 9 Foch succeeded in plugging every gap in the line opened by Hausen's continuing offensive and did, at the day's end, actually manage to organise a counter-attack. Merely by holding his front, Foch achieved a sort of victory.

On the Ourcq, meanwhile, September 9 was also a day of crisis. Kluck's First Army was now fighting as an independent entity, separated from Bülow's Second Army by a forty-mile gap. With four corps in line, it still outnumbered Maunoury's Sixth Army and, overlapping the flanks of the French to north and south, still retained the chance of winning an encirclement battle. The weight of his deployment was in the north, where von Quast's IX Corps was positioned and prepared to fall on the French, turn their flank and drive into the rear of the defenders of Paris. On the morning of September 9 von Quast began his attack. When his troops came up against the positions of the 61st Reserve Division, they drove the French infantry to flight, so that by early afternoon they were poised to sweep forward into undefended territory. The balance of advantage on the Marne seemed once more to have tilted the Germans' way.

German wounded, taken prisoner at the Battle of the Marne, under guard of a French dragoon, September 9, 1914. Churches were commonly used as temporary hospitals during the fighting, both because they provided space and because, as traditional places of sanctuary, it was expected that they would not be shelled by enemy artillery. Two of the men in the front row are medical orderlies, with white armbands. The others are "walking wounded," who have suffered only slight injuries. Contemporary military medicine could offer anaesthetics and antiseptic surgery but not blood transfusion or antibiotics. Death from shock or infection was as a result all too common.

ZEPPELIN

Germany, thanks to the experimental work of Count Zeppelin, had the largest and most successful fleet of dirigible airships by 1914. In August 1914 the army had seven military Zeppelins and had taken three civilian models into service; the navy had one. They were intended for use in reconnaissance but also as bombers.

Z-6 attacked Liège on the night of August 6–7, 1914. It soon became apparent, however, that Zeppelins were very vulnerable to damage by weather and ground fire. Four were lost in August, one to bombing in its shed by a British aircraft. As the envelope was filled with hydrogen, Zeppelins readily caught fire.

During 1915 the Zeppelin works produced the P-type, able to carry a bomb load of 2,500 pounds, with which raids were mounted against military targets, including Verdun, but also Paris and London, first bombed on May 31. Losses continued, however, as Zeppelins began to be attacked by Allied fighters.

New models introduced in 1916 had a higher ceiling and allowed the Zeppelins to mount heavier raids on London, by four or five airships at a time. The year saw twenty-two of the fifty-three raids suffered by Britain during the war. British air defences were improving, however, and a fighter pilot, Lieutenant Lief-Robinson, won the Victoria Cross for bringing down a Zeppelin at Cuffley, on London's outskirts.

By the end of 1916, the German army had decided to abandon the Zeppelin bombing campaign. Strategic attacks were continued by heavy bombers. The German navy, however, remained committed to its airship fleet, which had taken part in the Battle of Jutland. A naval X-type Zeppelin, with a ceiling of 25,000 feet, was shot down in the last raid on Britain on August 5, 1918.

Germany flew a total of 115 military Zeppelins during the war, of which 77 were destroyed, 7 captured, 22 scrapped and 9 surrendered to the Allies at the Armistice.

Above: Lieutenant Warneford shoots down a Zeppelin near Brussels, June 7, 1915. For this Warneford won a Victoria Cross.

Left: German Naval Airship L31 and the dreadnought *Ostfriesland.*

Opposite: *Rigid 29 and NS 7 at East Fortune Aerodrome,* starting point for British airships of the North Sea Air Patrol, by Sir John Lavery (1856–1941), British.

The parish priest of a French village watches a French infantry battalion passing his church during the Battle of the Marne, September 1914. The Third Republic was officially secular and did not appoint military chaplains. Priests of military age were conscripted and obliged to serve in the ranks. In practise they were usually allowed to do duty as medical orderlies. France, whatever the policy of its political class, was still heavily Catholic and soldiers sought the ministrations of priest-soldiers. One of the most notable was Father Teilhard de Chardin, the illustrious Jesuit intellectual, who was awarded the *Croix de Guerre* and the *Médaille Militaire*, the highest French award for bravery, while on active service as a soldier-priest during the war.

THE MISSION OF LIEUTENANT COLONEL HENTSCH

That was the local reality. Von Quast sensed no resistance to his front. His soldiers were elated by success. The way to the French capital seemed to lie open. Then, at two o'clock in the afternoon, Quast received a telephone call from Kluck's headquarters. The offensive was to be discontinued. An order for retreat had been received. Local reality was dissolved in a larger reality. The great advance, the sweep through Belgium and northern France, the masterstroke that was to end the war in the west before the fortieth day, had failed. Schlieffen's vision had evaporated in the heat of battle.

Not just the heat of battle. The cool appraisal of a military technician had decided that the position of the German First, Second and Third Armies was untenable. The technician was a middle-ranking officer of the general staff, Lieutenant Colonel Richard Hentsch. Moltke felt unable to make what would be a time-consuming journey himself. His well-informed intelligence chief was perfectly qualified to bridge the gap. Hentsch set off by motorcar from Luxembourg at eleven o'clock on the morning of September 8. In the evening he arrived at Second Army's headquarters. When Bülow returned, he and the Hentsch party settled to survey the situation. The result of their discussion was to be decisive for the outcome of the campaign in the west. Bülow proposed to avert disaster by a "voluntary concentric retreat." The retreat that followed was orderly but precipitate. Once Second Army moved, First and Third were obliged to conform, as by the working of interlocking parts. Mechanistically, Fourth, Fifth and Sixth fell in with the retrogression. Along a front of nearly 250 miles, the German infantry faced about and began to retrace its steps over the ground won in bitter combat during the last two weeks. Moltke gave the orders himself for the retreat of the left wing, and in person. When Hentsch at last returned to Supreme Headquarters in the afternoon of September 10, the Chief of Staff decided to visit his subordinate army commanders himself. The positions to which he directed them were those on the Aisne and its tributaries. "The lines so reached," he stipulated, "will be fortified and defended."

Those were the last general orders Moltke issued to the German armies; on September 14 he was relieved of command and replaced by General Erich von Falkenhayn, the Minister of War. They were also the most crucial orders to be given since those for general mobilisation and until those initiating the armistice four years and two months later. For the "fortification and defence" of the Aisne initiated trench warfare. Whatever the technical factors limiting the German army's capability to manoeuvre, none constrained its power to dig. It was better provided with field engineer units than any army in Europe and better trained in rapid entrenchment. The German soldier had been obliged to use the spade on manoeuvre since at least 1904. "From 1906 onward, foreign observers [of German manoeuvres] noted that German defensive positions frequently consisted of several successive trench lines linked by communication saps, often with barbed wire entanglements strung in front of them."

When, at the end of the second week of September, therefore, the French and British troops came up against the Germans, they found their counter-offensive halted by entrenchments which ran in a continuous line along the crest of the high ground behind the Aisne and its tributaries. The line ran on beyond, turning south-west at Verdun and following the River Meurthe until it climbed away through the precipitate Vosges to reach the Swiss frontier near Basle. The Aisne had now become the critical front and there, between September 13 and 27, both sides mounted a succession of attacks; the Allies in the hope of pressing their pursuit further, the Germans with that of holding their line. The Allies began in optimistic mood. They were shortly to discover that the days of "open warfare" were over.

Joffre's object, not yet fully formulated, was to deploy across the rear of the Germans' thickening front on the Aisne and so to regain possession of the northern departments lost to France during August. While from September 14 Sir John French was ordering his troops to entrench wherever they occupied ground on or above the Aisne, Joffre was seeking means for this new manoeuvre. On September 17 he instructed his armies to "keep the enemy under threat of attack and thus prevent him from disengaging." Three days earlier, Falkenhayn, the new German Chief of Staff, had likewise ordered counter-attacks along the whole front with a similar object. Both commanders had grasped that opportunity in the campaign in the west now lay in the hundred-mile sweep of ter-

ritory standing, denuded of troops, between the Aisne and the sea. Whoever could find an army to operate there might still outflank the enemy and so triumph.

This outflanking attempt has come to be called "the Race for the Sea." A race it was; not for the sea, however, but to find a gap between the sea and the Aisne position before it was exploited by the other side. Both sides could economise force in the burgeoning entrenchments to send formations northward. The largest was the new French Tenth Army, which from September 25 onwards began to deploy beyond the River Somme on the great stretch of open chalk downland

Opposite top: The beginnings of trench warfare. An artist's impression of French infantry attacking earthworks during the fighting on the Western Front, September 1914. Both sides improvised field defences at the eastern end of the line from an early stage. After mid-September, the Western Front was formally entrenched by the Germans all the way from the River Aisne to the Swiss frontier.

Opposite bottom: Sailors of the German 1st Naval Division in action at Lombarteyde in Belgium, September 11, 1914. The division was formed from the sailors surplus to the need of the High Seas Fleet and from the navy's pre-war landing parties, who wore military uniform. They were known respectively as Marine Fusiliers and Marine Infantry. There were eventually three naval divisions which were usually deployed on the Belgian coast, where this scene, an episode in the German pursuit of the Belgian army from Antwerp to the River Yser, is set.

Right: A rearguard of Belgian regular infantry, distinguishable by their round caps, defending a railway bridge at Termonde, after blowing the central span, during the retreat from Antwerp to Nieuport, September 18, 1914. The tiny Belgian army, personally commanded by King Albert, had conducted a heroic defence, first on the frontier with Germany, then in the forest of Antwerp, to which it had retreated after Liège and Namur had been lost. Following a German attack in overwhelming strength on the perimeter of Antwerp, King Albert ordered the fortress to be abandoned and led the survivors of his army, only 60,000 strong, in a fighting retreat along the coast to the estuary of the Yser River where, on October 27, he ordered the floodgates to be opened. The resulting inundations formed an impermeable barrier to further German advance throughout the war.

that sweeps northward above the steeper countryside of the Aisne. Even as it began to deploy, however, an equivalent German mass was marching forward to oppose it. Falkenhayn's plan was to use this Sixth Army to mount an offensive westward towards the Channel. The outcome Falkenhayn intended was a new drive through northern France, leaving the Germans in possession of all the territory above the Somme and thus positioned to march down towards Paris from lines that outflanked the French entrenched zone between the Aisne and Switzerland.

Part of the Falkenhayn plan succeeded. At Antwerp, General von Beseler had by September 27 devised an effective scheme to crack the Belgian entrenched camp's three lines of defences. With the siege train of super-heavy guns that had reduced Liège and Namur, he began by bombarding the outermost ring and then launched his infantry through the breach gained on October 3. A British inter-

On a fine autumn day, October 5, 1914, French dragoons pass a party of British soldiers of the 1st Cameronians. The Battle of the Aisne is over and the British and French are heading northward, attempting to turn the right flank of the German army while the Germans try similarly to outflank them. This stage of the campaign in the west became known, misleadingly, as "the Race to the Sea." Although the opponents' outer flanks did eventually come to rest on the sea, at Nieuport in Belgium, each was still hoping in October to win a victory in open country. The Cameronians, part of the 19th Brigade, have been marching by night and are about to settle down to sleep, out of view of German reconnaissance aircraft.

vention temporarily stayed the crisis. On October 4 an advance guard of the Royal Naval Division, which had landed at Dunkirk on September 19, arrived in Antwerp by train. In its wake appeared the First Lord of the Admiralty, Winston Churchill, thirsting for action and glory. The Royal Marines and sailors temporarily halted the German advance. On the night of October 5, however, Beseler's men managed to penetrate the second ring of forts at an unguarded point. The German artillery quickly began to break up their antiquated masonry, forcing the Royal Naval Division and what remained of the Belgian field army to evacuate towards the westernmost corner of Belgium on the River Yser. On October 10 General Deguise, the heroic Belgian commander of Antwerp, delivered up his sword to a German colonel.

Two other elements of Falkenhayn's plan foundered. Between October 1 and 6 the offensive of the new Sixth Army was checked and defeated by the French Tenth Army; it was then and there that Foch, acting as Joffre's deputy, issued the celebrated order, "No retirement. Every man to the battle." Finally, the great sweep of the eight German cavalry divisions was rapidly blunted by the appearance, west of Lille, of the French XXI Corps and its own supporting cavalry.

THE FIRST BATTLE OF YPRES

Thus, by the end of the second week of October, the gap in the Western Front through which a decisive thrust might be launched by one side or the other had been reduced to a narrow corridor in Belgian Flanders. It was here, between October 8 and 19, that the five corps now comprising the British Expeditionary

Zouaves with a Hotchkiss machine gun in the Yser position near Nieuport, October 1914. Zouaves, though originally North African regiments that wore "Turkish" caps and baggy trousers, were by 1914 recruited from native Frenchmen. The line along the estuary of the Yser ran through flat, featureless country, so waterlogged that trenches could not be dug. Instead breastworks of sandbags were built up. Though they offered protection against rifle and machine-gun fire, they were vulnerable to shelling and needed constant repair. Fortunately for the defenders on both sides, the Yser sector was so wet that neither high command judged it worthwhile to mount large-scale offensives across the estuary, which became one of the most static stretches of the Western Front.

A British cavalry regiment passing through the Grand Place at Ypres, October 13, 1914, three days before the beginning of the First Battle of Ypres. The buildings, including (left) the Cloth Hall, are intact. By the end of the battle in mid-November, Ypres would lie in ruins. After 1918 it was completely rebuilt as it had been before the fighting. This scene would be instantly recognisable today to the tens of thousands of British tourists who visit Ypres, which has become the centre of British pilgrimage to the Western Front, each year. The soldiers carry full cavalry equipment. During the coming battle they would abandon their horses and go into the line as infantrymen, part of the trickle of reinforcements which just succeeded in blocking the German offensive and retaining Ypres, the last sizable unoccupied town in Belgium, for the Allies.

Force arrived by train and road To the B.E.F.s north the remnants of the Belgian army had made their way along the coast to Nieuport, the town at the mouth of the Yser River. On the Yser, a narrow but embanked river that forms a major military obstacle in the waterlogged coastal zone, the Belgians quickly erected barricades and laid plans to inundate the surrounding countryside if the river line were breached. The resulting inundation created an impassable zone two miles wide between Nieuport and Dixmude.

South of Dixmude the line of the Yser and the Ypres canal was held by the French as far as Langemarck, on the outskirts of Ypres. From Langemarck south-

Belgian soldiers defending the west bank of the River Yser, north of Ypres, October 1914. The sea lies to the left, just out of view. This was the northernmost point of the Western Front and proved an impassable barrier to the Germans. After October 27 the defences were strengthened by the Belgians' decision to let in the sea through the flood controls, creating an inundated zone ten miles long, reaching almost to Ypres.

The Cloth Hall at Ypres after the First Battle. The largest and most magnificent example of high medieval secular architecture in Europe, the Cloth Hall was shelled constantly throughout the war, eventually being reduced to a pile of shattered masonry. The tower, however, was never quite obliterated, a deformed shoulder remaining even to the end. It was completely rebuilt after 1918 and now houses a museum commemorating the three battles of Ypres, in 1914, 1915 and 1917.

ward the arriving British had pegged out an advanced line that ran in a circle around Ypres towards the low ridge of higher ground at Passchendaele and then southward again across the River Lys to the La Bassée canal. The length of their line was thirty-five miles, to hold which Sir John French had available six infantry divisions, with one in reserve, and three cavalry divisions. The only reinforcements on which he could count were another infantry division, some additional regular cavalry and volunteer horsed yeomanry and the advance guard of four infantry and two cavalry divisions of the Indian army. These, composed of British and Indian units in a ratio of one to three, were scarcely suitable for warfare in

a European winter climate. Weak in artillery and without experience of high-intensity operations, they did not promise any enhancement of the B.E.F.'s offensive capacity.

Yet, at the outset of what would swell into the First Battle of Ypres—in which Indian units would fight gallantly and effectively both in defence and attack—Field Marshal French still preserved hopes of mounting an attack that would carry the Allies to Brussels. His hope was shared by Foch, who now commanded the northern wing of the French armies. Both deluded themselves. Falkenhayn not only disposed of the relocated Sixth Army and of Beseler's III Reserve Corps, but of an entirely new collection of war-raised formations, eight divisions strong.

These belonged to a group of seven Reserve Corps raised from volunteers who had not previously undergone military training. Of those the best were students exempted while they pursued their studies. The recruits received two months' training and then left for the front. Of these thirteen new divisions, two went to

Russia, one to the front in Lorraine, ten to Flanders. It was those which, in the third week of October, would open the assault on the B.E.F. between Langemarck and Ypres.

The battle that ensued raged almost continuously from early October until late November, when both sides accepted the onset of winter and their own exhaustion. Geographically it divided into four: a renewed offensive by Beseler's corps against the Belgians, nullified by the inundations; an attempt by the French under Foch to drive north of Ypres towards Ghent; the Battle of Ypres itself, between the B.E.F. and the German volunteers; and, to the south, a defensive battle conducted by the right wing of the B.E.F. against the regular divisions of the German Sixth Army. Fighting on the three latter sectors merged effectively into one battle. British survivors were content to say they had been at "First Ypres."

Arriving in stages from the Aisne, the B.E.F. began by pressing forward east of Ypres towards the ridges that swell some five miles beyond. The names of these low heights—Passchendaele, Broodseinde, Gheluvelt, Messines—were to recur throughout the four coming years of war. As the British arrived, so did fresh Ger-

Survivors of the First Battle of Ypres in the line at Houplines on November 18, 1914, a week after the battle's official end. The photograph is from the unique archive of the 1st Cameronians, who had fought throughout the campaign in the west since the beginning of August. The officer (left) wears the regimental Glengarry, the soldiers their woolen cap-comforters. In the background is the defensive breastwork, built up above the waterlogged soil to form a front line. The battle exhausted both sides and also their stocks of artillery ammunition. An artificial period of quiet resulted, allowing this party to cook without risk of smoke from their fire attracting shelling.

man corps. Under pressure, the British fell back. Their IV Corps was driven close to the ancient ramparts of Ypres. The arrival of I Corps, commanded by General Douglas Haig, on October 20 secured Ypres itself, but that exhausted the army's strength. It was on October 20 that a general German offensive began against the whole front, twenty-four divisions against nineteen, though the latter total included the six terribly weakened Belgian. The line was held by the superiority of the British in rapid rifle fire. By the end of October the wider German offensive had failed, at enormous cost. At their cemetery at Langemarck today the bodies of 25,000 student soldiers lie in a mass grave. Dominating the hecatomb are sculptures by Käthe Kollwitz, herself a bereaved parent of 1914, of a mother and father mourning their lost son. They represent tens of thousands of bourgeois Germans whom this phase of the battle disabused of the belief that the war would be short or cheap or glorious, and introduced to the reality of attrition.

Fighting around Ypres would flicker on until November 22, the date chosen by the official historians to denote First Ypres's termination. The British survivors, whose unwounded numbers were less than half of the 160,000 which the B.E.F. had sent to France, were by then stolidly digging and embanking to solidify the

The captured colours of a German infantry regiment is paraded before troops of the French XV Corps at Montzeville, October 1914, after the Battle of the Marne. The XV Corps (29th and 30th Divisions) formed part of de Castelnau's Second Army during the battle. The British had not taken their regimental colours into action since the nineteenth century but some French and German units did so as late as 1915. Inevitably, some fell into the hands of the enemy, a dire disgrace to the regiments which lost theirs, far outweighing the intended morale value of displaying the symbol of regimental identity to hard-pressed soldiers.

line. The French, too, were digging in to secure the territory for which they had fought both north and south of the city. At best the line ran a little more than five miles to the eastward; elsewhere it stood much closer. Everywhere the Germans held the high ground, dominating the shallow crescent of trenches the British would call "the Salient." Its winning had cost uncountable lives. The Germans had lost even more heavily. At least 41,000 of the German volunteers, the Innocents of Ypres, had fallen outside its walls.

They represented but a fraction of all the dead of the Battles of the Frontiers, the Great Retreat, the Marne, the Aisne, the "Race to the Sea" and First Ypres itself. The French army, with a mobilised strength of two million, had suffered by far the worst. Its losses in September exceeded 200,000, in October 80,000

French prisoners under German cavalry escort, near St. Mihiel, December 8, 1914.

and in November 70,000; the August losses, never officially revealed, may have exceeded 160,000. Fatalities reached the extraordinary total of 306,000; 45,000 of those under twenty had died, 92,000 of those between twenty and twenty-four, 70,000 of those between twenty-five and twenty-nine. Among those in their thirties, the death toll exceeded 80,000. All deaths had fallen on a male population of twenty million. Germany had lost 241,000, including 99,000 in the twenty–twenty-four age group, out of a male population of thirty-two million. Belgium, out of 1,800,000 men of military age, had suffered 30,000 dead. The total was the

The Christmas Truce, 1914. Early on the morning of Christmas Day, the Germans in the line opposite the British, between Ypres and Messines, began to sing Christmas carols and display Christmas trees on their parapet. Germans then came forward into no-man's-land and proposed a break in the fighting. Parties from both sides began to mingle, to exchange tobacco and drinks, to sing together and, in one place, to organise a football match. They also agreed to allow burial of the dead in no-man's-land. The truce persisted the following day and in places for some days afterwards but the high command on both sides disapproved and took measures to stop the fraternisation. There was none on the French front. In this photograph Private Turner, of the London Rifle Brigade, a recently arrived Territorial regiment, stands behind two German officers, one of whom wears the ribbon of the Iron Cross.

same as that for British deaths, with the difference that the British dead had almost all belonged to the regular army. It was the arrival of the Territorial Force in strength in 1915 that alone allowed the British army to sustain its share of the war effort in France and to participate in the offensives mounted by Joffre in the Artois and Champagne sectors of the Western Front.

The prospect of any offensive, either by the Allies or the Germans, looked far away as winter fell in France at the end of 1914. A continuous line of trenches, 475 miles long, ran from the North Sea to the mountain frontier of neutral Switzerland. Behind it the opposing combatants crouched in confrontation across a narrow and empty zone of no-man's-land. The room for manoeuvre each had sought in order to deliver a decisive attack at the enemy's vulnerable flank had disappeared. The hope of success in frontal attack had temporarily disappeared also. The experience of the French in Alsace and Lorraine in August, of the British in the Aisne in September, of the Germans in Flanders in October and November had persuaded even the most bellicose commanders that offensives unsupported by preponderant artillery would not overcome. A sort of peace prevailed.

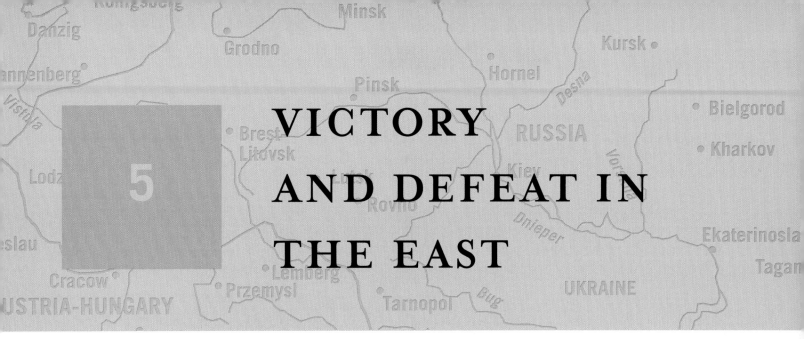

VICTORY AND DEFEAT IN THE EAST

5

"In military operations, time is everything," wrote Wellington. Time had also oppressed Schlieffen: time to mobilise, time to concentrate, time to march to the crucial objective. It was his calculations of timing that had persuaded him, and those who inherited his plans, to wager almost all the force Germany commanded in the west and to let the east wait upon victory over France. Russia's known weaknesses had convinced Schlieffen and Moltke, his successor, that forty days would elapse before the Tsar's armies could appear in strength on Germany's eastern border.

It seemed that space might also be made to work for Germany on its side of the frontier. The division of territories between the three empires of Germany, Austria and Russia might superficially be regarded to favour the latter in war, for Russian Poland, centred on Warsaw, thrust forward in a great salient between the Carpathian mountains in Austria to the south and East Prussia to the north. The Polish salient, however, might also be regarded as a region of operational exposure since its flanks were overlapped on either side by difficult terrain. The Carpathians form a chain of sally-ports against invaders from the north-east, while East Prussia confronts any advancing army with a jumble of lakes and forest. The Masurian lakeland was a region of small communities largely isolated from the outside world. Beyond Masuria, moreover, lay a chain of German fortresses protecting the populated regions of East Prussia, at Thorn, Graudenz and Marienburg on the River Vistula, matching the Austrian Carpathian fortresses at Cracow, Przemysl and Lemberg (Lvov). The Russian high command had long recognised the ambiguous strategic character of the Polish salient and it had accordingly starved the region of railway and road building that might aid an enemy counteroffensive. It had also cautiously designed two westward strategies, Plan G, which held a strong force in reserve, as well as Plan A, which thrust it forward.

Under French pressure the Russian high command in 1914 had committed itself to Plan A. Two-fifths of the peacetime army was in any case stationed around Warsaw, from which its strategic deployment against East Prussia and the Carpathians might easily be achieved. Common sense and intelligence alike dictated that

Advance of the 2nd Prussian Cavalry Division through Pabolwiamy.

the bulk of Russia's western forces would have to go towards the Carpathians, for Austria-Hungary, unlike Germany, could count on waging a one-front war—the Serbian army appearing at the outset to be of no account—and so deploy its main strength there. Nevertheless, sufficient force could be found, by Russian staff calculations, to mount an offensive on the East Prussian frontier that would, while leaving the Austrians with their hands full, assure a crisis for Berlin in its backyard.

Germany had indeed little left over from the great western *Aufsmarsch* with which to hold the Prussian heartland. Its war plan allotted only one of its eight armies to the Eastern Front, the Eighth Army, commanded by General Max von Prittwitz, a Prussian of Prussians, and consisting of the I, XVII and XX Corps, the

Opposite top: The staff of the German Ninth Army outside the Magistrature in the Russian Polish town of Lenschitza, after the Battle of Tannenberg. In the center, with thumb locked in pocket, is the commander. General, later Field Marshal, August von Mackensen (1849–1945) had led the Eighth Army until succeeded by Hindenburg. He was an extremely successful Eastern Front commander, responsible for the breakthrough at Gorlice-Tarnow in May 1915. He was said to be of Scottish descent, a story he had encouraged before the outbreak of war. He was in fact a Prussian of Prussians who remained a fervent monarchist even during the Nazi years.

I Reserve Corps, and the 1st Cavalry Division. To it was added on mobilisation a collection of reserve formations, raised from younger and older reservists, which added to it perhaps the strength of a whole corps. The army's soldiers, many of them locals, could be counted upon to fight with tenacity against any invasion of their homeland.

They were, nevertheless, outnumbered by the force the Russian high command had earmarked to mount the East Prussian operations, the First and Second Armies of the North-Western Front. Together these opposed nine corps to Prittwitz's four and seven cavalry divisions to his one. Rennenkampf, commanding First Army, and Samsonov, commanding Second, were moreover both veterans of the Russo-Japanese War while Prittwitz had no experience of war at all.

A German infantry regiment on the march in East Prussia, August 1914, with its horse-drawn regimental transport. The scene—scrubby pine trees, clouds of dust raised by the soldiers' boots from the light, sandy soil—is typical of the setting of the campaign. Both Germans and Russians marched enormous distances as they manoeuvred against each other in the days before and during the Battle of Tannenberg. Later, as the campaign moved into Poland, the Germans would abandon their heavy iron-tyred carts for the light, flexible *panje* wagons.

General Paul von Rennenkampf (1853–1908), commander of the Russian First Army at Tannenberg. His failure to co-operate with the commander of Second Army, Samsonov, contributed greatly to the Russian defeat. His German ancestry led to accusations against him of treachery, which were unfounded.

Their formations were very big, divisions having sixteen instead of twelve battalions. Though they were weaker in artillery it is untrue that they were much less well provided with shells; all armies had grossly underestimated the expenditure that modern battle would demand and, at an allowance of 700 shells per gun, the Russians were not much worse off than the French fighting on the Marne.

The enormous preponderance of Russian strength—ninety-eight mobilised infantry divisions, thirty-seven cavalry divisions—should, moreover, have ensured the *Stavka,* the Russian high command, an overwhelming majority over the German Eighth Army, had Rennenkampf and Samsonov been able to move together and keep together. The wings of their armies should have easily completed a pincer movement that surrounded Eighth Army and secured either its destruction or its precipitate flight, thus opening West Prussia and Silesia to a deeper Russian invasion.

Geography was to disrupt the smooth onset of the Russian offensive. Less excusably, timidity and incompetence were to disjoint it. The Russians made the mistake of exposing themselves to defeat in detail: that is, of allowing a weaker enemy to concentrate at first against one part of the army, then against the other, and so beat both. The way in which geography worked to favour the Germans' detailed achievement is the more easily explained. Though eastern East Prussia does indeed offer a level path of advance to an invader, the chain of lakes that feed the River Angerapp also poses a significant barrier, tending to drive them apart. Strategically, the easier option was to pass north and south of the Angerapp position rather than to force it frontally, and that was what the commander of the North-Western Front, General Y. Zhilinsky, decided to direct Rennenkampf and Samsonov to do.

Unfortunately, he allowed Rennenkampf to strengthen his flank on the Baltic coast, which was not at risk, and Samsonov to detach troops to protect his connections with Warsaw, equally not threatened. The result of these dispositions was a diversion of effort which left both armies considerably weakened to undertake the main task. Having commenced the deployment with a superiority of nineteen divisions against nine, Rennenkampf and Samsonov actually marched to the attack with only sixteen between them.

Worse, the two armies arrived on their start lines five days apart in time. First Army crossed the East Prussian frontier on August 15, but Second not until August 20. As the two were separated in space by fifty miles of lakeland, neither would be able to come rapidly to the other's assistance if it ran into trouble.

The superiority of German over Russian intelligence-gathering clinched the issue. Armed with the knowledge that Rennenkampf led Samsonov by several days, Prittwitz could decide to deploy the bulk of Eighth Army north of the Masurian lakes without undue anxiety. When the Russians opened their offensive with a probing attack at Stallupönen on August 17, they were driven back. When their main body arrived in strength, at Gumbinnen three days later, the German I Corps was actually advancing to attack them under cover of darkness. The commander, von François, was as aggressive as he looked, and his troops took their spirit from him. They belonged to some of the most famous of Prussian regiments and fell fiercely on the Russians they found opposite. Unfortunately, the enemy had prepared overnight trenches and fortified farm buildings and houses. The harder the Germans pressed forward, the higher rose their casualties. The Russian artillery was well positioned and added to the carnage. By mid-afternoon, I Corps had come to a halt. Its neighbouring corps, XVII, commanded by the famous Life Guard Hussar von Mackensen, was meanwhile attacking north-eastward into the Russians' flank. It did so without reconnaissance which would have revealed that the Russians were entrenched. From their positions they poured a devastating fire into the advancing German infantry who broke and ran to the rear. By late afternoon the situation was threatening to turn from a tactical reverse to a strategic catastrophe. To the right the I Reserve, under von Bülow, counter-attacked to protect Mackensen's flank against a Russian advance. At Eighth Army headquarters, however, even the news of that success could not stay the onset of panic. There Prittwitz was yielding to the belief that East Prussia must be abandoned and the whole of his army retreat beyond the Vistula.

At O.H.L., Moltke was appalled by the reports of Eighth Army's sudden predicament, which undermined the whole substance of belief in the possibility of postponing crisis in the east while victory was gained in the west. Only twenty of the vital forty days had elapsed, and Schlieffen's timetable threatened to crumble before O.H.L.'s eyes. Moltke decided first that a director of operations of the first quality must be

Russian soldiers and their officer in a trench, East Prussia, August 1914. They are wearing the *ghymnasterka*, the practical loose blouse adopted as service dress after the Russo-Japanese War, and are carrying their possessions in a sack slung over the shoulders, worn in action when it was impractical to be encumbered with the blanket roll in which they normally packed their kit. Some of the blanket rolls have been discarded on the parapet, for collection after the fighting. It was also a Russian practise to keep bayonets fixed, whether needed or not, though it detracted from marksmanship. The Russian army of 1914 laid emphasis on shock action rather than fire superiority.

Above: General Alexander Samsonov (1859–1914), commander of the Russian Second Army at the Battle of Tannenberg. A cavalryman, and former Governor of Turkestan in Russian Central Asia, Samsonov was pessimistic of his army's chances. He also got on badly with his fellow commander, Rennenkampf. After the battle he fell into a deep depression, blaming himself for the defeat and seeking to escape from the supervision of his staff. In a moment of their unwatchfulness, he rode off alone and committed suicide on the night of August 29–30.

Right: General Hermann von François (right) in conversation with General Kluiev, commander of the Russian XIII Corps, taken prisoner at Tannenberg. François (1856–1933) was, like many other Prussian officers, of Huguenot descent. Though a capable officer, he proved insubordinate in command of a corps in 1914, wishing to attack the oncoming Russians when his orders were to stand on the defensive. He briefly commanded the Eighth Army but was relieved after his poor performance in the Battle of the Masurian Lakes in October.

sent instantly to the east to take charge. He chose Ludendorff, who had twice so brilliantly resolved crises in Belgium. He next determined to dispose of Prittwitz altogether. In his place he promoted Paul von Hindenburg, a retired officer noted for his steadiness of character if not brilliance of mind. As a lieutenant in the 3rd Foot Guards, Hindenburg had fought in the Franco-Prussian war. He had left the army in 1911, aged sixty-four, but applied for reappointment at the war's outbreak. He and Ludendorff, unalike as they were, were to unite from the start in what Hindenburg himself called "a happy marriage." Their qualities, natural authority in Hindenburg, ruthless intellect in Ludendorff, complemented each other's perfectly and were to make them one of the most effective military partnerships in history.

It was, nevertheless, to Ludendorff that Hindenburg looked for an initiative when the two arrived at Eighth Army on August 23. On August 24, the two generals went forward to confer with Scholtz, commanding XX Corps opposite Samsonov's Second Army, which was advancing to contact. Scholtz was nervous. He wanted to withdraw. Ludendorff was adamant that he must hold his ground. Assistance would reach him, but he must stand and fight.

The help on its way had been started forward by the superseded Prittwitz, who had grasped that François had halted Rennenkampf and so freed forces to be used elsewhere. Old war games, some played by Schlieffen himself, had taught Prittwitz's generation of officers that the correct strategy for defending the East Prussian frontier was to defeat one Russian army on one side of the lakes, then to send forces to the other side and repeat the process. With remarkable moral courage he decided that Rennenkampf could be counted as beaten and, before

Hindenburg's arrival, had already initiated the movement of I and XVII Corps to meet Samsonov on the southern front. Ludendorff did not, therefore, have to devise a plan but merely to endorse one already in execution.

On the Russian side, Rennenkampf correctly sensed that the German forces in front of him were thinning out but inferred that they were withdrawing to the Königsberg fortress on the Baltic coast. That the Germans had left only a screen of cavalry to hold their former positions he did not guess. He believed he was faced with the burden of a deliberate siege of Königsberg. He formed the conclusion that the task lay with Samsonov, now breasting up to contact with the Germans south of the lakes, who must be cut off by him from escape across the lower Vistula. To ensure the necessary encircling movement, he ordered his left wing even further away from Rennenkampf, who was meanwhile probing forward slowly with cavalry and transmitting orders for the planned siege of Königsberg by radio.

Lack of Russian radio security has become part of the legend of the Tannenberg campaign. In its most sensational form, the story has Rennenkampf's and Samsonov's headquarters signalling detailed reports of the two armies' intentions to each other in plain language, to be acted upon with deadly effect by their German opposite numbers. The reality is less simple and more mundane. There was

The headquarters staff of the German army on the Eastern Front (*OberOst*) awaits a visit by the Kaiser. Hindenburg stands in center foreground, Ludendorff to his left. Field Marshal Paul von Hindenburg (1847–1934) was recalled from retirement to replace Prittwitz in East Prussia on August 22, 1914. General Erich Ludendorff (1865–1937) became his chief of staff. Under their command, Eighth Army succeeded in inflicting a crushing defeat on the Russian First and Second Armies at Tannenberg, later repeated at the Masurian Lakes. They then diverted the advance into Russian Poland. Hindenburg, essentially a figurehead, owed the victory to the operational ability of Ludendorff, though he in turn owed it to the brilliance of his chief staff officer, Max Hoffmann. The photograph is a study of German military finery, with hussar, uhlan, and jäger officers in field-grey versions of their ceremonial uniforms surrounding the grandees.

a good deal of Russian signalling *en clair*, but the Germans were guilty also. The reason, on the Russian side, was difficulty in distribution of code books, on the German side lack of time. German operators often transmitted uncoded messages on the calculation that they would be missed by listeners, just as they knew their own listeners missed so many Russian messages.

On the morning of August 25, however, Hindenburg had a stroke of luck. He was passed the transcript of a complete Russian First Army order for an advance to Königsberg, which revealed that it would halt well short of the city on August 26. Furnished with this assurance, he met von François, whose corps was just beginning to arrive on Samsonov's flank, in confident mood. Distance was working for him and so now too was time.

Then François interrupted the smooth unrolling of a plan that should have brought his corps successively into action against Samsonov's flanks. Claiming that he was awaiting the arrival of his artillery, he was slow off the mark to attack on August 25, and the next day. Ludendorff arrived to energise the offensive, but François's hesitation had meanwhile had a desirable if unintended result. Unopposed to his front, Samsonov had thrust his centre forward, thus exposing lengthening flanks both to François and to Mackensen and Scholtz, who were marching their corps down from the north. On August 27 François pushed his men on. Samsonov, disregarding the danger to his rear, pressed on also. On August 28 his leading troops broke through almost to open country, with the Vistula beyond. Ludendorff ordered François to detach a division to oppose them. François drove every battalion he had eastward at best speed. With the weight of Samsonov's army moving westward by different routes, there was little to check them. On the morning of August 29, François's leading infantry reached Willenberg, just inside East Prussia from Russian territory, and met German troops coming the other way. They belonged to Mackensen's XVII Corps, who had been attacking southward since the previous day. Contact between the claws of the two pincers announced that Samsonov was surrounded.

"Cauldron" battles were to be a repeated feature of the fighting in the Second World War, particularly in the east. Victories of encirclement were almost never to be achieved in the First. That was one reason which made Tannenberg—as Hindenburg decided to call the battle—so singular. The Germans counted 92,000 Russian prisoners, besides 50,000 enemy killed and wounded. Tannenberg became for the Germans their outstanding victory of the First World War. Not only had it saved the Prussian heartland from occupation by the enemy but it had also

An artist's impression of the Battle of Tannenberg, August 26–31, 1914. A line of Russian riflemen in a hastily dug field entrenchment are being counter-attacked by troops of the German Eighth Army. Although the Russians invading East Prussia greatly outnumbered the German defenders, lack of co-ordination between the commanders of the First and Second Armies, Rennenkampf and Samsonov, allowed Hindenburg to manoeuvre between them as they advanced and defeat each in turn. The victory made him a German national hero and the German people chose to regard Tannenberg as the epic victory of the war. Hindenburg was buried in 1934 at the Tannenberg Memorial. It was destroyed on Hitler's orders in 1945 and Hindenburg's body was subsequently reburied at the ancestral home of the Hohenzollern dynasty in southern Germany. The colours of the Tannenberg regiments were preserved at the post-war German cadet school at Hamburg.

Cossacks in East Prussia, 1914. The Imperial Russian army maintained large numbers of cavalrymen in peacetime and mobilised twenty-four divisions of cavalry in 1914. Six were Cossack. There were other Cossack units in the Imperial Guard and a Circassian Cavalry Division, from the Caucasus, which wore Cossack dress. The Cossacks were originally escaped serfs who made their way to the steppe frontier with Muslim Central Asia, where they lived a free life but made war on the nomadic horse people who preyed on the settled peasants of Russia proper. In time they came to form an irregular cavalry arm bound to the Tsar by personal loyalty. They were recruited not individually but by tribe, each tribe having to provide and maintain a fixed numbers of soldiers in time of war. In 1914 about 100,000 Cossacks were mobilised. Though difficult to discipline, they excelled as scouts and skirmishers.

Russian prisoners taken by the German Eighth Army at the Battle of Augustov, October 1–9, the last episode of the Tannenberg campaign of 1914. Fighting persisted in the forest of Augustov, the last primeval wilderness in Europe, until February 1915, when Bulgakov's XX Corps was encircled and forced to surrender. Over 12,000 Russian prisoners passed into German hands. A principal casualty of the battle was the surviving stock of auroch, Europe's last wild bison. Despite their vast number, the Russians taken prisoner by the Germans did not suffer death by privation as those captured by the *Wehrmacht* in the Second World War would do. The majority survived to return home after the Revolution.

Above: An artist's impression of German troops reoccupying an East Prussian village during the Tannenberg campaign, 1914. The villagers welcome the advancing German soldiers as liberators from Russian invasion. Most of the German troops engaged in East Prussia in August 1914 were locally recruited. They included units of the I, XVII and XX Corps, all belonging to the active army but based in peacetime in East Prussia, the 1st Cavalry Division, also of the active army, and a large number of second- and third-line troops, the I Reserve Corps and East Prussian *Landwehr* and even *Landsturm* (overage fourth-line) units. Whatever their age and state of training, these East Prussian soldiers, defending what was both their own homeland and that of the German monarchy, fought with battle-winning ferocity to repel the Russians.

Left: The ruins of Soldev, East Prussia, after the Battle of Tannenberg.

averted the danger of a deeper advance into industrial Silesia and towards Berlin. Tannenberg was a deliverance, and celebrated as such. After the war the colours of the regiments that fought there were displayed in a monumental Tannenberg memorial, modelled on Stonehenge, in which the body of Hindenburg was interred after his death as President.

Tannenberg had a military importance greater than its symbolic significance. It reversed the timetable of Germany's war plan. Before the triumph, victory was expected in the west, while the front in the east was to be held as best it might be. After Tannenberg, disaster in the east no longer threatened, while victory in the west continued to elude week after week. Tannenberg temporarily devastated the Russians. Yet, for all the incompetence of their commanders and inadequacy of their means to fight, the Russians retained resilience. They were to show it immediately in 1914. Despite Samsonov's collapse, Rennenkampf refused in the aftermath of Tannenberg to accept defeat. When Hindenburg turned against him the whole weight of Eighth Army, he handled his troops with dexterity. It was they who were now outnumbered. First Army, Hindenburg's target, still only counted nine divisions, against the Germans' eighteen, but in what came to be called the Battle of the Masurian Lakes, launched on September 7, it evaded all Hindenburg's efforts to organise an encirclement. François, directing the first stage, succeeded in cutting off some units in the heart of the lakeland. Thereafter Rennenkampf conducted a fighting retreat, in and above the lakes, switching units from one flank to another as need arose. On September 13 he crossed back into Russian territory, having extricated his whole army, drawing the Germans behind him. By September 25 delaying actions had allowed him the time and room to organise for a counter-attack and on that day he unleashed it, driving the Germans from their positions and in places returning to the lines reached on the Angerapp during the August invasion.

GALICIA AND SERBIA

The high point of the Masurian Lakes counter-offensive, however, was a tactical rather than a strategic success, for it engaged only a fraction of Russia's forces. The majority were deployed across the southern face of the Polish salient, facing the Austrians, whose main line of resistance ran along the crests of the Carpathians, through which the strategic passes led down. This was an enormous front, of three hundred miles, and defended by large fortifications, of which those at Lemberg (Lvov) and Przemysl had recently been modernised. The Russian war plan required the concentration on this sector of four armies, Third, Fourth, Fifth and Eighth, forming the South-Western Front. They were to attack as soon as deployed. The Austrians, too, intended to attack as soon as mobilisation was completed. Because of confusion over choice between the fronts in Galicia and Serbia, however, the Austrians were slower to concentrate their force than they should have been, while the Russians were quicker. The result was that, by the end of August, the Russians had fifty-three infantry and eighteen cavalry divisions in place, while the Austrians had only thirty-seven infantry and ten cavalry divisions to oppose them. The Russian formations, moreover, were larger than

WOMEN AT WAR

During 1914–18, women, for the first time in the history of warfare, took a uniformed place in the ranks. In 1917 Britain raised a Women's Auxiliary Army Corps (WAAC) and a Women's Royal Naval Service (WRNS), to provide substitutes for men as cooks, signallers, clerks and transport drivers. Women had already begun to replace men enlisted for war service in Britain on a large scale, following the establishment of the Register of Women for War Service in March 1915. By August 1916, 750,000 British women held men's jobs, and 350,000 others held jobs created by the war economy. The creation of the Land Army attracted 240,000 women into agriculture by 1918.

In other countries, which lacked Britain's long tradition of female industrial employment, women tended to remain at home, even if, as in France, taking up more of men's work in the fields than before the war. As the war progressed, however, financial want, often caused by the death of a breadwinner, drove women into factory employment in large numbers, as also occurred in Germany. One of the inequities of the war was that a mother with children enjoyed quite generous state support as long as her husband was alive; his death in action terminated state benefits, leaving her dependent on the skimpiest of pensions. By November 1918 there were 630,000 war widows in France, more in Germany. Most were forced to seek employment, often of the most menial sort and at depressed wages, to support themselves and their families.

Women's contribution to the war effort in Britain lent impetus to the strong political emancipation movement and led to the grant of the parliamentary vote, to women over thirty, in January 1918. In the United States, all women became eligible to vote in 1920, partly as a result of their war work in 1917–18. Elsewhere the war did little to improve women's lot and much to worsen it, leaving not only several million widows but also millions more of the unmarried without the prospect of finding husbands. There were also nearly ten million bereaved mothers. The First World War was a woman's tragedy.

Above: A woman at a machine.

Left: Russian women working in a munitions factory in Germany.

Opposite top: Women trucking clay to a moulding house for silica brick making, Wales.

Opposite bottom: *For King and Country* (women in munitions factory), by E. F. Skinner (1888–1919).

Above: A woman making airplane propellers at the Frederick Tibbenham LTD airplane factory in Ipswich, England. Here, she fits sections to template.

Right: Women working in a British munitions factory.

the Austrian; and while Russia was under pressure from France to mount operations that would divert German forces from the Western Front, Austria was under even heavier pressure to act in relief of the outnumbered German Eighth Army in East Prussia.

Austria's principal emotional war aim, however, remained the punishment of Serbia, which had precipitated the July crisis. Sense would have argued that Austria deployed its whole strength forward of the Carpathians to engage the Russians. Outrage demanded the defeat of the Belgrade government. Conrad von Hötzendorf, the Austrian Chief of Staff, had long had prepared a plan to deal with Serbia alone, a situation known as "War Case B." During 1912–13, however, increasing consideration was given to the likelihood that a crisis with Serbia would precipitate a Russian war, "War Case R," demanding that the Balkan army be reduced to strengthen that in Galicia. The general staff tinkered with the deployment of three groups: the "A-Staffel" that would go to Galicia in the event of a Russian war, the "Balkan Group" that would attack Serbia, and the "B-Staffel" that would participate in either campaign, depending on the promptness of Russian mobilisation. The railway planning section prepared timetables accordingly.

In the event, the Austrians muddled. Conrad claimed as mobilisation began that Russia's military intentions were not clear and that it was safe to send B-Staffel to join the Balkan group, which it did. When it became clear that Russia intended to attack in Galicia, he decided, as he had to, that B-Staffel must go north; but as it was on its way south, he allowed it on August 1 to proceed after all and to take part in the attack on Serbia before re-entraining to the Galician front. It was given the mission of making a "demonstration," to draw Serbian forces away from the main axis of the Austrian invasion.

The idea of a demonstration revealed how little the Austrians understood the Serbs' military qualities. In Vienna they were thought of as backward semi-barbarians. Moreover, the Austrians, despite the known impassability of Serbia's terrain, high, forested mountains cut by deep river valleys, with few roads and almost no railways, expected a

Opposite: A German column climbing a mountain road in Montenegro in pursuit of the retreating Serbian army, 1915. The Serbs had defended their country against the Austrians with astonishing success in 1914. In October 1915, however, a concerted effort by Austrians, Germans and Bulgarians forced the Serbs back from one position to another until, at the end of November, they abandoned the effort to resist and set out, in the depths of a harsh Balkan winter, to march over the mountains of Montenegro and Albania to the Adriatic. The aged King Peter marched with them, the Voivode (War Leader), Putnik, being carried in a sedan chair. Although about 200,000, including many civilians, set out, only 100,000 survived to reach the sea. They were evacuated to the Greek island of Corfu, re-equipped and sent to the Allied encampment at Salonika.

Below: Russian troops entering the town of Czernowitz, March 1915, during their Carpathian counter-offensive against Austria.

walkover. In fact the Serbs, if barbarian in the cruelty with which they waged war, were not militarily backward at all. Their system of conscription mobilised a higher proportion of the male population than in any other European country and their soldiers were naturally warlike as well as fiercely patriotic. They were also frugal and hardy. Their arms were varied; but every man had a weapon and the first-line units retained most of the modern weapons acquired during the Balkan Wars, including a hundred batteries of artillery and four machine guns per infantry regiment. With a third-line reserve of men aged forty to forty-five and "capable soldiers of sixty and seventy," Serbia could put 400,000 men into the field, almost as many as those in the Sixth, Fifth and Second Armies of Austria's B-Staffel.

The Austrians nevertheless began with an advantage, for the Serbian commander, Radomir Putnik, expected an attack from the north across the Danube towards Belgrade. Instead, Conrad's plan was for an attack from the west into the salient enclosed by the Rivers Drina and Sava. There was sense in it, for the salient is one of the few areas of level terrain in the whole of the country, and at first the advance, began on August 12, went well. Had Putnik hurried his troops forward, they might have been encircled and trapped. The canny veteran declined the

risk. Instead he organised his main line of resistance along the River Vardar and the high ground beyond. The defenders did not arrive until the night of August 14, but, once in place, brought devastating fire to bear on the attackers. Potiorek, the Austrian commander, signalled Conrad to request the intervention of Sec-

An Italian artist's impression of the fighting on the River Sava between Austrians and Serbs, August 1914. The Austrian intention was to trap the Serbs between the Sava and the Danube but Putnik, the Serb Commander-in-Chief, turned the tables and forced the Austrians back across the Sava. By August 24 the Austrians had withdrawn from Serbian territory altogether. The Serbs then unwisely followed up their advantage and three months of savage fighting followed, during which Belgrade, the Serbian capital, was temporarily lost. Not until December was the situation stabilised. The Serbs then enjoyed nine months of respite until their enemies' resumption of the offensive in October 1915.

ond Army. Conrad refused, despite Potiorek's report of a "frightful heat" in the fighting. He appealed again on August 16 and a third time on August 17, when the request was granted, on condition that the "swing" formation's departure for Galicia was not delayed. The battle on the Drina and Sava now involved the Austrian Fifth and Sixth Armies, part of the Second and the whole of the Serbian, which, driven back and forward by the weight of Austrian artillery fire, always

Street fighting in Belgrade, October 9, 1915. The Germans and Austrians, under the command of the formidable von Mackensen, bridged the Danube and Sava Rivers on October 7 and, outnumbering the Serbs with seventeen divisions, attacked to the east. The Serbs, hardened by almost continuous fighting since the First Balkan War of 1912, resisted with their customary tenacity but were too few to repel their enemies. They eluded encirclement nevertheless and conducted a successful fighting retreat out of the country.

returned to the attack. On August 19 the commander of the Austrian Fifth Army had withdrawn it across the Sava. The Second Army made a final, ineffective intervention on August 20, before departing to join the A-Staffel in Galicia. The Sixth Army had never been properly engaged and joined the general withdrawal. By August 24 the Serbs had expelled the enemy from the whole of their territory.

That was not the end of the fighting. On September 6 the Serbs crossed into Austrian territory. It was an unwise manoeuvre and they lost nearly five thousand casualties when forced to withdraw. Later in the month, however, the Serbs found a weak spot on the Drina, crossed into Bosnia and raced towards Sarajevo. The Serbian occupation of eastern Bosnia lasted only forty days. On November 6,

Potiorek opened a general offensive and, by concentric attack, drove the Serbs back from one line to another in north-eastern Serbia as far as the line of the Morava, eighty miles from the Bosnian frontier. Twice Putnik ordered a general disengagement and retreat, through hills covered with three feet of snow. On December 2 Belgrade fell and King Peter released his soldiers from their oaths, to go home without dishonour if they chose. He announced that he intended to continue the fight and appeared in the front line, carrying a rifle. His example may have marked a turning point. Putnik, believing the Austrians over-extended, launched a new offensive on December 3 which broke the Austrian

line and in twelve days of fighting drove the enemy clear of Serbian territory. Over 40,000 out of the 200,000 who had campaigned against Serbia since November were lost. The Austrians and Germans would not resume their effort to conquer the kingdom until the autumn of 1915. Then the Serbian epic would take a grimmer turn.

THE BATTLES OF LEMBERG

The Serbian campaign, however, had never been more than a sideshow to Austria's great battle in Russian Poland. There, both the Austrians and Russians had pre-war plans to attack as soon as deployment was completed. Conrad's plan was to strengthen his left and attempt an encirclement in the great Polish plain south of Warsaw, while conducting an "active defence" on his right, where he could use the great fortresses of Lemberg and Przemysl as a buttress. The Russian plan was also for an encirclement in western Galicia but for rather more than active defence in the east; but there had been divided counsels on the Russian side. A sort of

Kalémegdan, the great fortress that dominates Belgrade, from its hilltop above the Danube. A mixture of Austrian and Turkish work, it stood to the Serbs as a symbol of hated Ottoman power. It was one of the targets of the Austrian gunboats, which on July 29, 1914, fired the initial shots of the First World War. Immensely strong, despite its antiquity, it was scarcely scratched then or during the subsequent fighting in the capital in 1914. In October 1915, however, the Germans and the Austrians deployed such a superiority of artillery that the Serbs were forced to abandon it. Today it houses the Serbian national military museum, telling the story of the Serbs' struggle for independence against Turks, Austrians and Germans.

compromise plan for a "double envelopment" was devised, but the Russians lacked the strength to impose equal pressure in both sectors. The opening phase was, in consequence, to be confused and indecisive.

Yet physical circumstances favoured the Russians. The terrain suited their enormous formations of hard-marching infantry and their plentiful cavalry. So did the geographical features. The Austrian positions on the forward slope of the Carpathians formed a salient. The Vistula, running north, boxed in the Austrians on the left, the Dniester, running south-east, gave the Russians a strong support to any thrust they might make from the right. Geography thus forced the Austrians to advance into a pocket.

At the first encounter, the Austrians prevailed. They deployed thirty-seven infantry divisions and a screen of ten cavalry divisions spread out ahead. The Russians, moving forward in an arc opposite, deployed fifty-three divisions of infantry and eighteen of cavalry. Despite the Russians' superiority in numbers, Conrad's first thrust succeeded. His left wing ran into the Russian right at Krasnik on August 23, and attacked. The leading Austrian formation was the First Army, which fought fiercely in a three-day battle against the Russian Fourth Army, which had come forward without waiting for its reserves. The Russian general staff recorded that things went from bad to worse. By August 26, the Russians had retired twenty miles towards Lublin. On the same day the Austrian Fourth Army encountered the advancing Russian Third at Komarov, just short of the River Bug. By the conclusion, the Russians were almost surrounded.

Then the geographical insecurity of the Austrian position began to assert itself. East of Komarov, the frontier with Russia made a sharp turn to run south-eastward towards the border with neutral Romania. Superficially, this flank offered was easily defensible, since a succession of river lines ran behind it at intervals of twenty or thirty miles; the headwaters of the Bug, moreover, were protected by the great fortress of Lemberg, with a second even stronger fortress at Przemysl not far in its rear. The Austrian Third Army should have easily been able to present a strong resistance to the Russians, since the Second Army in Serbia was now sending back to it the divisions attached to the Balkan Group. Third Army, however, had been disfavoured by Conrad's decision to give it an "active defensive" role, while First and Fourth attempted the encirclement of the Russian flank in western Galicia. As a result, it was deployed well inside Austrian territory, standing on the River Gnita Lipa. There it should have been safe, had it stayed put. On August 25, however, Brudermann, its commander, decided to act offensively and moved forward. It was the day, moreover, when he lost XIV Corps, called northward to Second Army. When the encounter came, less than a hundred Austrian infantry battalions, supported by 300 guns, ran headlong into nearly two hundred Russian battalions, supported by 685 guns. In three days of fighting in the broken country between the two Lipa rivers, the Austrians were first defeated at Zlotchow, twenty-five miles short of Tarnopol, and then driven back in confusion, sometimes panic; some of the defeated Austrians fled as far as Lemberg.

Had the Russians followed up their victory, the whole of the insecure Austrian wing might have been overwhelmed. Ruzski, the responsible general, did not follow up and Brudermann's Third Army survived. It was an odd situation, though

The value to armies of the balloon was appreciated almost as soon as the first ascent in 1783. As a tethered observation platform, it served in the American Civil War and subsequent conflicts, as it would widely on the Western Front from 1915 to 1918. Not until the development of the dirigible, perfected by Count Zeppelin in 1900, did the balloon promise a useful reconnaissance function, however; and not until the Wrights' success with heavier-than-air flight in 1903 was the role of their aeroplane as a flexible weapon of war foreseen.

The first use of the aeroplane in war was by the Italians against the Turks in Libya in 1911–12. By 1914, however, the British, French and Germans all had military aviation services, of which the French was the largest. It played an important reconnaissance role in the Marne campaign. Air crews soon began to attack each other and by 1915, two distinct types of aircraft, fighters and scouts, were emerging. Again, the French took the lead, but Germany soon followed; British aircraft design lagged behind. German fighters, including the Fokker models, dominated in 1915–16, largely due to the early adoption of "interrupter" gear, which allowed machine guns to fire through the propeller arc. By 1917, however, new generations of French and British fighters, including the Nieuport 17, Spad 13, Sopwith Camel and S.E.5, allowed them to fight on equal terms with such enemy types as the Halberstadt D, Albatros D-III and the Fokker Triplane. By 1918, despite the deployment of the advanced Junkers J-1 armoured fighter by the Germans, the Allies had achieved air superiority over the Western Front. All air forces were deploying fighters en masse; the Richthofen "Flying Circus" was the most famous of these groups.

Bombing from aircraft began early in the war, with little effect. By 1917, however, the Germans had developed several types of strategic bomber, including the Gotha-G, which, with Zeppelins, carried out raids on London. The British Independent Air Force, equipped with the Handley Page O/400, responded with attacks on German industrial zones. The real pioneers of strategic bombing were, however, the Russians, whose Sikorski 1M aircraft determined the pattern all other air forces would eventually follow.

Right top: *Dogfight between German and French aircraft near Reims, 1914, by Achille Beltrame, Italian.*

Right: Damaged British plane, S.E.5 type, from the 2nd Squadron AFC, March 24, 1918.

Above: *British DH4 biplanes attacking German Fokker triplanes,* by George Horace Davis, British.

Left: German Fokker DI triplane with its crew.

not unprecedented in war before or since. Each side misappreciated the extent of its own achievements. Ruzski believed he had won no more than "a fine defensive success," and paused to regroup his forces. Conrad believed that, if he reinforced Brudermann, he could further the double envelopment which was the basis of his war plan. By August 30 he had increased Austrian strength opposite Ruzski to 150 battalions, supported by 828 guns, largely through the return of most of the Balkan Group to Second Army. Since Ruzski was not advancing, Conrad judged the moment ripe to reopen the offensive, largely with Second Army fighting on Third's right, the two forming an army group under the successful commander of Second Army. Under Conrad's orders, Second Army attacked again on August 29 between the Lipa rivers, this time with results even more disastrous than at first. Russian strength opposite now exceeded 350 battalions, supported by 1,304 guns, and, in the ensuing maelstrom, 20,000 Austrians were captured and thousands more killed and wounded.

In the face of all the evidence, Conrad continued to believe he was winning. He persuaded himself that he could allow Third and Second Armies to make a deep withdrawal behind Lemberg, drawing the Russians after them and then bring Fourth Army down from the north to attack the enemy in flank. The main line of resistance was to be the River Wereszyca between Lemberg and Przemysl. He was motivated in part towards this doomed enterprise by a desire to emulate the success of Hindenburg and Ludendorff in East Prussia. He was also stung by the growing impatience of his allies with the Austrians' failure to pull their weight. "Our small army in East Prussia," Kaiser Wilhelm remarked acidly in early September to Conrad's representative at O.H.L., "has drawn twelve enemy corps against it." The Kaiser exaggerated; but, since Conrad was opposed at most by fifteen corps, the taunt stung. He was determined to drive his tired and battered armies to victory.

In the event, the plan nearly worked. The Russians were slow to follow up the abandonment of Lemberg. The Third and Second Armies actually won some success on the Wereszyca position, thus delaying for a few days the closure of the Russian encirclement of the Austrian centre, the imminent danger of which was becoming even more evident. Conrad continued to ignore the threat. The Fourth Army marched on until, at Rava Russka, thirty miles north of Lemberg, it fell on September 6 into heavy combat with a concentration of the Russian Third Army and was halted. Conrad's efforts to outflank with a weaker force a stronger force that was attempting to outflank him now threatened catastrophe. A huge gap had opened between his First Army still battling against the Russians in the north and his other three, locked in conflict behind Lemberg. He had no reserves of his own. The Russians, gathering reinforcements daily, stood with open jaws ready to close on the Austrian Fourth, Third and Second Armies. Sixteen Russian corps now faced eleven Austrian, most of which were bunched in a narrow pocket which the enemy dominated from both sides. First Army, moreover, was suffering a battering it could not resist in its isolated situation to the north. Conrad appealed to the Germans for help; the Kaiser replied, "Surely you cannot ask any more of [Hindenburg and Ludendorff] than [they] have already achieved." He forced Second and Third Armies into a renewed offensive on the Wereszyca. When that failed he had no recourse but to order a general retreat, first to the River San, then to the Dunajec, a tributary of the Vistula only thirty miles east of Cracow. Przemysl, the huge fortress guarding the gaps in the Carpathian chain where the Rivers San and Dniester rise to flow into the Polish plain, had been abandoned, leaving its garrison of 150,000 soldiers surrounded behind Russian lines. Austrian territory to a depth of 150 miles had been surrendered. The Habsburg Emperor had lost 400,000 men out of the 1,800,000 mobilised, including 300,000 as prisoners.

THE BATTLES FOR WARSAW

The Austrian collapse on the Carpathian front precipitated one of the first great strategic crises of the war. Not only was the Hungarian half of the Austrian empire, beyond the mountain chain, threatened with invasion, but the territory of heartland Germany suddenly lay under threat of a Russian drive into Silesia, towards the great cities of Breslau and Posen. East Prussia was not out of danger, while at the far southern end of the front, Brusilov, best of the Russian generals, was menacing the Carpathian passes. Even Moltke could find time to turn his attention from the Battle of the Aisne to the affairs of the Eastern Front, and on his last day as Chief of Staff, before his supersession by Falkenhayn on September 15, he telephoned Ludendorff to order the formation of a new "southern" army to fill the gap between the victorious Eighth Army and the crumbling Austrians. Falkenhayn, on September 16, announced that most of Eighth Army would leave East Prussia to join the new army, numbered the Ninth, with Ludendorff as chief of staff and Hindenburg as commander. On September 18 Ludendorff motored to meet Conrad and agree with him a new plan to avert the danger under which the Austro-German front lay. The Ninth Army, instead of standing to await a Rus-

General Erich von Falkenhayn (1861–1922) was a favourite of the Kaiser. In 1914 he was Minister of War; after the removal of the younger von Moltke on September 14, he combined that office with the Chief of the Great General Staff, until February 1915. At first he took the strategic view that the Eastern rather than Western Front offered the better prospect of a decisive result and was responsible for transferring troops to launch the successful offensives at Gorlice-Tarnow in May and against Serbia in October. Neither, however, brought decisive victory in the east and he succumbed to pressure to resume the offensive in the west, authorising the additional attack at Verdun in February. Its failure led to his resignation in August, to be succeeded by Hindenburg, the hero of Tannenberg. He subsequently held lesser commands in Romania, which he successfully conquered, and over Turkish-German forces in Mesopotamia and Palestine, where he failed. He retired for good in February 1918.

Right: A Russian popular print. The caption reads "Germans, no matter how strong you are you will never see Warsaw." The Germans entered Warsaw on August 4, 1915.

Нѣмцы! Сильны хоша вы, А не видѣть вамъ Варшавы
Лучше бы въ Берлинъ поперли Всѣ пока не перемерли.

sian offensive into Silesia, would attack across the upper Vistula and drive towards Warsaw, the Russian centre of operations on the Polish front.

The Russians, however, had plans of their own. During September, in fact, they had too many plans, the supreme command, the *Stavka*, having one, and the North-Western and South-Western Fronts others. The Russian General Staff reports record "dissension between [them], resulting in different directives." The North-Western Front, now commanded by Ruzski, was, by his estimation, dangerously exposed as a result of the German successes in East Prussia and must retreat a long way, perhaps as far as the River Niemen, a hundred miles east of the Masurian Lakes; if necessary, Warsaw itself must be abandoned. The South-Western Front, by contrast, wanted to press its victorious pursuit of the Austrians westward towards Cracow. The *Stavka* had a radical alternative: the bulk of the Russian force on the Eastern Front would disengage, concentrate around Warsaw and the great fortress of Ivangorod, upstream on the Vistula, and then

Russian soldiers are photographed after their entry into Stallupönen, East Prussia, on August 17, 1914. They were soon driven out but in the subsequent fighting around Gumbinnen, the German Eighth Army was severely mauled by Russian artillery and Russian riflemen who had constructed field entrenchments. The setback persuaded von Moltke, the German Chief of Staff, to send Ludendorff, who had performed so brilliantly in the west, to take charge as operations officer of the Eighth Army. Shortly afterwards he decided to replace the army commander, von Prittwitz, with the dependable Hindenburg. Thus began the Hindenburg-Ludendorff partnership, which resulted in the victory of Tannenberg and led to their joint command of the German armies throughout the war.

launch a concerted offensive towards Silesia, with the purpose of taking the war directly into Germany.

By September 23, the *Stavka* had acquired clear intelligence that the German Ninth Army was concentrated in Silesia and was advancing towards Warsaw. The Grand Duke Nicholas, who had now taken control of the *Stavka,* accordingly decided to withdraw most of his forces from contact and await the German advance. Meanwhile, Brusilov would be left to menace the eastern Carpathians, while the Tenth Army would be despatched to mount a new offensive against East Prussia. When Hindenburg's and Ludendorff's Ninth Army appeared in the centre, the Russian Fourth and Ninth Armies would advance from Warsaw to oppose it, while the remainder of the *Stavka*'s strategic mass, Second, Fifth and First Armies, would sweep down to take it in flank.

This was war on a titanic scale. The Russians, who were beginning to receive important reinforcements from distant Siberian military districts, successfully

A Russian popular print of the army's entry into East Prussia, August 1914. The regimental band heads the column, with the regiments' singers behind them. East Prussia was the heartland of the German state and its military class, so the appearance of the Russians in the ancestral lands from which so many of its officers sprang exerted a profound shock. Many Prussian soldiers were committed to the campaign in the west and, as they advanced on Paris, were transfixed by anxiety about events in the east. Its defenders, however, were largely local, particularly the troops of I, XVII and XX Corps, who, fighting to protect their homeland, would display an extraordinary tenacity.

transferred most of their units engaged in the Carpathians to the Warsaw area in late September, without attracting the enemy's attention; the Austrians, finding their front had been thinned out, followed, but to their eventual disadvantage. All they gained thereby was the chance to relieve the garrison of Przemysl on October 9, soon to be surrounded again when they paid the penalty of joining the Germans in Ludendorff's ill-conceived offensive towards Warsaw. The *Stavka* also enjoyed the satisfaction of watching the Russian Tenth Army return to the fray on the East Prussian frontier. Though, in the Battle of Augustov (Septem-

ber 29–October 5), its attack was held, its intervention caused Hindenburg and Ludendorff considerable alarm. Eighth Army, overconfident after the glory of Tannenberg, had not bothered to entrench its positions and the Russians achieved some easy tactical successes before they were checked.

By early October there were really four fronts in the east: from north to south, a German-Russian front on the eastern border of East Prussia; an Austro-German–Russian front on the Vistula; a Russian-Austrian front on the San; and a Russian-Austrian front in the eastern Carpathians. The whole extent, from the Baltic to the Romanian border, was nearly five hundred miles, though with a gap of a hundred miles in the north between Warsaw and East Prussia, thinly screened by cavalry. It was in the centre, however, that the drama of a true war of movement was unfolding. There two complementary outflanking offensives were in motion: the German Ninth Army was marching down the west bank of the Vistula;

A Russian field battery emplaced outside Warsaw during the fighting in Russian Poland, September 1915. The artillery was traditionally the premier arm of the Russian army. Its officers were an élite and its equipment was excellent. The gun in the foreground is the 1902 model, of 76.2 mm, equivalent to the French 75-mm and the German 77-mm. The limber, to the left, contains its ready-use ammunition. The Germans eventually captured Warsaw, forcing the Russians back to the frontier of "Old Russia," but the positions it took there proved resistant to German offensives throughout 1916.

the Russians were preparing to cross the Vistula from the east below Ivangorod, to which the Austrians had imprudently advanced, and above Warsaw, there to launch the outflanking movement against Hindenburg and Ludendorff which they thought they were about to unleash on the Russians.

Had the Germans had any better means of mobility than the feet of their soldiers and horses they might have pulled the manoeuvre off, but the Kaiser's generals had no such means. Worse, the Russians had superiority of numbers: from Warsaw to Przemysl they deployed fifty-five infantry divisions against thirty-one Austrian and thirteen German. When Ludendorff appreciated, on October 18, that the Ninth Army was in imminent danger of defeat if he pushed it on towards Warsaw, he decided to withdraw it. Conrad, who had followed the Russians' deliberate retreat from Przemysl to the San, was less prudent. He tried to attack towards Ivangorod on October 22, was defeated and on October 26 was forced to retreat; Przemysl, with its garrison of 150,000 men, was left surrounded for a second time, an Austrian island in a sea of Russians, while 40,000 soldiers of Conrad's First Army were killed, wounded or captured. The Austrians ended up near Cracow, whither they had been pushed after their defeat in the Galician battles of August, the Germans only fifty miles from Breslau in Silesia, near their starting point for the march on Warsaw.

WINTER BATTLES IN GALICIA AND THE CARPATHIANS

The Battle of Warsaw was an undoubted Russian victory. Though it had not resulted in the encirclement the *Stavka* sought, it demonstrated the Russians' superiority in the warfare of manoeuvre and even in the strategy of deception. The question remained for the Russians: what to do next? The *Stavka* was not in doubt. It would resume its planned offensive and on November 2 issued the necessary directive. The continuing arrival of reinforcements from the Siberian, Central Asian and Caucasian military districts supplied the necessary force. As soon as dispositions had been made, the central mass, consisting of the Second and Fifth Armies, would press forward through Breslau and Posen towards Berlin. Meanwhile the southern armies would also go over to the offensive between Cracow and Przemysl, with the aim of "completing" the destruction of the Austrian forces in Galicia and the Carpathians.

There were two impediments to this plan. The first was the doubtful ability of the Russians to move their troops at the required speed to the point of encounter with the enemy. During the manoeuvre which had brought the Russian mass so skilfully to Warsaw and Ivangorod in October, the *Stavka* had been able to utilise the comparatively extensive rail network of central Poland. Western Poland, however, had deliberately been deprived of railways as a defensive measure. Moreover, during their retreat from Warsaw the previous month, the Germans had destroyed the rail network behind them for a depth of a hundred miles. The second impediment was positive rather than negative. Ludendorff was himself planning a resumption of the offensive with the object of taking the Russians in flank in the plains of western Poland and cutting them off from their Warsaw base. Making use of the undamaged rail link between Silesia and Thorn, he relocated thither the whole of Ninth Army by November 10. It consisted of eleven divisions, including reinforcements brought urgently from the Western Front at the demand of Hindenburg, who, on November 1, had become Commander-in-Chief in the east.

Ninth Army attacked on November 11. A gap of thirty miles was quickly opened. Although the Germans were outnumbered by the Russians on this front, by twenty-four divisions to fifteen, they had the advantage and pressed on. It was only on the fourth day of their offensive, sometimes called the Second Battle of Warsaw, that the *Stavka* realised it had a crisis on its hands; fortunately, it recognised almost simultaneously that the situation could be saved only by precipitate retreat. It ordered a disengagement, which was carried out with great efficiency. In two days of forced march, the Russian Second Army fell back on the great cotton-weaving town of Lodz. It was now the Germans' turn to be on the wrong foot. Russian out-flanking forces appeared from north and south and three German reserve divisions were for a time surrounded.

The Battle of Lodz ended on November 23 neither as a Russian defeat nor as a German victory. Ludendorff managed to represent it as a victory all the same and so extract from Falkenhayn the transfer of four German corps from west to east. The reinforcements deployed in the north were misused. During December they were committed to a series of frontal assaults which achieved the fall of Lodz on December 6 but then petered out.

Confronted by Russian trenches, the Germans dug also, so that the coming of winter found the central sector of the Eastern Front completely immobilised. It would remain frozen, militarily as well as physically, until the following summer.

In the south the arrival of the German reinforcements was to achieve quite different results. During November the Austrians had rallied and had staged a series of counter-attacks around Cracow. Joined by the right wing of the German Ninth Army, now commanded by Mackensen, and reinforced by Böhm-Ermolli's Second Army from the Carpathians, they succeeded, in confused fighting and at great cost, in gaining ground north of the Vistula between Cracow and Czestechowa. The Russian South-Western Front armies were present in greater strength, however, and were able to bring up reinforcements. After ten days of fighting, which began on November 16, Conrad had to accept defeat and draw his troops

Refugees from the fighting in Poland, 1915. The husband holds the reins of horses harnessed to a typical *panje* farm cart, a light, flexible wagon commonly requisitioned by the invading Germans and Austrians to negotiate the rutted, waterlogged roads during the spring and autumn *rasputitsa*, the seasons of thaw and downpour which make movement off unpaved roads on the Russian plains almost impossible.

back to positions closer to the German border than those from which he had started. South of Cracow things ended worse. Because the front in the Carpathians had been stripped of troops for the Cracow-Czestechowa offensive, the five main passes through the mountains stood exposed to a Russian advance. Brusilov captured the Lupkow pass on November 20 and by November 29 Boroevic, his Austrian opponent, faced the prospect of an enemy offensive against Budapest.

Then the Austrians' fortunes quite unexpectedly changed for the better, the result of their taking a well-judged initiative. Indecision, to which the Russian high command was so prone, further aided the Austrian initiative. On November 29 the Grand Duke Nicholas summoned Ruzski and Ivanov, the two front

A Jewish child begs a drink of water from German soldiers during the German occupation of Russian Poland, 1916. Although the German occupation included most of the Jewish "Pale of Settlement," the densest concentration of Jewish population in Europe and the focus of the "Final Solution" in 1942–44, German occupation policies were not anti-Semitic. Jews were favoured by the German occupation authorities because their use of Yiddish, a form of medieval German, allowed them to act as interpreters to the Slav population. Most of the volunteers to the proposed army of the Kingdom of Poland, a political revival cynically proposed by the Germans in 1917, were Jewish. The Austrians made similar use of Jews in their area of occupation in southern Russia.

commanders, to the *Stavka*'s headquarters at Siedlce to discuss future operations. They disagreed, as they had done so often before. Ruzski wanted to withdraw the North-Western Front to Warsaw. Ivanov, by contrast, wanted to regroup his forces and return to the offensive. "The way to Berlin lies though Austria-Hungary," he argued. He got his way; but his freedom of action depended not upon the permission of the Grand Duke but on availability of supplies and reinforcements. Reinforcements were plentiful, munitions were severely deficient. The artillery was rationed to ten rounds per gun per day.

Conrad struck while these circumstances prevailed. He had perceived a weak point in the Carpathians where, between the towns of Limanowa and Lapanow, a gap of nearly twenty miles yawned. Opposite he assembled the best of the troops available to him, the German 43rd Division and the Austrian XIV Corps. The German division was fresh, the XIV Corps was not. Surprise, nevertheless, was on the side of the task force and on December 3 it struck. In four days of fighting the Russians were pushed back forty miles. Then enemy reinforcements began to appear and on December 10 Conrad's drive was halted. It had, nevertheless, allowed Boroevic to go over to the offensive in the Carpathians and to secure new and stronger positions on the forward mountain slopes. As a result, the Battle of Limanowa-Lapanow not only blocked Ivanov's plan to thrust past Cracow towards Germany but also punctured the Russian dream of an advance on Budapest.

Yet, though a victory, Limanowa-Lapanow was also a last gasp. Never again would the Imperial and Royal Army unilaterally initiate or conclude a decisive operation on its own. Its victories thereafter would be won only because of German help and under German supervision. As it was, the army's victory at Limanowa owed much to the loan of German troops. Henceforward it would always fight as the German army's junior and increasingly failing partner. That was in large measure the result of its having entered the conflict with insufficient numbers and then suffering disproportionate losses. All the combatant armies had by December lost numbers that would have seemed unimaginable in July 1914. The Russian field army had been reduced from 3,500,000 men on mobilisation to two million; but it had perhaps ten million unconscripted men yet to call to the colours. Austria-Hungary, by contrast, had lost 1,268,000 men out of 3,350,000 mobilised but had less than a third as many potential replacements; the official figure put the number at 1,916,000. The steadfastness of the army was further undermined by the very heavy losses suffered at the outset among its regular officers and long-service N.C.O.'s. It was on its way towards becoming what the Austrian official history would itself call "a *Landsturm* [second-line] and militia army."

What that presaged was revealed when, the month after Limanowa-Lapanow, Conrad attempted to repeat the success further east in the Carpathians. He did so in concert with the Germans. Conditions did not favour success. The Beskids rise to 8,000 feet, then had few roads and are covered by deep snow in winter. The Germans, moreover, were ill-equipped for mountain operations. It was not surprising that the offensive, which began on January 23, made little headway. What was surprising was the early success of the Austrians who, in the Battle of Kolomea, drove the Russians down the eastern slopes of the Carpathians and reached Czernowitz at the junction of the Austrian-Russian-Romanian border. The territorial gains made were shallow, however, and a renewal of the offensive on February 27 was rapidly

Honved Hussars of the Austrian army enter the town of Limanova, December 1914. The Battle of Limanowa-Lapanow, south of Cracow, was the last purely Austro-Hungarian victory of the war. Conrad von Hötzendorf, the Austrian Chief of Staff, had perceived that a gap yawning between the Russian Third and Eighth Armies as they advanced westward invited a counter-attack. It was delivered on December 3 and drove the Russians back forty miles.

The *Honved* was the army of the Hungarian half of the Austro-Hungarian empire. Distinct from the Common Army, recruited throughout the empire, and the *Landwehr* of the German-speaking lands, it had been created in 1867 to satisfy Hungarian demands for a distinct military identity within the empire. It contained a disproportionate number of cavalry units, of which these hussars were one.

checked by Russian resistance. The Austrians lost over 90,000 men in these operations, without blunting Russian effectiveness. With the failure of these winter counter-offensives in the Carpathians, the morale of the enormous Austrian garrison of Przemysl, surrounded since October for the second time, collapsed. Its relief had been a primary object of the January operation. When that and its renewal in February failed, the commander of the fortress demolished as much of the fortifications as had survived Russian bombardment and, on March 22, surrendered. Two thousand five hundred officers and 117,000 soldiers passed into Russian captivity.

In Masuria the Russian Tenth Army still occupied the strip of East Prussia taken in the Battle of Augustow at the end of September and the Germans were determined to recapture it. Their plan, however, had two larger objects. The first was an encirclement of the Russian Tenth Army between Masuria and the forest of Augustow; the second was a wider encirclement of the whole Russian position in Poland, in concert with the Austrians' offensive in the Carpathians. Falkenhayn had wanted neither operation but he was overborne by Hindenburg, who, though his subordinate, enjoyed direct access to the Kaiser since his Tannenberg triumph. The troops were found, largely because of the German army's superior ability to create new formations from its existing structures. While the Russians and the Austrians merely made good losses as best they could with often untrained recruits, the Germans subdivided first-line divisions, upgraded second-line formations and organised new divisions out of reserves and fresh classes of conscripts. In this way, during November 1914, it created eight new divisions for the Eastern Front.

The "Winter Battle in Masuria" opened on February 9, 1915. Two armies, the old Eighth which had won Tannenberg and a new Tenth, attacked from north and south of the lake belt, broke through in terrible weather and quickly threatened the Russian with encirclement. The Russian infantry fought back but were progressively encircled. Russian intelligence was poor, consistently underestimating the strength of the Germans; the high command, which had provided the isolated Tenth Army with no reserves, complacently assured Sievers, its commander, that the Twelfth Army, far to its south, would solve its problems. He had warned, before the storm broke, that "nothing can prevent [my army] from being exposed to the same fate as [Rennenkampf's] in September." No notice was taken

An Austrian 305-mm siege howitzer in position in Galicia, 1915. Austria-Hungary had an advanced armaments industry, the Skoda works, in today's Czech Republic, producing weapons of the most modern design. The 305-mm howitzer, however, designated a "mortar" by the Austrian army, was lent to the Germans in 1914 to assist in the reduction of the fortresses of Liège and Namur. It was subsequently deployed against the Russian fortresses, notably Lemberg (Lvov) in the Ukraine, and later in the Italian campaign.

by his superiors, so that, by February 16, another Tannenberg did indeed threaten. The German pincers closed on February 21, when Bulgakov surrendered with 12,000 men. There had not been a second Tannenberg but East Prussia had been liberated from the danger of Russian invasion for good—at least in this war.

The winter battle in the Carpathians promised no such clear-cut result. There, in continuance of the efforts at Limanowa in December and in the Beskid mountains in January, the Austrians and their German loan troops renewed the attack in February, only to find the Russians respond with unexpected energy. The terrain and the weather in the Carpathians inflicted setbacks and terrible suffering on Conrad's soldiers. The Russian formations, which included a corps of Finns,

German troops operating with assault boats in the Masurian Lakes, East Prussia. The Battle of the Masurian Lakes in September 1914 completed the German victory of Tannenberg in August, but fighting between the Germans and Russians persisted in this region of forest, river, lakeland and swamp until February 1915. Conditions were extreme. Many on both sides perished of exposure in freezing conditions during the confused fighting in the winter of 1914–15.

perhaps the hardiest soldiers in Europe, were less affected. They answered Conrad's effort at an offensive with a counter-offensive of their own in late March which, despite the arrival of three German divisions to the Austrians' aid, pressed forward. By the beginning of April, the Russians dominated the Carpathian front and, despite losses throughout their army totalling nearly two million since the war's outbreak, were again contemplating a breakthrough over the crests to the Hungarian plains, with results decisive for the whole eastern campaign, as soon as better weather came. The Austrians, whose losses in the first three months of 1915 added 800,000 to the 1,200,000 already suffered in 1914, were at their last gasp. Without massive German help, whatever price was to be paid for that by way of political dependency and national prestige, the Habsburg empire faced a culminating crisis.

6 STALEMATE

By late November 1914, stalemate had fallen on the Western Front. Trench systems were continuous from Nieuport, on the North Sea, to Bonfol, on the Swiss frontier. The Germans had decided to stand on the defensive in the west, while prosecuting the war in the east. The British, though they occupied only a short sector of the front around Ypres, were already mounting trench raids and trying to dominate no-man's-land. The French had decided, while leaving certain sectors "inactive," to continue with their programme of counter-offensives. The First Battle of Artois, December 14–24, achieved no result. The winter battle in Champagne dragged on until March 14, costing 90,000 French casualties for no gain of territory. Joffre concluded that the French army must be greatly strengthened before it could attack with hope of success. The Germans were also studying their options. Geography occupied all their minds.

The strategic geography of the Western Front is easy to read and largely dictated the plans made by each side at the outset of trench warfare and in the years that followed. Much of the front was unsuitable for the style of major operations both sides envisaged, in which the power of artillery would prepare the way for large-scale infantry assaults, to be followed by cavalry exploitation into open country. The Vosges was such a front, and was accepted to be so by both French and Germans, who held it with second-rate divisions, reinforced by mountain infantry who occasionally disputed possession of the high points. Indeed, south of Verdun, neither side was to make any major effort between September 1914 and September 1918 and this stretch, 160 miles long, became "inactive." Elsewhere, the Argonne proved unsuited to offensives as, for different reasons, did the Flemish coastal zone. In the centre, the heights of the Aisne and the Meuse, though they were both to be contested in great battles, too much favoured the defender for offensive effort to be profitable. It was therefore only on the dry chalklands of the Somme and the Champagne that attacks offered the promise of decisive success. They were separated from each other by the high ground of the Aisne and Meuse, the bulge in the front to which they formed the shoulders. Military

Hussars in the trenches at Zillebeke (Ypres), January–February 1915.

159

Left and below: French rearward positions at Amblouville, department of the Marne, May 18, 1915. As artillery and ammunition became more readily available, after the shell shortage over the winter of 1914–15, the rear areas came under increasingly regular attack and had to be entrenched also. Woods, which provided cover from view, were defoliated and shredded. It will not be long before this sylvan scene will have disappeared, to be replaced by shattered tree trunks and upheaved earth.

Opposite top: A posed propaganda photograph of German soldiers enjoying the comforts of life underground in a dugout in the Argonne in 1915. The scene is not wholly misleading. Falkenhayn having decided in 1915 to stand on the defensive in the west, the German trench garrison settled in for a long stay, dug deep and furnished their dugouts with home comforts. Some even had electric light.

Opposite bottom: Above ground the Germans made their trenches as strong as possible. The sides here are revetted with wattle hurdles, to contain falls of earth, a besetting irritation for trench dwellers.

German troops loading supplies into a narrow-gauge Décauville railway in the Argonne, 1915. Because shell fire quickly destroyed the road network in the entrenched zone, all armies found it convenient to run light railways from the main lines up to the front. They were more easily repaired, when damaged by shell fire, than roads, which required tons of ballast and hardcore to be dumped for a hard surface to be restored. The load here consists partly of fodder for horses, the largest single item, by bulk, of stores shipped by all armies throughout the war.

logic therefore required that it was at those shoulders that the attackers should make their major efforts and defenders be best prepared to withstand an assault.

Who would be attackers and who defenders? In August 1914 it was the Germans who had attacked; Schlieffen's maps showing the "line of the 31st day" coincide in eerie accuracy with the early Western Front. In September the French counter-attacked; the engagements during "the Race to the Sea" follow the course of the stabilised line in Artois, Picardy and Flanders with an equivalent precision.

The trace of the railway network explains how these outcomes came about. Early in the campaign of 1914 the Germans took possession of the Metz-Lille line, running north-south within their area of conquest. The French, on the other hand, retained control of the Nancy–Paris–Arras line facing it. The latter is closer to the line of engagement than the former, and that proximity explains why the French were better able than their enemy to deliver reserves to the crucial point in time to win one battle after another. "The 'Race to the Sea' is thus best understood as a series of stalemated collisions along the successive rungs of a ladder whose uprights were formed by those vital parallel railways. Amiens, Arras and Lille, near which the principal engagements of the 'Race to the Sea' were fought are, as a glance at the railway map shows, all located on cross-country lines linking the two great north-south routes. Since the physical and human geography remained unaltered by the course of the fighting, the strategic advantage rested with the French, though the tactical advantage rested with the Germans, who had chosen the pick of the ground at the final points of contact."

French infantrymen snatch a meal after returning from the trenches at Les Eparges, April 13, 1915. Les Eparges was a German-held feature near Verdun, attacked in the First Battle of Champagne and taken on April 10. Losses there, and at other small places such as Tahure and la Main de Massiges, were heavy and were to be repeated in September during the Second Battle of Champagne. The landscape of Champagne, open dry chalkland, made it easy to defend. Before the war it had been a principal training area for the French army. The appearance of the troops, filthy and exhausted, testifies to the ferocity of the fighting. In the foreground, left, a *brancardier* (stretcher bearer) has flopped to rest. The soldiers are wearing the new horizon-blue uniform but have not yet been issued with steel helmets.

The geographical advantage enjoyed by the French disposed them to attack. Geography did not, however, supply the only argument for such a decision, nor for the complementary German decision to await attack on the Western Front. The real reasons were quite different. France, as the victim of Germany's offensive of August 1914, and the major territorial loser in the outcome of the campaign, was bound to attack. National pride and national economic necessity required it. Germany, by contrast, was bound to stand on the defensive, since the setbacks she had suffered in the east, in its two-front war, demanded that troops be sent from France to Poland for an offensive in that region. The security of the empire was at stake; so, too, was the survival of Germany's Austrian ally. The real

Soldiers behind the lines, at a wine merchant's. Poilus got a daily wine ration but preferred wine bought privately.

Behind the lines, June 1915. The earthwork is the embankment of the Somme canal. The French canal network was an important means of strategic transport in the northern sector of the front. A barge is moored above the shaving party. The wagon with chimney is a *cuisine roulante*, a horse-drawn cooker, common to all armies. On the march the cooks stood on the steps, preparing dinner as the wagon followed the regiment. In 1915 the Somme was a quiet sector, Allied attacks being concentrated to the north and south, in Artois and Champagne. In 1916 it would become the centre of the great British effort to push the Germans back from the centre of the Western Front.

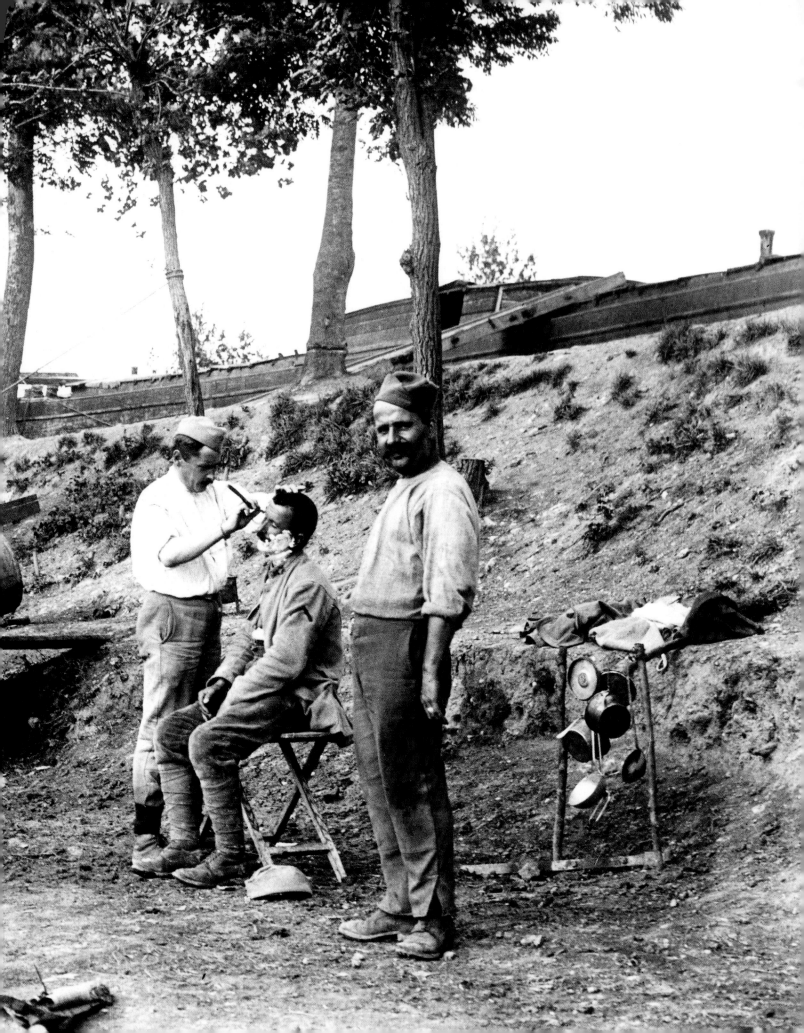

outcome of 1914 was not the frustration of the Schlieffen Plan but the danger of a collapse of the Central Powers' position in eastern Europe.

A piecemeal adjustment against that risk had been made as early as the last week of August, when the 3rd Guard and 38th Divisions had been transferred as a result of the Tannenberg crisis. They had been followed by ten more between September and December. Moltke had not wanted to let any go. His successor, Falkenhayn, resented the transfer of every one. He believed that the war had to be won by making the major effort in the west. There the French army was recovering from its losses of the opening campaign while French industry was gearing up for a war of material. The British were creating a whole new army of volunteers, while training the Territorial Force for active service; together these would produce nearly sixty divisions, besides those from Canada and Australia which were hastening across the Atlantic and Pacific to the motherland's aid. Of these figures Falkenhayn did not have exact intelligence but his impression of the gathering of a huge reinforcement was accurate enough. It would shortly double the force opposing the Germans on the Western Front, while they were already reaching the limits of expansion open to them from their manpower potential.

In the circumstances, Falkenhayn had convinced himself that 1915 must be a year of offence in the west and defence in the east, within the larger policy of bringing Russia to make a separate peace. He lacked, however, the authority to carry his case. Though the Kaiser had confirmed him in the appointment of Chief of Staff in January 1915, he was acutely aware that the real prestige of office attached to Hindenburg, as victor of Tannenberg, and his chief of the eastern staff (*OberOst*), Ludendorff. What they did not want, he could not insist upon. Moreover, Ludendorff was waging an active campaign to undercut his primacy, which the German system in any case did not

clearly define. Whereas Joffre exercised the powers of government within the Zone of the Armies, and Kitchener, appointed Secretary of State for War at the outbreak, effectively acted as Commander-in-Chief also, Falkenhayn was neither supreme commander, since that dignity belonged to the Kaiser, nor his immediate subordinate, since between him and Wilhelm II stood the Military Cabinet. It was through the Military Cabinet that Ludendorff began his intrigue. He was assisted by the Chancellor, Bethmann Hollweg, who shared the German people's admiration for Hindenburg in full measure. Bethmann Hollweg enlisted the help

Opposite top: After the terrible losses of the opening months of the war, the need in 1915 was to find new sources of manpower. Germany, which in peacetime had recruited only half its available manpower, had ample reserves. So did Britain, which had not practised conscription at all. In France over 80 per cent of young men had done military service. Replacement for the 300,000 dead of 1914 and reinforcements had largely to come from the annual "class" of young men reaching military age. Here some of the "class of 1916," those born in 1898, board a train at Gare Montparnasse, in Paris, for the training depot. They are in high spirits. As the war progressed, families would receive the call-up papers with increasing dread.

Opposite bottom: A regiment of Zouaves leaves Paris for the front, 1915. They have stuck flowers in their rifle muzzles and buttonholes. German troops did the same. Their stiff new uniforms show that they have recently been enlisted.

Right: A Pals battalion poses for a photograph in training camp, 1914. On August 8, 1914, Lord Kitchener, the British Secretary of State for War, called for "a hundred thousand volunteers." The response was immediate, large-scale and enthusiastic, over 500,000 young men volunteering by March 1915. Many came forward in groups from factories, offices, boys' clubs, churches or sports associations and were allowed to serve together in what became known as "Pals" or "Chums" battalions. Quite without training or knowledge of military life, they often appointed their own corporals and sergeants. Eventually thirty-six divisions of volunteers were formed, some of them providing the bulk of the force that attacked on the Somme, July 1, 1916. Losses among many Pals battalions were crippling, leaving some small towns virtually bereft of young men.

of both the Empress and the Crown Prince to argue for Hindenburg's and Ludendorff's eastern strategy. Falkenhayn fought back, first confronting Hindenburg with the demand that he resign his post, though that was impossible in the face of German public opinion, then securing Ludendorff's transfer from eastern headquarters to that of the Austro-German army in Galicia.

When Hindenburg appealed to the Kaiser for his return, he found he had gone too far. Wilhelm II decided that the hero of the day was challenging the authority of the supreme command. The result was a compromise. Falkenhayn

The First World War was a trench war. The sudden multiplication of firepower, produced by the magazine rifle, the machine gun and quick-firing artillery in the first years of the twentieth century, forced all the armies of Europe, soon after they encountered each other on open battlefields in August 1914, to dig to survive. In early September the German army took the deliberate decision to terminate its retreat from the Marne by entrenching a line on the River Aisne; the line soon reached from Switzerland to the North Sea. Following the Battles of Tannenberg and the Masurian Lakes, the Russians also entrenched the Eastern Front. Italy's front with Austria in the Alps was quickly entrenched also after May 1915.

All armies rapidly designed trench systems which resembled each other, as well as similar trench routines. The front line, protected by a barbed-wire entanglement, was paralleled by a support line some hundreds of yards to the rear, and a reserve line further back again. Communication trenches, running at right angles, connected the lines and protected troops moving up and down. No-man's-land, between the opposing front lines, might be as little as fifty yards or as much as half a mile wide.

Infantry battalions defending trenches in periods of static warfare conventionally rotated between front and rear on a two-weekly basis. They might spend five days in the front line, five in support, five in reserve but, even when out of the front line, would be required to go forward to carry supplies and to work at digging, usually at night. Hot food came forward in containers, though surreptitious cooking was possible at quiet times. Signalling between front and rear was by telephone cable which, by mid-war, was usually buried to protect it against

Trench scene on the Somme, by André Devambez (1867–1943), French.

artillery. Bombardment, often at predictable intervals, dawn or dinnertime, was part of trench routine. So, more occasionally, were trench raids at night, intended to take prisoners or "establish superiority." Often, however, particularly in sectors not held by élite troops, a "live and let live" regime prevailed. The opposing garrisons left each other alone. Such tolerance was by no means the norm, however; in the Ypres salient, on the Somme, at Verdun, trench routine was a deadly business of constant give and take and daily casualties.

Covered-in trenches on the south side of Ortler summit, 3,862 metres, the highest front of the war.

French troops in trenches in the Argonne, November 1915.

decided not to make the thwarting of his strategy a resigning issue, came to a personal accommodation with Hindenburg and acquiesced in the return of Ludendorff to the *OberOst* headquarters. Hindenburg contented himself with the hope that more troops could be extracted from the west if he could make a convincing case for mounting an offensive that would cripple the Russian army. In those hopes lay the germ of the plan for a renewal of battle east of Cracow which would result in the great breakthrough at Gorlice-Tarnow in the coming May. Meanwhile the debate between Germany's "westerners" and "easterners" would rumble on unresolved.

There was as yet no such division of opinion on the Allied side. Despite the absence of any supranational command organisation, the informal understanding between the British and French general staffs was working well. The Russian view was also represented through their liaison officers at both French and British headquarters. Field Marshal French was, in any case, of one mind with General Joffre, who had but one thought: to drive the invader from the national territory. French shared it, though curiously, he believed, like Hindenburg, that the war would be settled on the Eastern Front. Nevertheless, "until the Russians [could] finish the business," he was certain that the right policy for Britain was to commit all the troops available to Western Front operations. They were growing rapidly in number. Soon the British would be able to take over stretches of the line from their ally and find a striking force to mount offensives on their own initiative.

The question was, where? An early plan to make a major effort on the Belgian coast, with the Royal Navy supporting a combined Anglo-Belgian army, foundered on Admiralty warnings that its ships could not stand up to German coastal artillery. Plans to use troops against the Austrians were shown to be equally unrealistic. Militarily weak though Austria-Hungary was, geographically it was almost unapproachable by a maritime power. The only other region beyond the Western Front where Britain might use its growing strength in independent action was therefore in Turkey, which had joined Germany and Austria as a belligerent ally on October 31. The only active front Turkey had opened, however, was against Russia in the Caucasus, which lay too far from any centre of British power for an intervention to be contemplated there. Moreover the British government was as yet unwilling to divert troops from France, though it was prepared to consider deploying naval forces, if a promising use for them could be found. In January the British War Council began to consider the preparation of a naval expedition to the Turkish Dardanelles, with the object of opening a way to Russia's Black Sea ports. The mission was to be strictly naval, however; Britain's commitment to France remained, in every sense, complete.

Yet the Western Front presented not only militarily but also geographically a strategic conundrum. There was the initial difficulty of how to break the trench line; beyond that lay the difficulty of choosing lines of advance that would bring about a large-scale German withdrawal. During January the French operations staff at G.Q.G. began to analyse the problem. It turned on the rail communications which supported the German armies in the field. There were three systems that led back across the Rhine into Germany. The southernmost was short and easily defended. That left the two systems that supplied the Germans holding the great salient between Flanders and Verdun. If either, or preferably both, could be cut, the Germans within the salient would be obliged to fall back. The French and the British therefore agreed during January that the correct strategy during 1915 was for offensives to be mounted at the "shoulders" of the salient, thus threatening the Germans with encirclement as well as disruption of their supplies.

There was to be a spring offensive, jointly British and French in Flanders and Artois, French alone in Champagne. Indeed, this first agreement was to set the pattern for much of the Allied effort on the Western Front throughout the war. This, however, is to anticipate the failure of the spring offensive of 1915. Fail it did, however, for reasons to become tragically familiar with every renewal of the French and British efforts. There was, indeed, warning of failure before the spring offensive ever began, in the miscarriage of a minor and preliminary attack by the British at Neuve-Chapelle in March. All the contributing factors that were to bedevil success in trench offensives for much of the war were present. Among the structural were the relative immobility and total vulnerability to fire of advancing infantry and the absence of means of speedy communication between front and rear, between infantry and artillery and between neighbouring units. The unfolding of action at Neuve-Chapelle demonstrates the operation of all these factors as if in a military laboratory.

THE WESTERN FRONT BATTLES OF 1915

Neuve-Chapelle was launched because Sir John French was unable to comply with Joffre's request that the B.E.F. assist the preparation of the coming Artois offensive by taking over more of the French line. The plan was simple. Neuve-Chapelle, twenty miles south of Ypres, was to be attacked on March 10 by the British 7th and 8th Divisions and the Meerut and Lahore Divisions of the Indian Corps. The front of attack was about eight thousand yards, behind which five hundred guns had been assembled. There was to be a "barrage"—the term was French, meaning a dam or a barrier—of bursting shells fired behind the German trenches, to prevent reinforcements reaching their stricken comrades. The British and Indians would be supported by reserves moving forward to take further objectives, but only on the receipt of orders.

The bombardment took the Germans by complete surprise. That was an achievement rarely to be repeated. The defenders were overwhelmed. Their wire had been extensively cut, their front trench destroyed. When the British infantry assaulted at five past eight, they were not opposed and within twenty minutes a breach 1,600 yards wide had been opened in the German line. The makings of a victory had been won.

Then the factors making for failure started to set in. The British plan stipulated that, after the first objective was taken, the infantry was to pause for fifteen minutes while the artillery shelled the ruins of Neuve-Chapelle village in front of them. The intention was to disable any remaining defenders waiting there. In fact there were none. Those that had escaped were hurrying towards the strong-

The headquarters of the 21st Brigade, 7th Division, during the Battle of Neuve-Chapelle, March 10–14, 1915. In the spring of 1915 the French and British high commands agreed to mount offensives in Artois and Champagne, on either side of the Somme salient. Neuve-Chapelle was the initial British effort, mounted to seize dominating ground south of Ypres. The attacking force consisted of two British regular divisions, the 7th and 8th, and the Indian Meerut Division. The attack went well at first, the 8th Division seizing a wedge of territory inside the enemy positions, but the Germans rushed reinforcements forward to seal off the break-in. By the end of four days of fighting, casualties were about equal, 12,000 on each side, and the Germans had strengthened their line. It was a foretaste of failure to be frequently repeated in trench warfare.

points which had been built precisely to check such a break-in. After this second bombardment the British followed fast. Orders, however, now required that they should wait again. The commander of the battalion in the centre, belonging to 2nd Rifle Brigade, managed to send back a message requesting permission to disregard the order. Surprisingly—there were no telephone lines and this was the pre-radio age—it was received; even more surprisingly an answer was returned, wholly for the worse. Permission to move forward was refused.

It was now about half-past nine and the Germans were recovering their wits. Falkenhayn's tactical instruction of January 25 had laid down that, in the event

of an enemy break-in, the flanks of the gap were to be held and immediately reinforced, while reserves were to hurry forward and fill the hole. That was what was beginning to happen. On the British left, where the bombardment had left the German positions intact, two machine guns were brought into action on the right, the attackers had lost their way, an all too common occurrence, and stopped to get their bearings. Meanwhile, according to plan, fresh British battalions were crowding into the gap. By ten o'clock, "roughly nine thousand men [were squeezed] into the narrow space between Neuve-Chapelle village and the original British breastwork [where] they lay, sat, or stood uselessly in the mud, packed like salmon in the bridge pool at Galway, waiting patiently to go forward."

Unfortunately, the British artillery could not rapidly be informed of the deteriorating situation. Without radio, communication depended on flag signals or runners, the first usually obscured, the second slow and vulnerable.

At half-past eleven a bombardment was organised against the 11th Jägers' machine-gun positions, and an officer and sixty-three men came out to surrender, having killed about a thousand British soldiers. All the while the local German commanders were hurrying reserves to the flanks. By contrast, the British junior officers were passing their observations of the local situation, as the plan required, back up the chain of command so that authority could be granted for any alteration of the all-defining plan they requested. What all this meant, in terms of the actual rather than planned timetable in this particular battle, was that between nine o'clock in the morning, when the German line had been broken and the writing of firm orders to exploit the success at ten to three in the afternoon, nearly six hours elapsed. By the time those written orders had filtered down, via telephone and runner, another three hours were lost.

Dark was drawing in and so were the German reserves. The flanks of the break-in had been secured before midday. By nightfall fresh German troops were filling the open gap. Next morning the British renewed the offensive but the attack soon stopped. It was now the turn of the Germans to be frustrated because their counter-attack troops simply could not march fast enough to reach their desig-

Below: A ration party of the 4th Black Watch, a Scottish Territorial regiment, at Neuve-Chapelle, March 1915. Units of the Territorial Force, Britain's part-time civilian reserve army, began to reach France at the end of 1914. The reinforcements they provided were essential to British efforts to sustain their part in the war before the arrival of the new volunteer formations later in the year.

nated jumping-off positions. The attack was therefore postponed for a day. When, on the morning of March 12, the attack did go in, it was immediately stopped with heavy German losses. The British front-line commanders had used the pause imposed by mist the day before to consolidate their foothold and site twenty machine guns in commanding positions.

As a result, the "exchange ratio" of casualties, as it would now be termed, at Neuve-Chapelle was eventually almost equal: 11,652 British killed, wounded, missing and captured to about 8,600 German. The reasons are easy to identify. At the outset, the advantage lay with the attackers, as long as they could preserve a measure of secrecy. Almost as soon as the attackers entered the enemy's positions, however, the advantage tended to move towards the defenders. The attackers found themselves moving into unknown and confusing surroundings, and away from their supporting artillery the further they advanced, thus progressively losing contact with it as telephone lines were broken or left behind. Then, when the defenders counter-attacked, the advantage reversed. The attackers had familiarised themselves with the ground taken, organised its defences and re-established telephonic communication with their artillery. The physical product of offence and counter-offence was an ever thicker and more confused trench line, resem-

bling a layer of scar tissue, picked at and irritated, over the site of an unsuccessful surgical operation.

The British nevertheless judged Neuve-Chapelle a partial success. It was significant also because it anticipated in miniature both the character and course of the spring offensive in Artois, to which it was a preliminary, as well as its renewal in Artois and Champagne in the autumn. For a moment, indeed, during Neuve-Chapelle, the leading waves of British and Indian troops had glimpsed the way open to the crest of Aubers Ridge, which was to be the British objective during their part of the Artois attack. Before that could be launched, however, the British had undergone an offensive in the reverse direction, in Flanders, which came to be known as the Second Battle of Ypres. The First, which had secured the "Salient" at the end of 1914, had petered out in confused and ineffective fighting. By the beginning of April, however, Falkenhayn had decided, in order partly to disguise the transfer of troops to the Eastern Front for the forthcoming offensive at Gorlice-Tarnow, partly to experiment with the new gas weapon, to renew pressure on the Ypres salient.

Below: Photographs taken of soldiers at close grips with the enemy are rarities. These, taken by Private F. A. Fyfe, in private life a press photographer, show soldiers of his battalion, the 1/10th King's Regiment (Liverpool Scottish), assaulting German positions at Bellewaarde Farm, near Ypres, on June 16, 1915.

Right: Private Fyfe, one of the battalion bombers (hand-grenade throwers), has moved on with the leading wave to the lip of the German trench. The flag planted on the parapet is to show to observers in the British lines that the trench has been taken and that the attackers are moving on. The attack at Bellewaarde was a local offensive and did not lead to a breakthrough.

Opposite bottom: British and German wounded shelter inside devastated German trenches, Aubers Ridge, May 9, 1915. The British attack, part of the Anglo-French Artois offensive, was intended to seize high ground and to test new British tactical methods. For the Germans it also provided an opportunity to test new defensive methods, using concrete pillboxes and carefully sited machine guns to throw back a dense infantry assault. The German method succeeded. Over six thousand British and Indian troops of the 1st and Meerut divisions were killed or wounded, only nine hundred Germans.

GAS

The Germans were the first to employ gas as a weapon, at Neuve-Chapelle in October 1914, but the quantities launched, inside shrapnel shells, were too small to be noticed by the French. When xylil bromide (tear gas) was used in larger quantities at Bolimov on the Russian front in January 1915, low temperatures froze it. In April 1915, therefore, the Germans decided to try the lethal agent chlorine, which kills by causing the lungs to produce fluid in which the victim drowns. First tried against the French in the Second Battle of Ypres, April 1915, it panicked those not immediately killed or disabled into flight. A large gap was opened in the Allied lines but the German infantry, rightly suspicious of the new weapon, advanced too slowly to exploit it and a new front was formed. When the British used chlorine at the Battle of Loos, September 25, 1915, it blew back in the attackers' faces. Had they not been wearing the newly issued gas masks, unintended casualties would have been high.

During 1916 the combatants turned to the less fratricidal mustard gas, a blistering agent that could be fired by shell. Occasionally lethal, its principal effect was to disable, and also to pollute areas inside the enemy's territory, sometimes persisting for weeks. Increasing quantities of mustard gas were included in the great preliminary bombardments of 1917 and 1918, often in shells that also contained high explosive. Other gases, mainly of respiratory effect, employed were bromine, phosgene and chloropicrin.

The Germans were the largest users (68,000 tons), then the French (36,000) and British (25,000). Although hundreds of thousands of soldiers were affected by gas during the war, those killed amounted to only about 3 per cent of casualties. After-effects were, however, persistent, so that many veterans were troubled by breathing difficulties for the rest of their lives, had their lives shortened and were prone to common respiratory diseases. Gas aroused a peculiar horror among all combatants. It was not accidental that the first effective and universal measure of post-war arms control was the prohibition of the use of lethal gas, a ban which has remained generally effective since 1925.

Opposite: Troops advancing to the attack through gas. This photograph was taken by a member of the London Rifle Brigade on the first day of the Battle of Loos, September 25, 1915.

Above: *Dressing the Wounded during a Gas Attack.* The casualty wears a PH gas helmet, as his box respirator is damaged. Pastel by Austin O. Spare.

Top right: A German soldier and horses wearing gas masks.

Right: British soldiers from the 1st Cameronians B Company preparing for a gas attack, Bois section, May 20, 1915.

Gas had been used by the Germans already, on the Eastern Front, at Bolimov, on January 3, when gas-filled shells had been fired into the Russian positions on the River Rawka, west of Warsaw. The chemical agent was lachrymatory (tear-producing), not lethal. It appears to have troubled the Russians not at all; prevailing temperatures were so low that the chemical froze instead of vaporising. By April, however, the Germans had a killing agent available in quantity, in the form of chlorine. Experiments with gas-filled shells had failed (though, with a different filling, gas shells would later be widely employed). The direct release of chlorine, from pressurised cylinders, down a favourable wind, promised better. By April 22, six thousand cylinders, containing 160 tons of gas, had been emplaced opposite Langemarck, north of Ypres, where the trenches were held by the French. Next to them was the Canadian Division, first of the imperial divisions to reach the Western Front; the rest of the Ypres salient was held by three British regular divisions.

The afternoon of April 22 was sunny, with a light east-west breeze. At five o'clock a greyish-green cloud began to drift across from the German towards the French trenches, following a heavy bombardment, and soon thousands of Zouaves and Algerian riflemen were streaming to the rear, clutching their throats, coughing, stumbling and turning blue in the face. Within the hour, the front line had been abandoned and a gap eight thousand yards wide had been opened in the Ypres defences. Some of the gas drifted into the Canadian positions but their line was held and reinforcements found to stem the advance of the German infantry who, in many places, dug in instead of pressing forward. Next day, the gas was quickly identified for what it was and, as chlorine is soluble, Lieutenant Colonel Ferguson proposed that cloths soaked in water be tied round the mouth as a protection. The Germans attacked the Canadians with gas again on April 24, but the effect was less than on the first day and more reinforcements were at hand. Efforts at counter-attack were made by both the French and the British. On May 1 there was another gas attack in the jumble of broken ground known to the British as Hill 60, the Dump and the Caterpillar. The line was held, nevertheless, and the Ypres salient, though pushed back to within two miles of the city, was thereafter never dented. Gas in a variety of forms, the more deadly asphyxiant phosgene, and the blistering "mustard," would continue in use throughout the war, and chlorine would kill thousands of Russian troops in German offensives west of Warsaw in May. Its intrinsic limitations as a weapon, dependent as it was on wind direction, and the rapid development of effective respirators, ensured, however, that it would never prove decisive, as it might have done if large reserves had been at hand to exploit the initial surprise achieved by the Germans in the Second Battle of Ypres.

Le Petit Journal

ADMINISTRATION
61, RUE LAFAYETTE, 61
Les manuscrits ne sont pas rendus

5 CENT. SUPPLÉMENT ILLUSTRÉ 5 CENT.

26ᵐᵉ Année — 44 — Numéro 1,278

DIMANCHE 20 JUIN 1915

ABONNEMENTS

Victimes de leur propre barbarie
Soldats allemands asphyxiés par les gaz qu'ils avaient lancés contre les Russes et qu'un coup de vent rejette sur leurs tranchées

"Victims of their own barbarity" reads the caption to this reconstructed picture of a German gas attack in Russian Poland, on the Bzura River, west of Warsaw, June 1, 1915. A change in wind direction has blown the gas back into the attackers' trenches. The Germans, though the first to employ asphyxiating chlorine gas at Ypres in April 1915, were soon imitated by the French and the British. The rapid development of effective gas masks reduced the new weapon's effectiveness. Armies subsequently made more use of blistering (mustard) gas, incorporated in the filling of shells and spread by artillery fire. A disabling rather than killing agent, its effect was to pollute ground, so denying it to the enemy.

British troops in defensive positions behind the ramparts of Ypres, near the Menin Gate, 1915. Ypres was the location of the first German gas attack on the Western Front and of heavy fighting in the spring of 1915. The seventeenth-century fortifications were incorporated by the British into their defensive system. The city, though almost destroyed by shell fire, was not entered by the Germans throughout the war. The Menin Gate, rebuilt as a war memorial, records the names of the more than 50,000 "missing" who died in the battles around Ypres, 1914–18, and whose bodies were not found. Atop the ramparts today is one of the most beautiful of the many cemeteries that surround Ypres.

The Allies had no technological surprise with which to inaugurate either of their offensives on the Western Front in 1915, and both failed. In May, the French and British attacked in Artois, the British against Aubers Ridge on May 9, the French against Vimy Ridge a week later. Although the French had artillery and ammunition available in quantity while the British had not, the difference between their achievements was negligible. Douglas Haig's First Army was simply stopped in its tracks. The French gained the summit of Vimy Ridge, to look down into the Douai plain through which the crucial rail tracks in enemy hands ran, only to be decisively counter-attacked by reserves reaching the summit before their own, positioned six miles in the rear, could join them.

When the offensive was renewed in September, this time in Champagne as well as Artois, the results were scarcely different. The plan of attack had been

proposed to Sir John French by Joffre on June 4. It required as a preliminary that the British take over more of the French line. The British now held most of the line from Ypres to the Somme, leaving a short length near Vimy from which the French Tenth Army would attack as soon as preparations for Joffre's plan were completed.

That took time. Both allies were learning that a large-scale attack against trenches could not be launched extempore; roads had to be built, stores dumped, battery positions dug. The date of the opening of what would be called the Second Battle of Champagne was postponed from the end of August to September 8, then, because Pétain demanded time for a lengthy bombardment, until September 25.

The Germans profited from the delay, and the undisguisable signs of impending attack, to strengthen the portions of their line against which they detected the offensive was preparing. The German positions in the Western Front were becoming impregnable, certainly against an offensive planned to achieve breakthrough on the first day. Worse still for the attacker, German defensive doctrine required that the second position be constructed on the reverse slope of any height occu-

Above: A British attack on the Hohenzollern Redoubt, during the latter stages of the Battle of Loos, October 13, 1915. The white lines are banks of upturned chalk, marking the parapets of British trenches. Shells are falling on the German positions, which dominate the ground over which the British had to attack. On the first day of the offensive, September 25, the two British divisions principally engaged lost over 8,000 out of 30,000 men. In the fighting up to October 13, 16,000 British soldiers were killed, 5,000 German. The German line was scarcely penetrated.

Left: A British battalion coming out of the line after the Battle of Loos. The platoon the young officer is leading has lost a third of its strength. The troop-carrying London omnibuses carry the insignia of the Royal Naval Division, then fighting in the Gallipoli campaign.

pied so that it was protected from the Allied artillery fire designed to destroy it. The role of the German artillery was, by contrast, not to bombard trenches but to attack the enemy infantrymen as they assembled and then to lay a barrage in no-man's-land once they moved forward; those who penetrated that barrier of fire were to be left to the machine gunners, who, experience was showing, could stop an attack at ranges as close as two hundred yards or less.

The effectiveness of the Germans' preparations was proved all too painfully on September 25, 1915, at Loos, the site of the B.E.F.'s offensive in Artois, at nearby Souchez, where the French renewed their assault on Vimy Ridge, and in distant Champagne, where the French attacked alone. In both sectors the offensives were preceded by a discharge of chlorine gas. At Loos, the gas hung about in no-man's-land or even drifted back into the British trenches, hindering rather than helping the advance. In any case the British divisions engaged were quickly stopped by machine guns. They were ordered to resume the advance next morning, which they spent marshalling for the attack. In early afternoon they moved forward in ten columns "each [of] about a thousand men, all advancing as if carrying out a parade-ground drill." The German defenders were astounded by the sight of an "entire front covered with the enemy's infantry." They stood up, some even on the parapet of the trench, and fired triumphantly into the mass of men advancing across the open grassland. The machine gunners had opened fire at

Waterlogged trenches at Laventie, near Ypres, December 1915. After constant minor and two major efforts to break the German line on the Western Front during 1915—the big offensives were in Artois and Champagne, on either side of the great Somme salient, in May and September respectively—stalemate had once more set in. These two officers of the Scots Guards stand outside their dugout, built of sandbags in the breastwork. Duckboards provide a path through the flooding. Graves have been dug just behind the front line.

British and French prisoners being marched under German guard through a ruined street in Lille after the Battle of Loos, September 27, 1915. Most of the British are wearing the kilt belonging to the Highland regiments of the 9th Scottish Division. The French are in the new horizon-blue uniforms, with the recently issued Adrian helmet. There was heavy fighting around Lille during the Battle of the Frontiers in August 1914. It then fell into German hands and remained occupied, the largest French city to be captured by the enemy, until October 1918.

1,500 yards' range. The effect was devastating. "The enemy could be seen falling literally in hundreds, but they continued their march in good order and without interruption" until they reached the unbroken wire of the Germans' second position. "Confronted by this impenetrable obstacle the survivors turned and began to retire."

The survivors were a bare majority of those who had come forward. Of the 15,000 infantry of the 21st and 24th Divisions, over 8,000 had been killed or wounded. Their German enemies, nauseated by the spectacle of the "corpse field of Loos," held their fire as the British turned in retreat, "so great was the feeling of compassion and mercy after such a victory." A German victory Loos was; though the British persisted with attacks for another three weeks, they gained nothing but a narrow salient two miles deep. The battle had been a terrible and frustrating initiation to combat for the soldiers of the New Armies, though the Scots of the 9th and 15th Divisions, in particular, seem to have shrugged off casualties and taken setback only as a stimulus to renewed aggression. Yet Loos, in strategic terms, was pointless and so, too, were the efforts of Pétain's Second Army and

Moroccan spahis (*spahis morocains*) bundled up against the snow on the Aisne, 1915. Spahis were North African irregular cavalry, recruited both in Algeria, a French colony, and Morocco, a protectorate since 1912. They retained their picturesque uniform up to the outbreak of war, a voluminous white cloak and turban, baggy trousers and a red jacket. During 1915 they adopted the khaki of the colonial army but this regiment is at a halfway stage. Moroccan soldiers had a high reputation as warriors but the French high command found little use for cavalry after the entrenchment of the Western Front. Spahi regiments, being run by their French officers according to tribal discipline, did not easily adapt to modern warfare.

A sentimental German trench Christmas card for 1915. The sentry gives permission for a Christmas angel to take presents to the front line. Christmas was celebrated in Germany more elaborately than any other European country and the effort to observe the Christmas spirit was widely made in 1914 on the Eastern Front and on parts of the Western Front. The British reciprocated, the French did not. Efforts to repeat the "Christmas truce" of 1914 were not successful.

A French listening post below Vimy Ridge, December 1915. Possession of the heights of Vimy Ridge, unsuccessfully attacked in May and September 1915, allowed the Germans to dominate a wide area of the front between Arras and Ypres during 1914–17. It was eventually captured by the Canadians in April 1917. The French trench sentry in rear is watching no-man's-land through a camouflaged periscope.

de Langle's Fourth in the offensive in Champagne that opened the same day. There twenty divisions attacked side by side on a front of twenty miles, supported by a thousand heavy guns and behind a gas cloud similar to that launched at Loos. The results were equally unavailing. The attempts on the Champagne heights nowhere gained more than two miles of ground. The Germans' second line was not penetrated and, when the fighting ended on October 31, their positions remained intact, though 143,567 French soldiers had become casualties.

It had been a doleful year for the Allies on the Western Front, much blood spilt for little gain and any prospect of success postponed until 1916. The Germans had shown that they had learnt much about the methods of defending an entrenched front, the Allies nothing about means of breaking through. It was a bitter lesson for the French, all the more so because, in a widening war, their allies seemed bent on seeking solutions elsewhere, leaving the main body of the enemy implanted in their territory. Yet the defeat of the enemy through victories outside France looked no closer a prospect than breakthrough towards the Rhine. In Russia, where German intervention had rescued Austria from collapse, on the new Italian front which had opened in May, in the Balkans, on the Turkish battlegrounds, the course of events favoured the enemy. Only at sea and in Germany's distant colonies had the Allies established an advantage, and, as they knew, in neither the naval nor the colonial theatres could success bring them victory.

7

THE WAR BEYOND THE WESTERN FRONT

By the end of 1915, none of the original combatants was fighting the war that had been wanted or expected. Germany had expected a one-front war fought in two stages: first against France, while a token force held its Eastern Front, then another victorious campaign against Russia. Instead, it was heavily engaged on both the Western and Eastern Fronts, on the latter sustaining substantial forces on Austrian territory to prop up its Habsburg ally. Austria, which had thought the war might be limited to a punitive expedition against Serbia, had reaped the whirlwind of its folly, and found itself locked in combat not only with Russia but Italy as well. Serbia had reaped the whirlwind of its intransigence and found extinction as a state. Britain, which had committed itself at the outset only to providing an expeditionary force to widen the French left in Flanders, found itself assuming responsibility for ever longer stretches of the Western Front, while simultaneously finding men to fight the Turks at Gallipoli, in Egypt and in Mesopotamia, to assist the Serbs and to reduce the garrisons of Germany's African colonies; men had also to be found to reinforce the crews of ships denying the North Sea to the German High Seas Fleet, dominating the Mediterranean, chasing the enemy's surface commerce raiders to destruction and defending merchant shipping against U-boat attack. The war that men were already beginning to call the Great War was becoming a world war and its bounds were being set wider with every month that passed.

THE WAR IN THE GERMAN COLONIES

Germany had had to become an empire itself, the Second Reich, proclaimed in the Hall of Mirrors at Versailles in January 1871, before it could join Europe's great powers in the competition for empire. Their extensive conquests left the new state few pickings. North Africa was by then French, Central Asia and Siberia Russian, India British. It was German traders who supplied the impulse to enter the African continent. Between 1884 and 1914, they had established commercial enclaves in Kamerun, Togo and South-West Africa (Namibia) on the west

Italian gunners in the Alps hoisting a field gun up a mountain.

coast, and what is now Tanzania on the east coast. Purchase (from Spain) and deliberate imperial effort had meanwhile secured Papua, Samoa and the Caroline, Marshall, Solomon, Mariana and Bismarck Islands in the south and central Pacific. The coastal region of Kiaochow, and its port of Tsingtao, had been seized from China in 1897.

On the outbreak of war, the British and French at once took action to reduce the garrisons of Germany's colonies; the Japanese, who had entered the war (on August 23) to improve their strategic position in the Pacific at Germany's expense, likewise moved against Tsingtao and the central Pacific islands. Japan occupied the Marianas, Marshalls and Carolines during October. Samoa fell to a New Zealand force on August 29. German New Guinea (Papua) was surrendered unconditionally to an Australian expedition on September 17, together with the Solomons and the Bismarcks. The reduction of Tsingtao took longer. The Japanese, taking no chances, landed fifty thousand men and commenced a deliberate siege. They were later joined by troops from the British treaty port of Tientsin. Three lines of defence confronted the attackers. The first two were abandoned by the Germans. Against the third, the Japanese opened a bombardment with 11-inch howitzers. On the night of November 6–7 an infantry assault was delivered and the following morning Captain Meyer Waldeck, the naval officer serving as governor, surrendered his force. His marines had lost two hundred men killed, against 1,455 Japanese fatal casualties. It had been a brave, if purely symbolic, resistance.

In Africa, the tiny territory of Togo, sandwiched between the British Gold Coast (now Ghana) and French Dahomey (now Benin), was quickly overrun (August 27). Kamerun (now Cameroon), equal in size to Germany and France combined, proved more difficult to conquer. The garrison numbered about a thousand Europeans and three thousand Africans. The Allied force eventually rose to a strength of 25,000. Despite its preponderance of numbers, distance, climate and topography blunted its early efforts. Three British columns were in motion by the end of August, each separated from the other by 250 miles of roadless terrain. Near Lake Chad one was advancing towards Mora; a second was approaching Yarua, five hundred miles from the sea; a third, near the coast itself, was directed at Nsanakang. All three encountered strong resistance. The French did better, seizing a coastal bridgehead and winning a small battle just south of Lake Chad. The arrival of reinforcements then gave the British the advantage and, with the assistance of cruisers and a fleet of small craft, they secured the coast and started inland up the rivers. The objective was Yaounda, 140 miles inland, where the enemy had an ordnance depot. Skilful German resistance delayed the renewal of the advance until October 1915. Finally, as the dry season opened in November, the Allies pushed forward into the central mountainous region and forced most of the Germans to seek internment in the neutral enclave of Spanish Guinea. The last German post at Mora surrendered in February 1916.

The campaign which opened in German South-West Africa in September 1914 was of a different quality altogether. "German South-West" was an enormous territory, six times the size of England, arid, infertile and populated then by only

The British blow up the gateway of the German fort at Dschang, Cameroons, January 1915. The Cameroons, of nearly 300,000 square miles, but with a population of less than four million, was Germany's largest West African colony. It was surrounded by British and French territory. The Allies regarded it as important to capture because of the radio station at Duala, a link in Germany's overseas communication system. Invading columns entered via the coast and from the north, beginning in August, but the Germans, who blew up the radio station but retreated with equipment to set up another, retired into the interior. They conducted a skilful delaying campaign and did not surrender until March 4, 1916. The Allies had deployed 18,000 troops against 3,000 German, mostly African, soldiers. Most of the German survivors escaped into the neutral Spanish colony of Rio Muni at the end. Over 4,000 Allied troops died, largely of disease.

eighty thousand Africans. The Germans had hoped, as elsewhere in their African possessions, to avoid a conflict in "South-West"; they put their trust in a vague, mutual, pre-war commitment to neutrality in Africa between the colonial powers. The British, however, were determined otherwise and they embarked at once on an expedition by sea and land. Some sixty thousand troops were available. A few, the South African Permanent Force, were regulars, wholly loyal to Britain. The Citizen Force was divided; some of its units were Anglo–South African and loyal to the crown. Others were a touchier proposition. Of the leading commanders of the Boer War now in British service, General Louis Botha had made his peace and would not shift. Christiaan de Wet and Christiaan Beyers went into active

rebellion. At the very outset, therefore, Britain found itself engaged both in a colonial campaign against the German enemy and in a Boer rebellion.

The rebellion, fortunately for the British, did not take fire. About eleven thousand Afrikaners joined in but, opposed by thirty thousand loyalists, Boer and British, they had all been forced into surrender or into German territory by January 1915. The war against the Germans then began in earnest. The army was formed into four columns. Mainly mounted, it converged on the German centres of resistance from the coast, from the Orange River and from Bechuanaland, the enormous protectorate to the north of the Union. The objective was Windhoek, the German colonial capital, on which the Germans fell back in a fighting retreat. The Germans were in a hopeless position. Outnumbered many times without any prospect of resupply from outside, they eventually surrendered unconditionally on July 9, 1915.

By 1916, the last centre of German resistance in the colonial empires was in "German East," today Tanzania. The war in that enormous colony, almost exactly the size of France, had begun on August 8, when the British cruiser *Astraea* had bombarded its port of Dar es Salaam. Hostilities then lapsed. When resumed,

VON LETTOW-VORBECK

Paul von Lettow-Vorbeck was, with Lawrence of Arabia, one of the few truly individualist leaders of the First World War; in duration and scale, his operations in East Africa far exceeded those of Lawrence in the desert.

Von Lettow, a colonel aged forty-four in 1914, was an experienced colonial campaigner. He had served in the German contingent sent to suppress the Boxer Rising in China in 1900 and subsequently in the defeat of the Hereros in German South-West Africa. Command of the *Schutztruppe* in German East Africa, Germany's most important colony, was a mark of his standing. When war came, the German governor, like his British opposite number in Kenya, hoped to except the territory from fighting. Fighting, nevertheless, soon broke out and Lettow scored an early success by defeating a landing of British and Indian troops at Tanga in November 1914. He originally had fewer than 3,000 askaris (black African soldiers) and 200 white officers. Those opposing him, including British, Indians and South Africans, and askaris from the Belgian Congo, Portuguese Mozambique and Britain's East and West African colonies, eventually numbered 350,000 soldiers and as many porters.

During 1915 both sides built up their strength (Lettow's final strength reached 20,000). The only notable events were the destruction of the German cruiser *Königsberg* in the backwaters of the Rufiji River (its crew and guns joined Lettow) and of German gunboats on Lake Tanganyika by British gunboats dragged overland from the coast. In 1916 General Jan Smuts, bringing troops from South Africa, took command. Lettow slipped away before him, leading his enemies on a dance that took them over the course of the next three years from British Kenya, to Portuguese Mozambique and to British Northern Rhodesia. He was never cornered and inflicted one distinct defeat on his enemies at Mahiwa, in German East Africa, in October 1917. His supremely loyal askaris also proved far more resistant to disease and hardship than their opponents. While their numbers held up well throughout the war, Allied troops and porters suffered nearly 600,000 "non-battle" casualties.

Lettow, cut off from news of the Armistice, eventually surrendered at Abercorn, Northern Rhodesia (modern Zambia), on November 25, 1918. He returned to Germany an undisputed hero, as he remains to many post-colonial Africans.

Opposite: "Mimi" and "Tou-Tou" passing over one of the bridges during the Tanganyika expedition, 1915.

Above: 1st Gold Coast Regiment crossing the Mgeta River during the campaign in German East Africa, December 1916. The German Residency is in the background.

Right: Company of askari troops on the march.

One of the 4.1-inch (105-mm) guns of the German commerce-raiding cruiser *Königsberg*, mounted on an improvised carriage, being dragged from the wreck to join von Lettow-Vorbeck's little army in the interior of German East Africa (modern Tanzania). After sailing from Dar es Salaam on July 31, 1914, *Königsberg* sank only one merchant ship, but her successful attack on the British light cruiser *Pegasus* in September concentrated the Royal Navy's efforts against her. She was eventually located in the estuary of the Rufiji River and sunk. Her crew joined von Lettow and fought as soldiers during the next three and a half years of his campaign.

they were to last until after the negotiation of the European armistice in November 1918, testimony to the extraordinary tenacity and prowess of Colonel Paul von Lettow-Vorbeck, commander of the colony's *Schutztruppe*. Lettow-Vorbeck, aged forty-four in 1914, was an experienced imperial campaigner; he had served previously in the German contingent sent to suppress the Boxer Rising in China and in German South-West Africa. Appointment to German East Africa was a denomination of his standing. German East Africa, bounded by British Uganda and Kenya to the north, the Belgian Congo and Rhodesia to the east, British

Nyasaland and Portuguese Mozambique to the south, straddled the Great Lakes region, the most romantic and potentially productive part of the continent.

At the outset it seemed that the pre-war understanding between the powers to exempt black Africa from hostilities might prevail. The German governor, Schnee, forbade offensive operations; the Governor of Kenya declared his colony had no "interest in the present war." Moreover, neither governor disposed of any force with which to fight. They reckoned without the aggressiveness of the young men on both sides. Lettow-Vorbeck simply ignored Schnee and began assembling his forces, few though they were, about 2,500 askaris and two hundred white officers. Nairobi, capital of Kenya, meanwhile began filling up with bellicose young settlers and white hunters, all bearing arms and demanding uniforms and a mission.

The home governments wanted war also. A German cruiser, the *Königsberg*, opened hostilities by sinking a British warship, H.M.S. *Pegasus*. Small though she was, her loss drove the admiral commanding the South African station to concentrate all his force against *Königsberg*. She was soon driven into the swampy

Indian soldiers of the British Expeditionary Force B under guard at Tanga, German East Africa, after the collapse of the British effort to take the port, November 2–5, 1914. The British made no effort to conceal their intentions and even sent emissaries to renounce a local non-aggression pact on November 2. As a result von Lettow, with 1,000 troops present, had no difficulty in dispersing the 8,000 landed by the British. Most, admittedly, were from undertrained and badly officered contingents of the Indian princely forces rather than the Indian army proper. Force B's supplies were shamefully abandoned on the beach, providing von Lettow with several hundred rifles and 600,000 rounds of ammunition, which greatly eased his re-supply difficulties at the beginning of his four-year campaign.

depth of the Rufiji River, where her captain conducted a brilliant exercise in evasion that lasted 255 days. The cruiser was eventually sunk. Even as a hulk, however, she continued to contribute to the campaign. Many of her crew went ashore to serve with Lettow-Vorbeck's askaris and some of her guns were dismounted and used as field artillery. Lettow's aggressiveness had by then caused Britain to prepare a full-scale military expedition against him. The most important reinforcement was two brigades of British and Indian troops from India. The expedition's first landing at Tanga on November 2, 1914, ended in humiliation. The

The wreck of the German light cruiser *Königsberg* in a branch of the delta of the Rufiji River, July 1915. After a brief and unsuccessful passage as a commerce raider in East African waters, *Königsberg* went into hiding from searching British ships while waiting to be re-fuelled by German coalers. Those in the vicinity could supply her only with small quantities. Eventually one was captured by the British with documents aboard that revealed *Königsberg*'s presence. She was blockaded, while two shallow-draught gunboats, *Severn* and *Mersey,* were sailed from Britain to track her down in the Rufiji's backwaters. The gunboats, their fire directed by aircraft, eventually succeeded in disabling her, on July 11, 1915.

Indians ran away, the British got lost; though outnumbered eight to one, the Germans easily drove their enemies back to the beaches, where they re-embarked on November 5, leaving sixteen machine guns, hundreds of rifles and 600,000 rounds of ammunition behind. These supplies would help to sustain von Lettow's campaign throughout 1915. Better British troops arrived; he won a small victory at Jassin. The cost in German lives there and in ammunition taught Lettow "the need to restrict myself to guerrilla warfare." That, thereafter, would be his strategy. In March 1916, Jan Smuts arrived from South Africa. He began to plan a convergent offensive, from Kenya, Nyasaland, the Belgian Congo and Portuguese Mozambique, designed to crush Lettow's little army in the interior. Lettow had no intention of being caught. Since his soldiers could live off the land, and resupply themselves with ammunition by capture from the enemy, his capacity to evade defeat in the enormous spaces of the bush was almost limitless, as he would demonstrate throughout 1916, 1917 and 1918.

CRUISER WAR

Before Lettow set off on his extraordinary venture into the vastness of the African interior, another, briefer but dramatic campaign had been mounted by the overseas squadrons of the Imperial German Navy in the depths of the Atlantic and Pacific Oceans. Germany maintained small forces in the Pacific, at Tsingtao and in the islands. In August, the cruisers *Scharnhorst* and *Gneisenau* were in the Carolines, *Emden* was at Tsingtao, *Dresden* and *Karlsruhe* were in the Caribbean, *Leipzig* was off the Pacific coast of Mexico and *Nürnberg* was en route to relieve her; the *Königsberg* was on a lone mission off East Africa. Though few in number, these eight ships represented a major threat to Allied shipping, particularly to convoys bringing Australian and New Zealand troops to European waters, for they were of recent construction, fast, well-armed and commanded by officers of ability, notably Admiral Maximilian Graf von Spee. It was a major weakness of British naval planning that its own cruiser fleet consisted either of "armoured" ships too slow to catch their German equivalents or of light cruisers which had speed to match that of the Germans but lacked the firepower to fight.

Two of the raiders were swiftly run down. *Königsberg*, the least well-handled, ceased to count after she was driven into the Rufiji delta. *Emden*, under an energetic captain, Karl von Müller, caused havoc in the Pacific and Indian Oceans, though pursued at times not only by British but also French, Russian and Japanese ships. She was eventually intercepted and sunk by the Australian cruiser *Sydney* at Direction Island in the Cocos and Keeling group on November 9, 1914, after the local wireless station managed to get off a signal before the German landing party destroyed the transmitter. That was not quite the end of *Emden's* remarkable cruise. The commander of the landing party on Direction Island evaded the Australians, appropriated a schooner, sailed it to the Dutch East Indies, got passage aboard a German steamer to Yemen in Arabia, fought off Bedouin attacks, reached the Hejaz railway built to bring pilgrims to Mecca and eventually arrived to a justifiably extravagant welcome in Constantinople in June 1915.

Karlsruhe was destroyed by a mysterious internal explosion off Barbados on November 4, after sinking sixteen merchant ships. *Leipzig* and *Dresden*, with varied adventures behind them, rendezvoused with *Scharnhorst* and *Gneisenau* in South American waters in October; *Nürnberg* had joined them earlier. These five ships then formed the most formidable threat to Allied control of the seas outside the North Sea. Admiral von Spee exploited his advantage. Deterred from

The German light cruiser *Emden* driving ashore, under fire from the Australian heavy cruiser *Sydney*, on Keeling Island in the Cocos and Keeling group in the Indian Ocean, November 9, 1914. *Emden* had had great success as a commerce raider, sinking sixteen British cargo ships, together with a Russian cruiser and a French destroyer in three months. Müller, her captain, also bombarded the British port of Penang, doing serious damage to its oil storage tanks. His strict observance of the rules of war, together with his will-o'-the-wisp capacity to elude pursuit and turn up where least expected, won him a legendary reputation among his enemies and made him a national hero in Germany. His luck ran out only because a heavily escorted Australian troop convoy was passing close to the Cocos and Keeling archipelago when he decided to attack its radio station.

An artist's impression of the Battle of Coronel, November 1, 1914, with Admiral Cradock's flagship, *Good Hope,* and its consort *Monmouth* under fire by the German battle line. Graf Spee, the German admiral, commanded a force of five modern cruisers, which could both outgun and outrun the ancient *Good Hope* and *Monmouth.* His clever use of wireless transmissions concealed the strength of his squadron from Cradock, who imprudently sailed to attack without waiting for reinforcements. Whether *Canopus,* his supporting battleship, could have held the Germans at bay is problematic, however. Her big guns were outranged by those of the German cruisers. Winston Churchill, First Lord of the Admiralty, eventually decided to delay battle but his signal was not sent until Cradock was dead.

operating in the northern Pacific by the menace of the large Japanese fleet, Spee acted against the French possessions in Tahiti and the Marquesas but met resistance and found coaling difficult. With bold strategic sweep, he therefore decided to transfer from the Pacific to the South Atlantic, signalling *Dresden, Leipzig* and his colliers to meet him near Easter Island, the most remote inhabited spot on the globe.

Interception of his insecure signals alerted the British admiral commanding the South American station, Christopher Cradock, of his intentions. Passing through the Straits of Magellan, Cradock brought his squadron into Chilean waters. The light cruiser *Glasgow* went ahead; Cradock followed with the cruisers *Monmouth* and *Good Hope* and the battleship *Canopus,* so old (1896) and slow that it was left to escort the accompanying colliers. *Monmouth* and *Good Hope* were almost as old and poorly armed. They steamed to join *Glasgow,* which had put into the little Chilean port of Coronel. Intercepted intelligence then gave Spee the advantage. Hearing that *Glasgow* was at Coronel, he waited outside for the old cruisers to appear. When they did, on the evening of November 1, he kept out of range until darkness fell, then opened fire in the gloaming. *Monmouth* and *Good Hope* were quickly sunk, not one of the 1,600 sailors aboard surviving. *Glasgow* escaped to warn *Canopus* and save her from a similar fate.

CRUISE OF THE EMDEN

Germany's naval war plan in 1914 was, while keeping the High Seas Fleet at home to wait for a favourable moment to engage the British Grand Fleet in the North Sea, to deploy its cruisers based on the German colonies as commerce raiders in the great oceans.

The most successful of these was to be *Emden,* based at Tsingtao in China and commanded by Captain Karl von Müller. He sailed her into the Pacific on August 6, 1914, to avoid capture by watching British warships. After meeting the squadron commander, von Spee, in the Mariana Islands, he was ordered to cruise in the Indian Ocean. He left on August 13, together with *Markomannia,* a collier.

Arriving in the Bay of Bengal, Müller sank six steamers between September 10 and 14, captured two as colliers and sent a third away with prisoners. On September 22 he bombarded oil tanks at Rangoon, then made for the remote island of Diego Garcia, to coal. He sank five ships in October and again kept another as a collier and sent a second away with prisoners. Proceeding to

Penang, in Malaysia, he surprised and sank two warships belonging to the large Allied force pursuing him, the Russian cruiser *Zhemtchug* and the French destroyer *Mousquet.*

Emden's terrorisation of commerce in the Indian Ocean had also delayed the sailing of troop convoys from Australia to Europe. By early November, three British and three Japanese cruisers were hunting Müller, who had become a household name. On November 9, however, the radio station on Direction Island, which he had landed sailors to destroy, managed to get off an emergency signal. The Australian cruiser *Sydney,* escorting one of the delayed troop convoys, was close by and rapidly wrecked the outgunned *Emden.*

The men of the landing party escaped capture and managed to make their way, via the Dutch East Indies and Arabia, home to a hero's welcome. Müller had meanwhile become something of a hero to his enemies. Not only was his cruise a model of offensive action, he had also scrupulously observed the rules of war and compromised the safety of his own ship by the care he had taken to ensure the survival of his captives.

In reply please quote
No.

H.M.A.S. "Sydney",

at sea,

9th November 191 4.

Sir,

I have the honour to request that in the name of humanity you now surrender your ship to me. In order to show how much I appreciate your gallantry, I will recapitulate the position.

(1) You are ashore, 3 funnels and 1 mast down and most guns disabled.

(2) You cannot leave this island, and my ship is intact.

In the event of your surrendering in which I venture to remind you is no disgrace but rather your misfortune, I will endeavour to do all I can for your sick and wounded and take them to a hospital.

I have the honour to be,

Sir,

Your obedient Servant,

John C.T. Glossop.

Captain.

The Captain,
H.I.G.M.S. "Emden".

Opposite, inset: The *Emden*'s Captain, Karl von Müller.

Opposite: A German naval landing party prepares to leave Direction Island after the *Emden* sounded the alarm at 9:30 a.m., November 10, 1914.

Above: A letter from Captain Glossop, of the Australian ship H.M.A.S. *Sydney,* to the Captain of the *Emden,* demanding his surrender.

Above right: The wreck of the *Emden*.

Right: A Japanese portrayal of the sinking of the *Emden*.

期 最 之 ンデムエ艦獨 　（三十四其）報畫亂戰大洲歐

THE ILLUSTRATION OF THE GREAT EUROPEAN WAR. NO. 49   THE BRITISH SYDNEY FORCED THE GERMAN EMDEN TO FIGHT AND THE SHARP ACTION THAT ENSUED.

Coronel was the first British defeat at sea for a hundred years. The outrage it caused was enormous, far exceeding that following the loss of *Hogue, Cressy* and *Aboukir,* three other old cruisers sunk by submarine *U-9* off Holland on September 22. Admiral Sir John Fisher, who had become First Sea Lord on October 31, at once set in motion a pan-oceanic redeployment of forces designed to intercept Spee wherever he moved. Most dangerously for Spee, Fisher decided to detach two of his precious battlecruisers, *Invincible* and *Inflexible,* from the Grand Fleet. Spee might still have remained free to cruise for a long time had he not decided to attack the British Falkland islands in the South Atlantic. He arrived off Port Stanley on December 8. Fatally for the Germans, Admiral Sir Doveton Sturdee, commanding the battlecruiser squadron, had also decided to visit Port Stanley when the Germans appeared. Making steam in haste, Sturdee left harbour and worked up speed to run the five German ships down. Bravely, Spee turned to cover the escape of the others but was overwhelmed by salvoes of 12-inch shells at ranges his 8.2-inch guns could not match. Two of his light cruisers were also run down by Sturdee's light cruisers. Only

Opposite top: The British battlecruiser *Invincible*, Admiral Sturdee's flagship at the Battle of the Falklands, December 8, 1914. With *Inflexible*, also mounting eight 12-inch guns and capable of 28 knots, it completely outmatched Graf Spee's best ships, the *Scharnhorst* and *Gneisenau*, whose heaviest guns were 8.2-inch and best speed was 22 knots. Spee might nevertheless have inflicted delaying damage on the British battlecruisers had he attacked when he found them coaling at Port Stanley early in the morning. Alarmed by a salvo fired by H.M.S. *Canopus*, the old battleship which had missed action at Coronel, he decided to make off into the Atlantic. *Inflexible* and *Invincible*, leaving harbour with coaling uncompleted, inexorably ran down the slower German ships. Spee tried to cover the escape of his light cruisers but four of his five ships were sunk in late afternoon. Only 215 of the 2,200 German sailors in *Scharnhorst*, *Gneisenau*, *Leipzig* and *Nürnberg* survived.

Opposite bottom: An artist's impression of *Scharnhorst* sinking at 4:17 p.m. *Gneisenau*, shown under British fire, survived only until 5:45.

Below: British cruisers in formation in the North Sea. Before the general adoption of oil as a fuel, the heavy black smoke produced from coal-fired boilers betrayed the position of ships at long range, often from over the horizon, and frequently obscured both targets and fall of shot.

Dresden got away, to skulk for three months in the sub-Arctic inlets around Cape Horn, until cornered and forced to scuttle on March 14, 1915, by a British squadron that included the only survivor of the Coronel disaster, H.M.S. *Glasgow*.

Sturdee's victory terminated the high seas activity of the German navy. After the Falklands, indeed, the oceans belonged to the Allies and the only persistent naval surface fighting, pending a clash of the capital fleets in the North Sea, took place in landlocked waters: the Black Sea, the Baltic and the Adriatic. The Mediterranean was wholly controlled by the French and Royal Navies, assisted by the Italian after Italy's entry, and their command of it was to be disturbed only by the appearance of German U-boats there in October 1915. Inside the Adriatic, cordoned at its bottom end by an Italian mine barrier anchored on Otranto, the Austrians waged a tit-for-tat war with the Italians, of which the only strategic point was to deny the Allies more direct amphibious access to the Balkan war zone than the Mediterranean coast allowed. A similar war was waged in the Baltic between Germany's light forces and pre-dreadnoughts and Russia's Baltic fleet. There was much mine-laying, which deterred the Russians risking their dreadnoughts far from Finnish ports, coastal bombardment and, eventually, some daring British submarine operations.

In the Black Sea, where Russia maintained the second of her three fleets—the third, in the Pacific, played a minor part in the conquest of Germany's possessions there—her command was complete. The Turks, after their declaration of hostilities in November 1914, had neither sufficient nor good enough ships to challenge, and the Russians mined Turkish waters and attacked Turkish ports and shipping at will. Yet Turkey's navy was, nevertheless, to prove, indirectly, one of the most significant instruments in the widening of the world crisis. The Ottoman government, under the control of the "Young Turk" nationalists since 1908, had spent the years since taking power in modernising the empire's institutions. The

Young Turks welcomed German military advice and commercial investment. The railway system benefited from German money, the Ottoman army was re-equipped with Mauser rifles and Krupp guns. The Young Turks nevertheless looked to Britain, as all emergent powers of the period did, for naval armament and in 1914 were about to take delivery from British yards of two magnificent dreadnoughts, the *Reshadieh* and the *Sultan Osman*. On the outbreak of war with Germany, Britain peremptorily purchased both. Two days earlier, however, on August 2, Turkey had concluded with Germany an alliance against Russia, her oldest enemy. Germany at once sailed its Mediterranean squadron, comprising the battlecruiser *Goeben* and light cruiser *Breslau*, into Turkish waters, evading a mismanaged

S.M.S. (His Imperial Majesty's Ship) *Goeben*. This German battlecruiser, mounting ten 11-inch guns and capable of 28 knots, was one of the most modern capital ships in the High Seas Fleet. It was the backbone of the *Mittelmeer division* (Mediterranean squadron), Germany's naval presence in southern waters before 1914. The German government's decision to transfer the *Goeben*, together with its escorting cruiser *Breslau*, to the Turkish government on August 3, 1914, transformed the naval, and military, situation in the Mediterranean. It gave warning that the Ottoman empire was aligned towards Germany and Austria-Hungary in the developing world war. It also posed a direct threat to the French and Russian navies. The Royal Navy attempted to intercept the two German ships but failed to do so. Two days before Turkey declared its commitment to the Austro-German alliance, on October 31, *Goeben* and *Breslau* initiated actual hostilities by bombarding Russian Black Sea ports. As *Sultan Yavuz Selim* and *Middile* respectively, with their German crews wearing Turkish naval uniform, they were then officially incorporated as units of the Ottoman navy.

British effort to head them off. On arrival at Constantinople, they hoisted the Turkish flag.

For the next three months, *Goeben* and *Breslau* remained peacefully at anchor off Constantinople. The conditions for Turkey's entry into the war were, however, already in place, for the treaty pledged her to assist Germany in the event of the latter having to support Austria-Hungary against Russia, a diplomatic circumstance already in force when it was signed. Enver Pasha, the leading Young Turk and Minister of War, was meanwhile completing his military preparations. Liman von Sanders, his senior German military adviser, expected him to open hostilities by an expedition into the great plains of the Russian Ukraine. Instead, Enver chose to make his attack into the wild mountains of the Caucasus, where terrain and the Muslim loyalties of the population would, he believed, work to Turkey's advantage. As a public signal of precipitation of the new war, however, he sent *Goeben* and *Breslau* to attack the Russian ports of Odessa, Sebastopol, Novorossisk and Feodosia. Three days later, Russia declared war on Turkey and by November 5 Turkey was at war with France and Britain also.

THE WAR IN THE SOUTH AND EAST

Turkey's entry did not merely add another member to the alliance of the Central Powers or another enemy to those the Allies were fighting already. It created a whole new theatre of war.

Indeed, Turkey's undisguised inclination towards Germany from August 1914 onwards had already decided Britain to secure its position at the head of the Persian Gulf, which was Turkish territory, by military occupation. The obvious source of troops for the operation was India and in September part of the 6th Indian Division was shipped to Bahrein, then the most important of the Gulf sheikhdoms. On Turkey's declaration, the British government also took the opportunity to recognise the separate sovereignty of Kuwait, while the convoy carrying the division proceeded to the mouth of the Shatt al-Arab, the confluence of the Tigris and Euphrates Rivers in Turkish Mesopotamia, bombarded the Turkish port and landed troops on November 7. The expeditionary force then marched inland and by December 9 had occupied Basra, the chief city of southern Mesopotamia and advanced to Qurna, where the two rivers join. There it paused, while decisions were taken about its future employment. They were to prove among the most ill-judged of the war.

Meanwhile, the Turks had taken an initiative of their own in another corner of their enormous empire. Egypt remained legally part of it but, since 1882, had been under the administration of a British "Agent" with powers of government. On Turkey's entry, the British declared a protectorate over Egypt, which was meanwhile filling up with troops, Territorials sent from Britain, Australians and New Zealanders staging to Europe. By January 1915 their numbers had risen to seventy thousand. It was at this moment that the Turks, at German prompting, chose to attack the Suez Canal, which Britain had illegally closed to enemy belligerents at the outbreak of war. The conception was faultless, for the canal was the most important line of strategic communication in the Allies' war zone. The difficulty was in execution, for the Turkish approaches to the canal lay across the hundred waterless miles of the Sinai desert. Nevertheless, careful preparations had been made. Pontoons for a water crossing were prefabricated in Germany and smuggled, through pro-German Bulgaria, to Turkey and then sent by rail across Syria to Palestine. The Ottoman Fourth Army was now concentrated at Damascus in November, with a German officer, Colonel Franz Kress von Kressenstein, as chief of staff. The approach chosen promised well, a direct march across the sands rather than down the traditional coastal route. Nevertheless, even in this very early age of aerial surveillance, a large army could not hope to pass unnoticed in terrain totally without cover during a journey of several days. It was, indeed, detected by a French aircraft before it reached the canal, near Ismailia, above the central Great Bitter Lake, on February 3. The British were well prepared and, though fighting lasted a week, only one Turkish platoon managed to drop its pontoon, so laboriously transported from Central Europe, into the canal's waters. The single outcome of the campaign was to keep in Egypt a larger British garrison than necessity dictated during 1915.

The third front opened by Turkey's entry into the war, that in the Caucasus,

Overleaf: Armenian refugees, displaced from their homeland in Turkey, 1915. The Armenians, a Christian people who in the early Christian era had ruled an extensive empire in the Caucasus, were in 1914 subjects of the Russian and Persian as well as Ottoman empires. They sought independence and, during the Russo-Turkish Caucasian battles of 1914–15, some enlisted in the Russian army. The Turks decided to regard all Turkish Armenians as political dissidents and expelled them from their traditional Turkish homeland into the desert, where hundreds of thousands died. These "Armenian massacres" have poisoned Turkish-Armenian relations ever since.

Overleaf, inset map: Turkey, on entering the war in 1914, was forced to conduct campaigns on four fronts. At the outset, Enver Pasha, military leader of the Young Turks, opened a campaign against Russia in the Caucasian mountains. It dragged on until the outbreak of the Russian revolution in 1917. The Turks also attacked the British in Egypt, but were themselves later counter-attacked in Palestine. The British meanwhile mounted a seaborne invasion of Mesopotamia (Iraq). In 1918, they also intervened, via Persia, against the Turks and Germans in revolutionary southern Russia.

Black Sea

Caspian Sea

RUSSIA

Poti
Batum • Tiflis
Trebizond
Kars
Baku

TURKEY

Euphrates

Tigris

Tabriz
Enzeli
Resht
Kazvin

Aleppo

MESOPOTAMIA

Mosul

*Mediterranean
Sea*

Damascus

Hamadar
Kermanshah

200 mls

Ramadi
Baghdad

PERSIA

Kut

Tigris

Gaza

Euphrates

EGYPT

Aqaba

Basra

*Persian
Gulf*

▨	Turkey's war zones, autumn 1918
⇨	Turkish offensives, autumn 1918
⇨	German advances, June 1918
➡	British advances, autumn 1918
⇢	British "Dunsterforce" expedition, 1918
⇢	Proposed British cavalry advance to link both British fronts, 2 Oct 1918

was by far the most important, both by reason of the scale of the fighting it precipitated and because of that fighting's consequences. The Ottoman advance into Russian Caucasia so alarmed the Tsarist high command that it prompted an appeal to Britain and France for diversionary assistance, and so led to the campaign of Gallipoli.

Enver, whose conception the Caucasus campaign was, chose the theatre for a variety of reasons. It was far from the main areas of deployment of the Russian army in Poland, and therefore difficult to reinforce. It was of emotional importance to the Turks, as a homeland of fellow Muslims, many speaking languages related to their own. It was, Enver believed, a potential centre of revolt against Russian rule, which had been imposed by brutal military action in the first half of the nineteenth century. Enver counted on the memories of these atrocities to bring the "Outside Turks" to Turkey's side. His plans, indeed, went wider, envisaging a dual-pronged offensive—of which the advance to the Suez Canal was one, that into the Caucasus the other—that would result in the raising of revolt in Egypt, Libya and the Sudan and in Persia, Afghanistan and Central Asia.

Enver's grand design was flawed on two counts. The first was that the non-Turkish peoples of the Ottoman empire, who formed the majority of the Sultan's subjects, were already awakening to their own nationalisms; they included not only the Arabs, who outnumbered the Turks, but such important minorities as the Muslim Kurds. In the circumstances, "Outside Turks," whatever their historical associations with the Ottoman caliphate, were unlikely to a respond to his appeal to holy war. The second flaw in Enver's plan was graver still, being unalterably geographical. "The Caucasus," the Russian general Veliaminov had written in 1825, "may be likened to a mighty fortress, marvellously strong by nature . . . Only a thoughtless man would attempt to escalade such a stronghold."

Enver was worse than thoughtless. His decision to attack the Caucasus at the beginning of winter, during which temperatures descend to twenty degrees of frost, was foolhardy. He had superior numbers, about 150,000 in the Third Army, to the Russians' 100,000, but his line of supply was defective since, beyond the single railway, the troops depended on the roads, which were too few and snowbound to bear the weight of necessary traffic. His plan was to draw the Russians forward and then strike behind to cut them off from their bases. The first stage of the scheme succeeded, for the Russians favoured him by advancing during November as far as the great fortress of Erzerum. The Ottoman Third Army, however, brought with it 271 pieces of artillery and proceeded ponderously. The weather, too, slowed its advance; one division lost four thousand of its eight thousand men to frostbite in four days of advance. On December 29, 1914, the Russian commander, General Mishlaevski, counter-attacked at Sarikamis and triumphed. The victory was complete by January 2, when the whole of the Turkish IX Corps surrendered, and in mid-month no more than 18,000 of the 95,000 Turks who had fought the campaign survived. Thirty thousand are said to have died of cold. The victory was, however, to have one lamentable local outcome. Among the troops the Russians had employed was a division of Christian Armenians, many of them disaffected Ottoman subjects, who took the opportunity offered by Russian sponsorship to commit massacre inside Turkish territory. Their participation in the campaign, and the declaration in April 1915 of a provisional Armenian government, underlay the Ottoman government's undeclared campaign of genocide against their Armenian subjects which, between June 1915 and late 1917, led to the deaths of nearly 700,000 men, women and children, force-marched into the desert to die of starvation and thirst.

Turkey's decision to attack Russia in the Caucasus, its attempt against Egypt and its need to find forces to oppose the British expedition to the Tigris and Euphrates, created a military vacuum in the eastern Mediterranean that could be exploited by those with ambitions on its territory. Greece had such ambitions and tilted towards joining the Allies. It was deterred by its military weakness and its common border with pro-German Bulgaria. Italy's territorial ambitions lay towards Austria first, from which it had failed to "redeem" the Italian-speaking parts of the Tyrol and Slovenia in the last Austro-Italian war of 1866. Diplomatically, Italy was still a party to the Triple Alliance of 1906, binding her to Germany as well as Austria, but had wriggled out of its provisions in August by a narrow interpretation of its terms. The Italian navy, though recently modernised, was outgunned by the Allied Mediterranean fleets. Moreover, while Austria proved unwilling to offer any transfer of territory as a bribe, the Russians had made free with promises of Austrian territory which aroused hopes that the other Allies might do likewise. In March the Italian ambassador in London began negotiations with the British about what Italy might be offered and the talks proceeded into April. With Germany heavily engaged in France and Russia, Austria in the

Conrad von Hötzendorf (foreground, left) on the Italian front, May 1916. Italy's decision to enter the war on the side of France and Britain was motivated by its desire to liberate *Italia irridenta* (unredeemed Italy) from Austrian occupation. The principal Italian-speaking portions of the Austro-Hungarian empire lay in the Alpine regions of the Trentino, the Alte Adige and the Isonzo. Conrad, the Austrian Chief of Staff, reacted to Italy's attack with as much outrage as he had shown toward Serbia in 1914, regarding it as a betrayal of the pre-war Triple Alliance. Austria successfully repelled all Italian offensives and in October 1917 mounted, with the Germans, a counter-offensive at Caporetto which almost knocked Italy out of the war.

throes of a military crisis and Turkey overcommitted at the Asiatic borders of her empire, the reversion of alliance appeared not only risk-free but potentially highly profitable.

Territorial avarice prodded Italy towards a declaration of war throughout March and April. The German ambassador laboured to check the momentum, even offering Italy the Austrian territory Vienna had previously been unwilling to give. The majority of Italians, people and parliamentarians alike, had no enthusiasm for the dangerous adventure. The impetus came from Salandra, the Prime Minister, Sonnino, the Foreign Minister, the King, Victor Emmanuel II, and a collection of political and cultural revolutionaries, including Mussolini, then a socialist. The final stages of war preparations were conducted as a virtual conspiracy between Salandra, Sonnino and the King. On April 26 the Treaty of London was signed in secret with Britain, France and Russia, committing Italy to go to war within one month. On May 23 she declared war on Austria, though not yet against Germany.

From the outset things went badly, as any realistic appreciation should have warned. The whole of the Italian frontier with Austria rested against the outworks of the highest mountains in Europe, from the Tyrol in the west to the Julian Alps in the east, along which the enemy everywhere held the crests. At the western end, the Trentino, nine routes led through passes into the mountains; at the eastern end, where the Isonzo River cuts through the curtain, there is an avenue of advance. The Trentino, however, was a detached pocket of Austrian territory and so an unprofitable objective, while beyond the Isonzo valley the ground rises to form two desolate plateaux, the Bainsizza and the Carso.

Italy's plan for the opening of the war promised a rapid breakthrough that would avert losses. Choosing the Isonzo as the front of attack, Cadorna, the Chief of Staff, foresaw an advance through the gateways cut by the Rivers Drava and Sava to Klagenfurt and Agram (Zagreb) and thence into the heartland of the Austrian empire. Cadorna's hopes were misplaced. When the Italian army attacked in what would become known as the First—of twelve, though the future kindly hid that from those involved—Battle of the Isonzo, beginning on June 23, 1915, its advanced guards did little more than establish contact with the enemy front line. The Italian infantry, moving forward with great bravery but little tactical skill, were stopped in no-man's-land. Nearly two thousand were killed and twelve thousand wounded. The very high proportion of wounded was to prove a recurrent feature of the campaign, rock splintered by exploding shells becoming secondary projectiles which caused frequent injury, particularly to the head and eyes.

There were to be three more battles of the Isonzo in 1915, in July, October and November, each incurring a heavier toll of killed and wounded, 6,287, 10,733, 7,498 dead respectively, for almost no gain of ground at all. The Austrians also suffered heavily, since artillery had the same effect on defenders in their rock-cut trenches as on attackers in the open, and by the end of the Fourth Battle they counted 120,000 killed, wounded and missing. Nevertheless, they had held their positions and were beginning to receive reinforcements to strengthen the over-pressed trench garrisons which had borne the brunt of the first months of fight-

Count Luigi Cadorna (1850–1928), Italian Chief of Staff, May 1915–November 1917. Cadorna belonged to the professional military class of the old Kingdom of Savoy, which had led the campaign for Italian liberation and unification in the nineteenth century. A cold, northern Italian technocrat, he showed little understanding of the spirit of the army of the United Kingdom of Italy, whose soldiers were drawn in the majority from the south. He drove them pitilessly into eleven unsuccessful offensives on the Isonzo front, a harsh region of rock and mountain gradients where over half a million Italians perished in 1915–17 for little gain of territory. The twelfth Isonzo battle was a German-Austrian triumph, which threw the Italians back into the plains. Cadorna was relieved of command in the aftermath.

Opposite: An Austrian mountain unit excavating a rock face, Italian front, 1915. Both the Austrian and Italian armies deployed large numbers of specialist mountain troops, who sought to dominate positions by seizing vantage points at high altitude. These soldiers are well equipped, with climbing rope, alpenstocks and heavily nailed boots. Resupply was the main difficulty for mountain troops established at great height. A system of fixed ropes had to be installed to bring rations and ammunition up from lower ground.

An antiquated Austrian 280-mm howitzer in position on the Isonzo front, 1915. Although the Austrian arms industry produced some excellent modern equipment before 1914, notably the 305-mm howitzer, quantities were too small to equip all the units mobilised for war and much ancient material was pressed into service. Fortresses were stripped of their armament to send guns into the field. High-angle weapons, such as this, were essential to the artillery in the mountains, to enable fire to be directed out of valleys and over high ground.

ing. By the end of 1915 the Isonzo front had been stabilised and no longer posed a major hazard to the strategic provisions of the Central Powers.

Italy's decision to go to war had, in truth, been ill-timed. If taken earlier, during the desperate battles around Lemberg, which tried the Austrians so hard, or later, when the British army had developed its full fighting strength and the Russians had staged their military recovery, an Italian initiative might have precipitated a real crisis for the German and Austrian general staffs. As events fell out, the First Battle of the Isonzo was narrowly anticipated by a genuine German-Austrian victory, the breakthrough at Gorlice-Tarnow.

Gorlice-Tarnow was to be a second Limanowa-Lapanow, the battle that had saved Austria-Hungary from disaster in December 1914, but with far more dramatic consequences. Like Limanowa, Gorlice was launched on a narrow front, in the gap between the River Vistula and the Carpathian Mountains; unlike Limanowa, it was to be a German rather than an Austrian victory for, though Conrad von Hötzendorf contributed sizeable numbers to the striking force, its cutting edge was German and so was its direction. The plan was Austrian, nevertheless, in its conception. Conrad was aware that the Russian army, for all its superiority of numbers, was in severe material difficulty. Between January and April, its divisions on the Eastern Front, excepting the small number in the Caucasus, received from the factories only two million shells, at a time when preparatory bombardments with several hundred thousand shells were becoming the norm. In 1915, Russia's deficiency was serious, and compounded by inefficiency in distribution. For the Gorlice-Tarnow offensive, the Germans accumulated a stock of a million shells, a quantity available to the Russians only in a few fortified sectors, such as Novogeorgevisk and Kovno, where shells were stockpiled in quantities not disclosed by the fortress commanders to the general staff.

A German Jäger (light infantry) battalion, identifiable by their distinctive cloth-covered shakos, detraining on the Italian front. In October 1917 Germany lent several divisions of light infantry and mountain troops to Austria in order to mount the offensive at Caporetto (Karfreit), designed to inflict an irrecoverable defeat on the Italians, whose last (Eleventh) offensive on the Isonzo had tested the Austrian defenders to the limit. The Italian army was driven down into the plains of the Po, with heavy loss of life, and had to be saved from total collapse by the transfer of British and French troops from the Western Front.

The covert concentration of men, shells and guns on the Gorlice-Tarnow sector during April 1915 therefore predisposed towards a victory. The front was short, only thirty miles. On the Russian side, it was defended by the fourteen infantry divisions of Third Army; opposite the assault sector, between Gorlice and Tarnow, the front was held by only two divisions, the 9th and 31st. Against them the Germans had positioned some of the best of their troops, including the 1st and 2nd Guard Divisions. On the whole attack front, the Germans and Aus-

The attack at Zamecyskoberg by the 3rd Bavarian Infantry Regiment, May 2, 1915, a painting by Ludwig Putz of an episode of the German-Austrian offensives of Gorlice-Tarnow. Falkenhayn, who had succeeded von Moltke as German Chief of Staff the previous September, planned the Gorlice breakthrough as a means both of relieving Russian pressure on the Austrians and of achieving a decision outside the stalemated Western Front. Although a brilliant technical success, Gorlice did not prove a decisive victory, since the Russians could afford to surrender space without compromising their strategic position.

trians had a superiority of over three to two in men and a very large superiority in guns, generously supplied with ammunition. The plan for the offensive was Falkenhayn's, who entrusted its execution to Mackensen, victor in the East Prussian battles of 1914.

His operation order stressed the importance of a break-in rapid and deep enough to prevent the Russians bringing forward reserves to stem the flow. "The attack of Eleventh Army must, if its mission is to be fulfilled, be pushed forward fast . . . Two methods are essential: deep penetration by the infantry and a rapid follow-up by the artillery." These orders anticipated the tactics which would be employed with such success against the British and French in 1918. The Germans were as yet insufficiently skilled to make them work against the densely defended trench fronts in the west. Against the Russians in Poland, where barbed-wire barriers were thin, entrenched zones shallow and supporting artillery short of shell, they were to prove decisive. The preparatory bombardment, which began on the evening of May 1, devastated the Russian front line. By May 4 the German Eleventh Army had reached open country and was pressing forward. By May 13 the German-Austrian front had reached the outskirts of Przemysl in the

German soldiers resting on the banks of the Vistula, June 1915, after their advance into central Russian Poland, following the breakthrough at Gorlice-Tarnow in May. In the enormous spaces of the Eastern Front the effort to turn breakthrough into decisive victory was consistently frustrated by distance during 1915–16, however hard soldiers marched.

When threatened by encirclement, the enemy simply retreated into the hinterland. Some of the soldiers in the picture are wearing the coal-scuttle steel helmet, which had just been issued to combat troops. The group in the far right foreground, wearing white armbands, are the battalion's medical section.

south and Lodz in central Poland. On August 4 the Germans entered Warsaw and between August 17 and September 4 the four historic Russian frontier fortresses of Kovno, Novogeorgevisk, Brest Litovsk and Grodno were surrendered to the enemy. The number of Russian prisoners taken had risen to 325,000 and three thousand guns had also been lost.

The scale of the Austro-German victory encouraged Ludendorff during June to press for reinforcements that would enable him to mount a wide sweeping movement from the Baltic coast southward, cutting off the Russian armies as they retreated eastward and so, he argued, bringing the war in the east to an end. Falkenhayn, concerned as ever for the security of the Western Front, disagreed, demanding a net withdrawal of divisions from Poland to France. Conrad wanted to send troops to the Italian front. Mackensen was for persisting in his demonstrably successful offensive in the centre. He, with Falkenhayn's consent, got his way.

Outraged though Ludendorff was by what he saw as the supreme command's timid refusal to embrace the grand solution, Falkenhayn was reading the strategic situation more accurately than he. The Russians had been hard hit at Gorlice-Tarnow and had surrendered more ground than they would have freely chosen to do. By late July, however, they had accepted that the state of their army and its shortage of weapons and ammunition left them no recourse but retreat. The Germans had the impression of breasting forward against an undefended front. The Russians knew that they were deliberately retreating, shortening their front by withdrawal from the great bulge in central Poland and consequently length-

A soldier's snapshot taken during the Gorlice-Tarnow campaign. The handwritten inscription reads, "Cooling off just behind the front."

ening the enemy lines of communication as the Germans struggled to follow, across country deficient in railways and roads, particularly all-weather roads.

By September the Russians had, by abandoning the Polish salient, shortened their front by nearly half, from a thousand to six hundred miles, an economy in space which produced a major economy in force, releasing reserves to oppose the German advance along the Baltic coast and in the centre. As the autumn *rasputitsa,* the liquifying of the surface under seasonal rain, set in, the German advance came to a halt on a line that ran almost perpendicularly north-south from the Gulf of Riga on the Baltic to Czernowitz in the Carpathians. Most of Russian Poland had been lost but the territory of historic Russia remained intact and so, too, did the substance of the Tsar's army. It had suffered great losses, nearly a million dead, wounded and missing, while three-quarter of a million prisoners had been captured by the enemy. On September 1 the Tsar had taken the grave step of assuming executive supreme command himself, with Alexeyev as his Chief of Staff, the Grand Duke Nicholas being transferred to the Caucasus. All these outcomes of the German advance brought disadvantage to Russia's military situation. Nevertheless, the Russian army remained undefeated. Shell output was increasing—to 220,000 rounds a month in September—and its reserves of manpower still amounted to tens of millions. Four million men would be called up in 1916–17 but the real reserve approached eighteen million. Russia would be able to fight on. What it needed was a breathing space, while its armies re-organised and re-equipped. The Italian intervention had failed to divert significant numbers of Austrian troops. Serbia, whose unexpectedly successful resistance in 1914 had disrupted the Austrian mobilisation, could help no further. French and British plans for a great offensive on the Western Front could not be realised until 1916. Throughout the travails of 1915, Russian hopes for a strategic reversal, which would deter Turkey from further offensives and perhaps destroy her as a combatant, had therefore turned on the faraway campaign in the Dardanelles where, in April, Britain and France had opened an amphibious operation designed to break through to the Black Sea and Russia's southern seaports.

GALLIPOLI

The original proposal was French but the idea was then taken up by Winston Churchill, as First Lord of the Admiralty. By the spring of 1915 he had persuaded his Cabinet colleagues to allow a naval attempt on the Narrows, the Mediterranean mouth of the Dardanelles. The grand advance began on March 18, with sixteen battleships, twelve British, four French, mostly pre-dreadnoughts, but including the battlecruiser *Inflexible* and the almost irreplaceable superdreadnought *Queen Elizabeth,* arrayed in three lines abreast. They were preceded by a swarm of minesweepers and accompanied by flotillas of cruisers and destroyers. At first the armada made apparently irresistible progress. Between 11:30 in the morning and two in the afternoon it advanced nearly a mile, overcoming each fixed and mobile battery as it moved forward. Then, suddenly, at two o'clock, the balance of the battle swung the other way. The old French battleship *Bouvet,* falling back to allow the minesweepers to go forward, suddenly

Opposite top: Austrian soldiers kneeling as a military chaplain elevates the host. The "field mass" was an important ceremony in the Habsburg military tradition.

Opposite bottom: A derogatory display of puppets fabricated by German soldiers behind the lines in Poland, 1916. They represent the Tsar; President Poincaré; Lord Kitchener, the British War Minister; and the Italians, labelled "Tutti Frutti."

Left: The antiquated French battleship *Bouvet*, sunk by a mine during the naval attempt to force the Narrows of the Dardanelles at Gallipoli, May 18, 1915. *Bouvet*, launched in 1896, was a "fierce face" warship, designed to intimidate the enemy by its ugliness. It lacked underwater protection and its internal compartmentation was defective. The explosion was devastating, since there were no survivors, although the Narrows are only a mile wide at the point *Bouvet* sank. The decision to use only obsolete warships in the attempt on the Narrows made sense strategically, since any loss left the fighting strength of the modern dreadnought fleets untouched. The human consequences were, however, tragic. The small Turkish steamer which laid the mines with such devastating effect is today preserved at Chanakalle, opposite Gallipoli.

suffered an internal explosion and sank with all hands. Later it became known that, on the night of March 7, a line of mines had been laid by a small Turkish steamer parallel to the shore and had remained undetected. In the confusion that followed, the minesweepers, manned by civilian crews, began to fall back through the fleet and, as it manoeuvred, the old battleship *Irresistible* was damaged also and fell out of the line. Next *Ocean*, another old battleship, also suffered an internal explosion and soon afterwards the French pre-dreadnought *Suffren* was severely damaged by a plunging shell. As *Gaulois* and *Inflexible*, the modern battlecruiser, had been damaged earlier, Admiral de Robeck, the commander, now found himself with a third of his battle fleet out of action. By the end of the day, *Ocean* and *Irresistible* had, like *Bouvet*, sunk. *Inflexible, Suffren* and *Gaulois* were out of action and *Albion, Agamemnon, Lord Nelson* and *Charlemagne* had suffered damage. As darkness fell, de Robeck drew his fleet away. The ten lines of mines laid across the Narrows, numbering 373 in all, remained unswept and most of the shore batteries, though they had shot off all their heavy shell, preserved their guns.

By March 22, when Admiral de Robeck met General Sir Ian Hamilton, the nominated commander of the military force, to discuss whether the naval advance should be resumed, it was quickly agreed that it could not, without the assistance of strong landing parties. Bold spirits, who included Commodore Roger Keyes, commanding the minesweepers, were for pressing on regardless of loss. Keyes believed the Turks were demoralised and out of ammunition. The more cautious officers thought more risk-taking must lead to more losses. The cautious party prevailed. By the end of March, the decision for landings had been taken and the only question remaining to be settled was where the landings should take place and in what strength. The intelligence service estimated that the Turks had 170,000 men available. That was an exaggerated guess; Liman von Sanders, their German commander, had six weak divisions with 84,000 men to guard 150 miles of coastline. There were, however, only five Allied divisions in the Mediterranean Expeditionary Force—the 29th, Royal Naval, 1st Australian and the Australian and New Zealand Divisions, and the *Corps expéditionnaire d'Orient*, of divisional strength provided by the French. From a hastily established base in Mudros Bay on the nearby Greek island of Lemnos, they would be embarked as soon as possible and got ashore. In the month between the naval defeat of March 22 and the eventual D-Day of April 25, an extraordinary improvisation was carried forward.

Nothing was more improvised than the plan. It had to be based on guesses as to where landings would be least opposed and do most good. Along much of the seaward side of the peninsula, steep cliffs descend to the water. Only at one place was there a practicable beach, which was allotted to ANZAC—the acronym for the Australian and New Zealand troops. The only other possibilities were at Cape Helles itself, where there is a chain of narrow beaches giving onto the summit of the headland. As it could be covered all round by fire from the fleet standing offshore, Helles was chosen as the objective of the 29th Division. The Royal Naval Division was not to land at once, but make a demonstration at Bulair and the French were to do likewise on the Asiatic shore, at Kum Kale, near Troy, before

Opposite bottom: H.M.S. *Queen Elizabeth*, the Royal Navy's most modern battleship, shelling Turkish positions, May 18, 1915. Its inclusion in the naval effort to force the Narrows violated the principle that only old warships should be used.

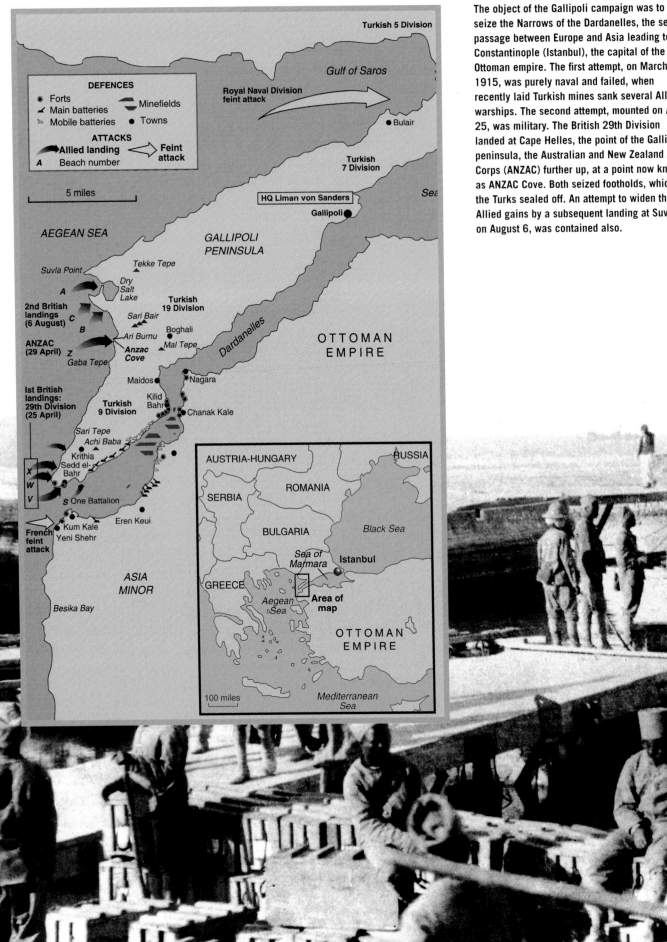

The object of the Gallipoli campaign was to seize the Narrows of the Dardanelles, the sea passage between Europe and Asia leading to Constantinople (Istanbul), the capital of the Ottoman empire. The first attempt, on March 18, 1915, was purely naval and failed, when recently laid Turkish mines sank several Allied warships. The second attempt, mounted on April 25, was military. The British 29th Division landed at Cape Helles, the point of the Gallipoli peninsula, the Australian and New Zealand Army Corps (ANZAC) further up, at a point now known as ANZAC Cove. Both seized footholds, which the Turks sealed off. An attempt to widen the Allied gains by a subsequent landing at Suvla, on August 6, was contained also.

DEFENCES

- Forts
- Main batteries
- Mobile batteries
- Minefields
- Towns

ATTACKS

- Allied landing
- Feint attack
- *A* Beach number

5 miles

Turkish 5 Division

Gulf of Saros

Royal Naval Division
feint attack

Bulair

Turkish
7 Division

Sea

HQ Liman von Sanders

Gallipoli

AEGEAN SEA

GALLIPOLI
PENINSULA

Suvla Point

Tekke Tepe

Dry
Salt
Lake

A

2nd British
landings
(6 August)

C

B

Sari Bair

Turkish
19 Division

Ari Burnu

Boghali

ANZAC
(29 April)

Z

Anzac
Cove

Mal Tepe

Gaba Tepe

Dardanelles

OTTOMAN
EMPIRE

Maidos

Nagara

1st British
landings:
29th Division
(25 April)

Kilid
Bahr

Turkish
9 Division

Chanak Kale

Sari Tepe

Achi Baba

Krithia

X

Sedd el-
Bahr

W

V

S One Battalion

Eren Keui

French feint
attack

Kum Kale

Yeni Shehr

ASIA
MINOR

Besika Bay

AUSTRIA-HUNGARY

RUSSIA

SERBIA

ROMANIA

BULGARIA

Black Sea

Sea of
Marmara

Istanbul

GREECE

Aegean
Sea

Area of
map

OTTOMAN
EMPIRE

Mediterranean
Sea

100 miles

French Senegalese troops unloading stores from the *River Clyde*, run ashore at V Beach on April 25 as a landing ship, later used as a pier. The sand spit built out to the ship can still be seen.

The landing from the *River Clyde*, April 25, 1915. Holes had been cut in the bow of the ship leading to gangplanks, down which the soldiers of the British battalions, from the Hampshire Regiment and the Royal Munster Fusiliers, charged onto the beach. The bridge between the ship and the beach was formed by lighters. Perfectly sited Turkish machine guns caught the Munsters and Hampshires as they emerged and caused hundreds of casualties. Two sailors who stood in the water to hold the lighters in place as the infantry tried to land were awarded the Victoria Cross, Britain's highest award for bravery. The survivors found shelter under the lip of V Beach and eventually drove off the Turkish defenders, who numbered only thirty. They had killed several hundred British soldiers.

landing later alongside the 29th Division. Five beaches at Helles were selected, lettered, Y, X, W, V and S.

In retrospect, it is possible to see that Hamilton's plan could not work. The only certainly successful scheme would have required the deployment of a force large enough to land at and hold Bulair, Helles and the Asiatic shore simultaneously. Such a force was not available nor could it have been assembled speedily enough to bring urgent aid to the Russians. Hamilton's only hope of achieving success in the essentially diversionary mission he had been given, therefore, lay in the Turks mismanaging their response to the landings.

The soldiers of the 29th Division and ANZAC expected to succeed. Those of the 29th Division were regulars of the pre-war army. The ANZACs, staging through Egypt to Europe, were citizen soldiers, products of the most comprehensive militia system in the world. Out of a male population of half a million, New Zealand could provide fifty thousand trained soldiers aged under twenty-five. Australia furnished proportionate numbers. Together they were to create units of formidable offensive power, as the Germans would later acknowledge and the Turks were soon to discover. Before dawn on April 25, two hundred merchant ships, supported by most of the bombardment fleet that had been turned back from the Narrows on March 18, stood in towards ANZAC Cove and Cape Helles. *Queen Elizabeth* was flagship and headquarters, though its 15-inch guns were also to join in the preliminary bombardment by the older battleships. They were also troop carriers, however; from them, and other warships, the landing parties were to move to the beaches in "tows," lines of rowing boats pulled in column behind steam pinnaces. As the shore shelved, the tows were to be cast off and

An artist's impression of the Australian and New Zealand landings at ANZAC Cove, April 25, 1915. The ground behind the cove, which is broken up into steep gullies and dead ends, rises at forty-five degrees or more and, in 1915, was covered with thick scrub. Many of the ANZACs lost direction in the confusing conditions. The Turkish counter-attackers, coming downhill, were able to choke off the ANZACs' advance and deny them the crests. Both sides then dug in, the prelude to bitter trench fighting which lasted until the end of the year.

the boats rowed ashore by bluejackets. Only one specialised landing ship had been included, the collier *River Clyde*, which was to be grounded off V Beach. Holes had been cut in its bow through which the soldiers of the Royal Munster Fusiliers and the Hampshire Regiment were to run down gangplanks on to lighters and so onto the beaches, under the covering fire of machine guns positioned behind sandbags on the forecastle.

The bombardment began at dawn and soon the tows for all beaches were moving inshore. For reasons never satisfactorily explained, perhaps human error, perhaps a last-minute but inadequately communicated change of plan, the forty-eight boats of the ANZAC tows touched ground a mile north of the beach originally selected, under steep slopes that give onto a succession of ridges, rising in three jumbled steps above the cove. To north and south, high ground comes down to the sea, so that ANZAC Cove takes the form of a tiny amphitheatre dominated on three sides by high ground. Unless the Australians and New Zealanders could reach the crests before the enemy, all their positions, including the beach, would be overlooked, with calamitous effect on subsequent operations. The ANZACs knew the importance of getting high quickly and, after an almost unopposed landing, began climbing the ridges in front of them as fast as their feet could take them. The reason their landing had been unopposed soon, however, became apparent. The enemy were few because the Turks had dismissed the likelihood of a landing in such an inhospitable spot. One crest was succeeded by another even higher. Organisation dissolved in the thick

Below: A British 60-pounder at full recoil, near Cape Helles, Gallipoli. The gunner to the right of the piece has just pulled the firing lanyard; the soldier in the foreground is adjusting the fuse of the next shell. The 60-pounder was the principal equipment of the medium batteries of the British divisional artillery throughout the war. Another gun of the battery can be seen on the skyline. The main role of medium batteries was "counter-battery fire," attack on the enemy's artillery.

Right: A Turkish field gun in a camouflaged position on the Gallipoli peninsula. The Turkish artillery was equipped with German guns, chiefly the Krupp 77-mm. Its officers were well trained, often by German military missions, and performed efficiently against their Allied opponents.

scrub, which separated group from group and prevented a coordinated sweep to the top. If even some of the twelve thousand ashore could have reached the summits of the Sari Bair ridge, two and a half miles above ANZAC Cove, they would have been able to look down on the Narrows. Their maximum depth of penetration by early afternoon, however, was only a mile and a half and, at that precipitous point, they began to come under counter-attack by the assembling Turkish defenders.

Ten miles south, at Cape Helles, day had also broken to the crash of heavy naval gunfire, under which the ninety-six boats of the tows and the crammed *River Clyde* moved shoreward. On the flanks, at S, Y and X Beaches, the attackers met little or no opposition and soon established themselves ashore. Across the water, at Kum Kale on the Asiatic shore, the French also found their landings unopposed. The Turks in the vicinity were disorganised and badly led. The British landing parties sunned themselves, made tea, humped stores up from the shore and wandered about in the pretty country-side, as if the war was miles away. At W and V Beaches, just down the coast, the Lancashire Fusiliers and the Dublins, Munsters and Hampshires were fighting for their lives and dying in hundreds. The two beaches are separated by the headland of Cape Helles itself. To the west, on W Beach, ever afterwards known as Lancashire Landing, the Lancashire Fusiliers were struck by a hail of rifle and machine-gun fire a hundred yards from the shore. Most of the boats beached, nevertheless, only to find themselves in front of barbed wire at the water's edge, behind which Turks in trenches were shooting every man who rose from the sea.

Amid these ghastly scenes, a few Lancashire Fusiliers managed to struggle through the wire and find a way round. Out of the 950 who landed, over five hundred were killed or wounded but the survivors pressed inland. On the other side of the headland, at V Beach, the scenes were even worse. The Dublin Fusiliers thought themselves unopposed until, as the boats touched bottom, they fell under a hail of bullets. As the *River Clyde* grounded and the Hampshires and Munster Fusiliers struggled to find a way out of the ship, four Turkish machine guns opened fire. The columns on the gangplanks tumbled one after another to fall bleeding into the sea. Yet some survived, found shelter under the lip of the beach, gathered their force and drove the Turks from their trenches.

What should have alarmed the British commanders—Hamilton of the Mediterranean Expeditionary Force (M.E.F.), Hunter-Weston of the 29th Division, Birdwood of ANZAC—was that the injuries done to their brave soldiers had been the

Above: British soldiers examining the wreck of the 9.4-inch gun at the Turkish Fort No. 1, above V Beach, after the landings of April 25, 1915. The fort was destroyed by fire from H.M.S. *Queen Elizabeth* during the preliminary bombardment. Gallipoli had been heavily fortified by the Turks in the pre-war period. In the Italo-Turkish war of 1911–12, the Italian navy had attempted to penetrate the waterway, but was turned back at the Narrows. During February and early March 1915, the British landed marines at several points and bombarded the forts, achieving little but compromising surprise. The Turkish defences were still largely intact on April 25, apart from Fort No. 1. Its gun and emplacement are still easily recognisable today.

Opposite top: Mustapha Kemal (1881–1939), the victor of the Gallipoli campaign. Kemal, a regular army officer, was an early adherent of the cause of the Young Turks, who sought to modernise the Ottoman empire and seized power in 1908. In 1915, however, he was still only an obscure divisional commander. His 19th Division, however, happened to be stationed on the Gallipoli peninsula, just above the spot at which the ANZACs landed on April 25. Rapidly appraising the situation, he brought reinforcements forward, counter-attacked and contained the ANZAC landing. His rise thereafter was inexorable. During the collapse of the Ottoman regime, he took command of Turkish forces in the war against the Greeks, re-established Turkish independence and became the first President of the Turkish Republic. As President he added "Ataturk" to his name, meaning, appropriately, "Father of the Turks."

Below: Australian soldiers, of the 2nd Light Horse, at Queen's Post, Gallipoli. One is observing the Turkish positions through a periscope, another is using a periscope-sighted rifle.

work of so few of the enemy. The number of troops deployed by Liman von Sanders on the Gallipoli peninsula was only a fraction of his force, the rest being dispersed between Bulair and Kum Kale, between Europe and Asia. The assault area was held by a single division, the 9th. In places there were single platoons of fifty men, in some places fewer men or none: at Y Beach none, at X twelve men, at S a single platoon. Even at ANZAC Cove there was only one company of two hundred men, while V and W Beaches were defended by single platoons. The massacre of the Lancashire, Dublin and Munster Fusiliers and the Hampshires had been inflicted by fewer than a hundred desperate men, survivors of the naval bombardment, and killing so that they should not be killed.

Some of the Turks, nevertheless, had run away; those at Kum Kale surrendered to the French in hundreds before the withdrawal on April 26. More might have turned tail on the peninsula had not reserves been close at hand and under the command of an officer of outstanding ability and determination, Mustapha Kemal. Kemal, reacting instantly to the sound of the naval bombardment, forced the march of his 19th Division, himself at the head. Having reached the crest of Sari Bair, the dominating ground that was the ANZAC objective, "the scene which met our eyes was a most interesting one. To my mind it was the vital moment of the [campaign]." He could see warships offshore and, in the foreground, a party of Turks of the 9th Division running towards him. They told him that they were out of ammunition and he ordered them to lie down and fix bayonets. "At the same time I sent [my] orderly officer . . . off to the rear to bring up to where I was at the double those men of the [57th Regiment] who were advancing [behind me] . . . When the men fixed their bayonets and lay down . . . the enemy lay down also . . . It was about 10:00 hours when the 57th Regiment began its attack."

The Australians had seen Kemal on the crest and fired at him, without effect. Their failure to hit him and to push forward to the top in those minutes may indeed be judged "the vital moment of the campaign," for Kemal, as soon as his troops were to hand, began a series of counter-attacks against the Australian bridgehead that lasted until nightfall. Almost everywhere the Australians were overlooked, and a constant rain of enemy bullets sent a steady stream of wounded back to the narrow beach, an only slightly more numerous stream of reinforcements coming up to replace them. That scene, wounded

down, fresh troops up, was to be repeated every day the campaign lasted and remained every ANZAC's most abiding memory of those precipitous hillsides.

By May 4 both sides at ANZAC Cove were exhausted. The Turks had lost fourteen thousand men, ANZAC nearly ten thousand. After a final attack on May 4, Kemal recognised that the enemy was too tenacious to be driven into the sea, and ordered his men to dig in. On the lower ground at Cape Helles, the days after the landing had also been filled with savage fighting, as the 29th Division, and the French withdrawn from Kum Kale, struggled to connect the beachheads and push the line inland. On April 26, the castle and village of Sedd el-Bahr were

captured and next afternoon there was a general advance. The objective was the village of Krithia, four miles inland. A deliberate assault was made on April 28 and another on May 6. Neither reached the village, despite the arrival of an Indian brigade from Egypt and parts of the Royal Naval Division. By May 8 the British were stuck just short of Krithia, on a line that ran from Y Beach to a little north of S Beach, three miles from Cape Helles.

There it remained throughout an unbearably hot summer, balmy autumn and freezing early winter. The War Council sent more troops, first one and then three more Territorial divisions, then three Kitchener divisions. The French also added, reluctantly, to the expeditionary corps, and in August the 2nd Australian Division and 2nd Mounted Division were sent to Lemnos. To break the stalemate,

Opposite: The 1st Battalion, Australian Imperial Force, at Steele's Post, above ANZAC Cove, May 3, 1915. The terrain on the west side of the Gallipoli peninsula above ANZAC Cove is steep, in places sheer. The Australians survived by choosing positions sheltered by higher crests from Turkish fire and by constructing scrapes and dugouts. They also had to shelter during daylight from the fierce Mediterranean sun, stretching blankets and groundsheets over their rifle pits. The front line lies above the top of this photograph, and the men seen here are waiting to go up. Day after day, there was a constant flow of reinforcements up, wounded down. The line was held, nevertheless, until the moment of evacuation in January 1916.

Right: Dead Turks in no-man's-land at Aryne, on the Gallipoli peninsula. British troops are arranging the bodies for burial during a local truce, on May 24, 1915. The Turks, from Kemal's 19th Division, are casualties of the fighting for Krithia, the main village immediately north of Cape Helles. The British soldiers are probably from the 29th Division, which made the landing on April 25. Despite the ferocity of the fighting, both sides observed traditional rules of war during the campaign. "Johnny Turk" was regarded as an honourable opponent by British and ANZACs alike and, after the war, Kemal Ataturk raised a monument to the dead of both sides, inviting forgiveness and reconciliation.

Opposite top: Australians making grenades out of empty ration cans at Gallipoli. Before the issue of government hand grenades, the Mills bomb, British trench garrisons made their own, usually filling old meat or vegetable cans with explosives and fixing a friction or percussion fuse.

Opposite bottom: The 2nd Battalion, Australian Imperial Force, about to charge at the Second Battle of Krithia, May 8, 1915. The attacks on Krithia were intended to enlarge the Cape Helles bridgehead and link up with ANZAC. The efforts did not succeed.

A French 75-mm battery in action near Sedd el-Bahr during the Third Battle of Krithia, June 4, 1915. The French made a large contribution to the Gallipoli campaign. This section of colonial artillery (*bigors*) is a model of their professionalism. The gun is perfectly positioned, with its limber to the left, the ready-use ammunition neatly arranged and a pile of reloads stacked to the rear. The gun commander is about to give the order to fire.

A supply dump below Plugge's Plateau, ANZAC Cove, Gallipoli, 1915. There being no port on the peninsula, supplies had to be run directly onto the open beaches and then carried by man or mule up to the front line. Much of the Allied-held area was under Turkish observation and little was protected from Turkish fire. The wounded had to be evacuated as quickly as possible, away from the danger of being re-wounded in the advanced dressing stations, one of which is visible center left. Enormous quantities of stores were abandoned when the Allied footholds at ANZAC Cove, Suvla and Cape Helles were evacuated in January 1916. The men, however, were got away almost without loss, by a remarkable deception plan, the only successful episode in the whole tragic campaign. ANZAC Cove, with its eleven hauntingly beautiful military cemeteries, has become a place of national pilgrimage for present-day Australians and New Zealanders.

General Sir Ian Hamilton decided on a fresh amphibious assault north of ANZAC Cove at Suvla Bay. It took place on August 7 but Kemal, now appointed to command all Turkish troops in the northern sector, was soon on the scene determined to pen the Allies close to the sea. By August 9 he had succeeded and no addition of force by the British could gain ground. The attackers and defenders dug in and Suvla Bay became simply the third shallow and static enclave maintained by the Allies on the Gallipoli peninsula. The Turks now had fourteen divisions in place against an exactly equal number of Allied. There had been calls within the Dardanelles Committee of the War Council for evacuation earlier. In November they became overwhelming. Between December 28 and January 8, 1916, the garrison began to slip away, little troubled by the Turks who had failed to detect that a complete evacuation was in progress. By January 9, ANZAC Cove, Suvla and Cape Helles were empty. The great adventure was over.

The Turks had probably lost 300,000 men killed, wounded and missing. The Allies had lost 265,000. The 29th Division had lost its strength twice over, while the New Zealanders, of whom 8,566 served on the peninsula, recorded 14,720 casualties, including wounded who returned two or three times. Yet of all the contingents which went to Gallipoli, it was the Australians who were most marked by the experience and who remembered it most deeply, remember it indeed to this day. Citizens of an only recently federated country in 1915, they went as soldiers of the forces of six separate states. They came back, it is so often said, members of one nation. The ANZAC ordeal began to be commemorated at home in the following year. Today the dawn ceremony on April 25 has become a sacred event, observed by all Australians of every age and ANZAC Cove is a shrine. The Gallipoli peninsula, now preserved as a Turkish national park, in which a memorial erected by Mustapha Kemal Ataturk magnanimously recalls the sufferings of both sides, has reverted to nature, a beautiful but deserted remoteness on the Mediterranean shore.

Nothing at Gallipoli can fail to touch the emotions of those who descend from the soldiers of any nation that struggled there. The village of Kum Kale has disappeared but the overgrown cemetery of Muslim headstones remains to mark the furthest limit of the French advance of April 25. The war cemetery above W Beach is full of the dead of Lancashire Landing, while at Sedd el-Bahr the Dublin and Munster Fusiliers lie in graves only a few yards above the water's edge where they gave their lives for a state many of their countrymen, at Easter 1916, would confront with rebellion. Most poignant of all Gallipoli memorials, perhaps, is that of the white marble column on the Cape Helles headland, glimpsed across the water from the walls of Troy on a bright April morning. It is difficult to say which epic Homer might have thought the more heroic.

"The Australian and New Zealand troops have indeed proved themselves worthy sons of the Empire."
GEORGE R.I.

A patriotic postcard celebrating the ANZAC effort. The Australian and New Zealand contingents were en route to Britain in 1914 but were disembarked in Egypt for training. They were therefore on hand when the decision was taken to mount landings on Gallipoli. After the withdrawal in January 1916 the New Zealand and Australian divisions went on to fight in France where, in 1918, they became a principal offensive element in the British Expeditionary Force's final assault on the German line. Both countries made exceptional contributions to the war effort. Over half the eligible male population of New Zealand served, most of them as volunteers, and 17,000 were killed out of 124,000 enlisted. Among Australians, 60,000 were killed and 212,000 wounded, out of 332,000 enlisted, the highest proportion of casualties suffered by any army during the war.

SERBIA AND SALONIKA

General Sarrail and his staff at Salonika, April 1916. While the Gallipoli campaign was failing, Britain and France agreed to open another subsidiary front in northern Greece, with its base at the port of Salonika (Thessaloniki). The troops initially came from the Gallipoli force. The intention was to assist Serbia and attack Bulgaria, which had recently joined the German-Austrian alliance. In the event, the Serbs were defeated before the Salonika expeditionary force became effective. The Allies nevertheless continued to reinforce Salonika, until 100,000 soldiers were concentrated in an enormous fortified camp. The Salonika army achieved little throughout the war, though suffering very high casualties through sickness. The soldiers in the picture include Russians, French, British and Serbs, the Serbian army being transferred to Salonika after its escape to Corfu in the winter of 1915–16.

Gallipoli had failed as a military campaign. It had also failed in its secondary purposes, the bringing of relief to Serbia, encouraging Greece to join the Allies and deterring Bulgaria from joining the Central Powers. Moreover, the magnitude of the German victory at Gorlice-Tarnow in May impressed the Bulgarians and a month later they entered into negotiations. The dual stalemate on the Italian and Gallipoli fronts convinced the political leadership of Bulgaria that their best interests lay in alliance with the Central Powers and on September 6, 1915, four treaties were signed. The terms included financial subsidy and future transfer of territory at Serbia's expense; more critically and immediately, Bulgaria undertook to go to war against Serbia within thirty days. The purpose of the campaign, in concert with Germany and Austria, was "decisively to defeat the Serbian army." It was at once transmitted to Mackensen, the victor of Gorlice-Tarnow, who proceeded to assemble an army. Serbia ordered general mobilisation on September 22.

Since the failure of the second Austrian offensive in December 1914, the Serbian army had remained deployed on the northern and eastern frontiers. Mackensen's plan was to extend the front of attack far south, where Bulgaria could force the Serbs to dissipate their numbers in the defence of Macedonia. They had only eleven weak divisions, particularly weak in artillery. Against them the Bulgarians could deploy six divisions, the Austrians seven, and the Germans ten. The odds overwhelmingly disfavoured the Serbs. Their commander, Putnik, disposed of 200,000 men, of very varying quality, Mackensen of 330,000, with 1,200

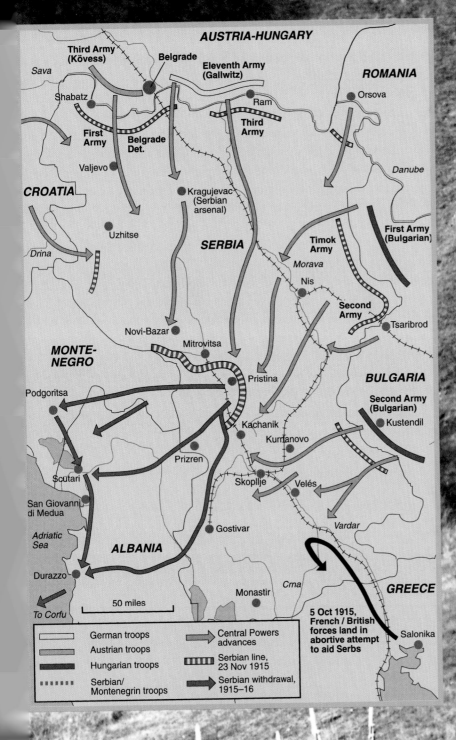

AUSTRIA-HUNGARY

Third Army (Kövess)
Belgrade
Eleventh Army (Gallwitz)
ROMANIA
Sava
Shabatz
Orsova
Ram
First Army
Belgrade Det.
Third Army
CROATIA
Valjevo
Danube
Kragujevac (Serbian arsenal)
Uzhitse
SERBIA
First Army (Bulgarian)
Drina
Timok Army
Morava
Nis
Second Army
Novi-Bazar
Tsaribrod
MONTE-NEGRO
Mitrovitsa
Podgoritsa
Pristina
BULGARIA
Second Army (Bulgarian)
Kachanik
Kustendil
Scutari
Prizren
Kurfianovo
San Giovanni di Medua
Skopllje
Velés
Adriatic Sea
ALBANIA
Gostivar
Vardar
Durazzo
Monastir
Crna
GREECE

50 miles

To Corfu

5 Oct 1915, French / British forces land in abortive attempt to aid Serbs

Salonika

German troops	→	Central Powers advances
Austrian troops	▥	Serbian line, 23 Nov 1915
Hungarian troops	→	Serbian withdrawal, 1915–16
Serbian/ Montenegrin troops		

In October 1915 the Germans agreed to assist Austria-Hungary in defeating Serbia, which had successfully resisted Austrian invasion in 1914. Bulgaria, recently allied, joined in. The Serbs skilfully disengaged and fought three delaying actions but their army was eventually driven out of the country and forced to flee through the mountains of Montenegro and Albania to the coast, whence it was evacuated first to Corfu and then Salonika. In October the British 10th and French 156th Divisions, transferred from Gallipoli, attacked the Bulgarians from Salonika but were repelled. The Salonika front then became static until the last months of 1918.

Bulgarian troops attacking a Serbian position, October 1915. The Serbian line can be seen to the right of the smoke from the supporting artillery barrage, in a photograph that unusually shows both attacking and defending troops.

guns to the Serbs' 300. Serbia's only hope of altering the balance lay in attracting Allied troops into the Balkans, via the Greek port of Salonika. On the day Bulgaria mobilised, the Greek Prime Minister, Eleutherios Venizelos, advised the British and French governments that if they would send 150,000 troops to Salonika, he was confident of bringing his country into the war on their side, under the terms of an existing Serbo-Greek treaty.

Venizelos viewed the organisation of aid to Serbia as both realistic and essential. He had, however, overestimated the strength of his position at home. King

Left: British troops landing on a beach near Salonika from boats rowed by British blue-jackets. The British and French presence at Salonika was only doubtfully legal, since the Greek government was divided over the issue of entry into the First World War. The Allies chose to regard the policy of the Prime Minister as legitimate, rather than that of the King, and simply walked in. The intervention proved ill-judged, for their Salonika army achieved nothing. Its soldiers would have been better employed in Mesopotamia or Palestine, perhaps even on the Western Front.

Opposite: Serbian soldiers conveying the Voivode Putnik out of Serbia in a sedan chair during the retreat to the Adriatic in December 1915. Radomir Putnik (1847–1917) had led the Serbian armies in the First and Second Balkan Wars of 1912–13 against Turkey and Bulgaria respectively and was a war leader (Voivode) of outstanding ability. In July 1914 he was taking a health cure at an Austrian resort. The Emperor Franz Josef, as an act of personal courtesy, allowed him to return home. The act was strategically ill-judged. Putnik, a brilliant tactician, directed the operations which defeated both Austrian offensives against Serbia in 1914. His conduct of operations in 1915 failed before the overwhelming strength of the German-Austrian-Bulgarian attack but the army was saved. Putnik's failing health was broken by the ordeal of the winter retreat and he died at Nice in May 1917. He was one of the few truly great soldiers of the First World War.

Constantine was not only the Kaiser's brother-in-law but believed his kingdom's interests best served by preserving its neutrality. On October 5 he dismissed Venizelos from office. The Allies, however, took matters into their own hands. Greece, as a neutral without the means to resist, was obliged to acquiesce in the arrival of a Franco-British (and later also Russian) expeditionary force, formed in part by withdrawals from Gallipoli, in the transformation of Salonika into a vast Allied base and in the despatch in October of an Allied advance guard into Serbian Macedonia.

Its arrival came too late to assist the Serbs. On October 5 the Germans and Austrians began a bombardment across the Sava and Danube, and the bridging of both rivers on October 7. As agreed a month earlier, the Bulgarians crossed the frontier from the east on October 11, simultaneously sending troops south to oppose the British and French in Macedonia, while the Germans and Austrians pressed down from the north. The plan, logical on paper, took insufficient account of the Serbs' pre-modern capacity to endure hardship. Hard as the Germans and Austrians pressed their pursuit after the fall of Belgrade, they found it impossible to corner the Serbs against any obstacle. Thrice they seemed to have succeeded, thrice the Serbs disengaged and slipped away, towards the brother-Serb principality of Montenegro, Albania and the sea. Only an army of natural mountaineers could have survived the passage through Montenegro, and many did not. Of the 200,000 who had set out, however, no less than 140,000 survived to cross in early December into Albania. Thence by ship, the survivors, with thousands of miserable Austrian prisoners forced to accompany them on the retreat, were transferred to Corfu. In their wake the Austrian Third Army took possession of

Serbian cavalry retreating, December 1915. The Serbian army was largely an infantry force and the Serbian military system embraced all male Serbs fit enough to serve. Centuries of resistance to Turkish oppression had hardened the population to military duty. Enlistment was compulsory at the age of seventeen in the junior class of the reserve, leading to two years of full-time service at twenty-one, further reserve service from twenty-three to forty-six and a final obligation in the senior reserve from forty-six to fifty. White-haired "grandfathers" were a familiar element in Serbian regiments, valued for their experience, hardihood and example. Among all the combatant nations of the war, the Serbs stood out as the supreme warrior race, tough, wily and apparently indefatigable.

A French artist's impression of the Serbian retreat through Montenegro, December 3, 1915. Many civilians accompanied the army on its gruelling march, being unwilling to submit to Austrian or Bulgarian rule of their occupied country, and as many as 200,000 are estimated to have died in the winter conditions. The Serbian government also accompanied the army and Serbia's fierce politics were continued in exile in Salonika, between those who favoured the continuation of a small ethnic Serbia and the supporters of a union of all South Slavs (Yugoslavia). Eventually the Yugoslav ideal prevailed, leading to the creation after the war of a Kingdom of Serbs, Croats, and Slovenes, largely formed out of former Austro-Hungarian territories. Its monarchy, however, was Serb and disputes between the three ethnic groups persisted up to the outbreak of the Second World War, as they do to this day.

Montenegro, while the Bulgarians turned back from the border to join in the counter-offensive against the Allied invasion of Macedonia.

Other Bulgarian troops had already blunted the French and British effort to relieve pressure on the Serbs in Macedonia and by December 12 the two Allied divisions that had crossed the Serbian frontier in October were back again on Greek territory. The British government, correctly judging the Salonika project useless, now pressed the French to agree to the withdrawal of the Allied troops altogether. The French demurred. Briand, who had replaced Viviani as Premier in October, had been pro-Salonika from the start and made support for the project a test of loyalty to himself and his government. He resuscitated his original arguments for the expedition: that it kept Greece and Romania neutral and that it posed a threat to the Austrian flank in the Balkans, which might be enlarged as later circumstances allowed. Between December 1 and 6, at Calais, at G.Q.G. at Chantilly, and in London, the British and French political and military leaders took decisions for and against Salonika in rapid succession. The British nearly prevailed. Eventually, however, they were persuaded, by fear of provoking a collapse of Briand's government and by the heartfelt plea of the Russians to sustain a western pressure in the eastern theatre of operations, to leave their troops in Salonika after all, useless as their presence was.

The year of 1915 thus ended on an inconclusive note. In the external theatres of war, the Western Allies had prevailed. Germany's colonies had been occupied, its colonial forces largely overcome and its cruising squadrons destroyed. Its Turkish ally had won a great, if local, victory at Gallipoli but had failed in its attempts to make either British Egypt or the Russian Caucasus diversionary fronts and was itself threatened by the British penetration of its Arab possessions in Mesopotamia. In southern Europe, Serbia had been overwhelmed and Bulgaria drawn into the Central alliance but Greece had been appropriated as an Anglo-French base and Italy persuaded to open an anti-Austrian front at its head of the Adriatic. On the two great fronts, Western and Eastern, the balance of success appeared to lie with the Central Powers. In France, the Germans had repelled every attempt by the French and British to break the trench line and had inflicted heavy losses on their enemies as the price of their efforts. On the Eastern Front, they had won a spectacular victory, at Gorlice-Tarnow, and pressed the Tsar's armies back to, and in some places, beyond the frontiers of old Russia. Poland and the Baltic coastline were theirs and the danger of a Russian invasion of Austria-Hungary across the crests of the Carpathians had been averted, apparently permanently. On the other hand, the fighting power of the Russian army had not been destroyed, the French army had sustained its aggressive spirit and the British army was transforming itself from a maritime expeditionary force of marginal significance into an instrument of continental offensive power. The coming year of 1916, all parties to the war recognised, would bring crisis on land, east and west, and at sea also. It would be a year of great battles between armies and fleets.

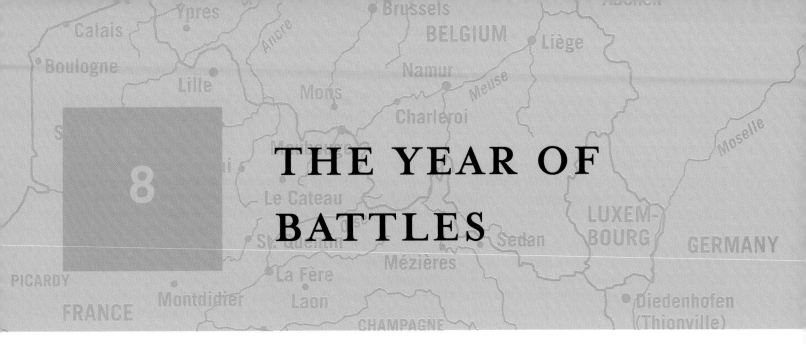

THE YEAR OF BATTLES

8

Italian sappers cutting through enemy trenches and defences, 1916, by Achille Beltrame.

WAR AT SEA

In a phrase to become famous, Winston Churchill told Admiral Jellicoe that he was "the only man who could lose the war in an afternoon." What he meant was that, if Jellicoe's Grand Fleet were beaten in the North Sea, the German High Seas Fleet could break out to dominate the world's oceans. It was the worst threat that Britain faced.

Germany's naval strategy, with a smaller navy, was to threaten Britain with "risk," keeping its squadrons always at high alert, in the hope of creating a situation in which the British would be caught at a disadvantage. Admiral Scheer, the High Seas Fleet commander, risked sorties into the Heligoland Bight in August 1914 and the Dogger Bank in January 1915 but was on both occasions driven back to harbour, the second time with serious loss. He nevertheless quickly resumed the policy of taking the fleet to sea in the search for action. He made two sorties in February and March 1916 and four in April and May; in April he succeeded in reaching the English east coast and, in a repetition of the raids of 1914, bombarding Lowestoft. The demonstration caused dismay in Britain but emphasised once again that, while the Grand Fleet at Scapa Flow closed the exit from the North Sea, and with the Battle Cruiser Fleet located at Rosyth, all that the Germans could do was raid, but they could not be brought to battle without considerable forewarning.

At the end of May, however, Jellicoe's squadrons got such forewarning. Scheer had been preparing another sortie for some time, on a scale elaborate enough to surprise Beatty's battlecruisers if they came sufficiently far south. Decryption of his signals, however, gave Jellicoe word of the German movements, so that, by the time Scheer had cleared the Heligoland Bight, not only were Beatty's battlecruisers at sea, so too were the Scapa Flow battleships. On the morning of May 31, over 250 British and German warships were steaming on convergent courses to a rendezvous, unanticipated by the Germans, off the Jutland coast of Denmark. They included, on the British side, twenty-eight dreadnoughts and nine

The naval situation in the North Sea. Britain's geographical position, astride both the narrows of the English Channel and the exit to the Atlantic between Scotland and Norway, allowed the Royal Navy to dominate the Imperial German Navy's ports on the estuaries of the Jade, the Weser and the Elbe. The British Admiralty had decided before the war to transfer the Grand Fleet to Scapa Flow in the Orkney Islands, so as to allow maximum warning time if the German High Seas Fleet emerged and made a break for the Atlantic. The Battle Cruiser Fleet was stationed further south at Rosyth, between Edinburgh and Scapa Flow, as an advanced scouting force. The dispositions worked perfectly, bringing the German fleet to action at the Battles of the Heligoland Bight, the Dogger Bank and Jutland.

SHETLAND ISLANDS

NORWAY

ORKNEYS

CHRISTIANIA

Northern mine barrage, 1918

Scapa Flow

Battle of Jutland, 1916

Edinburgh

DENMARK

Dogger Bank

Battle of Dogger Bank, 1915

COPENHAGEN

North Sea

Kiel canal

Manchester

Battle of Heligoland Bight, 1914

Kiel

Birmingham

HOLLAND

Jade Bay

Hamburg

Bremen

BRITAIN

Jade

Weser

Elbe

Ems

THE HAGUE

Amsterdam

LONDON

Zeebrugge

Southampton

Nieuport

Antwerp

GERMANY

BRUSSELS

English Channel

BELGIUM

Frankfurt

Rouen

LUXEMBOURG

PARIS

Marne

Rhine

Seine

Munich

Loire

FRANCE

Belfort

BERNE

H.M.S. *Lion*, one of the most powerful units of the Battle Cruiser Fleet, at the Battle of the Dogger Bank, January 24, 1915.

battlecruisers, on the German sixteen dreadnoughts and five battlecruisers. Jellicoe's arrangement of his fleet attached his four newest battleships, of the fast *Queen Elizabeth* class, to the six battlecruisers of Beatty's Battle Cruiser Fleet, deployed ahead of the Grand Fleet. Scheer's fleet, advancing fifty miles behind the First Scouting Group of five battlecruisers, included six *Deutschland*-class pre-dreadnoughts, which he appears to have brought with him for sentimental rather than military reasons. Their lack of speed made them a liability.

Scheer's decision to take the whole of the High Seas Fleet into the North Sea was predicated on the belief that the British would not have foreknowledge of his movements. Jellicoe's initial advantage was compromised at an early stage, however, by a procedural failure at the Admiralty. Mistrusting the ability of Room 40, the British interception and cryptologic service, to make operational judgements, the responsible staff officer asked a veiled question of the intelligence analysts and concluded from the answer that Scheer's battleships were still in harbour. He transmitted that false information to Jellicoe who, in consequence, limited his speed southward while allowing the battlecruisers to forge ahead. At a critical stage of the preliminaries, therefore, Jellicoe was making less than best speed, while his reconnaissance fleet of battlecruisers was hurtling to a potentially disastrous encounter with a superior force.

Jutland, as the impending battle would be called, fell into five phases: in the first Beatty's Battle Cruiser Fleet made a "run to the south" on encountering the weaker German battlecruiser force; then a "run to the north" when, on meeting the German dreadnoughts, it turned back to draw them into Jellicoe's Grand Fleet; then two encounters between

Admiral Jellicoe aboard his flagship *Iron Duke*. Sir John Jellicoe (1859–1935) commanded the Grand Fleet from August 4, 1914, the day Britain entered the war, until 1917. Modest and unassuming, he was much liked by his sailors and officers and showed great skill in command. The disappointing result of Jutland, which was not the second Trafalgar expected, cast a cloud over his career; he was relieved on December 24, 1917, to be replaced by the showier Beatty, commander of the Battle Cruiser Fleet.

S.M.S. *Blücher* sinking at the Battle of the Dogger Bank, January 24, 1915. *Blücher* was a misconceived design, based on inaccurate reports of the first British battlecruisers. It lacked both the speed and heavy guns of the British *Invincible* class but shared that class's lack of armoured protection.

the dreadnoughts, broken by a German "turning away" as heavier British fire-power told; and finally, after the German dreadnoughts had sought escape from destruction, a night action in which the light forces of both sides sought to inflict crippling damage by torpedo attack.

In the first phase Beatty's Battle Cruiser Fleet passed through Scheer's patrol line of U-boats without loss to arrive within fifty miles of Hipper's First Scouting Group undetected. Chance then directed them towards each other. Their light forces diverted to investigate a neutral merchant ship, found each other and brought the two groups of battlecruisers into contact. Fire was opened and, because of bad British signalling, the German told more heavily. It fell, more-over, on ships defective in armoured protection and in prudent ammunition-handling. First *Indefatigable,* then *Queen Mary* suffered penetrations, which set off fires in handling-rooms where too many propellant charges were lying ready to be sent into the turrets. Both blew up and sank. Beatty's superiority in num-bers was suddenly reduced from seven to five.

The appearance of his supporting fast battleships reversed the imbalance but then they and the surviving battlecruisers of the Battle Cruiser Fleet found that they had run down onto the main body of German dreadnoughts. When they

A coloured German newspaper picture of the crew of a capital ship's secondary armament in action during the First World War. H.M.S. *Dread-nought*, the original true capital ship, dispensed with secondary armament altogether, relying on its 12-inch guns for both offence and defence. The threat of attack by torpedo boats and destroyers subsequently led naval designers to a reconsideration. By 1914 dreadnoughts in all navies carried secondary batteries of lighter-calibre guns, from 3-inch to 6-inch, designed to engage the enemy's light forces. They also fired at other dreadnoughts when ranges shortened, though to little effect. The "all-big-gun" idea behind the original *Dreadnought* design was the correct solution to the problem of fleet action in the era of the capital ship.

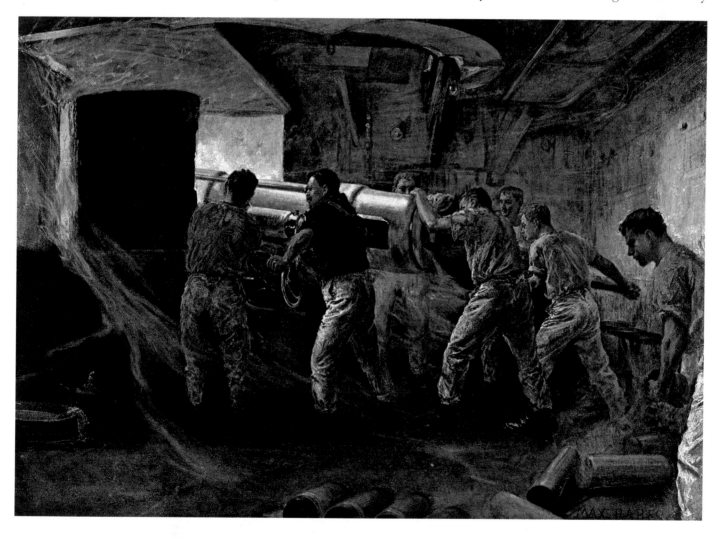

The 4th Battle Squadron of the Grand Fleet in the North Sea, from left to right H.M.S. *Iron Duke*, *Royal Oak*, *Superb* and *Canada*.

Right: Admiral Sir David Beatty, commander of the Battle Cruiser Fleet, 1913–17. Beatty (1871–1936) was the most prominent naval officer of his generation. He had won a dashing reputation in Britain's colonial wars and had married an American heiress. Impatient of convention, outspoken, often rude, he was greatly admired by civilians, less liked by fellow sailors. His handling of the Battle Cruiser Fleet at the Battle of Jutland, May 31, 1916, remains controversial. He replaced Jellicoe as commander of the Grand Fleet in December 1917, thus displacing in the opinion of many a worthier man.

Zur siegreichen Seeschlacht
am Skagerrak
am 31. Mai 1916

Above: Admiral Scheer (foreground) with Prince Henry of Prussia and the Crown Prince aboard Scheer's flagship.

Left: A German postcard of the "victorious sea battle of the Skagerrak" (Jutland), with portraits of the admirals involved: the Kaiser, von Capelle (Naval Minister), Tirpitz (creator of the modern German navy), Scheer (commander of the High Seas Fleet) and Hipper (commander of the battlecruisers).

Below: The German battlecruiser *Seydlitz,* badly damaged at Jutland, in dock after the battle, June 1916.

U-BOATS/SUBMARINES

The idea of an underwater warship is very ancient and the Americans had experimented with it both in the War of 1812 and the Civil War. The transformation of the idea into a practical reality came only with the building of the Holland X boat, by the Irish-American J. P. Holland, in 1901. His design enabled a submarine to dive and surface quickly, and to move at operational speed and launch a torpedo (itself a sort of unmanned submarine) against a surface target with crippling effect. Diesel engines supplied power for surface cruising and to recharge batteries; but underwater speed, by electric motor, was low and submerged endurance only a few hours.

The Royal Navy in 1914 possessed the largest fleet of effective submarines, seventeen D- and E-class boats, rising to 137 by 1918. France had a larger fleet, but of inferior boats. The Russian, Italian, Austrian and American submarine forces lacked numbers and efficiency. It was the Germans who, during the war, maximised the efficiency of their underwater (U-boat) flotillas. With the 390 U-boats built during the war, they conducted a highly effective campaign against Allied merchant shipping. Constrained at first by the rules of maritime warfare, which required an attacker to give a merchant captain warning, the boats were at first ineffective. During 1915, however, they progressively abandoned the rules until the sinking of the *Lusitania,* on May 7, with heavy loss of life, much of it American, brought a warning from the United States. In January 1917, however, the Germans returned to "unrestricted" U-boat warfare, seeing in it a means of securing victory increasingly frustrated on land. By April 1917, sinkings threatened Britain with starvation. The Admiralty then accepted the need to sail merchant ships in convoy, a procedure faulty operational analysis had previously ruled out. During the rest of 1917, sinkings dwindled as a result and in 1918, as anti-submarine technique improved, those of U-boats rose. By September 1918, it was clear that the German effort to win a war at sea that it was losing by land had failed. By then 178 U-boats had been lost, to a variety of causes, and 5,400 crew also.

Opposite top left: "Subscribe to 6th War Loan," Central Bank of German Savings Bank poster.

Opposite top right: *Submarine warfare: observation through periscope,* by Achille Beltrame, Italian.

Opposite bottom: *Submarine 53 of the German navy sinks a fishing-steamer,* watercolour by Claus Bergen.

Below: A German U-boat taking on stores at sea.

turned back towards Jellicoe's Grand Fleet, the "run to the north" began. During it the 15-inch gunfire of the fast battleships inflicted heavy damage on the following Germans, so that Scheer's battle line was in disarray when his dreadnoughts unwittingly fell under the fire of Jellicoe's a little after six o'clock in the evening. They were to inflict one more act of destruction, when *Invincible* was blown up, through the same causes that had devastated *Indefatigable* and *Queen Mary.* Then the concentration of British superior weight of shell proved so overwhelming that Scheer hastily ordered a retreat and disappeared into the gathering gloom of a misty North Sea evening.

There might have ended, inconclusively, an already unsatisfactory encounter. Scheer, however, then decided to turn back, perhaps because he judged that he could pass astern of Jellicoe's fleet and make his escape into the Baltic. Jellicoe, however, once again reduced speed, with the result that the German dreadnoughts, heading north-east, encountered the British heading south-east, and steering to pass their rear so as to cut them off from safety. At the moment of encounter, moreover, the British were deployed in line abreast, the Germans in line ahead, a relative position that greatly favoured the British. More of their guns

Battleships in Action at Jutland, an oil by Robert H. Smith. A dramatised but convincing impression of the Grand Fleet firing broadsides at the High Seas Fleet, whose shells are raising fountains in the foreground. The day of Jutland was much gloomier than the artist depicts, with low cloud and mist impeding observation.

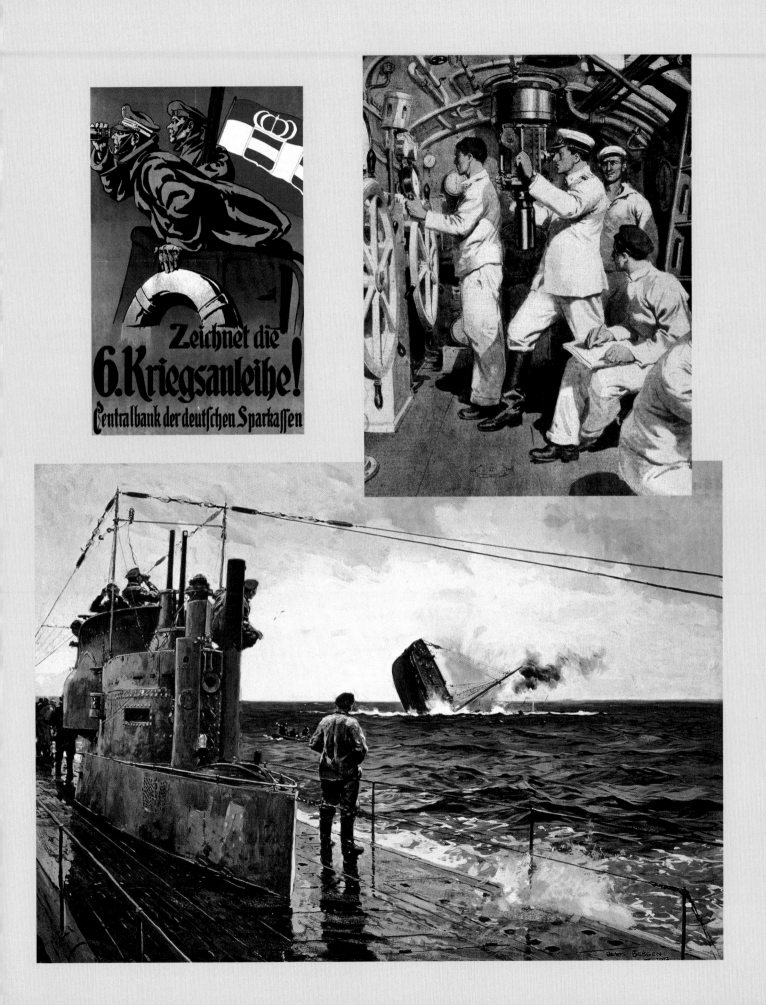

could be brought to bear than could those of the German fleet. Ten minutes of gunnery, in which the Germans suffered twenty-seven hits by large-calibre shells, the British only two, persuaded Scheer to turn away again into the dark eastern horizon, leaving his battlecruisers and lighter ships to cover his retreat. The torpedo threat they presented caused Jellicoe to turn away also—for which he has ever afterwards been reproached—and, by the time he turned back, Scheer had put ten miles between his dreadnoughts and the pursuit. Many German ships remained to cover Scheer's flight, including his squadron of vulnerable predreadnoughts, and in a series of dusk and night actions they suffered losses. So, too, did the British cruisers and destroyers that remained in contact. By the morning of June 1, when Scheer had his fleet home, he had lost a battlecruiser, a predreadnought, four light cruisers and five destroyers. Jellicoe, though remaining in command of the North Sea, had lost three battlecruisers, four armoured cruisers and eight destroyers; 6,094 British sailors had died, 2,551 German.

Nevertheless, though the High Seas Fleet had lost fewer ships than the Grand Fleet, it had suffered more damage to those that survived, so that in the aftermath its relative strength in heavy units fell from 16:28 to 10:24. In those circumstances it could not risk challenging the Grand Fleet outside coastal waters. Contrary to conventional belief, Jutland was not the German fleet's last sortie, nor its last action. There was an encounter between German dreadnoughts and British battlecruisers near Heligoland on November 17, 1917, while the High Seas Fleet steamed as far as southern Norway on April 24, 1918. It had accepted the verdict of Jutland nevertheless, pithily summarised by a German journalist as "an assault on the jailer, followed by a return to jail." Inactivity and discontent would eventually lead to serious disorder among the crews of Scheer's surface ships, beginning in August 1917 and culminating in full-scale mutiny in the last November of the war. After June 1, 1916, Germany's attempt to win a decision at sea would be conducted exclusively through the submarine arm.

OFFENSIVES ON THREE FRONTS

In the early summer of 1916, Germany saw as yet no need to reverse the policy of restricting U-boat operations it had adopted, for diplomatic reasons, the previous year, nor did the Allies apprehend the deadly danger that such a reversal would bring. Their thoughts were concentrated on the great offensives they jointly planned to deliver in the west and east, offensives which they believed would, after eighteen months of stalemate in France and Belgium, a year of defeats in Poland and six months of frustration in Italy, bring them decisive victories. On December 6, 1915, representatives of the Allied powers met at French headquarters at Chantilly to agree plans. Their forces had grown considerably since the beginning of trench warfare. Munitions output in all countries had grown enormously—by 2,000 per cent in Russia—and reinforcements had been found to make good losses and increase the size of the field armies. This was particularly the case in Britain where volunteering had increased the number of divisions almost tenfold since the last month of peace.

It was this enormous increment that allowed the French and British to promise their allies at Chantilly a continuation of their joint offensive efforts in 1916. It would, Joffre agreed on December 29 with Douglas Haig, the new commander of the B.E.F., take the form of a combined offensive in the centre of the Western Front, along the line of the River Somme, to which the British were to extend their line. As the movement would allow the French units north of the Somme to rejoin the main concentration of Joffre's armies to the south, the two armies would then share a clear-cut boundary which, Joffre argued, should be the axis of their great offensive in the coming year. Haig, who doubted the military logic of an operation that seemed likely at best to dent the huge salient left by the failed German advance in Paris in 1914, demurred but, in the interests of Anglo-French harmony, eventually concurred.

Plans made without allowance for the intentions of the enemy are liable to miscarry. So it was to prove in 1916. While Joffre and Haig were making their dispositions for the Somme, the Italians preparing to persist in the struggle for the heights above the Isonzo and the Russians contemplating retaliation for the loss of Poland, Conrad von Hötzendorf was laying the basis for an Austrian "punishment expedition" against the Italians from the unexpected direction of the Trentino, while Falkenhayn was devising a vast punishment expedition of his own against the French at Verdun.

Falkenhayn outlined his reasoning in a letter written to the Kaiser on Christmas Day, 1915. Germany's object, he insisted, must be to dishearten Britain, on whose industrial and maritime power the Alliance rested. He therefore argued that Britain's continental partners should be destroyed. Italy was too unimportant to deserve a major effort. Russia did not present the opportunity for a success decisive to the outcome of the war. He concluded that, since an offensive somewhere was necessary, because "Germany and her allies could not hold out indefinitely," it must be made against France. "The strain on France," he wrote, "has reached breaking point." The operational solution to his analysis was for a limited offensive at a vital point that would "compel the French to throw in every man they have. If they do so the forces of France will bleed to death."

He already had "the vital point" in mind, the fortress of Verdun in a loop of the Meuse, isolated during the operations of 1914, exposed to attack from three sides, badly provided with communications to the French rear area but lying only twelve miles from a major railhead in German hands. He quickly secured the Kaiser's agreement to what would be called Operation *Gericht* (Judgement) and, while a dissenting Conrad proceeded to prepare his own offensive against the Italians, began to mass the divisions that would try "the remarkable devotion" of the French to its limit.

Offensive at Verdun

Verdun was heavily fortified but, following the collapse of Liège and Namur to German heavy artillery in August 1914, the French had lost faith in all fortifications and Verdun's fortress guns had been sent away for use in the field. Verdun had become a "quiet sector" and its garrison had been whittled down until, in February 1916, it consisted of only three divisions.

Opposite them, Falkenhayn had assembled, during January and February, ten divisions, supported by an enormous concentration of artillery. Among the 542 heavy guns were thirteen of the 420-mm and seventeen of the 305-mm howitzers that had devastated the Belgian forts eighteen months earlier, and a stock of two and a half million shells. Falkenhayn's plan was brutally simple. The French, forced to fight in a crucial but narrowly constricted corner of the Western Front, would be compelled to feed reinforcements into a battle of attrition where the material circumstances so favoured the Germans that their defeat was inevitable. If the French gave up the struggle, they would lose Verdun; if they persisted, they would lose their army.

Operation Judgement was scheduled to begin on February 10. Bad weather postponed it from day to day but on February 19 the rains stopped, next day a warm sun dried the ground, and early in the morning of February 21 the bombardment opened. All morning it raged and on into the afternoon; in the Bois des Caures, 500 by 1,000 yards square, it is estimated that 80,000 shells fell before the German infantry appeared. Had the Germans attacked in strength they must have overrun the devastated enemy positions on the eight-mile front, but they did not. The philosophy of the operation was that artillery would destroy the French defences, which would then be occupied by the infantry in follow-up. On February 24, however, the whole of the outer trench zone was overrun, many of

The German Crown Prince watching German artillerymen in training. The wicker cases contain shells. During 1916, the Germans attached "infantry batteries," equipped with the standard 77-mm field gun, to infantry regiments, in order to provide close support during attacks. The experiment was discontinued after it was found that the guns were too heavy to manhandle through the broken surfaces of the trench zone. These gunners are carrying gas masks in cylindrical containers and some are wearing the wide-brimmed model of the standard steel helmet, issued in 1916.

Above left: A French machine-gun crew in the Casemate de Bourges, part of the defences of Fort Vaux. The Verdun forts had been largely stripped of their heavy guns to equip the artillery in the field, since many French generals lost faith in the value of fortresses after the rapid fall of the Belgian forts at Liège and Namur in August 1914. At Verdun, however, the forts, particularly Vaux, proved important as centres of resistance.

Above right: Philippe Pétain (1856–1951), commander of the French army, 1917–18. His rise was rapid. Only a colonel in 1914, he was an army commander the following year and in February 1916 was sent to take charge of the defence of Verdun, with which his name is always associated. He was made a Marshal of France in December 1918.

Opposite top: An artist's impression of a French counter-attack at Vaux, during the Battle of Verdun. Fort Vaux was a focus of fighting throughout the battle. It was captured by the Germans on June 7 but retaken on November 2, at the end of a local counter-offensive directed by General Mangin.

Below: A road-mending party on *la voie sacrée*, the road to Verdun. A minor highway, it led sixty kilometres from Bar-le-Duc. The road itself was reserved for supply trucks, which moved day and night. Wrecks were pushed off. The infantry going up and coming down marched in the road-side fields. Road mending was continuous as the surface near Verdun was kept constantly under fire by the Germans. At the height of the battle, 50,000 tons of ammunition and supplies were carried every week.

the defenders abandoning their positions in terror and fleeing to the rear. Only Forts Vaux and Douaumont stood as points of resistance on the forward slopes of the heights above the Meuse which, if taken, would allow German artillery observers to direct fire onto Verdun itself and the bridges across the Meuse which sustained the resistance. Then, on February 25, Douaumont fell, taken by a lone German sergeant of the 24th Brandenburg Regiment who, blown into the fort's moat by a near-miss, decided to explore the interior, found it occupied by only a handful of French troops and bluffed them into surrender. Verdun seemed on the point of falling.

Had it fallen the results might have been beneficial to the French conduct of the war, for it was indeed a death trap. On the morning of February 25, however, Joffre's deputy, Castelnau, who had commanded the Second Army at the Marne, arrived at Verdun, assessed the situation, and decided that the forward positions must be held. The decision he took on February 25 was the one for which Falkenhayn might have hoped and the soldier chosen to implement it, Philippe Pétain, the opponent Falkenhayn might himself have chosen. Pétain was not a man for

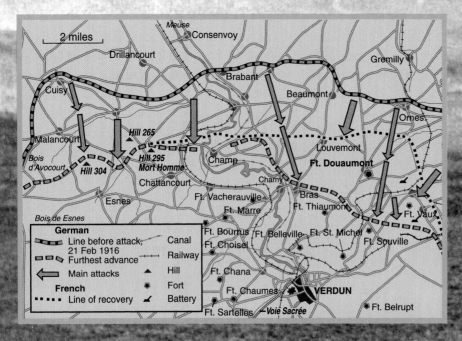

The object of the German offensive was to inflict unacceptable casualties on the French. Attacks began on the east bank of the River Meuse, against Fort Douaumont and Vaux. As French resistance stiffened, the Germans extended the front of attack onto the west bank, towards Hill 304 and the Mort Homme.

German
Line before attack; 21 Feb 1916
Furthest advance
Main attacks

French
Line of recovery

Canal
Railway
▲ Hill
● Fort
◢ Battery

2 miles

Meuse
Consenvoy
Drillancourt
Brabant
Gremilly
Cuisy
Beaumont
Ornes
Hill 265
Malancourt
Bois d'Avocourt
Hill 304
Hill 295
Mort Homme
Champ
Louvemont
Ft. Douaumont
Chattancourt
Charny
Esnes
Bois de Esnes
Ft. Vacherauville
Bras
Ft. Thiaumont
Ft. Vaux
Ft. Marre
Ft. Bourrus
Ft. Belleville
Ft. St. Michel
Ft. Choisel
Ft. Souville
Ft. Chana
Ft. Chaumes
VERDUN
Ft. Sartelles
Voie Sacrée
Ft. Belrupt

A unit of French infantry waiting to join a transport column in the early stages of the Battle of Verdun, April 8, 1916. The road—*la voie sacrée*—has not yet been doubled in width, as it would be soon under Pétain's orders. The soldiers wear cheerful expressions. The mood of fatalism, characteristic of the middle and later stages of the fighting, has not yet set in. As casualties rose, and divisions were rotated at more and more frequent intervals, 90,000 French soldiers would pass up and down the road each week.

giving up. He at once identified two essentials for the defence: to co-ordinate the artillery, of which he took personal control, and to open a line of supply. Henceforth it would be the Germans on whom fell a constant deluge of shells. Behind Verdun, the single road that led to Bar-le-Duc fifty miles away was designated a supply route for trucks alone; 3,500 were assembled to bring forward the 2,000 tons of stores the garrison needed daily. A whole division of Territorials was employed in road repairs and France was scoured for additional transport. Eventually 12,000 trucks would be used on what became known as the "*Voie sacrée.*"

A sanctified battle was what Falkenhayn had wanted France to fight. He had not counted upon the fervour the French would show. Already on February 27, the Germans recorded "no success anywhere." The XX "Iron" Corps had come into line and its soldiers were sacrificing themselves in a desperate effort to defend every foot of ground held; among those of XX Corps wounded—and captured—that day was Charles de Gaulle. The Germans sought to overcome the resistance of the French infantry by pushing their artillery ever closer to the front. An immediate result was appalling casualties among the horses of the gun-teams, yet, despite the growing weight of bombardment, the French line would not shift. By February 27, the Germans had advanced four miles and were within four miles of the city but no increase in offensive effort could push their front forward.

On the last day of February, Falkenhayn and the Crown Prince conferred and agreed on a new strategy. Since the narrow-front attack on the east bank of the Meuse had not achieved success, the offensive must be broadened to the west bank where, behind the heights of the Mort Homme and Côte 304, the French were hiding the artillery that flailed the German infantry. On the first day of the assault, March 6, the French 67th Division collapsed. The Germans were swiftly counter-attacked, however, the ground was regained and once again the line stuck fast. Simultaneous efforts on the east bank, in the direction of Fort Vaux, Douaumont's neighbour, were equally ineffectual. The ruins of the village of Vaux changed hands thirteen times during March, and yet the fort itself still lay tantalisingly beyond German reach. It was, moreover, defending itself resolutely. Both the French and the Germans were learning that the lessons of Liège and Namur were not as conclusive as had seemed. Even quite antiquated fortifications could stand up to intense and prolonged artillery bombardment if occupied by garrisons prepared to sit out heavy shellfire and wait for assault by unprotected infantry.

By the beginning of April, Falkenhayn's belief that he could win a victory of attrition was failing. At the beginning of April it was decided to attack across the extent of the whole front, now nearly twenty miles wide. The operation began on April 9 and lasted four days, until the descent of drenching rain stalled all activity for the rest of the month. On the first day the Germans reached what they thought was the crest of the dominating Mort Homme, only to find that the real summit lay just beyond their reach. The fight for the feature then resolved itself into an artillery combat. During May, after the bad weather relented, it was the Mort Homme that absorbed German efforts. On May 8 the French lost the true crest but clung on to the neighbouring slopes, against which the Germans picked step by step throughout the rest of the month. The final line of resistance delineated by Pétain on taking command was breached as they continued their advance

Above: Charles de Gaulle as a recently decorated young officer. He is wearing the *Croix de guerre.* In 1914 de Gaulle was a lieutenant in the 33rd Infantry Regiment, commanded by Colonel Philippe Pétain. He was wounded at Verdun and captured. As a prisoner, he learned to speak German fluently, a gift he used profitably in his efforts to re-establish Franco-German friendship after 1958, when he had become President of the Fifth French Republic. Pétain, who had become a Marshal and served as head of the wartime *État français*, the Vichy regime, died a prisoner in the fortress of the Ile d'Yeu, off the French Atlantic coast, in 1951. He had been condemned to death in 1946 but de Gaulle, then Prime Minister, had commuted the sentence.

Opposite: French soldiers of the 87th Infantry Regiment at Hill 304, Verdun, 1916. The improvised nature of the trench and the broken ground testify to the intensity of the fighting for this feature. First attacked by the Germans in March, it never fell into enemy hands. The 87th Regiment belonged to the 6th Division, from the Amiens military district. Eventually 259 of the 330 infantry regiments of the French army fought at Verdun. Over half a million French soldiers were killed or wounded there. The landscape was so heavily bombarded that several villages disappeared, never to be rebuilt, while the soil was so heavily polluted by explosives that parts of the pre-war forest have not regrown.

A French light machine-gun team in a shell scrape at Fort Vaux, Verdun, November 22, 1916. Shelling has reduced the surface of the soil to rubble and destroyed the natural contours. Trench lines have disappeared. The debris of battle litters the soldiers' surroundings—a broken shovel, tin cans, the relics of a barbed-wire entanglement. The battle is nearly over. Vaux and Douaumont have been retaken by the French, the Germans have lost the will to sustain the offensive. Apart from a few days of fighting in December, the Verdun front will not be contested again. Nearly a million soldiers, French and German, have been killed or wounded there.

but their progress was too slow to threaten the integrity of the Verdun position. Their casualties had now exceeded 100,000 killed and wounded and, though the French had suffered equally, most of the losses borne by the Germans had fallen on the same formations. While the French rotated divisions through Verdun, the Germans kept divisions in the line, making good casualties with replacements. By the end of April, forty-two French divisions had already passed through the Verdun sector, but only thirty German, and the disparity would persist.

Direct command of the Verdun sector had now passed from Pétain, whose disregard for casualties troubled even Joffre, to Nivelle, an artillery expert, fluent and persuasive in manner. He was already improving control of the French

A trench funeral at Verdun. The soldier has only just died. His bayonet is still attached to his equipment. The priest is probably a serving soldier who has put on his black *soutane* over his uniform; his crucifix is thrust between the buttons. The Battle of Verdun is far advanced, as the sombre, exhausted expressions of the dead man's comrades show. Death has come to seem a probability, rather than a possibility. Most of the French army's infantrymen had by now served spells on the Verdun battlefield, some twice or three times. The battle, begun in February and still raging in December, seems destined to go on forever.

guns, which were beginning to achieve dominance over those of the enemy. Meanwhile, however, the Germans sustained the offensive, pushing forward to the surviving French forts of Souville and Tavannes. From Souville, "it was downhill all the way to Verdun, less than two and a half miles away . . . and once the fort fell into enemy hands it would be but a matter of time before the city fell into enemy hands." German pressure continued unrelentingly after the fall of Vaux until on June 22 a new assault was preceded by a bombardment of an improved form of chlorine gas on six hundred of the 1,800 French guns at Verdun.

June 23 marked both the high point and crisis of the Verdun offensive. About twenty million shells had been fired into the battle zone since February 21, the shape of the landscape had been permanently altered, forests had been reduced to splinters, villages had disappeared, the surface of the ground had been so pockmarked by explosion that shell hole overlapped shell hole and had been overlapped again. Worse by far was the destruction of human life. By the end of June over 200,000 men had been killed and wounded on each side. The Germans made a final effort on July 11, which reached Fort Souville, but it was beaten off. Thereafter the Germans ceased their attempt to destroy the French army at Verdun and relapsed into the defensive. For a while it became a quiet sector until, in October, the French moved to recover the ground lost. On October 24 Douaumont was recaptured, on December 15 a wider offensive regained much of the ground lost on the east bank since the beginning of the battle. By then, however, another battle altogether, raging since July 1, had shifted the crux of the Western Front from Verdun to the Somme.

Offensive on the Somme

The Somme was to be the enterprise of Douglas Haig, who replaced Sir John French on December 16, 1915. Haig, commander of the B.E.F.'s First Army, had intrigued to gain the promotion. Although French had proved his incapacity to continue in supreme command, it was Haig who wielded the dagger. During a visit by King George V to France at the end of October, he told him directly that French was "a source of great weakness to the army, and no one had confidence in him any more." Haig was also enigmatic in personality and character, a devotee both of spiritualist practices and of fundamentalist religion. As a young officer he had taken to attending séances, where a medium put him in touch with Napoleon; as Commander-in-Chief he fell under the influence of a Presbyterian chaplain whose sermons confirmed him in his belief that he was in direct communication with God and had a major part to play in a divine plan for the world. His own simple religion, he was convinced, was shared by his soldiers, who were inspired thereby to bear the dangers and sufferings which were their part of the war he was directing.

Despite his strangeness, Haig was an efficient soldier, the superior to French in every branch of modern military practice, and his skills were not better shown than in his preparations for the Somme. That high and empty battlefield had not been contested since the first weeks of the war. On the enemy side, the Germans had profited from that to construct the strongest position on the Western Front. They had driven dugouts thirty feet below ground, impervious to artillery fire and linked to the rear by buried telephone cable and deep communication trenches. On the surface they had constructed a network of machine-gun posts, covering all angles of approach across the treeless downs, and in front of their fire trenches laid dense entanglements of barbed wire.

On the other side of no-man's-land, little had been done since 1914. The infrastructure for a great offensive was still not in place when Haig took command. Under his direction, the back area of the Somme was transformed into an enormous military encampment, cut by new roads and covered with shell dumps and gun positions. As a military technician, Haig could not be faulted. His talents as a tactician remained to be proved.

Haig's plan for the Somme was simple, akin to Falkenhayn's for Verdun, with the difference that he hoped to break the enemy's line rather than force him to

A French officer gives orders, les Eparges, January 1916. This sector lay between Verdun and the Somme, where the British army would open its great offensive on July 1. The landscape to the north, where the heights of the Meuse give way to the open downland of the Somme, offers a prospect of the nature of the fighting to come, a struggle to seize and hold positions under observed artillery fire and in full view of the enemy. Because of their losses at Verdun, the French were unable to fulfill their promised role in the Somme battle.

fight in a struggle of attrition. An enormous bombardment, to last a week and consume a million shells, was to precede the attack. As it died away on the date chosen for assault, July 1, nineteen British divisions and three French were to move forward across no-man's-land. So certain were Haig and most of his subordinates of the crushing effect the artillery would produce, that they had decided not to allow the inexperienced infantry to advance by the tried and tested means of "fire and movement." The tactical instruction for the battle, "Training Divisions for Offensive Action" (SS 109), and the associated instruction issued by

Soldiers of the 4th Battalion the Worcestershire Regiment cheering for a press photographer on their way up to the front line on June 28, 1916, three days before the opening of the Battle of the Somme. The bombardment had begun four days earlier and would deliver a million shells into the German positions, without cutting much of the enemy's wire or penetrating the deep dugouts in which the defenders sheltered. Although already heavily burdened, with extra ammunition bandoliers, these Worcesters would have been loaded with as much as sixty more pounds of equipment before going over the top.

Fourth Army, "Tactical Notes," both prescribed an advance by successive waves or lines of troops and a continuous movement forward by all involved. "The assaulting troops must push forward at a steady pace in successive lines, each line adding fresh impetus to the preceding line."

Almost everything that Haig and Rawlinson, commanding the attacking troops, expected was not to occur. The thirty-foot dugouts in which the German front-line garrison sheltered were almost impervious to any shell the British could fire. Even more ominous was the failure to cut wire. The general commanding the British VIII Corps, Hunter-Weston, who had been at Gallipoli, reported before July 1 that the enemy wire on his front was blown away and "the troops could walk in" but one of his junior officers "could see it standing strong and well."

Since uncut wire in front of defended trenches was death to attacking infantry, this complacent misappreciation by the staff was literally lethal.

The first day of the Battle of the Somme, July 1, 1916, was to be an awful demonstration of the penalties of poor infantry-artillery co-ordination. Its reality remains evident even today to anyone who returns to the centre of the Somme battlefield. Along it runs a line of the Commonwealth War Grave Commission's beautiful garden cemeteries. The cemeteries are a map of the battle. It tells a simple and terrible story. The men of the Fourth Army, the majority citizen volunteers going into action for the first time, rose from their trenches at zero hour, advanced in steady formation, were almost everywhere checked by uncut barbed wire and were shot down. Five divisions of the seventeen attacking entered the German positions. The infantry of the remainder were stopped in no-man's-land. Descriptions of zero hour on July 1 abound, of the long lines of young men, burdened by sixty pounds of equipment, plodding off almost shoulder-to-shoulder; of their good cheer and certainty of success; of individual displays of bravado, as in the battalions which kicked a football ahead of the ranks; of the bright sunshine breaking through the thin morning mist; of the illusion of an empty

The Tyneside Irish Brigade going over the top on the Somme one minute after zero hour—the start of the battle—on July 1, 1916. The Tyneside Irish Brigade consisted of four battalions, all "Kitchener" volunteers, of the Northumberland Fusiliers. It started from behind the front line, following up the leading waves, but was caught by German machine-gun fire in the open. Of its 3,000 men, most became casualties. One battalion lost 500 men killed or wounded, another 600. The brigade's advance was stopped inside the British position and never crossed the British front line. Yet its experience was not the worst suffered by British troops on the first day of the Somme.

battlefield, denuded of opponents. Descriptions of what followed zero hour abound also: of the discovery of uncut wire, of the appearance of the German defenders, manning the parapet at the moment the British creeping barrage passed beyond, to fire frenziedly into the approaching ranks, of massacre in the wire entanglements, of the advance checked, halted and eventually stopped literally dead.

Appalling loss of life was the result of the first day of the Somme along the whole front of the attack. When the two hundred British battalions that had attacked began to count the gaps in their ranks, the realisation came that, of the 100,000 men who had entered no-man's-land, 20,000 had not returned; another 40,000 had been wounded. In summary, a fifth of the attacking force was dead, and some battalions, such as the 1st Newfoundland Regiment, had ceased to exist. By contrast, the German 180th Regiment, for example, lost only 180 men out of 3,000 on July 1, while the British 4th Division, which attacked it, lost 5,121 out of 12,000. If the Germans had been shaken, it was by the "amazing spectacle of unexampled gallantry, courage and bulldog determination" and by their eventual revulsion from the slaughter inflicted; in many places, when they realised their

Crowds outside Charing Cross Station, London, waiting for the arrival of wounded men from the Battle of the Somme, 1916. Charing Cross Station was the main point of arrival and departure for the British Expeditionary Force during the First World War. It connects directly to the "Channel ports" where ferries leave for France in peacetime. It is also close to some of the larger London hospitals, including the Charing Cross Hospital, opposite, St. Thomas's, Guy's and the Westminster Hospital. Medical policy during the First World War was to evacuate the seriously wounded to Britain as soon as they were strong enough to stand the journey. Soldiers themselves classified wounds as "a Blighty one" (*Blighty* was Indian army slang for Britain) or not.

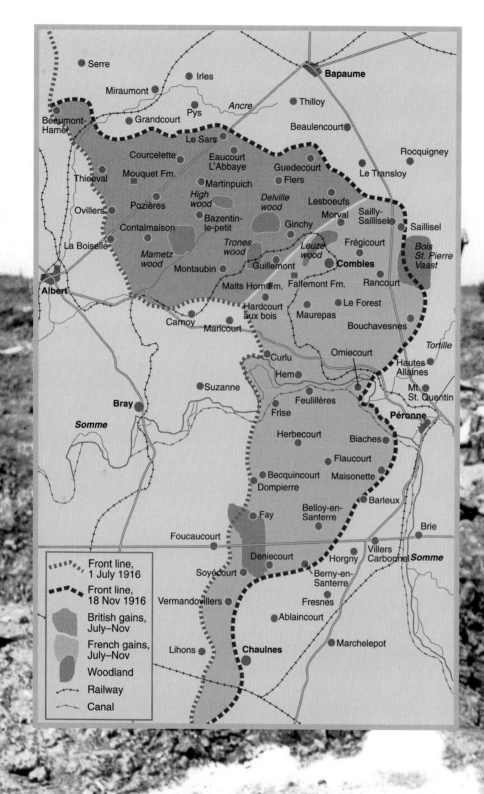

The more experienced French gained more ground than the British on the Somme, despite deploying fewer troops. Even so, the maximum depth of advance, over four months, was only eight miles, on a front of twenty miles.

Serre
Irles
Bapaume
Miraumont
Thilloy
Ancre
Pys
Grandcourt
Beaulencourt
Beaumont-Hamel
Le Sars
Rocquigney
Courcelette
Eaucourt L'Abbaye
Guedecourt
Le Transloy
Mouquet Fm.
Thiepval
Martinpuich
Flers
High wood
Delville wood
Lesboeufs
Pozières
Morval
Ovillers
Bazentin-le-petit
Ginchy
Sailly-Saillisel
Contalmaison
Saillisel
La Boiselle
Trones wood
Leuze wood
Frégicourt
Bois St. Pierre Vaast
Mametz wood
Combles
Montaubin
Guillemont
Albert
Malts Horn Fm.
Falfemont Fm.
Rancourt
Hardcourt aux bois
Le Forest
Camoy
Maurepas
Bouchavesnes
Maricourt
Tortille
Curlu
Omiecourt
Hautes Allaines
Hem
Suzanne
Mt. St. Quentin
Bray
Feuillères
Péronne
Frise
Somme
Herbecourt
Biaches
Flaucourt
Becquincourt
Maisonette
Dompierre
Barleux
Fay
Belloy-en-Santerre
Brie
Foucaucourt
Deniecourt
Horgny
Villers Carbonnel
Somme
Soyécourt
Berny-en-Santerre
Vermandovillers
Fresnes
Ablaincourt
Lihons
Marchelepot
Chaulnes

Front line, 1 July 1916
Front line, 18 Nov 1916
British gains, July–Nov
French gains, July–Nov
Woodland
Railway
Canal

British soldiers leaving their trenches for the attack at Morval, Battle of the Somme, September 25, 1916. The leading waves are already disappearing into the distance and smoke from the supporting bombardment is bursting on the skyline. Morval lies at almost the exact centre-point of the Somme battlefield, near Thiepval Ridge on which the vast memorial to the missing stands today. It also marks almost the furthest limit of ground gained during the battle since July 1. Fighting continued into October but for almost no advantage. As the Germans had done in attacking at Verdun month after month, the British had worn themselves out.

Left: Soldiers of the Border Regiment in improvised shelters, probably in the reverse face of a captured German trench. The soldiers of the Border Regiment, recruited in Cumberland and Westmoreland from hill farmers and shepherds, were notably hardy and self-reliant.

Below: The entrance to a German dugout at the northern corner of Bernafoy Wood, captured by the British on July 3, 1916. Along much of the Somme front, of which the Germans had been in undisturbed occupation since September 1914, they had sunk dugouts thirty feet below the surface, impermeable to British shell fire.

own lives were no longer at risk, they ceased firing, so that the more lightly British wounded could make their way back as best they could to their own front line. There was, for the worse wounded, no early rescue. Some were not got in until July 4, some never. A young British officer, Gerald Brenan, crossing subsequently captured ground in the fourth week of July, found the bodies of soldiers wounded on July 1 who had "crawled into shell holes, wrapped their waterproof sheets round them, taken out their bibles and died like that."

German defensive technique defied all Haig's efforts to exploit such success as had been achieved on July 1. Not until July 14, in the sector astride the Somme where the more experienced French had assisted the British to make a clear break-in to the German positions, was further ground gained. Haig's suspicion of night attacks was overcome by his subordinates and, in an assault at half-light, four British divisions rolled forward to take Bazentin Ridge, Mametz Wood and Contalmaison. Imperial troops, the 1st and 2nd Australian Divisions, veterans of Gallipoli, and the South African Brigade, renewed the advance during the second half of the month, taking Pozières and Delville Wood, but no opportunity for Haig's cavalry to intervene occurred. Like Verdun, the Somme was becoming an arena of attrition, to which fresh divisions were sent in monotonous succession— forty-two by the Germans during July and August—only to waste their energy in bloody struggles for tiny patches of

A British Mark I (Male) tank during the first tank attack in history, Flers-Courcelette, Battle of the Somme, September 15, 1916. "Male" tanks were armed with 6-pounder cannon, "Female" tanks with machine guns only. This "Male," bearing the name Clan Leslie, belongs to C Battalion of the Machine Gun Corps Heavy Branch, as the Tank Corps was first known. Terrifying to the German infantry, the early tanks moved at only two or three miles per hour, were prone to frequent mechanical breakdown and often ditched in broken ground.

ground, at Guillemont, Ginchy, Morval, Fleurs, Martinpuich. By July 31, the Germans on the Somme had lost 160,000, the British and French over 200,000, yet the line had moved scarcely three miles since July 1.

Following the attrition battles of August, a new effort was planned to open up the Somme front and tanks, some armed with machine guns, some with 6-pounder cannon, were allotted to the Fourth and Reserve (future Fifth) Armies, to lead an assault from Albert towards Bapaume between the villages of Flers and Courcelette. The appearance of the tanks terrified the German infantry defending the sector and the armoured monsters led the British infantry onward for 3,500 yards before mechanical breakdowns and ditchings in rough ground caused the advance to halt; a number, caught in artillery fire, were knocked out. The event resulted in one of the cheapest and most spectacular local victories of the

TANKS

The entrenchment of the Western Front behind entanglements of barbed wire in September 1914 quickly persuaded some soldiers that only a mechanical means of breaching the barrier would lead to breakthrough. Armoured cars had been developed before the war and saw service in Belgium, with the Royal Naval Air Service, the brainchild of Winston Churchill, in August. Wheeled vehicles, however, could not negotiate the trench battlefield and by December 1914 the idea of an armoured tracked vehicle had taken hold in Britain. Among those to be credited with its conception were Churchill himself but also such professional soldiers as Swinton, Stern and Sueter.

A prototype, "Little Willie," appeared in December 1915; a working prototype, "Mother," in January 1916. Weighing 28 tons and carrying 10 mm of armour, sufficient to keep out a rifle bullet, it was armed with four machine guns and two 6-pounder cannon; it could move, however, at only four miles per hour. By summer 1916, thirty-six were in France and the group took part, on September 15, 1916, in the Battle of the Somme. Though terrifying the Germans, the tanks were too few in number and too unreliable to achieve any decisive effect.

An improved model, the Mark IV, was available in much larger numbers in 1917 and at Cambrai, on November 20, a striking initial blow was delivered by 324 machines; a failure to exploit robbed Cambrai of result. By 1918, however, the Tank Corps was better organised and better equipped. The French, too, had created a tank force, equipped largely with the light two-man Renault (also supplied to the American Expeditionary Force). At Amiens, on August 8, over 400 British Mark IV's broke through; between September 12 and 26, the main Hindenburg Line was crossed, British and French tanks playing a major part.

The Germans, meanwhile, had notably failed to follow their enemies' lead. When a German model (the A7V) finally appeared in 1918, it proved a monstrosity, needing a crew of fifteen to work it and usually breaking down in action. The Germans resorted to repairing ditched British tanks for use in action but without effect on their declining fortunes. Not even the British, undoubtedly the pioneering tank nation, could claim, however, that their engineering achievements had a decisive effect on operations. Even their latest models were too primitive to be war-winning weapons.

Battle of the St. Quentin Canal, September 29, 1918. Tanks of the 8th Mark V Tank Battalion which were allotted to the 5th Australian Division.

Top left: Mark II tank ditched in crossing captured communication trench during the Arras offensive, April 1917.

Above: German tank captured at Villers Bretoneux by the 26th Battalion, July 14, 1918.

Above right: *Western Front: The Amiens Franco-British offensive,* 1918, by Achille Beltrame, Italian.

Right: *Camouflaged Tanks at Berles-au-Bois,* 1918, watercolour by John Singer Sargent.

war on the Western Front thus far, but its efforts were to be frustrated immediately by the disablement of almost all the thirty-six tanks that had crossed the start line.

October and November brought no change. Both the British and French attacked repetitively in increasingly wet weather that turned the chalky surface of the Somme battlefield into glutinous slime. By November 19, when the Allied offensive came officially to a halt, the furthest line of advance lay only seven miles forward of the front attacked on July 1. The Germans may have lost over 600,000 killed and wounded in their effort to keep their Somme positions. The Allies had certainly lost over 600,000, the French casualty figure being 194,451, the British 419,654. The holocaust of the Somme was overshadowed for the French by that of Verdun. To the British, it was and would remain the greatest tragedy of their military history.

The Ancre Valley in November 1916, during the last phase of the Battle of the Somme. The Ancre, in normal times a narrow, slow-flowing little river, had been transformed by months of shelling into an impassable swamp, which was nevertheless the scene of heavy fighting in the last stage of the Somme battle.

The Wider War and the Brusilov Offensive

While the great dramas of Verdun and the Somme were being played out in France, the war on the fronts elsewhere took a very varied form. In German East Africa, where Jan Smuts, the brilliant guerrilla opponent of the British during the Boer War, had arrived to take command in 1915, four columns set out in 1916, to make a concentric advance on von Lettow-Vorbeck's black army, encircle it and bring the campaign to a close. The Allied fighting troops numbered nearly 40,000, Lettow's about 16,000. Dividing his force, he had no difficulty in eluding Smuts with his main body and in beating a fighting retreat southward from Mount Kilimanjaro towards Tanga and Dar es Salaam. His African askaris, moreover, were resistant to most of the parasitic diseases that attack humans in the interior. His enemies, who included large numbers of Europeans and Indians, were not. Their enormously high toll of sickness—thirty-one non-battle casualties to one battle casualty—was the real cause of their failure to run Lettow to earth. At the end of 1916 his little army was as fit, capable and elusive as at the start of the war and would sustain resistance until after the armistice of 1918.

The Turks maintained the success they had achieved at Gallipoli. Though their efforts to revive their offensive against the Suez Canal were repulsed, in a limited campaign that took British forces to the Sinai border of Palestine, and though their army in the Caucasus suffered further defeats at the hands of the Russians, in Mesopotamia they inflicted a wholly humiliating defeat on the Anglo-Indian force that had landed at the mouth of the Shatt al-Arab in 1914. During 1915, Expeditionary Force D, as it was known, pushed up the River Tigris towards Baghdad until in November 1915 its advance guard was at Ctesiphon. Its situation looked promising. Somehow, however, the Turks managed to scrape together enough reinforcements to send troops down the Tigris and confront the expeditionary force. Its commander, Major-General Townshend, accordingly ordered a retreat to Kut al-Amara, a hundred miles down river. There the force entrenched itself in a loop of the Tigris to await support. It did not come. Kut was completely cut off from outside help and on April 29 surrendered. Townshend and 10,000 survivors of the expeditionary force went into captivity, four thousand of whom died in enemy hands. Kut was not retaken until the end of the year. Like Salonika, where the Allies continued to wage an unsuccessful campaign against very inferior forces throughout 1916, Mesopotamia had become a drain on resources instead of a threat to the enemy.

On the Italian front the defenders were also heavily outnumbered by the attackers. On May 15, 1916, the Austrians unleashed their "punishment expedition" between Lake Garda and the River Brenta, which leads towards the lagoons of Venice. The preliminary bombardment forewarned the defenders and they fought with heroic self-sacrifice to hold

Italian trench artillerymen launching French fin-stabilised mortar bombs at Austrian positions, Ortigarn, 1916. High-trajectory weapons were widely used in trench warfare and were particularly useful in mountain operations, where broken ground interfered with line-of-sight bombardment by conventional artillery. Although achieving considerable "area" blast effect, they were, however, inaccurate and frequently dangerous to their users.

Map, opposite: The progress of the Brusilov offensive, June–October 1916. Brusilov chose to attack on a front of 300 miles, thus depriving the enemy of the chance to mass reserves beforehand against a threatened point. The front was only thinly entrenched and wired and the Russians made rapid progress at the start. The offensive was one of the most successful of the war. Had Brusilov had adequate transport to follow up his leading attackers he would have recaptured even more ground than he did. A major handicap was the absence of good roads.

Background: An Austrian mountain battery, equipped with the M10 mountain howitzer. The gun was broken down into several sections for transport and pulled by horses working in tandem. This battery is at Prepolacsattel in the Carpathians, 1916.

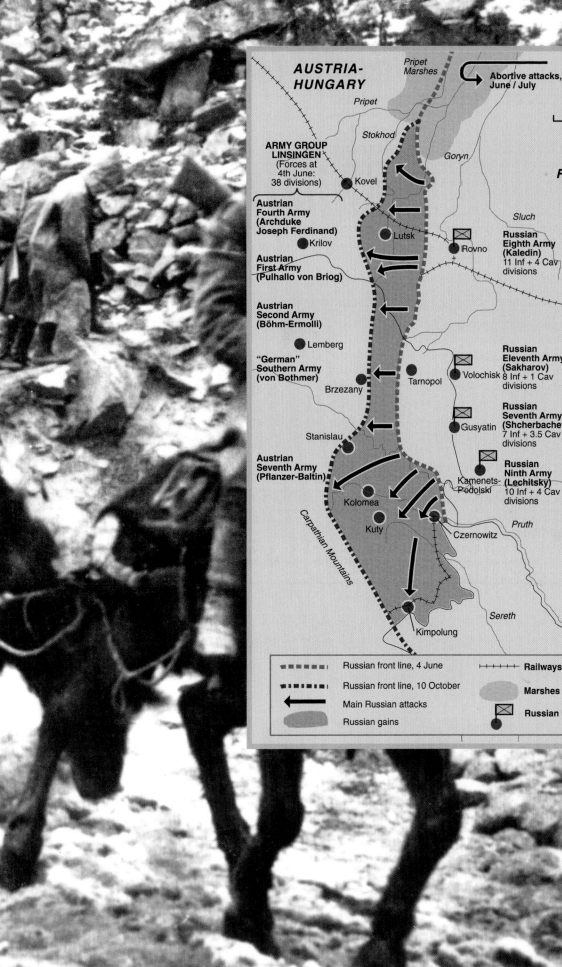

AUSTRIA-HUNGARY

Pripet Marshes

Pripet

Abortive attacks, June / July

Russian Third Army (Lesh)

Stokhod

Goryn

50 miles

RUSSIA

ARMY GROUP LINSINGEN (Forces at 4th June: 38 divisions)

● Kovel

Austrian Fourth Army (Archduke Joseph Ferdinand)

● Krilov

● Lutsk

⊠ ● Rovno

Russian Eighth Army (Kaledin) 11 Inf + 4 Cav divisions

Austrian First Army (Pulhallo von Briog)

Sluch

Brusilov's GHQ ⊠ ●

Austrian Second Army (Böhm-Ermolli)

● Lemberg

"German" Southern Army (von Bothmer)

● Brzezany

● Tarnopol

⊠ ● Volochisk

Russian Eleventh Army (Sakharov) 8 Inf + 1 Cav divisions

RUSSIAN SOUTH-WEST ARMY GROUP (Forces at 4th June)

⊠ ● Gusyatin

Russian Seventh Army (Shcherbachev) 7 Inf + 3.5 Cav divisions

● Stanislau

⊠

Russian Ninth Army (Lechitsky) 10 Inf + 4 Cav divisions

Austrian Seventh Army (Pflanzer-Baltin)

Kamenets-Podolski

Carpathian Mountains

● Kolomea

● Kuty

● Czernowitz

Pruth

Dniester

● Kimpolung

Sereth

	Russian front line, 4 June	┼┼┼┼	Railways
	Russian front line, 10 October		Marshes
←	Main Russian attacks	⊠ ●	Russian HQ / GHQ ⊠ ●
	Russian gains		

WAR IN THE ALPS

Italy's Alpine frontier with Austria-Hungary was to become, after her entry in May 1915, the scene of some of the most extreme fighting of the war. On the eastern Isonzo River, dividing Italy from modern Slovenia, the mountains rise to 1,500 feet, the Bainsizza plateaux being described as a "howling wilderness." In the Trentino, on the northern border with the Austrian Tyrol, crests stood at 6,000 feet. Italy maintained two groups of *Alpini,* 30,000 strong, experienced in mountain operations. The bulk of its army, however, was drawn from the lowland south. While Austria's élite was constituted by the *Kaiserjäger,* Tyrolean mountaineers, they were already committed to the desperate battles against the Russians in the high Carpathians of Hungary.

In the early stages of the Alpine war, therefore, Italian conscripts, largely untrained in the demands of mountain warfare, were sacrificed to win narrow slices of harsh upland territory from local reservists and militiamen who were learning their trade as soldiers in the heat of action. Neither side had adequate artillery, while the Italians were forced to construct roadways, tactical tracks, cablecar railways and precipitous gun positions as they edged their way forward. Troops found shelter in snow tunnels and trenches cut from the rock, those in the front line on both sides suffering a disproportionate number of head wounds from rock splinters.

The Italian army, in eleven Battles of the Isonzo between May 1915 and October 1917, nevertheless succeeded in advancing its front, and defeating an Austrian "punishment offensive" in the Trentino, although at a terrible cost in lives. On October 24, 1917, however, a joint German-Austrian army containing a high proportion of mountain troops, broke through on the Isonzo, captured nearly 300,000 prisoners and reversed all the gains won in the previous two and a half years. Thereafter the Italian war was fought in the lowlands of the Piave River valley where, in the last days of the war, an Allied army succeeded in winning a decisive victory.

Above: Stone and wooden steps on the precipice of Monte Corbin, in the Altopiano of the Asiago.

Left: At Monte Grappa, a seriously wounded soldier in a cable-car litter at Boccaor.

Opposite top left: German soldiers in the Tirol mountains.

Opposite top right: Light cannon on Monte Bombon.

Opposite bottom: Pulling artillery to the summit of Monte Moschin.

the invaders at bay. The Rome Brigade was almost wiped out in its defence of Piazza. As a result, the Austrians nowhere advanced more than ten miles and, though their losses were fewer than the Italian—80,000 to 147,000—the punishment expedition neither threatened a breakthrough nor deflected Cadorna, the Italian commander, from pursuing his relentless offensive on the Isonzo. The Sixth Battle opened in August and secured the frontier town of Gorizia, the Seventh, Eighth and Ninth followed in September, October and November. The bridgehead across the Isonzo at Gorizia was enlarged and a foothold on the harsh Carso upland secured. The Italian infantry, despite heavy losses, still seemed ready to return to the attack, even under Cardorna's aloof and heartless direction.

The course of operations in Italy during 1916 had one positive result: by attracting Austrian divisions from the Russians' southern front, it allowed the Tsar's armies to organise a successful counter-offensive against their weakened enemy. The architect, Alexei Brusilov, had proved his ability at lower levels of command and had also found the time to consider the problems of attacking entrenched positions covered by defending artillery with reserves in rear ready to stem a break-in. The solution, he had concluded, was to attack on a wide front, thus depriving the enemy of the chance to mass reserves at a predeterminably critical point, to protect the assaulting infantry in deep dugouts while they were waiting to jump off, and to advance the line as near as possible to the Austrian, by digging saps forward as close as seventy-five yards to the enemy trenches.

Brusilov's preparations worked admirably. Though his superiority of numbers over the Austrians on the twenty miles of chosen front was only 200,000 to 150,000, with 904 to 600 guns, the enemy was genuinely surprised when the attack opened on June 4. The Russian Eighth Army overwhelmed the Austrian Fourth and pushed on forty miles beyond the start line. Huge numbers of prisoners were taken, as the shaken Austrians surrendered to anyone who would apprehend them. The greatest success was achieved in the south, between the River Dniester and the Carpathians, where the Austrian Seventh Army was split in two, lost 100,000 men, mainly taken prisoner, and by mid-June was in full retreat.

At the beginning of July the Russian armies north of the Pripet Marshes also went onto the offensive, while Brusilov's army group sustained its success over the Austrians throughout July and August and into September, by which time it had taken 400,000 Austrians prisoner and inflicted losses of 600,000. The Ger-

Italian transport at Montebesso in the Dolomites, 1916. A Fiat artillery tractor hauls a 6-inch gun up the mountain road, an oxcart follows with water for the infantry. Both the technology and the personnel of Italy's war effort was very mixed. The artillery included the most modern models from Italy's advanced engineering works at Milan and Turin, the infantry was spearheaded by bold mountaineers from the Trentino and Julian Alps but the bulk of their soldiers were peasants from southern villages. Uncomplaining for two and a half years of the Isonzo offensives, they broke suddenly under German attack at Caporetto in October 1917.

man forces involved in opposing the Russian advance had lost 350,000 and a belt of Russian territory sixty miles deep had been taken back from the invaders. Had Brusilov possessed the means to follow up his victory, he might have recovered more of the ground lost in the great retreat of 1915. He possessed no such means. The rail system could not provide tactical transport across the battle zone, while the roads were unsuitable for heavy traffic. Nevertheless, the Brusilov offensive was, on the scale by which success was measured in the foot-by-foot fighting of the First World War, the greatest victory seen in any front since the trench lines had been dug on the Aisne two years before.

The Russian victory, though it also cost a million casualties, sealed the fate of Falkenhayn. His fall, and replacement by Hindenburg, came about, however, in a curiously indirect way. Romania, long courted by both the Allies and the Cen-

Above: General Alexei Brusilov (1853–1926), the most successful Russian general of the war. A cavalryman and an aristocrat, he commanded the Eighth Army on the southern front in the opening campaign in Galicia and the Carpathians, avoiding serious defeat. Appointed to direct the South-Western Front in 1916, he planned and carried through the offensive which bears his name. The Brusilov offensive took the Austrians by surprise and won back much ground. With ampler resources he might have recaptured Przemysl and Lemberg. He was one of the Russian military leaders who prevailed on the Tsar to abdicate and, though never a Bolshevik, accepted a position in the Red Army in 1917.

Above right: Russian infantry advancing during the Brusilov offensive.

tral Powers, had thus far prudently avoided choosing sides, though its neighbour, Bulgaria, had thrown in its lot with Germany and Austria in October 1915. Its chief national interest was in the addition to its territory of Transylvania, where three million ethnic Romanians lived under Austro-Hungarian rule. As Brusilov's advance pushed westward, apparently promising not only Russian support but Austrian collapse, the Romanian government's indecision diminished. On August 17, a convention was signed by which France and Russia bound themselves to reward Romania, at the peace, with Transylvania and the south-west corner of Hungary; in secret, the two great powers had previously agreed not to honour the convention when the time came. That the Romanians could not have known the treaty was made in bad faith does not excuse their entering into it. Good sense should have told them that their strategic situation, pinioned between a hostile Bulgaria to the south and a hostile Austria-Hungary to their west and north, was too precarious to be offset by the putative support of a Russian army which had only belatedly returned to the offensive.

The Romanians nevertheless went to war on August 27 in apparent high confidence in their army of twenty-three divisions, formed from their stolid peasantry, and in the belief that the Russian offensive north of the Pripet Marshes would prevent the transfer of German reserves towards Hungary, while Brusilov's continuing offensive would hold the Austrians in place. They appear to have made little allowance for the eventuality of Bulgarian or, as came to pass, Turkish intervention, and they overestimated the military potentiality of their armed forces. Alexeyev, the Russian Commander-in-Chief, actively discounted the value of the Romanians as allies, rightly reckoning that they would drain rather than add to Russian reserves.

The Romanians, in these deteriorating circumstances, opened an offensive all the same, not, as the commanders in Salonika had expected, against Bulgaria, but into Hungary through the passes of the Transylvanian Alps. Retribution was quick to come. The Austrians quickly organised the local defence forces into a First Army, while the Germans found the troops to position two armies in Transylvania and Bulgaria. While the Romanians, having occupied eastern Transylvania, then did nothing, their enemies made their preparations and struck. Assailed on three sides by four enemies, including the Turks, the Romanians were thrown into full retreat towards their remote eastern province of Moldavia, between the

Russian soldiers among Austrian dead killed at the end of the Brusilov offensive. Brusilov's tactics led to the capture of 400,000 enemy soldiers, and inflicted a million casualties, many on the Germans. Its success shook the German high command and led to the replacement of Falkenhayn as Chief of Staff by Hindenburg and Ludendorff. It also induced the Romanians to enter the war on the Allied side, tempted by promises of post-war territorial gains. Their entry was unwise. After the Brusilov offensive petered out, they found themselves vulnerable to attack by German, Austrian, Bulgarian and Turkish forces. At the end of the offensive the Romanian army had, like the Belgian, been pushed into a corner of its own country, where it hung on until the end of the war.

Sereth River and the Russian border. There, as winter closed in, they entrenched themselves to sit out the bad weather.

Their decision for war had been disastrous. They had lost 310,000 men, nearly half as prisoners, and almost the whole of their country. Their most important material asset, the Ploesti oil fields, had been extensively sabotaged by British demolition teams before they were abandoned to the enemy. The Allies' decision to entice Romania into the war had been ill-judged also. The addition of the

A Portuguese army band leading an infantry regiment to war, 1916. Portugal, historically Britain's oldest ally, declared war on Germany and Austria in March 1916. It eventually sent two divisions to the Western Front, armed and equipped by the British. Put into the line at Neuve-Chapelle, in the British sector south of Ypres, they were attacked during the second great German offensive of April 9, 1918, broke and ran. Large numbers of prisoners were taken. The Portuguese, an unsophisticated and rural people, were unsuited to the strains of industrial warfare and it was unwise of the Portuguese government to have taken sides. It would have been better advised to imitate Spain in standing apart.

nominal fighting power of lesser states—Portugal (which became a combatant in March 1916), Romania and even Italy—did not enhance the strength of the Allies but, on the contrary, diminished it, once they came to require resources to shore them up. The defeat of Romania not only necessitated, as Alexeyev had foreseen, the commitment of the Russian armies to rescue them from total collapse. It also delivered into German hands a million tons of oil and two million tons of grain, the resources that "made possible the . . . continuation of the war into 1918." By contrast, the accession of Greece to the Allied side, through a coup stage-managed by Venizelos but engineered by the Allies in June 1917, brought the Allies no advantage at all and, by its installation of a violently nationalist and anti-Turkish government in Athens, led to Greek mobilisation in the cause of the "Great Idea"—the recovery of the Greek empire in the east—which would complicate the Allied effort to resettle the peace of Europe for years after the war had ended.

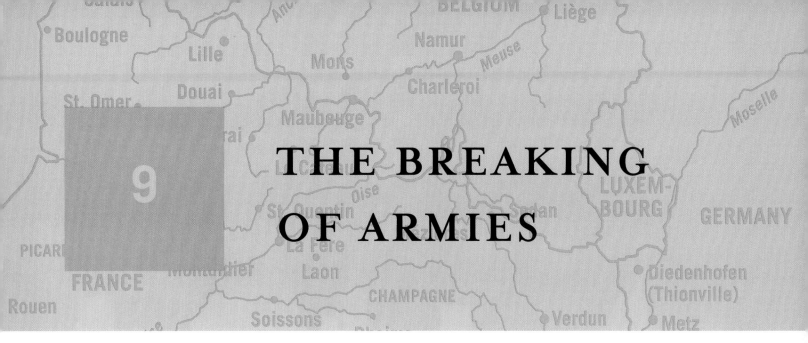

THE BREAKING
OF ARMIES

9

THE FRENCH MUTINIES

The year of 1917 was to be marked in France, Italy and above all Russia by a collapse of military morale. The accumulation of losses in the trenches, for little gain of territory, had depressed the spirit of all three armies, particularly so the Russian, which was also afflicted by the economic chaos into which war had thrown the country. The first manifestation of military breakdown was, nevertheless, to show itself in France.

A great offensive had been planned for 1917 at the meeting of Allied military representatives at French general headquarters, in November 1916. As in the year before, the Italians were to resume their offensives against the Austrians on the Isonzo and the Russians promised a spring offensive also. The great effort, however, was to be on the old Somme battlefield, by the French and British, to be followed by an offensive in Flanders aimed at "clearing" the Belgian coast and recapturing the bases of the U-boats which were operating with increasing effect against Allied shipping. Two events supervened to overtake these plans. The first was the replacement of Joffre by Nivelle, whose operational philosophy did not marry with a scheme for the resumption of the Somme battle. The Somme offered no terrain suitable for an abrupt breakthrough, of which Nivelle believed he had the secret. Under his control, a vast mass of artillery would drench the German defences with fire "across the whole depth of the enemy position," so that the attackers would pass unopposed into open country. Since the Somme was unsuitable for such tactics, Nivelle proposed to return to the terrain and the plan of 1915. He would attack at the "shoulders" of the great German salient on either side of the Somme. The French would take the southern Aisne sector, the Chemin des Dames, as their front of assault, while the British would reopen an offensive on the northern shoulder of the Somme salient, at Arras and against Vimy Ridge.

Fortunately for Nivelle's plan, the newly dug German Hindenburg Line stopped just short of the Chemin des Dames, where he planned to deliver the blow, as it

Fighting in Kudrinskaya Square in Moscow, October 1917.

291

Above: Nivelle at Ivry, March 24, 1917. General
Robert Nivelle (1856–1924) became commander of the French army in December 1916,
succeeding the displaced though still venerable
Joffre. He had had a rapid rise, due to his skills
as a gunner—his artillery tactics had led to the
recapture of Fort Douaumont at Verdun—and his
fluency in English; his mother was an English-
woman. He promised, on assuming command,
to break the German front in a few hours. The
Nivelle offensive of April 1917, at the Chemin
des Dames on the Aisne, was a physical and
psychological disaster, costing tens of thousands of lives and leading to the French
"mutinies" of May 1917. On May 15 Nivelle
was replaced by Pétain. He spent the rest of the
war in North Africa.

Right: Pyramids of British ration boxes at Rouen,
January 15, 1917. Rouen, an inland port on the
River Seine, which leads to Paris, is one of the
most important import centres in France and
remained throughout the First World War a principal supply center for the British Expeditionary
Force. Cross-Channel steamers restocked it
daily with food, ammunition and stores for the
British troops.

did also of the Arras–Vimy Ridge sector where the British and Canadians were to attack a little earlier. Unfortunately for the French, the defences of the Chemin des Dames were among the strongest on the Western Front. German artillery observers could overlook the positions in which the French infantry were to form up for the assault. Moreover, a new German defensive doctrine ensured that the front line would be held by divisions held just beyond the range of the enemy's artillery, so as to be able to "lock in" as soon as the leading waves of the enemy's attacking infantry had "lost" their own artillery's fire. While the French Sixth, Tenth and Fifth Armies awaited the day of attack, eventually fixed for April 16,

the B.E.F. prepared for its own supporting offensive, due to begin a week earlier. Its particular objective was the crest of Vimy Ridge, to be attacked by the Canadian Corps, from which a rapid advance by cavalry could link up with Nivelle's vanguards once they had cleared the Aisne heights at the Chemin des Dames, eighty miles to the south. An enormous weight of artillery and stock of munitions had been assembled.

These dispositions proved calamitous for the Germans. Their unfortunate infantry were pinned in their deep dugouts by the weight of the British bombardment, which had also torn their protective wire entanglements to shreds. When the British and Canadians appeared, plodding behind their creeping barrage, the defenders were either killed or captured below ground or, if they were lucky, had just enough time to run to the rear. The first day of the Battle of Arras was a British triumph. In a few hours the German front was penetrated to a depth of between one and three miles, nine thousand prisoners were taken, few casualties suffered and a way apparently cleared towards open country.

The Germans, however, had meanwhile inflicted a catastrophic defeat on the French. One way or another, the Germans had got ample warning of Nivelle's plan for *"rupture."* They had also put in place their own new scheme for "defence in depth," devised by Colonel von Lossberg, which left the front line almost empty, except for observers, while the "intermediate zone" behind was held by machine gunners dispersed either in strong points or improvised shell-hole positions. The supporting artillery, meanwhile, was deployed not in lines but in a haphazard pat-

tern to the rear, while the real strength of the defence lay in the reserves deployed outside artillery range 10,000 and 20,000 yards from the front. However successful, therefore, the French assault, and that was problematical, the attackers, when and if they achieved their final objectives, would immediately confront fresh troops whom, in their exhausted state, they would be hard-pressed to resist.

The over-rapid pace of the barrage left the foot soldiers behind. "Everywhere the story was the same. The attack gained at most points, then slowed down, unable to follow the barrage which, progressing at the rate of a hundred yards in three minutes, was in many cases soon out of sight. As soon as the infantry and the barrage became disassociated, German machine-guns . . . opened fire. The ground, churned up by the shelling, was a series of slimy slides with little or no foothold. Had the German guns been as active as their machine guns, the massacre that was going on in the front line would have been duplicated upon the helpless men in the crowded trenches and on the tracks to the rear." The massacre was comprehensive enough. Mangin, the hard colonial soldier command-

Opposite: Craonne on the Chemin des Dames, an artist's impression of one of the most heavily contested sectors of the Aisne front. At the centre of the front betweeen Soissons and Reims attacked during the Nivelle offensive, Craonne was defended by the XV Bavarian Reserve Corps. Assaulted by the French I Corps on April 16, it was taken on April 19 but no further ground was gained. It marked the furthest limit of Nivelle's success. Within the month, the French army, while promising to defend its front, would be refusing to mount new offensives. This "mutiny," which affected half the French divisions, brought down Nivelle and forced the British to assume a disproportionate share of the fighting during the rest of 1917.

Right: Canadian machine gunners organising shell-hole positions, Vimy, April 1917. Vimy Ridge, which dominated the front between Arras and Ypres, had been held by the Germans since the Battle of the Marne. It had resisted all efforts to take it, particularly by the French in the First and Second Battles of Artois, April and September 1915. The Canadian Corps, attacking on April 9, benefited from a heavy artillery preparation, including much gas, which killed German ammunition resupply horses. Vimy Ridge, on which an impressive Canadian war memorial now stands, has become to Canada what Gallipoli is to Australians and New Zealanders.

A British band playing in the Grand Place at Arras, April 1917. Though not as heavily bombarded as Ypres, Arras suffered heavily from German fire during the war and the magnificent buildings of its medieval and renaissance wool merchants were severely battered. Like that of Ypres, its Grand Place was completely reconstructed after 1918. The cellars of Arras, and the natural caverns over which the town is built, provided shelter to the British and Canadian divisions waiting to attack during the Battle of Arras.

ing Sixth Army, ordered that "where the wire is not cut by the artillery, it must be cut by the infantry. Ground must be gained." The order was entirely pointless. There was no breakthrough, no realisation of Nivelle's promise of *"rupture."* On April 29 he was removed and replaced by Pétain. The French losses, which included 29,000 killed, could not be replaced.

Nor could, for a time at least, the fighting spirit of the French army. Almost immediately after the failure of the offensive began what its commanders would admit to be "acts of collective indiscipline" and what historians have called "the mutinies of 1917." Neither form of words exactly defines the nature of the breakdown, which is better identified as a sort of military strike. The general mood of those involved—and they comprised soldiers in fifty-four divisions, almost half the army—was one of reluctance, rather than refusal, to take part in fresh attacks, though there was patriotic willingness to hold the line against attacks by the enemy. There were also specific demands: more leave, better food, better treatment for soldiers' families, an end to "injustice" and "butchery," and "peace." The demands were often linked to those of participants in civilian strikes, of which there was a wave in the spring of 1917, caused by high prices, resentment at war profiteering and the dwindling prospect of peace. Civilian discontent fed military discontent. The French crisis of 1917 was national. It was for that reason that the

government took it so seriously, as did its nominee to replace Nivelle, Philippe Pétain. For all his outward abruptness, Pétain understood his countrymen. He promised ampler and more regular leave. He also implicitly promised an end, for a time at least, to attacks by emphasising that the troops would be rested and retrained.

Nevertheless, the "movement"—indiscipline, strike or mutiny—was not put down without resort to force. Both high command and government, obsessed by a belief that there had been "subversion" of the army by civilian anti-war agitators, devoted a great deal of effort to identifying ringleaders, to bringing them to trial and to punishing them. There were 3,427 courts-martial, by which 554 soldiers were condemned to death and forty-nine actually shot. Superficially, order was restored with relative speed. By August, Pétain felt sufficient confidence in its spirit to launch a limited operation at Verdun, which restored the front there to the line held before the German offensive

Bottom: Soupir on the Chemin des Dames, one of the points of departure for French troops (XX Corps) during the Nivelle offensive. The Chemin des Dames, a pleasure walk for King Louis XV's daughters in the eighteenth century, followed the crest of the ridge above the Aisne.

of February 1916, and in October another operation on the Aisne drove the Germans back beyond the Ailette, the first-day objective of Nivelle's ill-fated offensive. In general, however, the objects of the mutinies had been achieved. The French army did not attack anywhere on the Western Front, of which it held two-thirds, between June 1917 and July 1918, nor did it conduct an "active" defence of its sectors.

REVOLT IN RUSSIA

It was not only the French army that recoiled from the mounting cost of the war in 1917. The Russian army too, never as cohesive or as "national" as the French, was creaking at the joints, even before its high command began to organise the spring offensives its representatives had promised at the inter-Allied Chantilly conference in December 1916. Yet the situations in France and Russia were not comparable. Even during the worst of its troubles, at the front and at home during 1917, France continued to function as a state and an economy. In Russia the economy was breaking down and thereby threatening the survival of the state. Industrial mobilisation, financed by an enormous expansion of paper credit and abandonment of budgeting balanced by gold, had created a relentless demand for labour, met by releasing skilled workers from the ranks and by a migration of exempt peasants, those who could show family responsibilities, from the land to the cities, where cash incomes were far higher than those won, often by barter, on the farm. Higher wages and paper money brought rapid inflation and inflation had a particularly disruptive effect on agricultural output. Large landowners took land out of production because they could not afford the threefold increase in wages, while peasants, unwilling or unable to pay high prices for trade goods, reverted to self-subsistence. At the same time the railways, though employing 1,200,000 men in 1917, against 700,000 in 1914, actually delivered less produce to the cities. By the beginning of 1917, supplies of fuel and food to the cities had

Opposite: A barricade in St. Petersburg (Petrograd), February 1917. Snow has fallen again, after the warm weather which encouraged the crowds to take to the streets on February 27. The Tsar, isolated at army headquarters at Mogilev, outside the capital, was unsure how to respond to the manifestations of revolt. He proved unwilling to use loyal forces to put the revolution down. Pulled this way and that by conflicting advice, he eventually decided to abdicate on March 2. Russia was effectively left without a government. The crucial influence was the attitude of the army, which had lost confidence in the imperial regime's conduct of the war.

Left: A cavalry patrol on the Nevsky Prospect, St. Petersburg, February 27, 1917, the first day of the February Revolution. The anti-government outbreak in February was not truly revolutionary but a demand for an alleviation of the harshness of war conditions. Alarmingly, however, the soldiers of the St. Petersburg garrison joined the protests. Thitherto, the Tsar had always been able to count on their loyalty, particularly that of the Imperial Guard regiments, including the Pre-obrazhensky and Semenovsky, which had been the prop of the regime since the days of Peter the Great.

almost broken down. In March, the capital, Petrograd, had only a few days' supply of grain in its warehouses.

The main outbreak of violent demonstrations was on February 27. By February 28 strikers and the whole of the Petrograd garrison had joined forces and revolution was in full swing. Tsar Nicholas, isolated at headquarters at Mogilev, preserved a characteristic unconcern. He seems to have believed, like Louis XVI in July 1789, that his throne was threatened by nothing more than a rebellion from below. He did not grasp that the army of the capital was in revolt against his rule and that the political class was following its lead. Russia's parliament, the Duma, was discussing its mandate in the Tauride Palace, while Soviets, committees of the common people, were passing resolutions and appointing represen-

Left: A demonstration in Kiev, Ukraine, during the February Revolution. The Russian mood during this first revolution was contradictory. Neither the people nor the common soldiers wished to give up the struggle against Russia's enemies, whom they suspected of wishing to perpetuate autocracy under an occupation regime. The soldiers, however, were generally unwilling to return to the front under the chaotic conditions prevailing there. Russia's will to resist German and Austrian aggression was still strong but ordinary Russians had unrealistic hopes that a change of government would bring victory. Ukrainian nationalists would shortly forge their own way out of the war.

Top: An officer distributing revolutionary newspapers in Moscow, February 1917.

Above: Crowds in Petrograd watch the burning of the Tsarist crest on February 27.

An anti-war demonstration in Petrograd, February 1917. The revolutionary mood was less anti-war than anti-government. It was economic mismanagement, resulting in runaway inflation and a shortage of affordable foodstuffs, which had alienated civilians, while the soldiers were disaffected by casualties and setbacks at the front. Russia did not want to leave the war but to win, under new leadership.

Opposite top: A revolutionary poster by T. Butschkin, 1917. The slogan reads "War Until Victory," the policy of the Provisional Government of the February Revolution.

Opposite bottom: A poster by Boris Kustodiev. "Do not let the enemy take back the victory you have won" was a theme echoed throughout the days of the Provisional Government.

tatives to supervise or even replace those in established authority. In Petrograd, the chief Soviet had nominated an executive committee, the Ispolkom, which was acting as the representative body of all political parties, including the Marxist Mensheviks and Bolsheviks as well as moderates. At the front, the officers of the general staff recognised the force of irresistible events. A proposal to despatch a punitive expedition to Petrograd under the command of General Ivanov was cancelled by the Tsar himself when he conferred with his military advisers at Pskov on March 1. There he also conceded permission for the Duma to form a cabinet. There, finally, on the afternoon of March 2, he agreed to abdicate.

The Tsar's abdication left Russia without a head of state, since the succession was refused by his nominee, the Grand Duke Michael, while the Duma would not accept that of the Tsarevitch. The revolution also shortly left Russia without the apparatus of government, since by an agreement signed between the Duma cabinet and the Ispolkom of the Petrograd Soviet, on March 3, all provincial governors, the agents of administrative power, were dismissed and the police and gendarmerie, the instruments of their authority, disbanded. All that was left in place outside the capital were the district councils, which were subject to the veto of the Ispolkom, which arrogated to itself responsibility for military, diplomatic

and most economic affairs, leaving the government to do little more than pass legislation guaranteeing rights and liberties to the population. Yet the two bodies at least agreed on one thing: that the war must be fought. They did so from different motives, the Provisional Government for broadly nationalist reasons, the Ispolkom, and the Soviets it represented, to defend the revolution. While they continued to denounce the war as "imperialist" and "monstrous," the Soviets nevertheless feared that defeat by Germany would bring counter-revolution and so, in their "Appeal to the Peoples of the World" of March 15, they called on them to join Russia in action for "peace" against their ruling classes and at the same time urged the army, through the Soviets of soldiers, to continue the struggle against "the bayonets of conquerors" and "foreign military might."

The soldiers, with a popular revolution to defend, rediscovered an enthusiasm for the war they seemed to have lost altogether in the winter of 1916. "In the first weeks of the [February Revolution], the soldiers massed in Petrograd not only would not listen to talk of peace, but would not allow it to be uttered"; the petitions of soldiers to the Provisional Government and Petrograd Soviet indicated that they "were likely to treat proponents of immediate peace as supporters of the Kaiser." The only supporters of immediate peace among all the socialist groups

A meeting at the front, March 1917. During the February Revolution, ordinary Russians formed Soviets—popular committees—all over the country, in towns, villages and factories. Soldiers formed their own Soviets in their regiments. They were rarely disrespectful to their officers but used the Soviets to represent their views. It was only later in the year, during and after the October Revolution, that Red soldiers showed violence, and then only in isolated incidents. Most Russian soldiers simply wanted to go home by the winter of 1917, to care for their families in disintegrating economic circumstances and to take land. Real ferocity between the old and new military leaderships broke out only after the inception of the Civil War.

represented on the Ispolkom, the Bolsheviks, were careful not to demand it and, with all their leaders—Trotsky, Bukharin and Lenin—currently in exile, were in no position to do so.

A renewed war effort needed leadership of its own, however, and neither the Ispolkom nor the original Provisional Government was headed by figures of inspiration. The Ispolkom's members were socialist intellectuals, the prime minister, Prince Lvov, a benevolent populist. Lvov had a high-minded but hopelessly unrealistic belief in the capacity of "the people" to settle the direction of their own future. The Bolsheviks, who knew what they wanted, were excluded from influence by the people's reborn bellicosity. In the circumstances it was to be expected that leadership should pass to a man of dynamism. He appeared in the person of Alexander Kerensky. He became Minister of War in May, and at once set about a purge of the high command, which he regarded as defeatist. Brusilov became Chief of Staff, while Kerensky's own commissars were sent to the front with the mission of encouraging an offensive spirit among the common soldiers.

Those in the Petrograd garrison demonstrated—"War for Freedom Until Victory"—safe in the knowledge that they would not be called upon to risk their lives; the seventh of the eight points of Ispolkom's notorious Order No. 1, abolishing governorship and police, stipulated that "military units that had participated in the Revolution . . . would not be sent to the front." Troops at the front, though they treated Kerensky as a popular idol on his tours of inspection, proved less enthusiastic for what has come to be called the "Kerensky offensive," of June 1917, launched to bring about the defeat of "foreign military might" for which there was so much verbal enthusiasm in the rear. On June 18, Kerensky's offensive opened, after a two-day preparatory bombardment, directed once again against Lemberg, pivot of the fighting in 1914–15. For two days the attack went well. Then the leading units, feeling they had done their bit, refused to persist, while those behind declined to take their place. Desertion set in, and worse. Fugitives from the front, in thousands, looted and raped in the rear. When the Germans, who were forewarned, counter-attacked with divisions already brought from the west, they and the Austrians simply recovered the ground lost and captured more themselves, driving the Russians back to the Romanian border.

While calamity overtook the Revolution's forces at the front, the Revolution itself was coming under attack in the rear. At the outset the extremists had been in exile. Lenin was in Zurich, Bukharin and Trotsky, the latter not yet a member of the Bolsheviks, in New York. By April, however, all had returned, Lenin through the good offices of the German government which, scenting the opportunity to undermine Russia's war effort by implanting the leaders of the peace movement in Moscow, had transported him aboard the famous "sealed train" to Sweden. From Stockholm the party proceeded to Petrograd, where it was welcomed not only by the local Bolsheviks but also by representatives of the Ispolkom and the Petrograd Soviet. Immediately after his arrival Lenin addressed a Bolshevik meeting where he outlined his programme: non-co-operation with the Provisional Government; nationalisation of banks and property, including land; abolition of the army in favour of a people's militia; an end to the war; and "all power to the Soviets," which he already had plans to bring under Bolshevik control.

Kerensky addressing troops leaving for the front, 1917. Alexander Kerensky (1881–1970) became leader of the Provisional Government set up after the February Revolution. A pre-war socialist member of the Russian parliament, the Duma, he had opposed the declaration of war but advocated its continuation after the February Revolution in order to protect Russia against German "militarism." As Minister of War he had planned a new offensive and oversaw its launching on July 1. Initially successful, it was soon checked when the Germans brought reinforcements, some from the Western Front. Its failure initiated the Russian army's eventual collapse.

A women's battalion being blessed by the Russian Orthodox patriarch before departure for the front, July 1917. The February Revolution attracted enthusiastic support among politically active women, some of whom volunteered for a Battalion of Death. It incorporated anomalous elements of modernism and traditionalism. Despite their shaven heads and combat uniforms, some of the soldiers in the photograph are making the sign of the cross, others are wearing high heels. The Battalion of Death joined in the defence of the Winter Palace in St. Petersburg against the Bolsheviks in October 1917. It numbered only 140. It is doubtful if the unit ever saw action against the enemy.

These "April Theses" failed to win support. Time, nevertheless, was on Lenin's side, time measured in the increasingly limited willingness of the field army to remain at the front. The collapse of the Kerensky offensive had dispirited even those soldiers who resisted the increasingly easy opportunities to desert. Their lapse of will allowed the Germans in August to launch a successful offensive on the northern front which resulted in the capture of Riga, the most important harbour city on the Baltic coast. Militarily, the Riga offensive was significant because it demonstrated to the Germans the effectiveness of their new system of breakthrough tactics. Politically, it was yet more significant, since it prompted a military intervention which, though designed to reinforce the authority of the Provisional Government, would shortly result in its collapse.

Kerensky had now become Prime Minister and he decided to replace Brusilov with an outspoken proponent of the anti-German war effort, General Lavr Kornilov. Kornilov was a man of the people who believed, for that reason, he would be followed in a personal campaign first against the defeatist Bolsheviks, then against

his country's enemies. On August 25 he ordered reliable troops to occupy Petrograd, with further orders to disperse the Soviet and disarm the regiments there should the Bolsheviks seek to take power. Militarily, his programme was entirely sensible. It was the only basis for continuing the war and for saving a government which, in a sea of defeatism, supported that policy. Politically however, Kornilov's programme confronted Kerensky with a challenge to his authority. Kerensky

could not throw in his lot with Kornilov, since he correctly doubted whether the general commanded sufficient force to combat the extremists. Equally, he could not turn to the extremists, since to do so would be to subordinate the Provisional Government to their power. In the event, Kornilov was manoeuvred by others into staging a coup he had not planned, which failed through the refusal of his soldiers to join in, and so was removed from command.

His fall ended any chance of sustaining the fiction that Russia was still fighting a war. The Provisional Government lost what remained of its authority in the aftermath, since Kerensky's dismissal of Kornilov lost him what support he retained among moderates and senior officers without winning him any from the forces of the left. The Bolsheviks were, indeed, now determined to mount the "second revolution" and Lenin, who had now established his absolute leadership over the

The German 1st Foot Guards crossing a pontoon bridge over the River Dvina, September 2, 1917, at the outset of the Riga offensive. The offensive, opened on September 1, was intended to terminate the Russian war effort by threatening an advance towards the seat of the Provisional Government in St. Petersburg. The Russian Twelfth Army, the last effective element of the old Tsarist army, began to retreat at once and had soon ceased to exist. The offensive, masterminded by General Hutier, was also a rehearsal of his new tactics of surprise artillery bombardment and infantry infiltration, to be used against the British and French with startling success in the spring 1918 offensives on the Western Front.

Provisional Government soldiers outside the Winter Palace, St. Petersburg, July 1917. On July 4, the Bolsheviks had staged a coup in the capital, with troops sympathetic to their cause, particularly the 1st Machine-Gun Regiment, Red Guards, workers from the factory districts and sailors from Kronstadt. The Bolshevik leadership was then seized by indecision and failed to carry the rebellion through. When troops loyal to the Provisional Government appeared at the Tauride Palace, seat of the Duma, the rebels began to disperse. Lenin went into hiding, to await a more favourable turn of events.

Above: Machine gunners demonstrating on the Nevsky Prospect, St. Petersburg, July 4, 1917.

Right: Cossacks outside the Winter Palace, July 1917. St. Petersburg was full of troops who declared their support for the Provisional Government and the continuation of war. Those who had taken part in the events of the February Revolution, however, had been promised that they would not be sent to the front and declined to go when requested.

Overleaf, inset map: The Bolshevik Revolution also led to the lapse of central authority over much of Russia. Although the Bolsheviks were able to win over the 900 Soviets which had replaced town and district councils in the provinces of the Russian heartland, the Ukraine declared independence and made a separate peace with Germany in February, while Poland, the Baltic States, Finland and the Caucasus were detached from the former empire. Following the Bolsheviks' refusal to implement the armistice agreed at Brest-Litovsk in December, the Germans simply launched an invasion to take as much of Russia as they wanted. It was unopposed, the Bolsheviks having no military force at their disposal.

∎∎∎∎∎	Eastern front at Brest-Litovsk Armistice (15 December 1917)
▬∎▬∎▬	Furthest gains of Central Powers
	Russian land under Central Powers after treaty (3 March 1918)
	Other lands under Central Powers
Frontiers after treaties	
••••	Russia relinquishes rights to area to west of this line
▬ ▬ ▬	Between Ukraine and Central Powers after treaty (9 Jan 1918)

ST. PETERSBURG (Petrograd)

STOCKHOLM

Revel

Tver

Pskov

Dvina

Moscow

Riga

Dvinsk

Vitebsk

Libau

Smolensk

Tula

Baltic Sea

Kovno

Vilna

Mogllev

Minsk

Desna

Orel

Königsberg

Grodno

Homel

Kursk

Danzig

Tannenberg

Vistula

Warsaw

RUSSIA

Bielgorod

← To Berlin

Brest-Litovsk

Kiev

Vorskha

Kharkov

Lodz

Dnieper

Ekaterinoslav

Don

Breslau

Cracow

Lemberg

UKRAINE

Taganrog

Rostov

Bug

GALICIA

Czernowitz

Dniester

Odessa

Sea of Azov

VIENNA

Budapest

Pruth

MOLDAVIA

BESSA-RABIA

CRIMEA

Novorossisk

AUSTRIA-HUNGARY

Sebastopol

Black Sea

Drava

BUCHAREST

Sava

WALLACHIA

BELGRADE

Danube

Railways

200 miles

A soldiers' meeting at the front, October 1917. No officers are present and the banners are inscribed "Revolution." The formation of a Bolshevik government on October 26, promising "socialisation" of agricultural land and offering the Germans and Austrians a three-month armistice, set in train the final disintegration of the Russian army. In Lenin's words, the soldiers "voted for peace with their feet."

party, was looking only for a pretext. It was given him by the Germans who, during September, enlarged their success at Riga by gaining positions in the northern Baltic from which they could directly threaten Petrograd. The Provisional Government reacted by proposing to transfer the capital to Moscow. The Bolsheviks, who represented the proposal as a counter-revolutionary move to consign the seat of the people's power to the Kaiser, won wide support for the creation of a defence committee with authority to defend Petrograd by every means. On the night of October 24–25, Lenin's Red Guards seized the most important places

in Petrograd, so that by next morning the Bolsheviks were in control. The Provisional Government put up a feeble resistance which was quickly overwhelmed. On October 26 Lenin announced the formation of a new government, the Council of People's Commissars, whose first acts were to proclaim the "socialisation" of land and an appeal for peace, to begin with a three-month armistice.

The three-month armistice effectively ended Russia's part in the First World War. The army at once began to melt away, as soldiers left the front to return to what they believed would be land for the taking in their villages. The Germans and Austrians, nervous at first of dealing with revolutionaries, were slow to react to Lenin's Peace Decree of October 26. When world revolution failed to erupt and the appeal to peace was repeated by the Bolsheviks on November 15, the

Germans decided to respond. On December 3, their delegation, and those of Austria, Turkey and Bulgaria, met the Soviet representatives at Brest-Litovsk. Discussions dragged on into 1918. The three-month armistice, tacitly accepted by the Germans, was rapidly running out, but the Bolsheviks, with no hand to play, continued to resist the enemy's terms, which were for the separation of Poland from Russia and wide annexations of territory further east. In the end, the Germans lost patience and announced that unless their terms were accepted they would take as much of Russia as they wanted. On February 17, their inva-

Opposite: Red Guards entering the Kremlin, November 2, 1917. The former capital remained under the control of anti-Bolshevik officer cadets on October 28. The Bolsheviks in Moscow might have been defeated had their opponents not agreed to negotiate. The Reds used the time gained to bring up reinforcements which, on October 31, attacked. In two days of fighting they seized the city and secured its surrender. On March 11, 1918, Lenin arrived from St. Petersburg to establish his headquarters in the Kremlin and to announce the transfer of the capital to Moscow. Declared a temporary measure, it soon became permanent.

Right: Decapitating the statue of Tsar Alexander III outside the Temple of Christ the Saviour, Moscow, 1918. The memory of Alexander III, a supreme autocrat, was particularly hated by the revolutionaries. During the Second World War, however, in order to strengthen Russian patriotism, the Communist Party, at Stalin's direction, deliberately revived memories of the nation's great figures of the past including Ivan the Terrible and Peter the Great, and heroic episodes of its history, such as the defeat of Napoleon in 1812. Traditional Tsarist insignia was restored to officers' uniforms, military decorations named after famous Tsarist generals were instituted, and the honourific title of "Guards" was conferred upon the most successful Red Army formations.

sion began. Within a week they had advanced 150 miles. Panic-struck, the Soviet government ordered its delegation at Brest-Litovsk to sign at Germany's dictation. The resulting treaty ceded to the enemy 750,000 square kilometres of territory, an area three times the size of Germany and containing a quarter of Russia's population and industrial resources and a third of its agricultural land.

Germany had already transferred the best of its eastern army to the Western Front, in preparation for what it planned to be the war-winning offensives against the French and British. The Russian army had disappeared, its soldiers, in Lenin's memorable phrase, having "voted for peace with their feet." Hundreds of thousands had walked away from the war even before the October Revolution, into enemy captivity. By the end of 1917 nearly four million Russians were in German or Austrian hands. The Russian peasant soldier simply lacked the attitude that bound his German, French and British equivalent to comrades, unit and national cause. Once the Bolsheviks began to sue for peace, disintegration became terminal. By the spring of 1918, after the German occupation of the Ukraine, the revolutionary government found that the only disciplined unit at its disposal was a band of Latvian volunteers, more committed to the cause of Latvia's national independence than Bolshevik ideology. The peasant mass had returned to the land, leaving in uniform only a residue of the rootless, the lawless and the orphaned, ready to follow the flag of any leadership which could provide food

and strong drink. Some of those leaders were ex-Tsarist officers, who, as opponents of Bolshevism, would raise "White" armies, others commissars who wanted a Red Army, but in either case desperate to find men, weapons to arm them, money to pay them. The Russian civil war was about to begin.

ROUT ON THE ITALIAN FRONT

In Italy, too, there was to be a breaking of armies in 1917, to follow that of the French and the Russian, though as the result of a great defeat, rather than a failed offensive or a social revolution. In October, at Caporetto, a small frontier town on the River Isonzo, the Germans and their Austrian allies would achieve a dramatic breakthrough of the positions the Italians had so painfully won in the thirty preceding months and dash the fragments of their army down into the plains.

It was highly creditable that the Italian army had persisted in eleven costly and

Top: Negotiations at Brest-Litovsk between the German and Austrian delegations and the Ukrainian representatives, February 8, 1918. Those present include the German von Kühlmann, the Austrian Count Czernin and the Ukrainian President, Redeslavov. The Ukraine agreed to a separate peace, which gave Germany and Austria access to the independent state's rich agricultural, industrial and mineral resources. The Ukraine's independence was short-lived. As a result of the Russian Civil War, it became a so-called Republic of the Soviet Union.

Above: The inauguration of the armistice between the Russian and German armies, December 15, 1917. Russian soldiers are saluting German officers at the border of the agreed neutral zone.

fruitless assaults on Austria's mountain borderland. The incidence of an offensive every three months, between May 1915 and August 1917, was higher than that demanded of the British on French armies on the Western Front and the contingencies more wearing; shellfire in the rocky terrain caused 70 per cent more casualties per rounds expended than on the soft ground in France and Belgium. Italian discipline was harsher also. It may have been, as the Italian Commander-in-Chief, General Cadorna, believed, that the social frailty of his army required punishments for infractions of duty of a severity not known in the German army or the B.E.F.: summary execution and the choosing of victims by lot. Nevertheless, it is unlikely that the British or Germans would have stood for such harshness and it is a tribute to Italy's sorely tried and uncomplaining peasant infantrymen that they did.

All armies, however, have a breaking point. That dividing line had been crossed for the French at the beginning of 1917, when the number of deaths suffered already equalled that of the infantry in the front-line divisions: the million and more French deaths exceeded the infantry strength of the army's 135 divisions. By the autumn of 1917 the Italian army, with 65 infantry divisions, or about 600,000 infantrymen in fighting units, had suffered most of the 571,000 deaths to be incurred during the war, and the sense of "one's number being up" may have become collective. "Fifty-one divisions . . . had been thrown into this massive struggle but by the second week of September the end of the war seemed as far away as ever."

Above: Joffre conferring with Cadorna, Italian front, summer 1917. Joffre had been relieved of command in December 1916 but had been created a Marshal of France and remained honoured and enormously popular in France. Cadorna was about to be relieved, following the disaster of Caporetto, and was heavily criticised in the official report on the defeat.

Right: The Italian front line at Monte Pasubio, 1917. The Austrian defenders of the Isonzo and Trentino fronts had been worn down by the successive Italian offensives of 1915–17 and by midsummer of 1917 were, in the opinion of their high command, ripe for defeat. It was for that reason that it called upon the Germans to lend soldiers for a relief operation.

German mountain troops pausing on an Alpine pass during the Caporetto offensive, October 1917. Germany had lent six divisions, mainly of mountain troops and including their illustrious Bavarian *Alpenkorps*, to spearhead the attack. Working along the valley of the Isonzo, from north and south, the attackers joined hands behind the Italian front in the Isonzo salient, cut the defenders off and took huge numbers of prisoners. Many other Italians fled in breakneck flight down the roads to the plain of the Po. The German mountain troops had acquired much experience of high-altitude operations in the Carpathians and the Balkans.

Passes secured by Italians 1915	Italian retreat from Caporetto, 25 Oct–10 Nov 1917
Isonzo gains by Italians, 1915–1917	Italian defence line stabilised after retreat from Caporetto
General area Trentino operations, summer 1916	Vittorio Veneto campaign, 1918
	Armistice line 4 November 1918

50 miles

AUSTRIA – HUNGARY

Stelvio

Giau

Ploken

Caporetto (Karfreit)

Tonale

Vittorio Veneto

Trent

Gorizia (Görz)

Guidriari

Asiago

Trieste

Heavy fighting June 1918

Venice

Gulf of Venice

ITALY

Not to the Austrians. On August 25, the Emperor Karl wrote to the Kaiser in the following terms: "The experience we have acquired in the eleventh battle has led me to believe that we should fare far worse in a twelfth. My commanders and brave troops have decided that such an unfortunate situation might be anticipated by an offensive. We have not the necessary means as regards troops." His request was for Germans to replace Austrians on the Eastern Front, so that the divisions thus released could be brought to the Isonzo. It was decided to commit seven German divisions, formed with six Austrian into a new Fourteenth Army, in a direct counter-offensive on the Isonzo. The German divisions were specially selected. They included the 117th, which had had a long spell of mountain warfare experience in the Carpathians, the 200th, which included ski troops,

and the illustrious *Alpenkorps,* a Bavarian mountain division, in one of whose units, the Württemberg Mountain Battalion, the young Erwin Rommel was serving as a company commander. Altogether the Austro-German force assembled for the "twelfth battle" numbered thirty-five divisions against the Italians' thirty-four, occupying bridgeheads across the Isonzo river which offered them the opportunity to drive down and up the valley from north and south and join hands behind the whole of the Italian Second Army.

Such was the Austro-German plan. The point divisions were the Austrian 22nd, locally recruited in Slovenia, followed by the 8th "Edelweiss" Division, largely composed of the élite Tirol *Kaiserjäger.* Attacking downstream, they were to follow the valley of the Isonzo towards Caporetto (called Karfreit by the Austrians), to meet the other point division, the *Alpenkorps,* attacking upstream. In the vanguard of the *Alpenkorps,* on October 24, marched the Bavarian Life Guards, supported by the Württemberg Mountain Battalion. Rommel, commanding a group

Left: Italian equipment abandoned on a road leading to the plains after the disaster in the mountains on the Isonzo front. The two guns in the foreground are 149 mm, the standard Italian medium gun, with a "footed" wheel, to facilitate movement over broken ground. Almost all Italy's medium and heavy artillery was lost in the retreat from Caporetto, necessitating re-equipment with French and British material. Almost everything else was lost also and, until requipment and reorganisation could take place, the Italian line was effectively defended by French and British troops rushed from the Western Front.

Opposite top: The future Field Marshal Erwin Rommel, after Caporetto. Rommel, a company commander in the Württemberg Mountain Battalion, attached to the Bavarian *Alpenkorps,* played a leading role in the German-Austrian breakthrough, pushing ahead of his accompanying regiment, the Bavarian Life Guards, to ambush Italians attempting to escape from the disaster in the mountains higher up. In command of fewer than 200 men, he eventually succeeded in taking 6,000 Italians prisoner. For his exploits he was awarded the Pour le Mérite, Germany's highest award for bravery, which in the photograph he is wearing around his neck.

Opposite bottom: Foch and Diaz in France, after the Caporetto disaster. Diaz replaced Cadorna in the aftermath of the defeat as commander of the Italian armies. Between Diaz and Foch stands Weygand, Foch's operations officer and commander of the French armies during the latter stages of their defeat in 1940.

of the battalion's companies, was no more content as a lieutenant with a supporting role than he would be as a panzer general in the 1940 blitzkrieg. He soon found himself separated from the Life Guards and out in front. There was little sign of the enemy and no resistance. "I then had to decide whether I should roll up the hostile position or break through in the direction of the Hevnik peak [a key height in the Italian rear]. I chose the latter. The elimination of the Italian positions followed once we had possession of the peak. The further we penetrated into the hostile positions, the less prepared were the garrisons for our arrival, and the easier the fighting." What Rommel was achieving on his tiny but critical sector was being repeated elsewhere. The Germans and Austrians, penetrating the steep defile of the Isonzo valley, by-passing Italian strong points and striking for the high ground, were biting out an enormous gap in the Italian front, fifteen miles wide, leaving behind them four Italian divisions isolated and surrounded. Moreover, the deeper the Austro-German Fourteenth Army advanced, the more they threatened the flanks of the larger concentrations of Italian troops to north and south, menacing the whole of Cadorna's eastern front with the collapse of its rear area. On October 26 Cadorna, a man beset by nightmare, realised that a general retreat to the Tagliamento, the next large river west of the Isonzo, was inevitable. The enemy, rampaging forward, did not allow him to rest there. Though the Italians blew the bridges behind them, their pursuers got across and by November 3 had pressed them back to the River Piave. In eleven days they had advanced eighty miles, to within striking distance of Venice, forced the retreat of the Italians from the whole length of their mountain frontier between the Tirol and its hinge on the sea, and captured 275,000 prisoners; Italian battle casualties amounted to the comparatively small total, by First World War standards, of ten thousand dead. Cadorna did his best to increase the number, by a ruthless and characteristic institution of the summary execution of stragglers. When, in the aftermath of Caporetto, he attempted to cast responsibility for the army's collapse onto defeatism in the rear he lost the government's support. On November 3, echoing sentiments expressed in France after the Nivelle offensive, he referred to the Caporetto retreat as "a kind of military strike." Five days later he had been removed from command, to be replaced by General Armando Diaz, who, like Pétain after the Nivelle catastrophe, would offer the common soldier a more indulgent regime of leave and comforts as an inducement to sustain the fight.

In practice, the Italian army, like the French, would not resume the offensive until the following year. When it did so, it would be in the company of a far stronger foreign contingent, largely British. Caporetto, one of few clear-cut victories of the First World War, was a triumph for the Germans, a vindication of the military qualities of their faltering Austrian allies and a major defeat for the Allies at the end of a year which had brought disabling setbacks to their cause. It had one positive effect, to force Britain and France to recognise that their haphazard system of directing the war effort could not continue if the war was to be brought to a conclusion in their favour. On November 5, an inter-Allied meeting was convened at Rapallo, at which it was decided to establish a permanent Supreme War Council to sit at Versailles under the aegis of the British, French and Italian Prime Ministers and the President of the United States.

German soldiers watch Italians
being marched into captivity after
Caporetto. About 280,000 Italians
were taken prisoner during October
and the first two weeks of November. The disaster brought down the
Italian government. The new Prime
Minister, Orlando, dismissed
Cadorna, the Commander-in-Chief,
and begged sufficient help from the
Allies, six French and five British
divisions, to stem the German-
Austrian advance. The Germans, in
any case, were anxious to recover
the troops they had lent, in order
to sustain their buildup on the
Western Front. In Italy a new front
was established on the River Piave,
a major defensive obstacle, twenty
miles north of Venice.

PALESTINE

Palestine in 1914 formed part of the Ottoman empire and was its outpost nearest to the Suez Canal, vital to Britain as the link between the home base and India. In February 1915, following Turkey's declaration of war the previous November, the Turkish governor of Syria launched an attack from Palestine across the Sinai desert towards the canal. Though defeated, the offensive greatly alarmed the British government, which thereafter maintained a large garrison in Egypt to guard against a future attack. Its commanders constructed defensive lines in Sinai, built railways and laid a water pipeline. A second Turkish thrust was turned back in August 1916, after which the British made a counter-offensive. In March 1917 the force in Egypt mounted an attack on Gaza, the nearest large town in Palestine. It was checked, as was another in April. Command then passed to General Sir Edmund Allenby, a successful leader brought from the Western Front. He had instructions from the Prime Minister, David Lloyd George, to take "Jerusalem before Christmas." He also brought reinforcements. The Turks now had considerable German assistance, however, and the advice of Generals Falkenhayn and Kress von Kressenstein. Nevertheless, Allenby was able in October to mount a successful Third Battle of Gaza and on December 9 to enter Jerusalem.

The Germans and Turks fought back, winning the Battle of Amman (in present-day Jordan), in March 1918. They were forced, however, to abandon plans for a drive to Baghdad (Operation *Yilderim*) and, under pressure from the Arab armies of Abdullah and Feisal, rebels against Turkish rule, to which T. E. Lawrence "of Arabia" had attached himself, also to surrender control of the Hejaz railway, the Red Sea coast and the desert flanks of Palestine and Syria. By September 1918, Allenby was poised for a decisive blow. It was delivered at Megiddo, in northern Palestine, on September 19. Assisted by the Arab army, Allenby's forces took the Syrian cities of Damascus on October 1 and Aleppo on October 26. Turkey was already seeking an armistice, which was granted at Mudros, from which the Gallipoli expedition had been launched in 1915, on October 30.

Left: In front is the British Military Governor of Jerusalem, Borton Pasha, followed by his two aides-de-camp, December 11, 1917.
Opposite top: *Action of the 6th Mounted Brigade at El-Mughar, November 13, 1917,* by J. C. Beadle.
Opposite bottom: *Camel Corps going into action at Magdabha,* 1916, by H. S. Power.

A camel ambulance stops to pick up a wounded man at Rafa. The swaying cacolets astride the camel's humps provided uncomfortable transport for the injured.

AMERICA, SUBMARINES AND PASSCHENDAELE

President Woodrow Wilson had said America was "too proud to fight," a sentiment that mirrored his own distaste for war. High-minded, idealistic, academic, he had formed the belief that plain dealing between nations in open diplomacy was the secret of averting and evading conflict. During 1916 he had, through his emissary, Colonel Edward House, made a determined but unsuccessful effort to bring the combatants to negotiation on terms he regarded as fair to all. He was not, however, unrealistic about the place of force in international affairs nor was he unwilling to use force if necessary. In 1915 he had brought Germany's campaign of "unrestricted" submarine warfare to a close by a threat to use American

naval power. As late as the spring of 1917, nevertheless, he had no intention of joining the war, nor was there enthusiasm for entry among his fellow citizens.

Two events changed America's outlook. The first was a clumsy German approach to Mexico, baited with the offer to return Texas, Arizona and New Mexico. This "Zimmermann telegram" was transmitted to the American government by British naval intelligence and caused outrage when it was published on March 1, 1917. The second was Germany's decision to resume the unrestricted U-boat campaign: sinking merchant shipping without warning in international waters. The policy allowed U-boat captains to sink by gunfire or torpedo at will. The proponent of the policy was Admiral Henning von Holtzendorff, chief of the German naval staff, whose argument was that only through an all-out attack on British maritime supply could the war be brought to a favourable conclusion. He demonstrated by statistical calculation that a rate of sinking of 600,000 tons of largely British shipping a month would, within five months, drive Britain to the brink of starvation, meanwhile also depriving France and Italy of the supply of British coal essential to the working of their economies.

Above: A U.S. Marine Corps recruiting poster, 1917. The Corps was the best prepared of American forces for war and fought in France as early as June 1918.

Left: The torpedo room of a German U-boat, 1917. The most numerous class of German patrol submarines had six torpedo tubes and displaced 750 tons surfaced, with a crew of forty. At the beginning of the war, U-boats observed the rules of commerce raiding, which required the captain to give a merchant ship warning of his intention to attack and to ensure the safety of its crew and passengers. In 1915 briefly, and again in 1917 until the end, Germany practised "unrestricted" submarine warfare, in which merchant ships were attacked without warning.

Overleaf, left: American troops and equipment disembarking in France, 1918. Over two million Americans, out of 5.5 million mobilised, had arrived in France by the Armistice. Their size and physique impressed Europeans, many of whose best men had already been killed or disabled during the early years of fighting. The American deficiency was in heavy equipment. The American artillery was largely equipped with the French 75-mm gun, its tank corps with French light Renault tanks and its air service with French aircraft.

Overleaf, right: Marshal Joffre reviewing West Point cadets in Washington, April 1917. After giving up command of the French armies at home, Joffre was appointed head of the French military mission to the United States.

The 1st Regiment, Illinois National Guard, steps out of its armoury on a recruiting march, 1917. The entire National Guard was mobilised on July 3, 1917, and eventually seventeen National Guard divisions served in France. The Guard, legally the "organised militia" of the individual states, could be brought under Federal control by presidential order. There were 80,000 National Guardsmen available for Federal service on April 1, 1917, and another 97,000 who had not yet taken the federal oath. The Guard was effectively the regular army's reserve, which had only 4,000 reservists of its own.

Hindenburg and Ludendorff responded enthusiastically to Holtzendorf's memorandum of December 22, 1916, urging the institution of unrestricted sinkings, and it was decided to take the risk. The campaign, in the seas around the British Isles, on the west coast of France and in the Mediterranean, began on February 1. The political effect in the United States was felt immediately and the severity of American reaction vastly exceeded German expectation. On March 15 German submarines made direct attacks on American merchant ships, sinking three. That was a direct challenge to the dignity of the United States as a sovereign power, one which Wilson reluctantly decided he could not ignore. On April 2, before a special session of Congress, he reviewed the development of the German submarine campaign, declared it to be a "war against all nations" and asked Congress "to accept the status of a belligerent which has thus been thrust upon it." Four days later Congress resolved that war against Germany should be formally declared. Declarations against Austria-Hungary, Turkey and Bulgaria followed, selective military conscription was enacted (May 18, 1917) and the armed forces of the United States began at once to prepare for operations in Europe.

The mobilisation of the United States Navy, with the second largest fleet of modern battleships in the world after Britain's, immediately altered the balance

of naval power unchallengeably in the Allies' favour; after December 1917, when five American dreadnoughts joined the Grand Fleet, the High Seas Fleet, outnumbered by thirty-five to fifteen, could not hope to stand against it in battle. The United States Army, by contrast, was in April 1917 only 128,000 strong; the federalisation of the National Guard, of 170,000 part-time soldiers, scarcely added to its effectiveness. The best American units belonged to the Marine Corps, but numbered only 13,000. Nevertheless, it was decided to form an expeditionary force of one division and two Marine brigades and send it to France immediately. Meanwhile, conscription would produce a first contingent of a million recruits. It was expected that two million men would arrive in France during 1918.

The spectre of America's gathering millions lent even greater urgency to Germany's attempt to starve out its European enemies by U-boat action. The first

months of unrestricted sinkings suggested that it might. During 1915 the U-boats had sunk 227 British ships (855,721 gross tons), the majority in the first unrestricted campaign. Sinkings then declined sharply when, after May 1916, the German Admiralty reverted to stricter observance of maritime law. From February, when unrestricted sinkings began again, the totals rose month by month to terrifying levels: 520,412 tons in February, 564,497 tons in March and 860,334 tons in April. Holtzendorf's target of the 600,000 tons of monthly sinkings necessary to win the war had been exceeded, and threatened to increase and to bring Allied defeat. The Admiralty could see no means to avert disaster. Arming merchant ships was pointless when U-boats attacked submerged with torpedoes. Mining the exits from the U-boat bases was ineffective. Hunting U-boats was like looking for a needle in a haystack. Trapping U-boats with apparently harmless decoys not worth a torpedo, the celebrated "Q" ships disguised as small merchantmen but heavily armed, worked on odd occasions until the German captains got canny.

Meanwhile the haemorrhage continued apparently unquenchably. U-boat losses were negligible: ten from October to December 1916, only nine from February to April 1917, two of which were to German mines.

There was a solution available—convoy—but the Admiralty resisted it. Sailing ships in groups, even under escort, seemed merely to offer a larger group of targets. The Admiralty analysis was, of course, wrong. In the spaces of the sea, a group of ships is little more conspicuous than a single ship, and, if not found by a U-boat, all would escape attack. Moreover, the Admiralty had been deluded by another mathematical misperception. In attempting to estimate the number of escorts it would have to find if it adopted convoy, it counted all sailings, which amounted to 2,500 weekly from British ports, and concluded it had insufficient warships. It was only under closer analysis that a more manageable picture was revealed. The number of weekly arrivals of the vital ocean-going merchant ships was only 120 to 140 a week, and for those sufficient escorts could easily be found.

By April 27 the senior admirals were convinced and on April 28 the first convoy was sailed. It reached Britain without loss on May 10. Thenceforward convoy was progressively introduced and losses began to decline. They stood, however, at 399,000 tons as late as December. Not until the second quarter of 1918 would they drop below 300,000 tons monthly, by which time, without convoy, nearly four million of the world's thirty million tons of shipping would have been sunk in a little over a year. It was convoy that had reversed the fatal trend; but important subsidiary measures included the systematic laying of mine barriers (70,000 in the Northern Barrier between Scotland and Norway), and the dedication of large numbers of aircraft and airships to anti-submarine patrols in narrow waters where air patrol, hydrophone and depth charge could more easily find U-boats, and minefields claim victims. Of the 178 U-boats lost during the war, out of 390 built, 41 were mined, only 30 depth-charged. Direct attack on U-boat bases, as on the famous Zeebrugge raid of April 23, 1918, interrupted submarine operations not at all. Nevertheless, Holtzendorf's war-winning total of sinkings was never achieved. If the British did not exactly win the U-boat war, the Germans still managed to lose it.

The unrestricted campaign nevertheless had the effect of driving Britain to undertake what would become its most notorious land campaign of the war, the Third Battle of Ypres, or Passchendaele. Haig had long nurtured a plan to make the Ypres salient the starting point for a counter-offensive that would break the German line. It was discussed at an Anglo-French conference held in Paris on May 4–5, 1917, when Pétain gave assurances that the French would support it with up to four attacks of their own. By June, with the truth of the French mutinies no longer deniable, it was clear that the British would have to fight alone. The matter of moment was to find a justification for them doing so. Haig was adamant that they should and believed they would win a victory. Local events in June, south of the Ypres salient, lent credence to his case. There, on June 7, Plumer's Second Army had mounted a long-prepared assault on Messines Ridge with complete success. Just before dawn nineteen enormous mines were detonated, and nine divisions moved forward. Nearly three weeks of bombardment had preceded the attack. When the assault waves arrived on the Messines crest they found such

Opposite top: The Royal Army Medical Corps evacuating casualties at Messines, June 1917. The Messines ridge, held by the Germans, had dominated British positions south of Ypres since October 1914. Beginning in January 1917, British and Australian tunnelling companies excavated twenty mine chambers under the ridge and filled them with 600 tons of explosive. Detonated on June 7, the mines killed 10,000 German defenders, obliterated much of the ridge and caused a shock wave felt in London. The Messines position was subsequently occupied by advancing British troops and a severe local defeat inflicted on the enemy.

Opposite bottom: An Australian soldier bringing in a wounded German prisoner after the Messines explosions.

defenders as survived unable to offer resistance. At a blow the British had driven the enemy from the southern wing of the Ypres salient. Haig's ambition to drive in the centre and thence advance to the Flemish coast was greatly enhanced.

The obstacle to another major Western Front offensive remained the hesitation of the then Prime Minister. David Lloyd George was oppressed by the rising tide of British casualties, already a quarter of a million dead, and the paltry military return gained by the sacrifice. In June he formed yet another inner committee of the Cabinet to assume the higher direction of the war. The Committee on War Policy first met on June 11. Lloyd George was relentless in his criticism. Haig was unshaken throughout two days of debate. Despite Lloyd George's fears about casualties, compounded by the difficulties in finding any more men from civil life to replace those lost, Haig insisted that "it was necessary for us to go on engaging the enemy . . . and he was quite confident, he could reach the first objective," which was the crest of the Ypres ridges. This was the nub of the difference:

Haig wanted to fight, Lloyd George did not. At the end, however, he felt unable, as a civilian Prime Minister, "to impose my strategical views on my military advisers" and was therefore obliged to accept theirs.

The consequences would be heavy. The "Flanders Position," as the Germans called it, was one of the strongest on the Western Front. From the low heights the enemy front line looked down on an almost level plain from which three years of constant shelling had removed every trace of vegetation and had destroyed the field drainage system so that the onset of rain rapidly flooded the battlefield's surface. To quagmire and absence of concealment the Germans had added to the B.E.F.'s difficulties by building a network of concrete pillboxes and bunkers, often constructed inside ruined buildings. The completed Flanders Position was actu-

Left: King George V at the front, 1917. George V was a frequent visitor to the British Expeditionary Force in France and Belgium. His evident humanity and concern for the welfare of his soldiers laid the basis for the enormous esteem in which he was held in post-war years. The Prince of Wales, his oldest son, the future King Edward VIII, also spent the war years with the B.E.F., but was not, to his frustration, allowed to serve in the trenches lest he be taken prisoner.

Below: A sergeant and tunnellers of the 1st Australian Tunnelling Company at work below Messines ridge, spring 1917. Many of the tunnellers were miners from Australian gold fields.

ally nine layers deep. The defenders of the Flanders Position belonged, in July 1917, to ten divisions, with 1,556 field and heavy guns deployed on seven miles of front. The British Fifth Army opposite had concentrated 2,299 guns, or one for every five yards, ten times the density on the Somme fourteen months earlier. It had also been allotted 180 aircraft, out of a total of 508 in the battle area; their role was to achieve air superiority above the front to a depth of five miles, where the German observation-balloon line began. Visibility, in good conditions, from the basket of a captive balloon, was as much as sixty miles, allowing the observer, via the telephone wire attached to the tethering cable, to correct the artillery's fall of shot with a high degree of accuracy and at speed. Improvements in wireless were also allowing two-seater observation aircraft to direct artillery fire, though laboriously, for two-way voice transmission was not yet technically possible. The war in the air, which in 1918 would take a dramatic leap forward into the fields of ground attack and long-range strategic bombing, remained dur-

Above: Lieutenant Ernst Udet (1896–1941), the highest-scoring German fighter ace to survive the war. He shot down sixty-two Allied aircraft, most during 1918. The air war over the Western Front reached its climax during 1918, with a genuine struggle for supremacy. The German air service, with 3,000 aircraft deployed, was committed not only to artillery observation and aerial combat but also to ground attack, its armoured Junkers J-1s taking part in the great offensives of spring and summer. Though less celebrated than Richthofen, Udet was more successful, surviving to become a leading light of the Luftwaffe after Hitler's rise to power.

Page 339, top: A British transport column moving out of Ypres up the Menin road, September 29, 1917, during the Third Battle of Ypres (Passchendaele). The hurdle in the foreground gives access to an extemporised ration and shell dump, off-loaded from wagons wrecked by German shell fire. The Menin road lay under German observation and was constantly swept by their shelling.

Page 339, bottom: A water cart bogged at Ypres during the Battle of Passchendaele. The horse on the left has gone off the brushwood track and has bogged. The man at far left is holding sacking to put under its hooves. Many horses had to be abandoned in the morass and men who lost their footing sometimes drowned in the mud, which in places was six feet deep.

ing 1917 largely stuck at the level of artillery observation, "balloon busting" and dog-fighting to gain or retain air superiority.

The French air service, though a branch of the army, was unaffected by the disorders which paralysed the ground formations during 1917. It operated effectively against the German air raids over the Aisne in April and May and lent important support to the Royal Flying Corps during the Third Battle of Ypres. Its best aircraft, the Spad 12 and 13, were superior to most of those flown by the Germans at the beginning of the year and it produced a succession of aces, Georges Guynemer and René Fonck the most celebrated, whose air-fighting skills were deadly. When Guynemer was killed during Third Ypres on September 11, the French Senate ceremonially enshrined the victor of fifty-three aerial combats in the Pantheon. The year was also to see, however, the emergence of the most famous German aces, including Werner Voss (forty-eight victories) and the legendary "Red Baron," Manfred von Richthofen (eighty eventual victories), whose achievements were owed not just to their airmanship and aggressiveness but also to the delivery to the German air service of new types of aircraft, particularly the manoeuvrable Fokker Triplane, which displayed a significant edge in aerial combat over the British and French equivalents. Aeronautical technology, during the First World War, permitted very rapid swings in superiority between one side and the other. "Lead times" in the development of aircraft, now measured in decades, then lasted months, sometimes only weeks; a slightly more powerful engine or a minor refinement of airframe could confer a startling advantage. During 1917 the Royal Flying Corps received three rapidly developed and advanced aircraft, the single-seater Sopwith Camel and S.E.5 and the two-seater Bristol Fighter, which provided the material to make its numbers, inexperienced as many of its pilots were, tell against the German veterans. It began also to produce its own aces to match those of the French and German air forces, the most famous being Edward Mannock, James McCudden and Albert Ball. McCudden, an ex-private soldier, and Mannock, a convinced Socialist, were cold-hearted technicians of dog-fighting from backgrounds wholly at variance with the majority of public school pilots whom Albert Ball typified.

The outcome of the Third Battle of Ypres would be decided, however, on the ground, not in the skies above it. The first objectives had been fixed six thousand yards away from the British start line, within supporting field-gun range. Once those had been taken, the artillery was to be moved forward until, bite by bite, the German defences had been chewed through, the enemy's reserves destroyed and a way opened to the undefended rear area. The bombardment, which had begun fifteen days earlier and expended over four million shells, reached its crescendo just before four o'clock in the morning of July 31. At 3:50 a.m., the assaulting troops moved forward, accompanied by 136 tanks. Though the ground was churned and pock-marked by years of shelling, the surface was dry and only two tanks bogged and the infantry also managed to make steady progress. By late morning, however, the familiar breakdown of communication between infantry and guns had occurred; cables were everywhere cut, low cloud prevented aerial observation, "the only news from the assault was by runners, who sometimes took hours to get back, if indeed they ever did." Then at two in the afternoon the Ger-

VON RICHTHOFEN

Manfred von Richthofen (1892–1918) was the leading German fighter ace and one of the most famous individual warriors of the First World War. A pre-war cavalry officer, he transferred in May 1915 to the air service, flying first as an observer, in accordance with the original German practise which allotted the pilot's role to a non-commissioned officer. In 1916, however, he became a single-seater fighter pilot in the *Jägdstaffel* (hunter squadron) of the already famous ace Oswald Boelcke. After Boelcke's death in combat, he succeeded to command in January 1917, by which time he had shot down 15 aircraft. By April he had, with 52 "victories," exceeded the score of both Boelcke (40) and the original German ace, Max Immelmann (15).

In June 1917 he took command of *Jägdstaffel* 1, to become famous as Richthofen's Flying Circus. Flying his distinctive bright red Fokker DR-1 Tri-plane, he then embarked on a highly aggres-sive campaign over the Western Front, directed particularly against the British, to whom he became during 1917 a figure of menace. Such was his propaganda value that his fellow pilots often softened up his chosen targets, leaving him to make the kill. By the spring of 1918 he had shot down 80 enemy aircraft, the highest score of any ace. On April 21, he was engaged in combat by Sopwith Camels of the Royal Air Force, brought down and killed. Despite his killer rep-utation, he was buried with full military honours by his adversaries. Controversy continues to surround his death, the destruction of his Fokker Triplane being ascribed to ground fire from Australian troops in the vicinity of the crash. Command of the Flying Circus subse-quently passed to Hermann Göring, the future chief of Hitler's Luft-waffe. The most famous equivalents of Richthofen on the other side were Fonck (75 victories) and Guynemar (54) of the French air force, Mannock (73) and Bishop (72) of the British and Ricken-backer (26) of the American.

Background image: *The squadron of Baron von Richtofen in action*, watercolour by Claus Bergen.

Top inset: Baron von Richtofen.

Right: Richtofen being buried by English soldiers.

man counter-attack was unleashed. An intense bombardment fell, so heavy that the leading troops were driven to flight. To the rain of German shells was added a torrential downpour which soon turned the broken battlefield to soupy mud. The rain persisted during the next three days, as the British infantry renewed their assaults and their artillery was dragged forward to new positions. On August 4 a British battery commander wrote of "simply awful [mud]. The ground is churned up to a depth of ten feet and is the consistency of porridge."

On August 24, after the failure of a third attack on the Gheluvelt plateau, Haig decided to transfer responsibility for the main effort at Ypres from Gough's Fifth Army to Plumer's Sec-

Left: The ruins of Ypres, 1917. The view is across the Grande Place towards the remains of the Cloth Hall. A 6-inch howitzer is parked on the right, waiting for a tow. The sky threatens rain. The autumn months of 1917 were wet even by the standards of Flanders, one of the wettest regions of northern Europe. The landscape surrounding Ypres, much of it reclaimed from the sea and in places below sea level, became completely waterlogged during the Third Battle (Passchendaele). The elaborate drainage system, put in place over centuries, had been destroyed by three years of shelling and the autumn rainfall, without means of escape, saturated the surface and subsoil.

Overleaf, left: French troops attacking across pontoons over the River Yser during the Third Battle of Ypres, August 1917.

Overleaf, right: 2nd Battery, Royal Australian Artillery, at Vormezeele, firing out of the Ypres salient, September 1917, during the Battle of Passchendaele. The gun is a 9.2-inch howitzer, principal weapon of the British heavy artillery. It threw a 380-pound shell up to 26,000 yards. The firing lanyard has just been pulled, and four of the crew are waiting to reload with the shell in a cradle. The loading crane is above their heads. The gun will have to be returned to the horizontal for the shell to be rammed into the breech. The camouflage netting is attached at one corner to a willow tree, common on the Flanders plain.

ond. Plumer had commanded the Ypres sector for two years, knew all its dangerous corners and had endeared himself to his soldiers by his concern for their well-being. He now decided that there must be a pause, to allow careful preparation for the next phase. There was to be one last action before the pause, on August 27, to attempt the capture of two long-vanished woods, Glencorse Wood and Inverness Copse, just north of the remains of Gheluvelt village. The official history admits that the ground was "so slippery from the rain and so broken by the water-filled shell holes that the pace was slow and the protection of the creeping barrage was soon lost." Edwin Vaughan, a wartime officer of the 1st/8th Warwickshire Regiment, describes the effort of his unit to get forward:

"Up the road we staggered, shells bursting around us. A man stopped dead in front of me, and exasperated I cursed him and butted him with my knee. Very gently he said, 'I'm blind, Sir,' and turned to show me his eyes and nose torn away

by a piece of shell. 'Oh God! I'm sorry, sonny,' I said. 'Keep going on the hard part,' and left him staggering back in his darkness."

Vaughan's experience was typical of what the Third Battle of Ypres was becoming. On September 4, Haig was summoned to London to justify the continuation of the offensive, even in the limited form proposed by the prudent Plumer. Lloyd George, reviewing the whole state of the war, argued that, with Russia no longer a combatant and France barely so, strategic wisdom lay in husbanding British resources until the Americans arrived in force in 1918. Haig insisted that, precisely because of the other allies' weakness, Third Ypres must continue. He got his way. Plumer's "step-by-step" scheme, for which the pause in early September was the preparation, was conceived in three stages. In each, a long bombardment was to precede a short advance of 1,500 yards. After three weeks of bombardment, the 1st and 2nd Australian Divisions attacked up the Menin road

east of Ypres. The accompanying barrage fell on a belt a thousand yards deep and, under that devastating weight of fire, the Germans fell back. The same results were achieved in the Battle of Polygon Wood, September 26, and of Broodseinde, October 4. "Bite and hold," Plumer's tactics, had been successful. The question was whether the next series of "bite and hold" attacks could be justified.

The only reliable assault divisions Haig had left were in his ANZAC and Canadian Corps, which had been spared the first stages of the battle. In what was called the "First Battle of Passchendaele," the New Zealand and 3rd Australian

Divisions tried on October 12 to reach the remains of the village. Caught in front and flank by machine-gun fire, the ANZACs eventually retreated to the positions from which they had started their advance on that sodden day. The New Zealanders alone suffered nearly three thousand casualties in attempting to pass through uncut wire. Having consigned the II ANZAC Corps to a pointless sacrifice, Haig then turned to the Canadians. General Sir Arthur Currie, commanding the Canadian Corps, had known the Ypres salient since 1915; he did not want to lose any more of his soldiers there. He nevertheless, after protest, complied with Haig's order. The early winter had brought almost continuous rain and the only way forward towards the top of the ridge was along two narrow causeways. On October

A British tank attacking a German pillbox at Polygon Wood during the Third Battle of Ypres, 1917. The wood, originally so called for its shape on aerial photographs, had long since been destroyed by shell fire. The German defenders of the Ypres front had constructed a network of reinforced-concrete pillboxes in the months before the battle opened, often inside existing buildings, to conceal the work from British observation. The pillboxes resisted artillery fire and had to be taken by infantry assault, at a heavy cost in lives.

26, the first day of the "Second Battle of Passchendaele," the Canadians broke the First Flanders Position and advanced about five hundred yards. The 1st and 2nd Canadian Divisions took over the front of attack for a fresh assault on November 6, which captured what was left of Passchendaele village, and a final assault was made on November 10, when the line was consolidated. The Second Battle of Passchendaele had cost the four divisions of the Canadian Corps 15,634 killed and wounded, almost exactly the figure Currie had predicted in October.

THE BATTLE OF CAMBRAI

There remained one means of offence against the Germans that the mud of Flanders had denied its potentiality: machine warfare. The main reserve of the Tank Corps remained intact. Its commander, Brigadier General H. Elles, had been seeking an opportunity to use it during the summer and had interested General Sir Julian Byng, commanding Third Army, in the idea of making a surprise attack with tanks on his front, which ran across dry, chalky ground. One of Byng's artillery officers, Brigadier General H. H. Tudor, of the 9th Scottish Division, had meanwhile been devising a plan of his own to support tanks with a surprise bombardment. Byng accepted both Elles's and Tudor's plans in August and Haig's headquarters approved them on October 13. By early November, with the bat-

A French artist's impression of a British tank attacking at Cambrai, November 20, 1917. This Mark IV is a "Male," mounting two 6-pounder guns in sponsons right and left. Over 300 tanks attacked. They were organised to work together in threes, the first suppressing enemy fire while the other two crossed the enemy trench in turn. The first tank was then to catch up and the pattern to be repeated. The tactics worked well at Cambrai but the tanks' intrinsic lack of speed, only three miles per hour, limited the depth of the break-in during the time available, and allowed the Germans to bring up reinforcements.

Above: Part of a German storm troop group manhandling a 75-mm mountain gun. By the beginning of 1918, most German divisions included storm troops, specially equipped and trained to lead attacks.

Below: German officers with a captured British Mark IV tank after Cambrai. Although Germany built its own tanks, most of those it used in 1918 were captured British models.

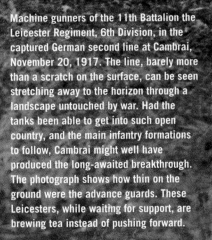

Machine gunners of the 11th Battalion the Leicester Regiment, 6th Division, in the captured German second line at Cambrai, November 20, 1917. The line, barely more than a scratch on the surface, can be seen stretching away to the horizon through a landscape untouched by war. Had the tanks been able to get into such open country, and the main infantry formations to follow, Cambrai might well have produced the long-awaited breakthrough. The photograph shows how thin on the ground were the advance guards. These Leicesters, while waiting for support, are brewing tea instead of pushing forward.

tle at Passchendaele lapsing into futility, Haig was anxious for a compensatory success of any sort and on November 10, at Byng's urging, gave his consent to the Elles-Tudor scheme. The offensive was to be launched at the earliest possible moment at Cambrai with over three hundred tanks. They were to be followed by eight infantry divisions and supported by a thousand guns. The nature of the artillery plan was crucial to success. Tudor had devised a method of registering guns by electrical means, so that the artillery commander could be confident his batteries would hit their designated targets without any of the preliminary registration which had always hitherto given offensive plans away.

All began well. The unfortunate German soldiers garrisoning the Cambrai sector were unprepared for the hurricane bombardment that descended upon them at 6:20 on the morning of November 20 and the appearance of dense columns of tanks, 324 in all, rolling forward with infantry following. Within four hours the attackers had advanced in many places to a depth of four miles, at almost no cost in casualties. The difference was in the centre. There the 51st Highland Division, gingerly following the tanks at some hundred yards' distance, entered the

German soldiers captured at Cambrai waiting at the roadside with British wounded for evacuation, November 20, 1917. Some 10,000 surrendered, mostly in the opening stages when stunned by the appearance of massed tanks. It was the largest number of German prisoners taken by the British in a single day during the war to that point. The defenders, mainly from the 20th and 54th Divisions, recovered quickly, as did the German high command. The success of its counter-attack on November 30 restored the position in the Cambrai sector.

defended zone of the German 54th Reserve. Its gunners began to engage the British tanks as they appeared and knocked them out one by one. Soon eleven were out of action, five destroyed by a single German sergeant who was killed by a Highlander when the 51st Division's infantry at last got up with tanks. By then, however, it was too late for the division to reach the objective so that, while on the left and right of the Cambrai battlefield, the whole German position had been broken, in the centre a salient bulged towards British lines, denying General Byng

The Kaiser and (to his right) Prince Rupprecht of Bavaria after the Battle of Cambrai. The Kaiser is wearing both the Iron Cross First Class and the Grand Class of the Iron Cross. His orderly is carrying his personal standard. Prince Rupprecht (1869–1955), heir to the throne of Bavaria, which retained considerable autonomy inside the German empire after its formation in 1871, commanded the Sixth Army during the Battle of the Frontiers in 1914. In 1916 he was promoted to field marshal and given command of the Northern Group of Armies. Greatly respected for both his personal and his professional qualities, he became convinced of the probability of Allied victory in the closing stages of the war.

the clear-cut breakthrough Elles's and Tudor's revolutionary plan should have brought him.

In England the bells rang out for a victory. The celebration was premature. Byng's cavalry was held up by wire the tanks had not cut and turned back. Then, on November 30, the German army demonstrated once again its formidable counter-attack power. In the ten days since the attack had been unleashed, twenty divisions had been assembled by Crown Prince Rupprecht, the local commander, and in a morning attack they took back not only much of the ground lost to the tanks on November 20 but another portion, which the British had held beforehand. The Cambrai battle thus ended on ambiguous terms along the line of the "Drocourt-Quéant Switch," a sinuous double salient which gave both the British and the Germans some of each other's long-held territory. It was an appropriate symbol of the precarious balance of power on the Western Front at the end of 1917.

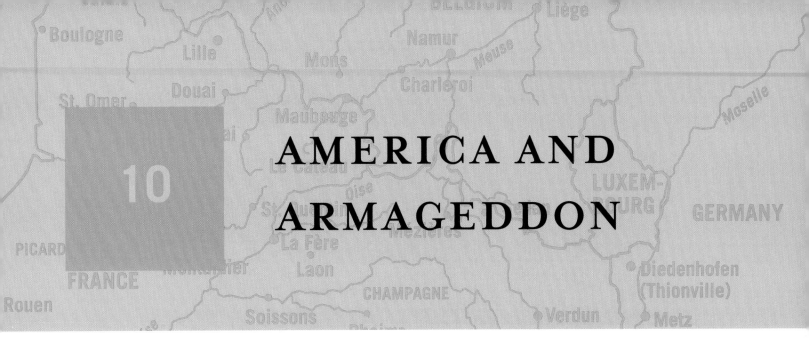

AMERICA AND ARMAGEDDON

10

"They will not even come," Admiral Capelle, the Secretary of State for the Navy, had assured the German parliament on January 31, 1917, "because our submarines will sink them. Thus America from a military point of view means nothing, and again nothing and for a third time nothing." At the beginning of 1917, four months before the United States entered the war on the side of the Allies, its army might indeed have meant nothing. It ranked in size seventeenth in the world. It had no experience of large-scale operations since the armistice at Appomattox fifty-two years earlier, and possessed no modern equipment heavier than its medium machine guns. Yet, by June 1917, the commander of the American Expeditionary Force, General John J. Pershing, had arrived in France and on July 4, elements of his 1st Division paraded in Paris. Throughout the following months, fresh units of an army planned to reach a strength of eighty divisions continued to disembark. By March 1918, 318,000 men had reached France, the vanguard of 1,300,000 to be deployed by August, and not one had been lost to the action of the enemy in oceanic transport.

Rare are the times in a great war when the fortunes of one side or the other are transformed by the sudden accretion of a disequilibriating reinforcement. By 1918, President Wilson's decision to declare war on Germany and its allies had brought such an accretion to the Allied side. Capelle's "they will never come" had been trumped in six months by an American's melodramatic "Lafayette, we are here." Yet the arrival of the Americans did not immediately threaten German defeat in 1917. By the end of the year, the Germans had turned a corner. The political collapse of Russia had released from the Eastern Front fifty divisions of infantry which could be brought to the west to attempt a final, war-winning offensive. Moreover, the German high command, which had for so long been compelled to sustain defensive strategy in the west, had given great thought and preparation to perfecting the offensive methods to be employed by the attack force. It was a grave deficiency that the army had no tanks. A clumsy prototype was under development, and British tanks captured during 1917 were being pressed into service, but no concentration of tanks such as was already available

American troops land in France, 1918, by
Achille Beltrame.

351

to the British and French stood to hand. Hindenburg and Ludendorff counted, in its absence, on a refinement of artillery and infantry tactics to compensate for German weakness at the technical level. The infantry had been re-equipped with large numbers of stripped-down machine guns and had been trained to "infiltrate" enemy positions, by-passing centres of resistance, rather than stopping to fight when held up directly to their front.

The emphasis of the German attack plan was on speed. Ludendorff had the necessary troops and guns and a realistic plan. The enemy was to be attacked both on a broad front—fifty miles—and in depth, to be achieved by concentrating an enormous weight of artillery firing the heaviest possible bombardment in a brief but crushing deluge of shells, lasting five hours. Ludendorff's bombard-

ment force amounted to 6,473 field, medium and heavy guns and 3,532 mortars of varying calibre, for which over a million rounds of ammunition were assembled. All the guns were "registered" beforehand, so that all would hit their designated targets. Explosive shell was also to be intermixed with varieties of gas projectiles, calculated to outwit the protection offered by enemy gas masks. Some combination of all these measures had been tried in the last offensive against the Russians at Riga in September 1917. Bruchmüller, Ludendorff's artillery supremo, there proved to his satisfaction that the firing of guns previously registered could create the surprise conditions in which an infantry assault would lead to victory.

It was with Bruchmüller's verified experiment in mind that Hindenburg had, at Mons on November 11, 1917, come to the decision to launch an all-or-nothing offensive in the west in the coming year. As Ludendorff expressed the mind of the high command in a letter to Hindenburg on January 7, 1918, "the proposed new offensive should create such conditions for peace with the Western Powers as are required by the security of our frontiers, our economic interests and our international position after the war." Those included control of Belgium's industrial economy and the incorporation of the French coal and iron basin of Longwy-Briey within the wider German industrial area. Yet, despite the weight of Germany's military preoccupation with preparation for the coming military offensive in the west, its political concerns for the future remained concentrated in the east.

THE WAR IN THE EAST CONTINUES

There, Germany correctly calculated, its opportunity to impose subordinate relationships on the peoples who had only just escaped from domination by the old Russian empire was promising. The Baltic peoples—Lithuanian, Latvian, Estonian—had retained their sense of association with the German-speaking lands for centuries; much of the land-owning class was German by origin. Finland, though it had enjoyed a degree of autonomy inside the Tsarist empire, was anxious to regain full independence and ready to accept German help to do so. Lenin's early policy was to allow the non-Russian peoples of the empire to secede if they chose, while encouraging the local left to stage pro-Soviet revolutions. In the Baltic lands, already under German occupation as a result of the successful offensives of 1916–17, Soviet revolutions were swiftly put down and semi-independent pro-German regimes were established. In Finland, where power was fairly evenly divided between left and right, the issue of what relationship with Germany the country should establish provoked civil war. The right had been pro-German throughout the European conflict. Its readiness to form a German alliance, after independence was declared in December 1917, provoked the left into forming a worker militia of its own; in January 1918 fighting broke out, the left seizing Helsinki, the capital, the right retiring into the northern provinces. The Germans sent arms, 70,000 rifles, 150 machine guns and twelve field guns, all of Russian

Opposite left: The officers of the 129th Artillery, American Expeditionary Force, at their headquarters in France, 1919. Third from right, second row, is Captain Harry S. Truman, from Independence, Missouri, future President of the United States.

Opposite right: General John J. Pershing (1860–1948), commander of the American Expeditionary Force. Pershing, a veteran of the Indian and Spanish-American Wars, had previously commanded the forces engaged against Pancho Villa in Mexico in early 1917. On appointment to the A.E.F. he made clear to the French and British from the outset his determination to keep it together and prevent them from using its soldiers piecemeal as replacements. They, desperate for men, resented his refusal to assist as they wanted but his insistence on America's military autonomy was eventually proved well judged. By September 1918 the A.E.F. was winning victories on its own account, while its sheer mass, backed by the prospect of almost limitless reinforcements, had a decisively disheartening effect on Germany's commanders and common soldiers alike.

Right: White Guards parading in Helsinki, June 1918. Finland, a province of the Russian empire since 1808, was bitterly divided by the October Revolution. The left wing responded to Lenin's appeal to join Russian workers in a struggle for world revolution. The right, pro-German throughout the war, was prepared to accept German hegemony. A third group of nationalists, led by the ex-Tsarist General Mannerheim, sought true independence. In the ensuing civil war, Mannerheim prevailed. He later became President of independent Finland.

origin; also from Russia came the commander who was to lead the right-wing forces, Gustav Mannerheim, a Baltic nobleman and ex-Tsarist officer, of formidable personal and military capacities.

Mannerheim had been commissioned into the Tsar's cavalry and had served under Brusilov. After the October Revolution, he decided, however, that he must transfer his loyalty to his homeland, made his way to Finland and secured appointment as the Commander-in-Chief of the anti-Bolshevik army. The Petrograd Bolsheviks had recognised the independence of Finland on December 31, 1917; but four days later, Stalin persuaded the Petrograd Soviet to alter the terms of independence and then offered the Finnish socialists Russian help to establish "socialist power." Its basis was already present on Finnish soil in the form of Russian units and the Finnish Red Guards. While Mannerheim consolidated his base in the western region of Ostrobothnia, the left took possession of the industrial towns.

During January and February 1918, both sides prepared for the offensive. The Reds had about ninety thousand men at their disposal, Mannerheim only forty thousand. His troops, however, were under the command of professional officers, while the Red forces lacked trained leadership. Moreover, while Germany was preparing to send an experienced expeditionary force, von der Goltz's Baltic Division, to the Finns' assistance, Lenin was increasingly nervous of taking any action that would provoke a German landing adjacent to Petrograd, where the military force at his disposal was inadequate to repel a foreign expeditionary force. After the signing of the treaty of Brest-Litovsk, which formally ended war between Russia and Germany, the Soviet actually began withdrawing what troops it had left in Finland.

Mannerheim seized the opportunity to push forward. The leader of the Finnish nationalists, Svinhufvud, was too pro-German for his taste, while he wanted no "part of another empire but . . . a great, free, independent Finland." In early March the Red advance into Mannerheim's area of control in Ostrobothnia petered out and he went over to the offensive. His plan was to organise a concentric advance which would squeeze the Reds between two convergent attacks.

Before he could consummate it, von der Goltz's Baltic Division appeared at the port of Hangö. On April 6, he took Tampere, the Reds' main stronghold in the south, a victory which allowed him to transfer forces south-eastward towards

German troops attacking across the railway line at Pysakki in 1918. The Germans intervened in the Finnish Civil War in order to prevent the Finnish Reds from seizing power, but also to bring pressure to bear on the Russian Bolsheviks, who threatened their occupation policy inside the former Russian empire after the enforced conclusion of the Treaty of Brest-Litovsk. Finland provided a base from which St. Petersburg, seat of the October Revolution, could be threatened. Germany was eventually forced to withdraw its intervention forces, but not until Mannerheim's accession to power after the Finnish Civil War did the country become truly independent of foreign influence.

Karelia. At his approach, the remaining Red forces beat a hasty retreat across the border into Russia, and on May 2 all resistance to Mannerheim's armies came to an end. Finland was free, both of German imperialism and of Soviet ideology. It was not yet independent, however. The Svinhufvud government was content to accept diplomatic and economic client status if that would guarantee German protection against the threat of renewed social revolution or Russian aggression. Mannerheim was not. On May 30 he resigned his command and retired to Sweden, from which he would return at the war's end to negotiate an honourable settlement of his country's differences with the victors.

German troops in Helsinki exchanging shots with Red Guards, 1918. Van der Goltz's Baltic Division, which landed in Finland at the old Tsarist naval base of Hangö (Gangut) in March 1918, found many Finnish supporters. Pro-German Finns had formed the 27th Jägers, a volunteer unit which fought very successfully against the Russians during 1915–17. In the uneasy and complex circumstances prevailing in the Baltic lands after Germany's defeat, Germanic militias, often organised by Allied forces, held uneasy sway between Reds and Whites until new states were consolidated.

Finland, though compromised by the German alliance, had had a swift and comparatively painless exit from the chaos of Russian collapse. Total casualties in the war numbered thirty thousand and, though that was a large figure in a population of three million, it would pale into insignificance beside the terrible toll of the civil war which was beginning to spread throughout Russia proper. That war would last until 1921 and take the lives of at least seven and perhaps ten million people, five times as many as had been killed in the fighting of 1914–17.

There need have been no civil war in Russia had the Bolsheviks not thrown away the advantages they had gained in the first months of revolution. Between November 1917 and March 1918 the Bolsheviks had won a great internal victory. During the so-called railway (*eshelonaia*) war, picked bands of armed revolutionaries had fanned out from Petrograd down the empire's railway system to make contact with the nine hundred Soviets that had replaced the official organs of administration in Russia's cities and to put down the resistance of groups opposed to the October Revolution. Then, with Russia in their hands, the Bolsheviks had prevaricated with the Germans over the terms of the peace settlement that would have confirmed their victory. Brest-Litovsk was a harsh peace. It required the Bolsheviks to accept that Russian Poland and most of the Baltic lands should cease to be part of Russia proper, that Russian troops should be withdrawn from Finland and Trans-caucasia and that peace should be made with the nationalists of the Ukraine. The Bolsheviks might, nevertheless, have signed without damage to their objective circumstances, since the territories were lost anyhow and there was always the prospect that they could be reintegrated when Germany's fortunes worsened and theirs improved. Trotsky, now Commissar for Foreign Affairs, succumbed, however, to the misconception that revolution was about to sweep Germany as it had Russia. He persuaded the Bolshevik Central Committee to challenge the Germans to do their worst, a worst which he believed would bring down the wrath of world revolution on the imperialists' heads, first in Germany itself, then elsewhere in the capitalist lands. There was to be "neither peace nor war." Russia would not sign; neither would it fight. In earnest of this extraordinary decision, the total demobilisation of the Russian army was announced on January 29, while at Brest-Litovsk Trotsky continued to fence with the Germans for another ten days. Then, on February 9, the Germans made a separate peace with the Ukraine, simultaneously issuing to the Bolsheviks an ultimatum requiring them to sign the treaty by the following day or else acquiesce in the termination of the armistice.

When Trotsky did not sign, the Germans swept forward during the next eleven days to what the ultimatum had called "the designated line." Operation *Faustschlag* (Thunderbolt) overwhelmed the Bolshevik forces in White Russia (Belarus), the western Ukraine, the Crimea, the Donetz basin and eventually, on May 8, the Don. In less than two months an area the size of France, containing Russia's best agricultural land, many of its raw materials and much of its industry, had been appropriated by the enemy. "It was the most comical war I have ever known,"

Opposite top: Red Guards arriving at Kagan, Uzbekistan, 1918, during the *eshelonaia* (railway) war.

Above: Lenin (center, with overcoat around shoulders) inspecting trainees of the embryonic Red Army in Red Square, Moscow, 1919. After precipitately proclaiming the disbandment of the old Russian army in January 1918, the Bolsheviks found themselves without the means to defend the Revolution or even maintain order. In May 1918 they reintroduced conscription and ordered all ex-Tsarist officers to register. Out of former soldiers, new recruits and mercenaries, among whom the Latvian Rifles were the most reliable and efficient, they were gradually able to create a Red Army to fight the Civil War which engulfed Russia in 1918–20.

Right: Trotsky arriving at Brest-Litovsk for peace talks with the Germans and Austrians, January 9, 1918. Leon Trotsky (1879–1940), who had returned from political exile in May 1917, became People's Commissar for Foreign Affairs on November 8. Although committed to the termination of military operations against Russia's enemies, he proved unwilling to negotiate from a position of weakness, believing that workers' revolutions in the capitalist countries would work to the Bolsheviks' advantage. His attempt to play for time was eventually terminated by Germany's unilateral seizure of Russian territory in February 1918.

Far right: Chicherin, Trotsky's replacement at Brest-Litovsk, arriving to conclude negotiations, in which the Bolsheviks conceded Germany's demands.

German occupation troops parading outside the Commercial Bank in Kiev, capital of the Ukraine, 1918. The Ukrainian Rada (parliament) set up an independent government after the collapse of central authority in Russia in 1917 and proclaimed independence, which Germany recognised on December 30. The Bolsheviks sent troops in an attempt to restore authority but on February 9 Germany and Austria signed a peace treaty with the Rada and at once sent troops of their own to occupy the country and to supervise the export of food to the west.

wrote General Max Hoffman. "We put a handful of infantrymen with machine guns and one gun onto a train and rush them off to the next station; they take it, make prisoners of the Bolsheviks, pick up a few more troops and so on." The results of the Bolsheviks' defeat were threefold. First, a number of Russia's minorities seized the opportunity to establish their own governments. Second, the failure of the Bolsheviks to resist the German irruption prompted the Western Allies—France and Britain, but also the United States and Japan—to establish a military presence on Russian soil, with the purpose of subjecting the German forces of occupation to a continued military threat. Finally, the collapse of Bolshevik armed force encouraged the opponents of revolution inside Russia to stage a counter-revolution that swiftly became a civil war.

Finland had been the first to strike for its freedom. The ethnic Romanians of the provinces of Bessarabia and Moldavia were next; they declared a Moldavian People's Republic in January 1918, which in April became part of Romania proper. Finally, in Transcaucasia the dominant nationalities—Christian Georgians and Armenians, Muslim and Turkic-speaking Azeris—declared, in April 1918, a Federative Democratic Republic. Federation lasted only a month, brought to an end by the revival of historic hostilities among the three ethnicities and independence, after the Bolsheviks decided to go back on their concession of political freedoms, only until 1921. In the interim, all three independent states had been drawn into the culminating stage of the Great War by the intervention of the major combatants.

Transcaucasia and Transcaspia, to its south-east, might have remained backwaters had not both contained resources of the greatest strategic value, oil and cotton. Under the Brest-Litovsk terms, Russia was obliged to supply a proportion of both to Germany. The Bolsheviks naturally wanted some for themselves. So did the Turks, who also cherished ambitions of incorporating the Turkic-speaking Transcaspians into the Ottoman empire. In the spring of 1918, the German forces in the Donetz basin began to push columns eastward towards the oil center of Baku; so did the Turks. At the same time, the British advanced their own troops into the region. A column, under General Dunsterville ("Dunsterforce"), had been started forward from Mesopotamia towards Baku in January. It was followed in June by a force of Indian troops, commanded by General Malleson, which crossed the North-West Frontier to establish a base in the Persian city of Meshed with the object of preventing German or Turkish penetration of Russian Central Asia.

The drama of the Great War in Central Asia, sensational though it potentially was, had an anti-climatic conclusion. Dunsterville was driven from Baku in September by a Turkish advance, which resulted in a massacre of Baku's Armenians by their Azeri enemies. Malleson's penetration of Central Asia was swiftly reversed, but not before the murder of twenty-six Bolshevik commissars, abducted from Baku by his Turkic confederates, had provided the Soviet government with the raw material to damn the British as "imperialists" to Central Asians for as long as Russian Communism would last. Neither the German nor Turkish interventions in the Caspian region would endure; Germany's would be ended by its defeat on the Western Front, Turkey's by the collapse of its imperial system after the armistice of October 31, 1918. In the long run, victory in Central Asia went to the Bolsheviks, though their wars against the insurrectionists there, among whom Enver Pasha made a brief appearance after the Ottoman defeat, would persist for years. The Central Asian episode, nevertheless, has its significance, for the British tentatives illuminate the diplomacy of the closing stages of the Great War in arresting focus.

The French and British but also the Americans and Japanese all sent troops to Russia during 1918. None, however, did so, initially, with the purpose of reversing the October Revolution. Indeed, the first soldiers to set foot ashore, a party of 170 British marines, who landed at the north Russian port of Murmansk on March 4, 1918, arrived with the encouragement of Trotsky. Trotsky and the British had a common interest. Murmansk was crammed with weapons and munitions sent by Britain to aid the Tsarist war effort. Following the victory of the anti-Bolsheviks in Finland, both Trotsky and Britain had reason to fear that the Finns and their German allies would seize the material.

Trotsky also wanted the store of British weapons for his own Red Army, which had effectively been brought into being by a decree creating a high command on February 3. The function of the Red Army would be to defend the Revolution against its real enemies, whom Trotsky identified, in a speech in April 1918, as "the all-powerful *external* enemies." By "external" enemies he meant the Germans, Austrians and Turks, who were extending their area of control over Russia's richest agricultural and resource-yielding regions in the Ukraine, Donetz and Caucasus. Thus, even as late as April 1918, despite the ideological hostility of the Bolsheviks to Britain, France and the United States, they and the Allies still retained a common interest, the defeat of the Central Powers. Pursuit of the common interest had faltered at times and, after the treaty of Brest-Litovsk the ratification by the Fourth Soviet Congress on March 15 seemed fated for extinction. Yet, thanks to the heavy-handedness of German occupation policy in the Ukraine and beyond, it might still have survived, had not haphazard and unforeseen events supervened to set the Bolsheviks and the West irredeemably at odds.

In the summer of 1918, the Western Allies became inextricably entangled with the Bolsheviks' Russian enemies. That had not been the Allies' intention. Sufficient realism prevailed in their policy-making to deter them from opening an irreparable breach with the regime that controlled Russia's capital city and what survived of its administrative system. The Bolsheviks' domestic enemies, though anti-German, were disorganised, disunited and dispersed around the margins of Russia's heartland. The most important groupings, the so-called Volunteer Army, led by former Tsarist officers, and the Don Cossacks, were too weak to threaten Bolshevik power. What changed everything—for the Bolsheviks, for their White enemies and for the Western Allies—in the unfolding of the struggle for power within Russia was the emergence to importance of a force none of them had taken into account, the body of Czechoslovak prisoners of war, originally belonging to the Austro-Hungarian army, released by the November armistice from captivity in the Ukraine. In April they began to make their way eastward out of Russia, via the Trans-Siberian railway, to join the armies of the Allies in the Western Front. Their journey pleased neither the British, who had hoped the Czechs would go north to assist in the defence of Murmansk, nor the French, who wanted the Czechs to remain in the Ukraine and fight the Germans. The Czechs, who were in direct contact with the foreign-based leaders of their provisional government, Masaryk and Benes, were adamant. Their objective was the Pacific terminal of the Trans-Siberian at Vladivostok, from which they expected to take ship to France. They intended that nothing should interrupt their transit.

It was nevertheless interrupted on May 14, 1918, when, at Cheliabinsk in western Siberia, an altercation broke out between the eastward-bound Czechs and some Hungarian prisoners being returned westward to the Habsburg army. When the local Bolsheviks intervened to restore order, the Czechs rose in arms to assert their right to use the Trans-Siberian Railway for their exclusive purposes. The loss of the Trans-Siberian was a serious setback to the Bolsheviks, since their seizure and retention of power was railway-based. Worse was to follow. The Western Allies, committed to the extraction of the Czech Corps for service on the Western Front, began to channel direct aid to the Czechs, who found a sudden enthusiasm not to leave Russia before they had dealt the Bolsheviks a death blow. At the same time, the Russian anti-Bolsheviks, including both the forces of a self-proclaimed Supreme Ruler, Admiral Kolchak, in Siberia and the original White forces in southern Russia, the Volunteer Army of Denikin, as well as the Don and

A camouflaged Czech train.

THE CZECH LEGION

Among the Austro-Hungarian empire's many minorities, the Czechs were the best educated and most economically advanced. Prague, after Vienna and Budapest, was the empire's third city and Brno and Pilsen centres of its industrial life. During the nineteenth century a strong nationalist movement had developed, fed by a popular revival of Czech language and culture and the support of Czech émigrés, particularly in the United States.

The Czechs were caught up in the initial enthusiasm for the war in 1914. Thereafter they served with increasing reluctance. By 1915 an embryonic government-in-exile had been formed under Tomas Masaryk and Eduard Benes, which by 1918 had been recognised by France, Italy, Britain and the United States, all eager to recruit Czech manpower for the culminating battles of the war. That available was formed into Czech "legions."

The largest, 40,000 strong, consisted of prisoners-of-war in Russia. Originally on good terms with the Bolsheviks, its leaders fell out with them while it was withdrawing along the Trans-Siberian railway en route to France via Vladivostok. A local fracas developed into full-scale confrontation, leaving the Czechs in control of the railway and overturning Bolshevik power in the Urals and Siberia. It had not been the Czechs' original intention to take sides in the burgeoning Civil War but they were nevertheless drawn in on the White side, and were then supplied with arms by the Western Allies who had taken a belated anti-Bolshevik stance. Czech numbers eventually reached 100,000 and the Legion took an active part in the operations of Admiral Kolchak's White army against the Bolsheviks in eastern Russia during 1919. It had by then established contact with an Allied force of Japanese and American troops sent to Vladivostok to expedite the Legion's transfer to France. It did not actually leave Russia until the spring of 1920. It and the legions recruited in France and Italy formed the nucleus of the army of the independent Czech Republic (subsequently Czechoslovakia), established in November 1918. The Czech Trans-Siberian saga is recognised as one of the most significant, if bizarre, episodes of early Soviet history.

Top: Volunteers in the trenches before Kungur, on the Perm-Ekaterinbourg Line, winter 1918.

Center: Czechs guarding their wagons at Kurgan.

Right: Arrival of T. G. Masaryk at Prague, December 21, 1918.

Below: Kolchak, 1919. Admiral Alexander Kolchak (1874–1920), a regular Tsarist naval officer, was commanding the Black Sea Fleet when revolution broke out. A successful commander, he was nevertheless deposed by a sailors' Soviet in June 1917 and sent by the Provisional Government to Washington as naval attaché. He returned to Vladivostok via Japan after the October Revolution and took command of White forces in Siberia. He set up a government at Omsk in February 1919 and proclaimed himself Supreme Ruler. Successful at first, his army was eventually defeated by the Red Army, and he was shot at Omsk in 1920.

Bottom: Japanese troops with the bodies of Russian railwaymen they have shot, at Vladivostok, 1919. Japan sent troops to assist Kolchak but they remained at Vladivostok until 1922.

Kuban Cossack Hosts, were heartened by the Czech success to return to the fray with renewed confidence. The apparent commonality of cause between them and the Czechs came to qualify them for Allied support also. Thus, by the late summer of 1918, the Allies found themselves effectively at war with the Bolshevik government in Moscow, supporting counter-revolution in the south and in Siberia, and sustaining intervention forces of their own, British in northern Russia, French in the Ukraine, Japanese and American on the Pacific Coast.

A war entirely subsidiary to the Great War ensued. In northern Russia a mixed French-British-American force made common cause with the local anti-Bolsheviks and pushed out a defensive perimeter two hundred miles to the south of the White Sea. It also cooperated generally with the commanders of the British intervention forces in the Baltic, which included military missions to the Baltic-German militias in Latvia and Estonia and to the armies of the emergent states of Lithuania, Latvia and Estonia, as well as Rear-Admiral Sir Walter Cowan's Baltic naval force. Meanwhile, in December 1918, the French landed troops in the Black Sea ports of Odessa and Sevastopol. In the Far East both Japanese and American troops disembarked at Vladivostok in August 1918, to consolidate a bridgehead for the evacuation of the Czech Corps. Both contingents eventually left for home, while the Czechs, whom they had been sent to assist, finally struggled out of Russia in September 1920. Allied intervention in the Russian Far East achieved nothing but the confirmation in Soviet eyes of the West's fundamentally anti-Bolshevik policy.

The reality was entirely contrary. On July 22, 1918, Prime Minister David Lloyd George told the War Cabinet that it was " 'none of Britain's business what sort of government the Russians set up: a republic, a Bolshevik state or a monarchy.' The indications are that President Wilson shared this view." It was a view that the French for a time shared also. France would later repudiate that position, to become the most sternly anti-Bolshevik of all the Allied powers. During the spring of 1918, however, it shared British and American hopes that the Bolsheviks could be used to reconstitute an Eastern Front on which military action would relieve the pressure in the west that threatened Allied defeat. Lenin and Stalin were later to represent their actions in terms of outright Allied hostility to the Revolution from the start. In truth, the Allies did not become commitedly anti-Bolshevik until the mid-summer of 1918 and then because the signs indicated, correctly, that the Bolsheviks had strayed from their own initially anti-German policy towards one of accepting German indulgence of their survival.

Until mid-summer the Germans had been equally puzzled to know how best to choose between Russia's warring parties. The army wanted the Bolsheviks "liquidated." The Foreign Office, by contrast, argued that it was the Bolsheviks who had signed the treaty of Brest-Litovsk and that it was in Germany's interest, therefore, to support the former at the expense of the Whites. On June 28 the Kaiser accepted a Foreign Office recommendation that the Bolshevik government be assured of German neutrality in the Russian civil war, an assurance that permitted Lenin and Trotsky to begin a counter-offensive that eventually unblocked the Trans-Siberian Railway, pushed the Czechs eastward towards Vladivostok and brought supplies and reinforcements to the Red

Armies fighting Kolchak's and Denikin's Whites in southern Russia and Siberia. The counter-offensive was to result in a Bolshevik victory in the civil war, a victory brought about not despite the Allies' eventual commitment to the Bolsheviks' enemies but because of Germany's positive decision to let Bolshevism survive.

Canadian troops parading through Vladivostok, November 15, 1918. The Allied contingents at Vladivostok also included Americans and Japanese. Allied intervention in Russia was an immensely complicated episode. Originally undertaken to prevent the large stocks of munitions shipped to the Tsarist army from falling into German hands after the Revolution, it only slowly developed into a conflict with the Bolsheviks. In Siberia, intervention was intended to expedite the evacuation of the Czech Legion, whose troops were awaited in France to assist resistance to the German offensives of 1918. Whatever the original motives, intervention soured relations between the West and Soviet Russia for decades afterwards.

THE CRISIS OF WAR IN THE WEST

While ignorant armies clashed at large over the vast spaces of the east, the garrisons of the narrow ground of the Western Front pressed closer for battle. The collapse of the Tsar's armies had re-created the strategic situation on which Schlieffen had predicated his plan for lightning victory: a strategic interval in which there would be no threat from Russia, leaving Germany free to bring a numerical superiority to bear on the axis of advance that led to Paris. The supe-

German troops moving through St. Quentin, on the Somme sector, before the launching of their great offensive of March 21, 1918, against the British Fifth Army. The collapse of the Russian army had allowed Germany to transfer the best of its divisions previously committed on the Eastern Front to the west. Hindenburg and Ludendorff planned to defeat the British and French in a series of offensives, beginning in March, before the arrival of the Americans in large numbers would permanently shift the balance on the Western Front to their disadvantage. The attack of March 21 inflicted heavy casualties on the Fifth Army and pushed the line back forty miles but the front was eventually stabilised outside Amiens.

riority was considerable. Having left 40 second-rate infantry and 3 cavalry divisions in the east, Ludendorff could deploy 192 divisions in the west against 178 Allied. They included most of the original élite of the army and they had been promised that the coming offensives would complete the record of triumph. What the German infantry could not know, though they might guess, was that they constituted their country's last reserve of manpower. Britain and France were in no better case. They, however, had superior stocks of material—4,500 against 3,670 German aircraft, 18,500 against 14,000 German guns, 800 against 10 German tanks—and, above all, they could look to the gathering millions of Americans to make good their inability to replace losses. Germany, by contrast, had by January 1918 embodied all its untrained men of military age. A double imperative thus pressed upon Hindenburg and Ludendorff: to win the war before the New World appeared to redress the balance of the Old, but also to win before German manhood was exhausted by the ordeal of a final attack.

German offensives

Michael	21 Mar–5 Apr
Georgette	9–11 Apr
Blücher–Yorck	27 Apr
Gneisenau	9 Jun
Marne–Rheims	15–17 Jul
– – –	Army boundaries

20 miles

HOLLAND

Flushing

Zeebrugge

Ostend
Bruges
Antwerp
Schelde

Nieuport
Dixmude
Ghent
German 4th Army

Dunkirk
Furnes
Thielt
Lys
BELGIUM

Calais
Belgian Army
Ypres
Roulers
Courtrai
Oudenarde

Cassel
Menin
Ancre

Boulogne
British Second Army
St. Omer
Hazebrouck
German 6th Army
BRUSSELS

Aire
Armentières
Lille
Rupprecht AGHQ

British GHQ
Béthune
Georgette
La Bassée
Mons

Montreuil
British First Army
Lens
Scarpe
St. Amand
Sambre

St. Pol
Douai
17th Army
Valenciennes

Frévent
Arras
Michael I
2nd Army
Maubeuge

Doullens
British Third Army
Cambrai
Michael II
Avesnes

Abbeville
Somme
Bapaume
Le Cateau
18th Army
Hirson

Amiens
Albert
Péronne
Michael III
Oise
Vervin

Aumale
British Fifth Army
Gneisenau
St. Quentin
7th Army

Nesle
Somme
Marle
Yorck

Montdidier
Roye
Ham
La Fère
Blücher
1st Army

Noyon
Laon
Rethel

Beauvais
Barisis
Craonne

Compiègne
Rheims

Clermont
French GHQ
Aisne
Vailly

Creil
Villers
Cotterêts
Soissons
Fismes

Chantilly
Oise
Marne
Rheims

Seine
French Sixth Army
French Second Army
French Fourth Army

FRANCE

Meaux
Dormans
Epernay
Châlons-sur-Marne

PARIS
Marne
La Ferté

Map: There were five German offensives in the
spring and summer of 1918, on the Somme in
March, at Ypres in April, on the Chemin des
Dames in May, on the Somme again in June and
on the Marne, again in June. This Second Battle
of the Marne led to a French counter-offensive
which marked the decisive turning point of
the war.

German assault troops practising for the spring
offensives of 1918. Select infantry groups were
trained to "infiltrate" the Allied front, bypassing
points of resistance and pushing in to the rear.
Supporting artillery did not open fire until just
before the moment of assault, in order to disguise the time and place of attack and achieve
maximum shock effect on the defenders.

The choice of front was limited: either another effort at Verdun or a strike against the British. The options had been reviewed at the fateful conference at Mons on November 11, 1917, where Colonel von der Schulenberg advocated a reprise of the offensive against Verdun, on the grounds that a defeat of the British armies, however severe, would not deter Britain from continuing the war, while if France were broken the situation in the west would be transformed. Ludendorff would have none of it. He announced that German strength sufficed for only one great blow and laid down three conditions on which it must be based. Germany must strike as early as possible, "before America can throw strong forces into the scale," and so if possible at the end of February or beginning of March. The object must be to "beat the British." He surveyed the sectors of the front on which such a blow might be launched and announced that an attack "near St. Quentin appeared promising." That was the sector from which the great strategic withdrawal to the newly constructed Hindenburg Line had been made the previous spring. By attacking there, Ludendorff suggested, the assault divisions, in an operation to be code-named Michael, could drive up the line of the River Somme towards the sea and "roll up" the British front. On March 10, the detailed plan was promulgated over Hindenburg's name: "The Michael attack will take place on March 21. Break into the first enemy positions at 9:40 a.m."

There were enough divisions which had served in Russia to bring to France some of the confidence won in a succession of victories there. The British, however, were not Russians. Better equipped, better trained and so far undefeated on the Western Front, they were unlikely to collapse simply because a hole was punched in their front. Ludendorff had, however, chosen better than he might have known in selecting the Somme as his principal assault zone. It was garrisoned by the Fifth Army, numerically almost the weakest of Haig's four armies and one that had suffered heavily in the Passchendaele fighting. It was also commanded by a general, Hubert Gough, whose reputation was not for thoroughness. Officers who served under him formed the opinion that lives were lost in the battles he organised because he failed to co-ordinate artillery support with infantry assaults, to limit his objectives to attainable ends, to curtail operations that had patently failed and to meet acceptable standards of administrative efficiency. Lloyd George had tried to have Gough removed, but Haig's protection had spared him from dismissal. He now had to cope with two problems which exceeded his capacity to handle.

Neither was of his own making. The first concerned a major reorganisation of the army. The underlying reason was simply a shortage of soldiers. The War Cabinet had calculated that the British Expeditionary Force would require 615,000 men in 1918, but that only 100,000 were available from recruits at home, despite conscription. The expedient accepted was to disband 145 battalions, and use their manpower as reinforcements for the remainder. Even so, nearly a quarter of the battalions had to leave the divisions in which they had served for years and find a new accommodation with unfamiliar commanders, supporting artillery batteries and engineer companies and neighbour battalions. Though reorganisation began in January, it was not completed until early March, and Gough's administrative failings then still left much work of integration to be done. Gough had also had to position his army not only on a difficult battlefield but, in parts, on an unfamiliar one. As a help to the French, after the breakdown of so many of their formations in 1917, Haig had agreed to take over a portion of their line precisely in the sector chosen by Ludendorff for his great spring offensive. Gough had therefore to extend his right across the Somme, into the notoriously ill-maintained French trench system, while at the same time attempting to deepen and strengthen the extemporised defences dug by the British in front of the old Somme battlefield after the advance to the Hindenburg Line a year earlier. The result was that while the first of the Fifth Army's three lines was complete and the Battle Zone well provided with strongpoints and artillery positions, the third had been excavated only to a foot's depth.

It was against these sketchy defences that the storm broke on the morning of March 21. A compact mass of seventy-six first-class German divisions fell upon twenty-eight British divisions, of unequal quality, the Germans advancing behind a surprise artillery bombardment across a front of fifty miles, on a morning of mist thickened by the use of gas. The barrage went on for five hours until the German troopers emerged from their trenches and began to penetrate the positions of the dazed defenders opposite. Enough of the British defenders and their supporting artillery survived the German bombardment to offer scattered resistance

German infantry making their way forward over the old battlefield of the Chemin des Dames, May 29, 1918. The German high command had hoped to break the British Expeditionary Force in its two opening offensives of March and April. Having failed to do so, it turned against the French on the Aisne. The defenders included some British divisions which had been sent to the sector to recuperate after their ordeal in March and April. The German advance, of nearly forty miles, brought their line nearer to Paris than their armies had been since September 1914.

as the Germans came forward. Firing largely blind by the "Pulkowski" method, which depended on meteorological observation, the German gunners had missed or overshot some key targets. As the Germans appeared out of no-man's-land, British guns and machine-gun nests sprang to life and surviving trench garrisons manned the parapet. "I thought we had stopped them," remembered Private J. Parkinson, "when I felt a bump in the back. I turned round and there was a German officer with a revolver in my back. 'Come along, Tommy. You've done enough.' I turned round then and said, 'Thank you very much, Sir.' I know what I would have done if I had been held up by a machine-gunner and had that revolver in my hand, I'd have finished him off. He must have been a real gentleman. It was twenty past ten. I know to the minute because I looked at my watch."

By this time almost all the British positions in the Fifth Army's Forward Zone had been overrun; only behind the obstacle of the ruined town of St. Quentin was a stretch of line still held. It would soon fall as the Germans pressed on to the main Battle Zone. Much better manned, the Red Line put up a stronger resistance. The British artillery, which steadfastly refused to surrender some gun positions though outflanked to left and right, also helped to sustain the opposition the attackers met. Much of the Red Line, however, was lost to the British during the afternoon, because the garrison either ran away or was overwhelmed by the power of the attack. The worst loss of ground occurred south of St. Quentin, at the point of junction with the French Sixth Army, which held the confluence of the Oise and Aisne Rivers. As the British divisions in Gough's southernmost sector gave ground the French were obliged to fall back also, opening a re-entrant that pointed towards Paris itself. In Gough's northern sector, where the Flesquières salient left by the Battle for Cambrai in the previous November bulged into the German line, the Germans achieved a dangerous envelopment menacing the security of the British Third Army and threatening to undercut the British hold on Flanders itself.

As evening fell on March 21, the B.E.F. had suffered its first true defeat since trench warfare had begun three and a half years earlier. Along a front of nineteen miles, the whole forward position had been lost, except in two places held heroically by the South African Brigade and another formed of three battalions of the Leicestershire Regiment, and much of the main position had been penetrated also. Guns had been lost in numbers, whole units had surrendered or fled to the rear and heavy casualties had been suffered by those that did stand and fight. In all, over seven thousand British infantrymen had been killed but twenty-one thousand soldiers had been taken prisoner. Day one of Operation Michael had undoubtedly been a German victory. The truth was that many of the British units, worn down by the attrition battles of 1917, were not in a fit state to defend their fronts, while Fifth Army's headquarters had no proper plan prepared to deal with a collapse should it begin to develop. "I must confess," wrote an experienced infantryman in a retrospect of the aftermath, "that the German breakthrough of March 21, 1918, should never have occurred. There was no cohesion of command, no determination, no will to fight, and no unity of companies or battalions." The question must be whether the collapse belongs to the same psychological order of events as the collapse of the French army in the spring of 1917, the collapse of the Russian army after the Kerensky offensive and the collapse of the Italian army during Caporetto. All four armies, if the British are included, had by then suffered over 100 per cent casualties in their infantry complement and may simply have passed beyond the point of what was bearable by flesh and blood.

If there is a difference to be perceived, it is in the extent of the psychological trauma and, in its containment. The French army exhibited signs of breakdown in over half its fighting formations and took a year to recover. The Italian army suffered a general crisis, never really recovered and had to be reinforced by large numbers of British and French troops. The Russian army broke down altogether and eventually dissolved. The crisis of the British Fifth Army was of a different and lesser order. Its defeat was undoubtedly moral rather than material in character, but its malaise did not infect the three other British armies, Third, Second or First; indeed, it was quite swiftly contained within the Fifth Army itself which, only a week after the German offensive's opening, had begun to recover and was fighting back.

The worst days of the German offensive for the British were the third, fourth and fifth, March 24–26, days in which the danger grew of a separation of the

A British 60-pounder firing near Bapaume, March 25, 1918, the fifth day of the German offensive on the Somme. The gun is at full recoil, the smoke is from the discharge; the target, beyond the horizon, may be 10,000 yards distant. Medium artillery normally fired from protected positions well behind the lines. It is evidence of the disorganisation caused by the German advance that the gun is in the open, the battery's equipment scattered about. Its camouflage net, which would normally have covered its gun pit, lies in the foreground. By every sign the gun crew is about to retreat again.

British from the French armies and of a progressive displacement of the whole British line north-eastward towards the channel ports. The spectre of a breaking of the front infected the French high command, just as it had done during the Marne campaign; but, while in 1914 Joffre had used every measure at his disposal to keep touch with the B.E.F., now Pétain, commanding the French armies of the north, took counsel of his fears. At eleven in the morning of March 24, he visited Haig at his headquarters to warn that he expected to be attacked himself north of Verdun and now had as his principal concern the defence of Paris. Haig instantly realised that he had an inter-Allied crisis on his hands. Two days later, at Doullens, near Amiens, directly in the line of the German axis of advance, an extempore Anglo-French conference was convened. The meeting did not begin well. Haig outlined what had happened to the Fifth Army and expressed his inability to do anything more. Pétain protested that he had sent all the help he could and that the aim must now be to defend Amiens. Amiens was twenty miles beyond the furthest point yet reached by the Germans. At its mention, Foch burst out,

"We must fight in front of Amiens, we must fight where we are now . . . We must not now retire a single inch." His intervention retrieved the situation. It was suddenly agreed that Haig would serve under the command of Foch, who would be "charged . . . with the co-ordination of the action of the British and French armies." Foch's authority would be extended, on April 3, to comprehend "the direction of strategic operations," making him in effect Allied generalissimo.

His appointment came only just in time. The Germans by April 5 had advanced twenty miles on a front of fifty miles and stood within five miles of Amiens. Nevertheless, the Germans were by this stage of their offensive in crisis also. Not only had the pace of their advance slowed, the advance itself had taken the wrong direction. Because the greatest success had been won on the extreme right of the British line, where it joined the French south of the Somme, it was in that sector that the German high command now decided to make the decisive effort. The object was to be the separation of the British and French armies by an advance north-westward towards the sea. The order marked an abandonment of the strategy of a single, massive thrust, and the adoption of a three-pronged advance in which none of the prongs would be strong enough to achieve a breakthrough.

The interior of Amiens Cathedral, sandbagged against enemy bombardment, 1918. Amiens, chief city of the Department of the Somme, was a principal objective of the German March offensive of 1918 but was just saved from capture by the hasty intervention of miscellaneous reinforcements, including American railway engineers. The thirteenth-century cathedral, one of the finest examples of French Gothic architecture, was damaged but survived. It contains a memorial to "the one million men of the British Empire who died in the Great War and of whom the greater number rest in France."

The accidents of military geography also began to work to the Germans' disadvantage. The nearer they approached Amiens, the more deeply did they become entangled in the obstacles of the old Somme battlefield, a wilderness of abandoned trenches, broken roads and shell-crater fields. Moreover, the British rear areas time and again tempted the advancing Germans to stop, plunder and satiate themselves. Colonel Albrecht von Thaer recorded that "entire divisions totally gorged themselves on food and liquor" and had failed "to press the vital attack forward."

Desolation and the temptation to loot may have been enemies as deadly to the Germans as the resistance of the enemy itself. On April 4, however, the British

A refugee with her cow in an Amiens street, March 1918. The approach of the Germans provoked a new wave of flight by country people from the battle area, recalling the scenes of 1914.

added to their difficulties by launching a counter-attack, mounted by the Australian Corps, outside Amiens and next day the German high command recognised that Operation Michael had run its course. While the Allied losses included men of all categories, from combat infantry to line-of-communication troops, the German casualties had been suffered among an irreplaceable élite. The cause of the failure, moreover, reflected Major Wilhelm von Leeb, who would command one of Hitler's army groups in the Second World War, was that "O.H.L. has changed direction. It has made its decisions according to the size of territorial gain, rather than operational goals."

Ludendorff, refusing to admit a setback, immediately inaugurated the subordinate scheme, Operation George, against the British in Flanders. The objective should have been easier to achieve than that of Operation Michael, for the sea lay only sixty miles beyond the point of assault; but the defences before Ypres, on which the B.E.F. had laboured since October 1914, were perhaps stronger than any part of the Western Front, and the British were familiar with every nook and cranny of its trenches. Mist again helped the Germans. Weight of fire won an opening advantage. It frightened Haig enough for him to issue a message to Second and First Armies which became famous as the "Backs to the Wall" order. "With our backs to the wall," it read, "and believing in the justice of our cause, each one of us must fight on to the end . . . Every position must be held to the last man. There must be no retirement." Retirement there was nonetheless, in part because Foch, now exerting to the full his power to allocate reserves, took the harsh but correct view that the British could survive without French help and must fight the battle out with their own reserves. The valiant little Belgian army took over a portion of the British line, the Royal Flying Corps operated energetically in close support, despite bad flying weather, and British machine gunners found plentiful targets as the German infantry pressed home their attacks almost in 1914 style. On April 24, south of Ypres, the Germans succeeded in mounting one of their rare tank attacks of the war, but it was checked by the appearance of British tanks, superior in both number and quality, and repulsed. On April 29, Ludendorff accepted that he had shot his bolt and must stop. The German official history recorded, "The attack had not penetrated to the decisive heights of Cassel and the Mount des Cats, the possession of which would have compelled the [British] evacuation of the Ypres salient and the Yser position. The Channel ports had not been reached. The second great offensive had not brought about the hoped-for decision."

Frustrated on the northern front, Ludendorff now decided to shift his effort against the French. From the nose of the salient created by the great advance of March, he might either have swung north-westward, as his original plan anticipated, or south-westward. Military logic was for the former option, which threatened the British rear area and the channel ports. The second, however, was favoured by the grain of the country, which offered an axis of advance down the valley of the Oise, and by the temptation of Paris, only seventy miles distant. For this third offensive the largest concentration of artillery yet assembled was brought to the front, 6,000 guns supplied from an ammunition stock of two million shells. Immediately after the bombardment ceased, fifteen divisions of the German Sixth Army, with twenty-five more following, crossed a succession of water lines to reach the summit of the ridge, roll over it and continue down the reverse slope to the level ground beyond. The plan required them to halt when open country was reached, as a preliminary to renewing the attack in the north, but the opportunity created was too attractive to relinquish. Ludendorff decided to exploit the gains of the first two days and during the next five days pressed his divisions forward as far as Soissons and Château-Thierry, until his outposts stood only fifty-six miles from the French capital. The Allies committed their reserves as slowly as they could but even so were forced to engage three divisions on May 28, five on May 29, eight on May 30, four on May 31, five on June 1 and two more by June 3. They included the 2nd and 3rd American Divisions, the latter containing a brigade of the U.S. Marine Corps, and at Belleau Wood on June 4 the Marines added to their reputation for tenacity by steadfastly denying the Germans access to the road towards Reims. At an

Black soldiers of the American 369th Infantry Regiment, 93rd Division, manning a trench at Maffrecourt, May 5, 1918. They are wearing French helmets and have French weapons, including a Chauchat light machine gun. The officer is white. The American army practised strict segregation during the war, never mixing white with black troops and subordinating blacks to white officers. Nearly 400,000 blacks were enlisted but only 200,000 sent to France, where they were used mainly as labour. Only 42,000 were allotted to enter combat and then in marginal assignments. The 93rd Division was actually allotted to the French army, where it was numbered as the 157th Division. France, with large numbers of African units on the Western Front, had no difficulty in accepting black troops as combat soldiers.

early stage of the battle in their sector it was suggested to a Marine officer by French troops retreating through their positions that he and his men should retreat also. "Retreat?" answered Captain Lloyd Williams, in words which were to enter the mythology of the Corps. "Hell, we just got here."

The Marine counter-attack at Belleau Wood was but one contribution to a general Allied response to the threat to Paris. Unknown to the Allies, the Germans had already decided to halt the third offensive on June 3. They had also lost another hundred thousand men and, while the Allies retained their ability to replace casualties, they did not. The Americans were now receiving 250,000 men a month in France and had twenty-five organised divisions in or behind the battle zone. Fifty-five more were being trained in the United States. On June 9 Ludendorff renewed the offensive, in an attack on the River Matz, a tributary of the Oise, in an attempt to widen the salient that now bulged westward between Paris and Flanders. The Matz, in any case a limited attack, was quickly broken off on June 14 when the French, with American assistance, counter-attacked and

German troops advancing through the village of Pont-Arcy, May 27, 1918, during the third spring offensive. The soldier in the foreground is stepping over telephone lines that have been brought down during the fighting.

Left: American machine gunners in action at Villers Tournelle, May 20, 1918. They are firing French Hotchkiss guns. The soldier on the right is about to feed a new strip into the breech. This is one of the earliest actions in which American troops took part.

Below: The Royal Scots Greys near Montreuil, May 6, 1918. This British cavalry regiment, the 2nd Dragoons, was so named after the colour of its horses. Montreuil was the headquarters of the British Expeditionary Force from 1915 to 1918. Cavalry was frequently sent into action, dismounted, during the German spring advances of 1918, to reinforce weakened sections of the line.

Troops of the American 23rd Infantry Regiment, in action at Belleau Wood, June 3, 1918. They are firing a French 37-mm cannon, a close-support weapon. This is one of the most famous photographs of the First World War, perhaps reproduced so often because it depicts a scene from the earliest official engagement of the American Expeditionary Force in France. The American divisions were released by General Pershing to reinforce the hard-pressed French during their defence of the Aisne. Belleau Wood was recaptured and the Americans went on to mount other counter-attacks between June 3 and 12.

brought the initial advance to a halt. The German inability to sustain pressure was also hampered by the first outbreak of the so-called Spanish influenza, in fact a worldwide epidemic originating in South Africa, which was to recur in the autumn with devastating effects in Europe but in June laid low nearly half a million German soldiers whose resistance, depressed by poor diet, was far lower than that of the well-fed Allied troops in the trenches opposite.

With his troop strength declining, Ludendorff now had to make a critical choice between the attack against the British in Flanders and a drive towards Paris. He took nearly a month to make up his mind. He remained, nevertheless, dedicated to military decision and on July 15 committed all the force he had left, fifty-two divisions, to an attack against the French, to be known as the Second Battle of the Marne. The temptation of Paris had proved irresistible. At first the offensive made excellent progress. The French, however, had had warning, from intelligence and observation experts, and on July 18 launched a heavy counter-stroke, mounted by the fiery Mangin with eighteen divisions in first line, at Villers-Cotterêts. It was the day Ludendorff travelled to Mons to discuss the transfer of

Americans attacking at St. Pierre Aigle, July 1918, during the Second Battle of the Marne. The battle began as the fifth German offensive but was transformed into a victorious French counter-attack when twenty-four French and two American divisions fell on the overextended Germans on July 18. The Americans took a leading role. At the end of seventeen days' fighting, the Germans had been pushed back to the positions they had held before their offensive had opened. Allied casualties were heavy—95,000 French, 13,000 British, 12,000 American—but were far exceeded by the German army's 168,000. After the Second Battle of the Marne the Allies' advance to victory began.

troops to Flanders for his much-postponed offensive against the British. The French attack brought him hurrying back but there was little he could do to stem the flood. The French had five of the enormous American divisions, 28,000 strong, in their order of battle, and these fresh troops fought with a disregard for casualties scarcely seen on the Western Front since the beginning of the war. On the night of July 18–19 the German vanguards which had crossed the Marne three days earlier fell back across the river and the retreat continued in the days that followed. The fifth German offensive was over and could not be revived. Nor could the Flanders offensive against the British be undertaken. Merely to make good losses suffered in the attacks so far, the German high command calculated, required 200,000 replacements each month. In six months, the strength of the army had fallen from 5.1 million to 4.2 million men and, even after every rear-echelon unit had been combed out, its fighting strength could not be increased.

Tirailleurs sénégalais at ease before the Second Battle of the Marne, July 1918. France had long recruited black regiments for its colonial wars and those raised in the West African colony of Senegal were particularly esteemed for their fighting qualities. As casualties among native Frenchmen rose, increasing numbers of black troops were sent to the Western Front.

The army's discontent with its leadership was beginning to find a voice. Though Hindenburg remained a figurehead above reproach, Ludendorff's uncreative and repetitive strategy of frontal attacks now attracted criticism from within the general staff. Lossberg, the great tactical expert, responded to the failure of the Second Battle of the Marne by arguing that the army should withdraw to the Siegfried Line of 1917, while on July 20 Major Niemann circulated a paper calling for negotiations with the Allies to be initiated at once. Ludendorff theatrically offered to resign but then recovered his nerve when the Allies did not move to exploit their success on the Marne. There was, he said, nothing to justify Lossberg's demands for a withdrawal and no sign that the Allies could break the German line.

Ludendorff's analysis was incorrect. A German army unable to make good its losses was now confronted by a new enemy, the U.S. Army, with four million fresh troops in action or training. More pertinently, its old enemies, the British and French, now had a new technical arm, their tank forces, with which to alter the terms of engagement. Germany's failure to match the Allies in tank development must be judged one of their worst military miscalculations of the war. Their own programme had resulted in the production of a monstrosity, the A7V. Moreover, industrial delays limited output to a few dozen, so that the German tank force chiefly depended on 170 tanks captured from the French and British. They, by contrast, had by August 1918 several hundred each, the French fleet including a thirteen-ton Schneider-Creusot model mounting a 75-mm gun, while the British possessed a solid mass of five hundred medium Mark IV and Mark V machines, capable of moving at five miles per hour over level ground and of concentrating intense cannon and machine-gun fire against targets of opportunity.

Ludendorff's belief during July that he retained the option of striking alternatively against the British or French was even more of a misconception. While his increasingly battle-worn infantry and horse-drawn artillery plodded forward over the worn battleground of the Marne, Foch and Haig were concentrating an enormous force of armour, 530 British tanks, 70 French, in front of Amiens, with the intention of breaking back into the old Somme battlefield and driving deep into their rear area. The blow was struck on August 8, with the Canadian and the Australian Corps providing the infantry support for the tank assault. Within four days most of the old Somme battlefield had been retaken and by the end of August the Allies had advanced as far as the outworks of the Hindenburg Line. On September 6 Ludendorff was advised by Lossberg that the situation could only be

An American regiment disembarking at Le Havre, July 12, 1918, with cased and uncased regimental colours. The number of Americans in France doubled between May and July, from 500,000 to one million. It doubled again by the end of the war, when over two million were present. The personal equipment of American soldiers was of the highest quality but the A.E.F. remained dependent on the British and French for heavy weapons throughout its time abroad.

retrieved by a retreat of nearly fifty miles to a line established on the Meuse. The advice was rejected, however, and during the rest of September the Germans consolidated their position in and forward of the Hindenburg Line.

Meanwhile the ever-stronger American army was taking an increasingly important part in operations. On August 30, General John Pershing, who had reluctantly lent formations and even individual units piecemeal to his allies, achieved his purpose of bringing the American First Army into being. It was immediately deployed south of Verdun, opposite the tangled and waterlogged ground of the St. Mihiel salient, which had been in German hands since 1914, and on September 12 launched the first all-American offensive of the war. The Germans opposite were preparing to abandon the salient, but were nevertheless taken by surprise and subjected to a severe defeat. In a single day's fighting, the American I and IV Corps, attacking behind a barrage of 2,900 guns, drove the Germans from their positions, captured 466 guns and took 13,251 prisoners. Pershing's army had won an undoubted victory.

Ludendorff paid it a tribute. He attributed the growing malaise in his

Above: Americans at ablutions in a German prisoner-of-war camp. Very few Americans were taken prisoner during 1918, though 50,000 were killed in action and another 50,000 died of disease, mainly in the great flu epidemic of 1918–19.

Right: Germans taken prisoner during the April offensive of 1918. Their shoddy uniforms and poor physique contrast notably with the appearance of their American opponents.

A British 14-inch naval gun, on a railway mounting, in action at Ballycourt, September 26, 1918. This was one of a small number of "super-heavy" cannon used to bombard key positions at long range. It threw a 1,400-pound shell up to 35,000 yards and its fall of shot was corrected by aerial observation. The target here was probably a road junction in use by German troops behind the Hindenburg Line, which was about to be successfully attacked in the following days.

army and the sense of "looming defeat" that afflicted it to "the sheer number of Americans arriving daily at the front." After four years of a war in which they had destroyed the Tsar's army, trounced the Italians and Romanians, demoralised the French and, at the very least, denied the British clear-cut victory, the Germans were now confronted by an army whose soldiers sprang, in uncountable numbers, as if from soil sown with dragons' teeth. A sense of the pointlessness of further effort rotted the resolution of the ordinary German soldier to do his duty. It was in that mood that, during September, the German armies in the west fell back to their final line of resistance, the Hindenburg Line. On September 26, in response to Foch's inspiring cry, "Everyone to battle," the British, French, Belgian and American armies began their culminating offensive.

Ludendorff had called August 8, when the British and French tank armada had overwhelmed the front at Amiens, the "black day of the German army." It was September 28, however, that was his own black day. Behind his expressionless and heavily physical facade, Ludendorff was a man of liquid emotions. "You don't know Ludendorff," Bethmann Hollweg had told the chief of the Kaiser's naval cabinet earlier in the war. He was, the German Prime Minister said, "only great at a time of success. If things go badly, he loses his nerve." Now he lost it altogether, giving way to a paranoid rage "against the Kaiser, the Reichstag, the navy and the home front." His staff shut the door of his office to stifle the noise

An American observation balloon company moving forward during the Argonne offensive, October 1, 1918. The front at this stage was moving too fast for the deployment of balloons, from which artillery fire was spotted, to be useful. Between September 26 and November 9, the French-American forces on the Argonne front advanced thirty-five miles. The Argonne, a region of dense woodland and small streams, was the A.E.F.'s major front during the war.

of his rantings until he gradually regained an exhausted composure. At six o'clock he emerged to descend one floor of headquarters to Hindenburg's room. There he told the old Field Marshal that there was now no alternative but to seek an armistice.

The domestic consequences were swift to follow. On September 29, a day when Germany's ally, Bulgaria, opened negotiations with the French and British for an armistice on the Salonika front, the high command received the Kaiser, the Chancellor, von Hertling, and the Foreign Secretary, von Hintze, at headquarters in Spa to advise them that Germany must now make terms. On January 8, 1918, President Wilson of the United States had presented Congress with fourteen points on which a peace honourable to all combatants could be made. It was

German soldiers taken prisoner after the breaking of the Hindenburg Line, at St. Quentin, October 2, 1918. The British Fourth Army attacked at St. Quentin on September 29, with 141 tanks and the support of 1,000 guns. After difficult fighting, 5,400 Germans surrendered. German morale, depressed by the failure of the five spring offensives and the appearance of Americans in increasing numbers, was at its lowest in this period. During the retreat to the Belgian border that followed it notably improved.

on the basis of the Fourteen Points that the German leadership decided to approach the Allies. Hintze proposed that any successful conclusion of negotiations would require the establishment either of dictatorship or full democracy. The conference decided that only democratisation would suffice and accordingly accepted the resignation of Chancellor Hertling. In his place the Kaiser appointed, on October 3, the moderate Prince Max of Baden. He was also an opponent of Ludendorff and, as a first act, secured from Hindenburg a written admission that

Opposite: British soldiers of the 136th Brigade lining the bank of the St. Quentin canal, which they have just captured, October 2, 1918. The canal, which was dry, had been incorporated by the Germans into the defences of the Hindenburg Line and formed one of the strongest positions on the Western Front. The Fourth Army's initial efforts to cross were defeated with heavy loss—5,400 American, 2,400 Australian—but a subsidiary attack by IX Corps at Bellenglise secured vital ground and led to a breakthrough. The action was the most important in the whole offensive to break the Hindenburg Line.

Right: A Crossley armoured car on the Amiens road at Harbonnières, during the great tank attack at Amiens, August 8, 1918, called by Ludendorff "the black day of the German army." Four hundred British tanks, attacking behind a surprise bombardment, overwhelmed the German line established at the end of the great offensive of March and pushed the defenders back towards the Hindenburg Line.

Below: Australians attacking the Hindenburg Line at Bellicourt, September 29, 1918, with a German concrete blockhouse on the skyline. The Australians suffered heavily but the line was broken four days later at Bellenglise.

"there was no further chance of forcing a peace on the enemy." That was prudent, for during early October Ludendorff began to recover his nerve.

So did the army, which started contesting the advance of the Allies towards the German frontier. It was in these circumstances that Ludendorff composed a proclamation to the army on October 24, which effectively defied the authority of the Chancellor and rejected the Wilson peace proposals.

An officer of the general staff managed to suppress the proclamation before it was issued. One copy, by mistake, however, reached the headquarters in the east, *OberOst,* where the signal clerk, an Independent Socialist, conveyed it to

British infantrymen of XI Corps entering Lille, October 18, 1918. Lille, a great textile centre and the largest French city to be occupied during the war, had been in German hands since 1914. The delight at their liberation is evident in the faces of the French children. The British did not stay. These soldiers are pressing on to the Belgian border, where bitter battles were fought in the last days of the war. The soldier in the foreground is carrying a Lewis light machine gun, the British infantry's principal close-support weapon.

Berlin. Prince Max, enraged by the insubordination, confronted the Kaiser with the demand that he must now choose between Ludendorff and himself. When Ludendorff arrived in Berlin on October 25, he was told to report to Schloss Bellevue, where the Kaiser was in residence, and there forced, on October 26, to offer his resignation. It was accepted with the briefest of words and without thanks. Hindenburg's, also offered, was declined. When the two soldiers left the palace, Ludendorff refused to enter Hindenburg's car and made his way alone to the hotel where his wife was staying. Throwing himself into a chair, he sat silent for some time, then roused himself to predict that "in a fortnight we shall have no Empire and no Emperor left, you will see."

THE FALL OF EMPIRES

Ludendorff's forecast was exact to the day. By the time, however, that Wilhelm II abdicated, on November 9, two other empires, the Ottoman and the Habsburg, had sued for peace also. The imminence of the Turkish collapse had been evident for some time. After the army's victories at Gallipoli and Kut, its vital energy had ebbed away. The continuing campaign in the Caucasus against the Russians had sapped its strength. Though the number of divisions doubled during the war, by 1918 all were weak, some scarcely as strong as a British brigade. The loyalty of the Arab divisions, moreover, was to be doubted after the Sherif of Mecca, Hussein, raised the standard of revolt in 1916. His Arab army, operating against the flanks of the Turks in Arabia and Palestine, under the direction of the later famous liaison officer, Colonel T. E. Lawrence, distracted sizeable forces from the main battlefronts, Mesopotamia and Palestine. Mesopotamia, south of Baghdad, had been conquered by the British during 1917 and late in 1918 they had advanced to the oil centre of Mosul. The real focus of their effort against the Turks, however, was in Palestine, where they established a foothold on the other side of the Sinai desert at Gaza in 1917. Several attempts to break the Turks' Gaza line resulted in the fall of Jerusalem on December 9. During 1918 the British commander, Allenby, reorganised his forces and pushed his lines forward into northern Palestine, where, by September, they opposed those of the Turks in northern Palestine at Megiddo.

Austrian plenipotentiaries at S. Leonardo-Borghetto, near Verona, with Italian officers, during the Austro-Italian armistice negotiations, November 3, 1918. A final Allied offensive on the River Piave, led by British and French troops, had resulted in the victory of Vittorio Veneto. The Austrians, who had expected to be allowed to surrender sooner, panicked in the face of the Allied advance and fled en masse. Over 300,00 were taken prisoner. The outcome was revenge for the humiliation of Caporetto, as some of the Italian expressions reveal.

Allenby's breakthrough on September 19–21 brought about the collapse of Turkish resistance. On October 30, the Turkish government signed an armistice at Mudros, from which the Gallipoli expedition had been mounted forty-two months earlier.

Austria's nemesis came on the soil, if not wholly at the hands, of its despised enemy, Italy. After the triumph of Caporetto the Habsburg effort had petered out. The Italians reorganised and, rid of the pitiless dictatorship of Cadorna, gained heart. The real defence of their country, however, passed to the British and French who, after Caporetto, succeeded in sustaining a substantial force there, despite withdrawals to cope with the crisis in the Western Front, throughout 1918. On June 24 the Austrians, whom the Russian collapse had allowed to build up their own numbers, attempted a double offensive out of the northern mountains and on the River Piave. Both attacks were swiftly checked, that on the Piave by the assistance of an unseasonal flood. Conrad von Hötzendorf was removed from command and the young emperor, Karl I, began to look for

LAWRENCE OF ARABIA

T. E. Lawrence—"Lawrence of Arabia"—remains perhaps the most celebrated and now widely remembered figure of the First World War. His exploits during the Arab revolt against the Turks were highly publicised at the time, while his own account of his adventures, *The Seven Pillars of Wisdom,* written in high-flown literary style, established him as one of England's leading cultural figures of the inter-war years.

Lawrence was born, illegitimately, to a baronet who had set up house with the nursemaid to his legal family. Educated at Oxford, Lawrence spent some of his pre-war undergraduate years travelling in the Near East, then part of the Turkish empire. His undergraduate thesis on Crusader castles would later secure his election to a fellowship at All Souls College, Oxford. When war came, Lawrence was recruited, because of his knowledge of Arabia and familiarity with the region, into the British army's intelligence section, the Arab Bureau, based at Cairo. He was soon sent to liaise with the dissident Arabs, led by Sherif Hussein's family, who were guardians of the Muslim holy places at Mecca and Medina and who sought independence from the Turkish empire.

Lawrence's ability to arrange arms supplies to the Arab rebels soon made him a leading figure in their attacks on the Hejaz railway and on Turkish garrisons along the Red Sea. Having escaped captivity by the Turks, during which he was physically abused, he went on to take part in the British victories in Palestine, Lebanon and Syria and in the Arab entry into Damascus, in 1918.

Lawrence represented Arab interests at the Versailles peace conference. Disillusioned by the Allies' post-war treatment of the Arabs, he retreated into obscurity, serving first in the ranks of the Royal Air Force, then as a private soldier in the Royal Tank Corps, finally again in the R.A.F.

He then retired to a cottage in Dorset, much visited by British intellectuals of the period. A motorcycle enthusiast, he was killed in a crash near his cottage in 1934.

Turkish prisoners at Akaba.

Above: T. E. Lawrence, painted by James McBey.

Below: Colonel Lawrence and his bodyguard at Akaba.

means to preserve his empire. On October 16, two weeks after he had already sent President Wilson word of his willingness to enter into an armistice, he issued a manifesto to his peoples that transferred the state into a federation of nationalities.

The manifesto came too late. On October 6, his Serb, Croat and Slovene subjects had already formed a provisional government of the South Slavs or "Yugoslavia." On October 7 the Habsburg Poles joined with their brothers to proclaim a free and independent Poland, on October 28 a Czecho-Slovak republic was organised in Prague, while on October 30 the Emperor Charles's German subjects claimed their freedom to determine foreign policy for a new German-Austrian state. Hungary, constitutionally an independent kingdom, declared itself so on November 1. The other imperial nationalities, Ruthenes and Romanians, were making their own arrangements. The uniformed representatives of all of them had already began to abandon resistance and, in some cases to set off for home. It was in these circumstances that Diaz, the Italian commander, launched the offensive of Vittorio Veneto on October 24. With extensive British and French help, the Italians succeeded in recrossing the River Piave, initiating an advance that culminated a week later on Austrian territory. The Austrians instituted a ceasefire on November 3. It was not recognised by the Italians until the following day. In the interval 300,000 prisoners fell into their hands.

By the first week of November, therefore, the German empire stood alone as a combatant among the Central Powers. Under Allied pressure, the army's resistance stiffened as it fell back towards Belgium and the German frontier. There was hard fighting at the rivers and canals, casualties rose—among the penultimate fatalities was the British poet Wilfred Owen, killed at the crossing of the River Sambre on November 4—and the war, to the Allied soldiers battling at the front, seemed to threaten to prolong. Behind the lines, in Germany, however, resistance was crumbling. On October 30 the crews of the High Seas Fleet broke into mutiny. Efforts to put it down resulted in the mutineers seizing weapons and taking to the streets. By November 3 the seaport of Kiel was in the hands of mutineers calling for revolution and next day the port admiral, Prince Henry of Prussia, the Kaiser's brother, had to flee the city in disguise.

The Kaiser had already left Berlin, on October 29, for headquarters at Spa, to be closer to the army, on whose loyalty he still believed himself able to count. There was wisdom in his departure, for power in the capital was shifting irrevocably to the forces of

Noske addressing German naval mutineers at Kiel, November 5, 1918. Gustav Noske (1868–1946), a moderate Socialist and supporter of the German war effort, later became a proponent of peace. In November he was sent to Kiel to negotiate with the sailors of the High Seas Fleet, who were threatening revolution. Those in the photograph are from the U-boat crews, who were much readier to continue the war than the men of the defeated battle fleet. Sailors were prominent in the armed revolutionary mobs which fought in the Berlin streets after the abdication of the Kaiser. In 1919 Noske became Minister of War in the republican government and was instrumental in organising the new German army.

revolution. The last achievements of Prince Max as Chancellor were to secure the appointment of a moderate general, Wilhelm Groener, as Ludendorff's successor and to insist that the delegation assembled to negotiate the armistice would include civilian as well as military representatives. He thus assured that the armistice would be an act from which the soldiers could not subsequently extricate themselves by objecting to its political terms. On November 9, with Berlin in turmoil and the moderate politicians threatened by street crowds orchestrated by Germany's Bolshevik leaders, Karl Liebknecht and Rosa Luxembourg, he transferred the office of chancellor to the Socialist Friedrich Ebert.

On the same day the Kaiser, at Spa, confronted his own deposition. Unrealistic as ever, he had spent his ten days at headquarters fantasising about turning

his army against his people, oblivious of the evidence that his soldiers now wanted only an end to the war. Ebert was anti-revolutionary and even a monarchist. By November 7, however, he knew that, unless he adopted the demands of the revolution growing in the streets his party would be discredited for good. That evening he warned Prince Max, "The Kaiser must abdicate, otherwise we shall have the revolution." Over the telephone to Spa, Max repeated the warning to the Kaiser. The Kaiser refused to listen, once again threatened to use the army against the nation and ended by rejecting any

Below left: The Kaiser leaves his Berlin palace for the last time, October 29, 1918. He went first to imperial headquarters at Spa in Belgium, in the hope of persuading the army to put down the growing revolution at home. When he recognised that the generals would not act, he accepted the necessity of abdication and left for exile in Holland on November 9. There were widespread demands in Allied countries to try him as a war criminal but the Queen of the Netherlands refused to extradite him and he died at the castle of Doorn in 1941.

Below: Rosa Luxembourg (1871–1919), German Marxist and, with Karl Liebknecht, leader of the revolutionary Spartacus League. Having tried but failed to raise a Bolshevik revolution in Berlin in the first two weeks of January 1919, she and Leibknecht were shot by the army on January 15.

Bottom: Revolutionary ex-soldiers in Berlin, 1918. The moderate Socialists, led by Ebert, proved much more ruthless than the German Bolsheviks, rapidly raised an improvisational army and put down disorder.

A member of the German armistice delegation in La Capelle, in the Department of the Aisne, on his way to the meeting with the Allied delegates in the forest of Compiègne, November 7, 1918. The terms dictated required the Germans to retire behind the Rhine, to surrender three bridgeheads over the river, to give up all their territorial conquests and to hand over vast quantities of military equipment. The German fleet was also to be interned in British waters. The Allied blockade was to continue in force until the signing of a final peace treaty.

thought of Prince Max resigning as Chancellor. "You sent out the armistice offer," Wilhelm II said, "you will also have to accept the conditions," and rang off.

The German armistice delegation had already crossed enemy lines to meet the French representatives at Rethondes, outside Paris. Until the issues of the abdication had been settled, however, the delegates could not proceed. The terms of the armistice had been presented to them by Foch, and stark they were. They required the evacuation of all occupied territory, including Alsace-Lorraine, the military evacuation of the western bank of the Rhine, the surrender of enormous quantities of military equipment and the internment of all submarines and capital units of the High Seas Fleet; the repudiation of the treaties under which the

Germans occupied their conquered territories in the east; the payment of reparations for war damage; and, critically, acceptance of the continuation of the Allied blockade. The continuation would eventually ensure Germany's compliance with peace terms, even harsher than those of the Armistice, to be imposed at the Versailles conference.

Left: The signing of the peace treaty between the Allies and Germany in the Hall of Mirrors at Versailles, June 28, 1919. Clemenceau is in the center. All Germans bitterly resented the Allies' insistence on maintaining the economic blockade of Germany until the terms of the treaty were agreed, believing it blackmail to force their acceptance of unfair conditions. The Allies, after four years of war, were not in a mood to agree that the terms were unfair. They were, however, perhaps untactful to arrange the signing of the treaty in the room where the creation of the German empire had been proclaimed in 1871.

Opposite top: The Kaiser's Christmas card to a British friend, sent from exile at Doorn, 1930. The Kaiser had many English habits, derived from his mother, Queen Victoria's eldest daughter. On arrival at Doorn, he had called for "a cup of good English tea." Widowed in exile, he took a second wife and seems to have lived quite contentedly into his eighties.

Opposite bottom: The entry of the French army into the city of Strasbourg, November 29, 1918, by the Shirmeck gate. Strasbourg, capital of the province of Alsace, had been incorporated into the German empire after the Franco-Prussian War in 1871. Its reintegration into France had been one of the highest hopes of the French ever after. The regiment, wearing colonial khaki, is the Colonial Infantry Regiment of Morocco (*Régiment d'Infanterie Coloniale de Maroc*), whose soldiers, despite the title, were native Frenchmen. It was the most highly decorated French regiment of the First World War. Their emphatic step speaks of overwhelming French pride in victory.

Two separate sets of events were meanwhile unrolling in Berlin and at Spa. In Berlin on November 9, Prince Max handed over the Chancellorship to Ebert. There was by then no alternative to the transfer of power. The streets were filled with revolutionary mobs, while Liebknecht and Luxembourg were already proclaiming a Bolshevik state. The last meeting between Max and Ebert was brief, "Herr Ebert," the Kaiser's brother-in-law announced, "I commit the German Empire to your keeping." The new Chancellor replied, "I have lost two sons for this Empire." Many German parents could have said the same. In Spa, on Novem-

ber 9, the Emperor met the leaders of his army. Wilhelm II still believed that, whatever disloyalties were being transacted by civilian politicians in Berlin, his subjects in field grey remained true to their oath of military obedience. Even on November 9 he continued to delude himself that the army could be used against the people. His generals knew otherwise. Hindenburg heard him out in silence. Groener found the sense to speak. He knew, from soundings taken among fifty regimental commanders, that the soldiers now wanted "only one thing—an armistice at the earliest possible moment." The price of that was the Kaiser's abdication. The Kaiser heard him with continuing incredulity. What about, he asked, the *Fahneneide*, the oath which bound every German soldier to die rather than disobey? Groener uttered the unutterable. "Today," he said, "the *Fahneneide* is only a form of words."

The fall of the House of Hohenzollern was swiftly concluded. Rejecting a suggestion that he should seek death in the trenches, as incompatible with his position as head of the German Lutheran Church, Wilhelm II departed by train to Holland on November 10. On November 28 he signed the act of abdication. As his six sons had each sworn not to succeed him, the Hohenzollern dynasty thereby severed its connection with the headship of the German state and even with the crown of Prussia.

American soldiers of Battery D, 105th Field Artillery, celebrating the Armistice, November 11, 1918, with one of their 75-mm guns, under the Stars and Stripes.

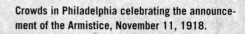

Crowds in Philadelphia celebrating the announcement of the Armistice, November 11, 1918.

Opposite: The celebration of the Armistice in the Place de la Concorde, Paris, November 11, 1918. Among the happy servicemen are a British gunner, an American lieutenant, an Australian and two French soldiers.

Above: *Armistice in Paris,* by Gaspard Maillol.

Right: Crowds on a Paris boulevard, November 11, 1918. It includes British as well as French soldiers and Frenchmen too young yet to have been called to military service.

Germany was by then effectively a republic, proclaimed on November 9. Yet it was a republic without substance, lacking an armed force to defend itself against its enemies. The last disciplined act of the old imperial army was to march back onto home territory, where it demobilised itself. The soldiers discarded their uniforms and weapons and went home. That did not empty the German republic of armed men. As elsewhere—in the new republics of Poland, Finland, Estonia, Latvia and Lithuania, in the nominal monarchy of Hungary, in German Austria— bodies of soldiers abounded. That ensured that hostilities would persist. The

Australians celebrating the Armistice in Martin Place, Sydney, November 11, 1918.

German soldiers returning from the Western Front in Berlin after the Armistice. Though the German people celebrated the news of the Armistice, they did so with apprehension, uncertain of what it might mean for their country's future.

The German dreadnought *Bayern* (Bavaria) sinking at Scapa Flow, June 21, 1919. One of Germany's two most modern battleships, *Bayern* mounted eight 15-inch guns and had a speed of 21 knots. She was successfully scuttled; her sister ship *Baden* settled in shallow water and was re-floated.

infant republic of Poland would have to fight for its borders, against German irregulars in the west and desperately against the Bolsheviks in the east. In Finland, in the Baltic states, in Hungary and in Germany itself, armed men threatened Red Revolution. It was put down in the east by civil strife. In Germany it threatened for a while to win by default, since constitutional republicanism could at first find no armed force to oppose it. Out of the wreck of the old imperial army, however, enough extemporised units were got together from men with no trade but soldiering to prevail in the battle of the streets in German cities, to repress German Bolshevism by brute force and to lay on the new republican government a permanent debt of gratitude to the improvised army's generals.

While Germany's political future was being settled by civil war, the armies of the Allies were advancing to take possession of the Rhine provinces and the three bridgeheads across the river, at Mainz, Coblenz and Cologne, under the terms of the armistice. The soldiers of the armies of occupation, the French excepted, were quick to fraternise with the population. Army rations made their way from cookhouses to family kitchens to feed people still subsisting on the skimpy wartime diet that the Allies' maintenance of blockade imposed. Hunger, even more than the threat of a full-scale invasion, was the measure that would eventually bring the German republic to sign the peace treaty on June 23, 1919. Two days earlier the High Seas Fleet, interned at the British anchorage at Scapa Flow, had been scuttled by its crews in final protest at the severity of the proffered terms.

There was historic irony in the Kaiser's naval officers choosing a watery grave for his magnificent battleships in a British harbour. Had he not embarked on a strategically unnecessary attempt to match Britain's maritime strength, fatal hostility between the two countries would have been avoided; so, too, in all possibility, might have been the neurotic climate of suspicion and insecurity from which the First World War was born. The unmarked graveyard of his squadrons inside the remotest islands of the

British archipelago, guarding the exit from the narrow seas his fleet would have had to penetrate to achieve true oceanic status, remains as a memorial to selfish and ultimately pointless military ambition.

It is one of the many graveyards which are the Great War's chief heritage. The chronicle of its battles provides the dreariest literature in military history. The war's political outcome scarcely bears contemplation: Europe ruined as a centre of world civilisation, Christian kingdoms transformed into godless tyrannies, the superficial difference between Bolshevik and Nazi ideologies counting not at all in their common cruelty to decent folk. All that was worst in the century which the First World War had opened, the starvation or exile of class enemies, the extermination of racial outcasts, the persecution of incorrect thinkers and artists, the extinction of small national sovereignties, the destruction of parliaments and

A temporary German cemetery at Sailly-sur-la-Lys, northern France, photographed on October 12, 1918. It contained 12,000 graves. France created deeply impressive cemeteries for its war dead after 1918, as did Britain, to which the French government granted rights of "perpetual burial" for the bodies of its soldiers. Almost a million are either buried or commemorated in cemeteries in France and Belgium. Neither France nor Belgium extended such ample courtesies to the Germans, whose dead are often buried in mass graves in obscure locations.

The sheer scale of loss of young men's lives in the Great War prompted a popular demand for commemoration. It was particularly strong in Britain, which, spared the shock of wars of national independence or unification undergone by many European countries during the nineteenth century, was unprepared for tragedy. In 1919, on the first anniversary of the Armistice of November 11, 1918, a temporary Cenotaph, so called after the Greek symbolisation of an empty tomb, was erected in the centre of Whitehall in London for the first victory parade. Designed by Sir Edwin Lutyens, the architect of the British war cemeteries, it proved so popular that it was re-erected in permanent form. At the same time, the British decided to re-inter the corpse of an Unknown Warrior in Westminster Abbey, the national and royal shrine. A body, which might have been that of a soldier, sailor or airman, was chosen from a battlefield in France and reburied, under the inscription, "They buried him among the Kings because he had done good toward God and toward his house."

The idea of the Unknown Warrior made an almost universal appeal in the combatant countries. In France, the tomb of an Unknown Warrior, honoured by an "eternal flame," was created under the Arc de triomphe in Paris. Similar memorials were set up in Italy, Greece and the United States. An attempt to erect a memorial to the Unknown Warrior in Germany in 1923, however, resulted in rioting between pro- and anti-war groups. The agony of defeat had there bitten too deep for the survivors to agree on an appropriate commemoration. The most important memorialisation became the monument at Tannenberg, scene of the heroic defence of East Prussia against the Russians in 1914. It was chosen as the burial place of President Hindenburg, victor of Tannenberg, in 1934. Removed in the face of the Red Army's advance in 1945, it is now located at Hamburg. In Turkey, one of the most poignant of all the war's memorials was established by Kemal Ataturk at Gallipoli, where he commanded the forces defending the peninsula against the British, Australians, New Zealanders, Indians and French in 1915. The inscription it bears generously requests all the bereaved to honour those who died as equal in sacrifice.

the elevation of commissars, gauleiters and warlords to power over voiceless millions, had its origins in the chaos it left behind. Of that, at the end of the century, little thankfully is left. Europe is once again, as it was in 1900, prosperous, peaceful and a power for good in the world.

The graveyards remain. Many of those who died in battle could never be laid to rest. Their bodies had been blown to pieces by shellfire and the fragments scattered beyond recognition. Many other bodies could not be recovered during the fighting and were then lost to view. Few Russian or Turkish soldiers were ever decently interred and many German and Austrian soldiers killed on the shifting battlefields of the Eastern Front simply returned to earth. On the fixed battlegrounds of the west, the combatants made a better effort to observe the decencies. War cemeteries were organised from the outset and when time permitted,

The procession carrying the body of the French Unknown Warrior, conveyed on the carriage of a 155-mm gun, to its final resting place under the Arc de Triomphe in Paris, November 11, 1919. Britain had inaugurated the idea of honouring an Unknown Warrior the previous year. It was subsequently imitated in most of the victorious combatant countries, including the United States. The photograph shows the cortege passing the statue of the Lion of Belfort, in the Place-Denfert-Rochereau, named for the principal French hero of the Franco-Prussian War.

chaplains and the dead men's comrades observed the solemnities. Even so, at the war's end, the remains of nearly half of those lost remained lost in actuality. Of the British Empire's million dead, the bodies of over 500,000 were never to be found. A similar proportion of the 1,700,000 French war dead had also disappeared. France buried or reburied the dead in a variety of ways. The Germans, working on foreign soil, and obliged to construct inconspicuous cemeteries, often excavated enormous mass graves; that at Vladslo in Belgium centres on a slab that covers the remains of over 20,000 young men.

The British chose an entirely different method of honouring the fallen. Each body was given a separate grave, recording name, age, rank, regiment and date and place of death. The names of those who had been lost altogether were inscribed on architectural monuments, the largest of which records the names of the 70,000 missing of the battle of the Somme. It was also decided that the cemeteries should each be walled and planted as a classic English country garden, with mown grass between the headstones and roses and herbaceous plants at their feet. There was also to be a Cross of Sacrifice as a centrepoint and, in the larger, a symbolic altar bearing the inscription composed by Kipling, "Their Name Liveth For Evermore." Over six hundred cemeteries were eventually constructed and given into the care of the Imperial War Graves Commission, which, working under a law of the French government deeding the ground as *sépultures perpétuelles*, recruited a body of over a thousand gardeners to care for them in perpetuity. All survive, much visited by the British, sometimes by the great-grandchildren of those buried within, as poignant remembrance cards testify, but also by the curious of many nationalities. None fail to be moved by their extraordinary beauty. In spring, when the flowers blossom, the cemeteries are places of renewal and almost of hope, in autumn, when the leaves fall, of reflection and remembrance.

The ribbon of British cemeteries running from the North Sea to the Somme stands as an idealised memorial to all those whose extinction on the battlefields of the Great War is not commemorated. Their number is enormous. To the million dead of the British Empire and the 1,700,000 French dead, we must add 1,500,000 soldiers of the Habsburg Empire, two million Germans, 460,000 Italians, 1,700,000 Russians and many hundreds of thousands of Turks. As a proportion of those who served, the death toll can be made to seem tolerable. It represents, for Germany, about 3.5 per cent of all who served. Calculated as a percentage of the youngest and fittest, the figures exceed by far what was emotionally bearable. One in three died. Little wonder the post-war world spoke of a "lost generation," that its parents were united by shared grief and that the survivors proceeded into the life that followed with a sense of inexplicable escape, often tinged by guilt, sometimes by rage and desire for revenge. Such thoughts were far from the minds of British and French veterans, who hoped only that the horrors of the trenches would not be repeated in their lifetime or that of their sons. They festered in the minds of many Germans, foremost in the mentality of the "front fighter," Adolf Hitler, who in Munich in September 1922 threw down the threat of vengeance that would sow the seeds of a second World War.

French soldiers working at the reburial of dead comrades in a permanent post-war cemetery, 1919

War, by Otto Dix (1891–1969), a triptych
painted between 1929 and 1932. Dix, who had
served at the front during the First World War,
became the most celebrated Expressionist
master of its horrors in the aftermath. The
painting is now in the Dresden Art Gallery.

BIBLIOGRAPHY

OFFICIAL HISTORIES

Neither Russia nor Turkey published official histories, the state structure of both empires having been devastated by the war and subsequent civil war. Nor is there an American official narrative history, though the United States government produced a number of volumes about specific aspects of the war. The most important official histories are the British, French, German, Austrian and Australian. The French history, though detailed, is desiccated in tone; the most useful volume is the tenth, divided into two parts, which contains the order of battle and records the movements and changes of command of divisions and higher formations. The Austrian official history also includes valuable orders of battle and provides a narrative less clinical than the French. The sixteen volumes of the German official history of operations on land was written in a detached general-staff style but is an indispensable record of the German army's activities; a companion series of informal battle narratives (e.g., Reichsarchiv, *Ypern, Gorlice*) is also useful. The British official series comprehends extended narratives of army operations in all theatres, a naval and an air force history, some technical volumes (medicine, transportation) and a subordinate and extremely detailed set of orders of battle, absolutely necessary to an understanding of Britain's part in the war. The Australian official historian, C. W. E. Bean, collected personal reminiscences from many participants. His series of volumes, as a result, has a human dimension none of the other official histories achieves, and anticipates in its approach that successfully adopted in the magnificent American official narrative of the Second World War. The titles of these official histories are as follows:

J. Edmonds, *Military Operations, France and Belgium, 1914–18*, London, 1925–48, and companion volumes on operations in Italy, Macedonia, Egypt and Palestine, the Dardanelles, Persia and East and West Africa by other authors. The naval history, *Naval Operations*, London, 1920–31, was written by J. Corbett and H. Newbolt. The aviation volumes are those of W. Raleigh and H. Jones, *The War in the Air*, Oxford, 1922–37.

Etat-major de L'armée, *Les Armées françaises dans la grande guerre*, Paris, 1922–39.

Reichsarchiv, *Der Weltkrieg*, Berlin, 1925–39.

Meaux, France, 1916

Bundesministerium für Landesverteidigung, *Österreich-Ungarns Letzter Krieg, 1914–18*, Vienna, 1930–8.

C. E. W. Bean, *Australia in the War of 1914–18*, Sydney, 1921–43.

GENERAL HISTORIES

There are few satisfactory general histories of the war, perhaps because of the miseries and rancours it left behind. The losers preferred to forget, while even among the victors there was little enthusiasm for recalling the events which had literally decimated their male populations. The British, who suffered proportionately least of the combatant great powers, produced the most successful general accounts. Theirs and others include:

J. Edmonds, *A Short History of World War I*, Oxford, 1951, a brief but comprehensive operational survey.

C. Falls, *The First World War*, London, 1960, incisive and compact.

M. Ferro, *The Great War 1914–18*, London, 1973, the first general history with a philosophical and cultural dimension.

A. J. P. Taylor, *The First World War: An Illustrated History*, London, 1963, characteristically succinct.

H. Herwig, *The First World War: Germany and Austria 1914–18*, London, 1997, is wider than its title suggests and surveys much modern scholarship.

H. Strachan, *The First World War* (projected 3 vols.; vol. 1, *To Arms*, Oxford, 2001), is expected to supplant C. M. R. F. Cruttwell, *A History of the Great War*, Oxford, 1934, dated but splendidly written.

ORIGINS

The peremptory transition from an apparently profound peace to violent general war in a few mid-summer weeks in 1914 continues to defy attempts at explanation. Historians, after abandoning efforts to assign war guilt, turned first to an examination of causes, which proved almost as contentious, eventually to an analysis of circumstances.

The bedrock of all discussion remains L. Albertini's *The Origins of the War of 1914* (3 vols.), Oxford, 1952–7, which provides a detailed chronology of the crisis and excerpts from the most important documents. A more recent and carefully balanced analysis of circumstances is provided by J. Joll, *1914: The Unspoken Assumptions*, London, 1984. Essential works on the unfolding of the crisis in each of the major combatant states are: I. Geiss, *Juli 1914*, Munich, 1965; J. Gooch, *Army, State and Society in Italy, 1870–1915*, New York, 1989; J. Keiger, *France and the Origins of the First World War*, New York, 1983; S. Williamson, *Austria-Hungary and the Origins of the First World War*, New York, 1991; and Z. Steiner, *Britain and the Origins of the First World War*, New York, 1977, which is particularly concerned with British official diplomacy. F. Fischer, in *Griff nach der Weltmacht*, Düsseldorf, 1961, and *Krieg der Illusionen*, Düsseldorf, 1969, controversially revived the issue of Germany's war guilt. Both, though causing outrage in Germany at the time of their publication, remain essential texts.

Two books on the mood of pre-war Europe are vital: M. Eksteins, *Rites of Spring*, Boston, 1989, and R. Wohl, *The Generation of 1914*, Cambridge, Mass., 1979.

WAR PLANS

In *The Schlieffen Plan*, New York, 1959, G. Ritter dissected the texts of the German chief of staff which launched his army on its disastrous campaign the year after his death; it is perhaps the single most important book ever published on the First World War. Valuable commentaries are supplied by G. Tunstall, in *Planning for War Against Russia and Serbia*, New York, 1993; A. Bucholz, *Moltke, Schlieffen and Prussian War Planning*, New York, 1991; D. Herrmann, *The Arming of Europe and the Making of the First World War*, Princeton, N.J., 1996; and the essays in P. Kennedy, *The War Plans of the Great Powers*, London, 1979.

CONDUCT OF THE WAR

The strategy of the war, as distinct from planning for it, has generated little scholarship. Its tactics, on the other hand, have always stimulated investigation, perhaps because a successful tactical solution was perceived to be the principal strategic necessity, particularly on the Western Front. In recent years a new generation of British, Australian and Canadian scholars have revived enquiry. Three leading writers are T. Travers' *The Killing Ground*, London, 1987, and *How the War Was Won*, London, 1992; P. Griffith, *Battle Tactics of the Western Front*, London, 1992, and *Forward into Battle*, Rambsbury, 1990; and H. Herwig, *The First World War: Germany and Austria-Hungary 1914–18*, London, 1997. None achieves the incisiveness of the British ex-official historian, G. C. Wynne, who, in *If Germany Attacks*, London, 1940, produced an analysis of British and French adaptations of their methods of the offensive against entrenched positions and of the German response which has not been surpassed. A valuable insight into the nature of trench warfare on the "inactive" sectors is supplied by T. Ashworth in *Trench Warfare: The Live and Let Live System*, London, 1980. Three important books on the war's generalship, casting much light on its strategy, are: R. Asprey, *The German High Command at War*, New York, 1991; M. Kitchen, *The Silent Dictatorship: The Politics of the German High Command under Hindenburg and Ludendorff*, London, 1976; and C. Barnett, *The Swordbearers*, London, 1963.

ARMED FORCES

There is a rich literature on the armed forces of the First World War, particularly on the British army. Among the best are: P. Simkins, *Kitchener's Army*, Manchester, 1986, a scholarly labour of love on the war's largest volunteer army; and I. Beckett and K. Simpson, *A Nation in Arms*, Manchester, 1985. Good books on the French army include D. Porch, *The March to the Marne*, Cambridge, 1981; L. Smith, *Between Mutiny and Obedience*, Princeton, N.J., 1994; and R. Challener, *The French Theory of the Nation in Arms*, New York, 1955. E. Weber, *Peasants into Frenchmen*, London, 1977, has illuminating passages on the acceptance of conscription by rural France before the war. G. Pedroncini, *Les mutineries de 1917*, Paris, 1967, is still definitive. B. Menning, *Bayonets Before Bullets: The Imperial Russian Army, 1861–1914*,

Piano di Vallarsa, Italy, 1918

Bloomington, 1994, is outstanding and is complemented by A. Wildman, *The End of the Russian Imperial Army*, Princeton, N.J., 1980. G. Rothenburg, *The Army of Franz Joseph*, West Lafayette, Ind., 1976, is the best book in English on the Austro-Hungarians, but J. Lucas, *Fighting Troops of the Austro-Hungarian Army*, Speldhurst, Eng., 1987, is packed with useful detail. There is still no good book in English on the German army. A Millett and W. Williamson's *Military Effectiveness*, I, Boston, 1988, has excellent chapters on national armies. J. Gooch, *Army, State and Society in Italy, 1870–1915*, New York, 1989, is excellent, and D. Omissi, *The Sepoy and the Raj*, London, 1994, on the Indian Army, is outstanding. Nothing comprehensive has yet been written in English on the Ottoman army of 1914–18.

There are several excellent studies of the German navy, including J. Steinberg, *Yesterday's Deterrent*, London, 1965, and H. Herwig, *Luxury Fleet*, London, 1980, and *The German Naval Officer Corps*, Oxford, 1973. On the Royal Navy, A. Marder, *From the Dreadnought to Scapa Flow*, 5 vols., London, 1961–70, remains the classic authority. M. Vego, *Austro-Hungarian Naval Policy 1904–14*, London, 1996, is interesting on the preliminaries to the Austro-Italian naval war in the Adriatic.

The technical literature of air fighting is considerable but there are few books of worth on air forces. An interesting study is D. Winter, *The First of the Few: Fighter Pilots of the First World War*, London, 1982.

BATTLES AND CAMPAIGNS

An early and now largely forgotten campaign history remains invaluable on the subject: S. Tyng, *The Campaign of the Marne*, Oxford, 1935. The best book on the contemporaneous battle in the east is D. Showalter, *Tannenberg*, Hamden, Conn., 1991. N. Stone, *The Eastern Front 1914–17*, New York, 1975, is indispensable. Important books on battles on the Western Front are: E. Spears, *Liaison 1914: A Narrative of the Great Retreat* and *Prelude to Victory*, London, 1939, on the Nivelle offensive; M. Middlebrook, *The First Day on the Somme*, London, 1971, and *The Kaiser's Battle*, London, 1978, on the opening of the German offensives of 1918; A. Horne, *The Price of Victory*, London, 1962, a classic account of Verdun; A. McKee, *Vimy Ridge*, London, 1962; and L. Wolff, *In Flanders Fields*, London, 1958, an impassioned account of Passchendaele. C. Falls, *Caporetto,* London, 1966, and A. Palmer, *The Gardeners of Salonika,* London, 1965, are the best studies of the Italian and Macedonian fronts in English. Gallipoli has produced an enormous literature, often of high quality. Good general books are: R. Rhodes James, *Gallipoli,* London, 1965; G. Cassar, *The French and the Dardanelles,* London, 1971; and A. Moorehead, *Gallipoli,* London, 1956, dated but highly readable. Useful books on the outer theatres of war are C. Falls, *Armageddon 1918,* London, 1964 (Palestine); A. Barker, *The Neglected War: Mesopotamia 1914–18,* London, 1967; and B. Farwell, *The Great War in Africa,* London, 1987. A compendium, *History of the First World War,* London, 1969–71, issued by Purnell in parts and edited by B. Pitt and P. Young, forming eight volumes, contains accounts of all the war's episodes, some by leading scholars. It is a valuable source, particularly for the more obscure campaigns (e.g., Tsingtao, the Caucasus). C. Ellis, *The Transcaspian Episode,* London, 1963, is a brilliant monograph on British intervention in South Russia in 1918. Allied intervention in Russia and on the military aspects of the Russian revolution and civil war are covered in J. Wheeler-Bennett, *Brest-Litovsk: The Forgotten Peace,* London, 1966; E. Mawdsley, *The Russian Civil War,* New York, 1989; R. Luckett, *The White Generals,* New York, 1971; J. Bradley, *Allied Intervention in Russia,* London, 1968; P. Kencz, *Civil War in South Russia,* New York, 1977; and M. Carley, *Revolution and Intervention,* New York, 1983.

Particular aspects of the naval war are well described in: J. Goldrick, *The King's Ships Were at Sea: The War in the North Sea, August, 1914–February 1915,* Annapolis, Md., 1984; P. Halpern, *The Naval War in the Mediterranean, 1914–18,* London, 1987; G. Bennet, *Coronel and the Falklands,* New York, 1962, and *Cowan's War: The Story of British Naval Operations in the Baltic, 1918–20,* London, 1964; and J. Terraine, *Business in Great Waters,* London, 1989, the best general account of the U-boat campaign. Among the enormous number of books on Jutland the following should be noted: N.

Campbell, *Jutland: An Analysis of the Fighting,* London, 1986; and A. Gordon, *The Rules of the Game,* London, 1996.

POLITICS AND ECONOMICS

Among notable books on the politics and economics of the war by academic writers are: V. Berghahn, *Germany and the Approach of War in 1914,* New York, 1973; G. Feldman, *Arms, Industry and Labor in Germany, 1914–18,* Princeton, N.J., 1966; D. French, *British Strategy and War Aims,* London, 1986; J. Galantai, *Hungary in the First World War,* Budapest, 1989; M. Geyer, *Deutsche Rüstungspolitik,* Frankfurt, 1984; P. Guinn, *British Strategy and Politics, 1914–18,* Oxford, 1965; and Z. Zeman, *The Break-up of the Habsburg Empire,* London, 1961.

CULTURE AND SOCIETY

French scholars have recently made notable contributions to the social and cultural history of the war. They include J.-J. Becker and S. Audouin-Rouzeau, *Les sociétés européennes et la guerre de 1914–18,* Paris, 1990; J.-J. Becker et al., *Guerres et Cultures 1914–18,* Paris, 1994; J.-J. Becker, *La France en guerre, 1914–18,* Paris, 1988; and J.-J. Becker, *The Great War and the French People,* Leamington Spa, Eng., 1985. Becker's English collaborator, J. Winter, has edited, with W. Wall, *The Upheaval of War: Family, Work and Welfare in Europe, 1914–18,* Cambridge, 1988. His *Sites of Memory, Sites of Mourning: The Great War in European Cultural History,* Cambridge, 1995, is a moving essay on the efforts made by soldiers and civilian communities to bear, rationalise and commemorate the griefs the war caused. More literary, and now one of the most famous of all Great War books, is Paul Fussell, *The Great War and Modern Memory,* Oxford, 1975, a study of the English literature, particularly novels and memoirs. An older but still valuable French equivalent is J. Norton Cru, *Témoins,* new edition, Nancy, France, 1993. Two important books on the German experience are L. Moyer, *Victory Must Be Ours,* London, 1995; and R. Whalen, *Bitter Wounds: German Victims of the Great War,* Ithaca, N.Y., 1984. In *The*

Myriad Faces of War, Cambridge, 1986, Trevor Wilson has constructed a multi-faceted portrait of the British war experience. An interesting American perspective is E. Leed, *No Man's Land: Combat and Identity in World War I,* Cambridge, 1979.

BIOGRAPHY

The military leaders of the First World War have found few retrospective admirers. This increasingly seems unfair. They were men presented with an almost insuperable problem—how to break a strong fortified front with weak, indeed inadequate means—and none was any much worse a general than another. An interesting collective portrait is presented by Correlli Barnett in *The Swordbearers,* London, 1963; his subjects are Moltke the Younger, Admiral Sir John Jellicoe, Commander of the Grand Fleet, Pétain and Ludendorff. Basil Liddell Hart's sympathetic biography *Foch: Man of Orleans,* 1931, stands the test of time. So does J. Wheeler-Bennett's *Hindenburg: The Wooden Titan,* London, 1936. D. Goodspeed is excellent in *Ludendorff,* London, 1966. Haig remains an enigma, an efficient military technician deficient in human feeling. John Terraine supplies a partisan defence of his achievements in *Haig: The Educated Soldier,* London, 1963; a more sceptical biography, emphasising the less rational side of his character, is by G. De Groot, *Douglas Haig,* London, 1988; also to be noted is *Haig's Command* by D. Winter, London, 1991. *The Private Papers of Douglas Haig,* edited by R. Blake, 1952, is indispensable. So, too, is Philip Magnus's *Kitchener,* New York, 1959. D. Smythe, *Pershing,* Bloomington, Ind., 1986, provides the best biography of the General of the (American) Armies. R. Holmes has written an excellent biography of Sir John French in *The Little Field Marshal,* London, 1981. Good biographies of British admirals are provided by R. Mackay, *Fisher of Kilverstone,* Oxford, 1973; A. Temple Patterson, *Jellicoe,* London, 1969; and S. Roskill, *Earl Beatty,* London, 1980.

The Angels of Mons, from a painting by W. H. Margetson

Notre Dame de Lorette, Pas de Calais, France

Anniversary of the Battle of the Marne,
Chambry, France, 1915

Monument for the dead of Douaumont, France

Visiting a battlefield after
the war, France

The Watch on the Rhine,
painting by
Sir William Rothenstein

A Note About the Author

John Keegan was for many years senior lecturer in military history at the Royal Military Academy, Sandhurst, and has been a fellow at Princeton University and a professor of history at Vassar College. He is the author of fourteen previous books, including the acclaimed *The Face of Battle, The Second World War* and *The First World War.* He lives in Wiltshire, England.

A Note on the Type

This book was set in Caledonia, a face designed by W. A. Dwiggins (1880–1956) for the Mergenthaler Linotype Company in 1939. It belongs to the family of types referred to by printers as "modern," a term used to mark the change in type styles that occurred around 1800.

Composition and color separations by North Market Street Graphics,
Lancaster, Pennsylvania
Printed and bound by Mohn Media,
Gütersloh, Germany
Designed by Wendy Byrne